Fodor'

VAN
& V

WELCOME TO VANCOUVER AND VICTORIA

Set on Canada's west coast, Vancouver and Victoria blend urban sophistication and multicultural vitality with spectacular settings near mountains, ocean, and rain forest. Both cities are famously livable: Vancouver gleams with towering skyscrapers; the smaller Victoria charms with its historic waterfront. To see the appeal, stroll and bike in Vancouver's Stanley Park, eat fresh seafood, sip cocktails, browse boutiques, and visit renowned museums and gardens. Sure, it rains out here, but take a cue from the laid-back locals in their chic, all-weather clothes.

TOP REASONS TO GO

★ **First Nations Cultures:** Museums, art galleries, and cultural centers provide insight.

★ **Neighborhoods:** From Vancouver's buzzing Yaletown to Victoria's scenic downtown.

★ **Outdoor Fun:** Terrific beaches, hiking, skiing, and whale-watching are all nearby.

★ **Food:** Granville Island's dazzling indoor market, top-notch seafood, superb Pacific Rim fare.

★ **Gardens and Parks:** Flowers in Butchart Gardens, the seawall in Stanley Park.

★ **Excursions:** Winter sports in Whistler; stormwatching and scenery on Vancouver Island.

Fodor's VANCOUVER & VICTORIA

Publisher: Amanda D'Acierno, *Senior Vice President*

Editorial: Arabella Bowen, *Editor in Chief*; Linda Cabasin, *Editorial Director*

Design: Tina Malaney, *Associate Art Director*; Chie Ushio, *Senior Designer*; Ann McBride, *Production Designer*

Photography: Jennifer Arnow, *Senior Photo Editor*; Jennifer Romains, *Photo Researcher*

Production: Linda Schmidt, *Managing Editor*; Evangelos Vasilakis, *Associate Managing Editor*; Angela L. McLean, *Senior Production Manager*

Maps: Rebecca Baer, *Senior Map Editor*; David Lindroth, Ed Jacobus, Mark Stroud, and Henry Colomb *Cartographers*

Sales: Jacqueline Lebow, *Sales Director*

Marketing & Publicity: Heather Dalton, *Marketing Director*; Katherine Punia, *Publicity Director*

Business & Operations: Susan Livingston, *Vice President, Strategic Business Planning*; Sue Daulton, *Vice President, Operations*

Fodors.com: Megan Bell, *Executive Director, Revenue & Business Development*; Yasmin Marinaro, *Senior Director, Marketing & Partnerships*

Copyright © 2015 by Fodor's Travel, a division of Random House LLC

Writers: Chloë Ernst, Carolyn B. Heller, Sue Kernaghan, Chris McBeath

Editors: Douglas Stallings, Caroline Trefler

Production Editor: Jennifer DePrima

4th Edition

ISBN 978-0-8041-4283-0

ISSN 1941-0301

SPECIAL SALES

This book is available at special discounts for bulk purchases for sales promotions or premiums. For more information, e-mail specialmarkets@penguinrandomhouse.com

PRINTED IN THE UNITED STATES OF AMERICA

10 9 8 7 6 5 4 3 2 1

CONTENTS

CONTENTS

MAPS

ABOUT THIS GUIDE

Fodor's Recommendations

Everything in this guide is worth doing—we don't cover what isn't—but exceptional sights, hotels, and restaurants are recognized with additional accolades. **Fodor's**Choice★ indicates our top recommendations; and **Best Bets** call attention to notable hotels and restaurants in various categories. Care to nominate a new place? Visit Fodors.com/contact-us.

Trip Costs

We list prices wherever possible to help you budget well. Hotel and restaurant price categories from $ to $$$$ are noted alongside each recommendation. For hotels, we include the lowest cost of a standard double room in high season. For restaurants, we cite the average price of a main course at dinner or, if dinner isn't served, at lunch. For attractions, we always list adult admission fees; discounts are usually available for children, students, and senior citizens.

Hotels

Our local writers vet every hotel to recommend the best overnights in each price category, from budget to expensive. Unless otherwise specified, you can expect private bath, phone, and TV in your room. For expanded hotel reviews, facilities, and deals visit Fodors.com.

Top Picks	Hotels &
★ **Fodor's**Choice	**Restaurants**
	⌆ Hotel
Listings	⤵ Number of
⌧ Address	rooms
⌧ Branch address	⍿⚬⍿ Meal plans
☎ Telephone	✕ Restaurant
🖶 Fax	⌔ Reservations
⊕ Website	⛫ Dress code
✎ E-mail	▭ No credit cards
⛳ Admission fee	⑀ Price
⊘ Open/closed	
times	**Other**
Ⓜ Subway	⇨ See also
⊹ Directions or	☞ Take note
Map coordinates	⚐ Golf facilities

Restaurants

Unless we state otherwise, restaurants are open for lunch and dinner daily. We mention dress code only when there's a specific requirement and reservations only when they're essential or not accepted. To make restaurant reservations, visit Fodors.com.

Credit Cards

The hotels and restaurants in this guide typically accept credit cards. If not, we'll say so.

EUGENE FODOR

Hungarian-born Eugene Fodor (1905–91) began his travel career as an interpreter on a French cruise ship. The experience inspired him to write *On the Continent* (1936), the first guidebook to receive annual updates and discuss a country's way of life as well as its sights. Fodor later joined the U.S. Army and worked for the OSS in World War II. After the war, he kept up his intelligence work while expanding his guidebook series. During the Cold War, many guides were written by fellow agents who understood the value of insider information. Today's guides continue Fodor's legacy by providing travelers with timely coverage, insider tips, and cultural context.

1

EXPERIENCE VANCOUVER AND VICTORIA

VANCOUVER AND VICTORIA TODAY

Separated from the rest of Canada by the Canadian Rockies, Vancouver and Victoria have always marched to a West Coast rhythm that is in many ways more similar to Seattle, Portland, and even parts of California than to their Canadian counterparts. Add to this their proximity to the sea and coastal mountains and you have winters that are mild, summers that are balmy, and landscapes that are lush with temperate forests and gardens. Nowhere else in Canada do daffodils bloom in February! And despite Victoria's old-English facades, these are young cities with active, outdoorsy, and health-conscious populations. Residents may exude a slightly smug, laissez-faire attitude, but who can blame them? They live in a place that is consistently ranked as one of the most beautiful and livable in the world.

The outdoors rule. Few cities have mountains, oceans, and pristine rain forests all on their doorstep. In both Vancouver and Victoria, locals take full advantage of these options themselves and have also realized the incredible opportunities in promoting ecotourism. Whatever your age or ability, the range of activities includes family whale-watching excursions; stellar golf, hiking, fishing, and white-knuckle rafting expeditions; and no-holds-barred extreme wilderness adventures. Victoria is a popular departure point for exploring the myriad culinary and eco-adventures on Vancouver Island, while Vancouver is the gateway to sophisticated Whistler and the more rugged interior regions of British Columbia. It's fair to say that all this fresh air makes for an extremely health-oriented population. Fitness clubs are part and parcel of many office and residential buildings, and smoking is prohibited in restaurants, bars, beaches, parks, and other public places. Stereotypes asides, many West Coast denizens really do live in fleece and yoga pants.

Entrepreneurs are in. The Vancouver Economic Commission, a city-run economic development agency, likes to boast about the region's combination of natural beauty and brains. As an example, they cite Meetup.com, the online network where people meet others with similar interests: in Vancouver, the largest Meetup group draws hikers, while the second largest is for entrepreneurs. Indeed, city coffee shops are full of laptop-tapping mobile workers, while in

WHAT'S HOT IN VANCOUVER AND VICTORIA TODAY

Bike lanes, breweries, and the booming real estate business continue to make headlines in Vancouver, Canada's third largest city. As part of Vancouver's "Green City" plan, which includes a significant increase in bike use, foot travel, and public transit, the city has

been adding bike lanes throughout the downtown core. Not without some controversy, the local government also closed a section of Kitsilano's waterfront Point Grey Road to extend the popular Seaside Greenway all the way to Spanish Banks.

A fresh batch of breweries and distilleries is amping up Vancouver's drinking scene and bringing "local"—long a food and wine catch phrase—to liquor. Thanks to recent changes in British Columbia's alcoholic beverage laws, several small-batch distilleries

the Gastown neighborhood, developers continue their conversion of once-seedy structures into offices for high-tech firms and design studios. Entrepreneurs around Vancouver and across Vancouver Island are also establishing agricultural, culinary, and tourism businesses that build on the region's natural assets.

Green is great. West Coasters are more eco-conscious than the average North American. New construction out here usually involves eco-oriented practices from thermal heating to energy-saving fixtures; rooftop gardens add to the relatively pristine air; and recycling is a daily ritual in business and at home. The area's hotels were among the first to introduce green practices when they started installing dual-flush toilets (that's two levels of flushes, not flushing twice) and asking guests to use towels more than once. Car-sharing services are commonplace, and bicycle lanes rule; Victoria has one of the highest percentages of two-wheel commuters in Canada, while at least 3,500 people bike to work daily in Vancouver. Many companies provide free or subsidized transit passes to employees who give up commuting by car, too. To do as the locals do, be sure to carry an eco-friendly water bottle and a reusable shopping bag. Maximize your use of public transit with a Day Pass (C$9.75), which is good on the SeaBus, SkyTrain, and local buses, or rent a bike to explore on two wheels.

Ethnic diversity is everywhere. The West Coast's easy access to Pacific Rim destinations has generated a great influx of Asian immigrants, making Vancouver the most Asian metropolis outside of Asia. News is delivered in 22 different languages; shops and ATMs post signs in English, Mandarin, Cantonese, Punjabi, Farsi, and even Vietnamese. Ironically, French, Canada's other official language, is rarely seen or heard except on the two Radio Canada stations. This diversity creates a cultural mosaic that comes vibrantly to life in various festivals (such as the Celebration of Light), community activities (including the Richmond Night Market), and, above all, in a range of superb restaurants. While Victoria is less diverse, that's beginning to change; the city's population of "visible minorities" rose by a whopping 40 percent between 1996 and 2006, and growing diversity remains on the upswing.

have opened and new craft breweries are springing up.

Not surprising for a city that's consistently voted one of the world's best places to live, the price of real estate is always a topic of conversation. A 2014 article in *The New Yorker* states, "The most expensive housing market in North America is not where you'd think. It's not New York City or Orange County, California, but Vancouver, British Columbia."

The city of Victoria has shaken off its reputation as a prim destination for proper afternoon teas and garden tours. Scones and snapdragons are still worthy draws but active and culturally sophisticated Victoria residents (and visitors) are just as likely to be hiking or cycling, eating at hip eateries, and enjoying the city's numerous festivals and cultural events.

WHAT'S WHERE

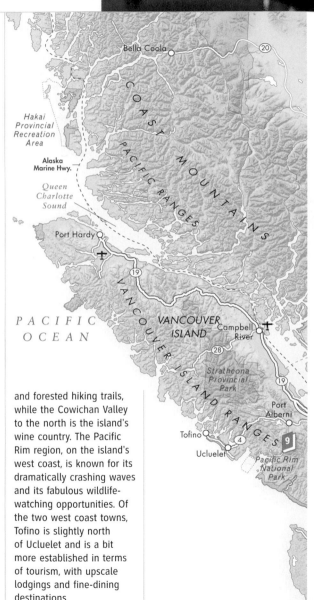

Numbers refer to chapters.

2 - **7** **Vancouver.** Many people argue that Vancouver is the most beautiful city in North America and situated as it is, between mountains and water, it's hard to disagree. The Vancouver area actually covers a lot of ground, but the central core—Downtown, the West End, Stanley Park, Gastown, Chinatown, and Yaletown—is fairly compact. An excellent public transportation system makes it easy to get around. When in doubt, remember the mountains are to the north.

8 **Victoria.** At the southern tip of Vancouver Island, British Columbia's capital is a lovely, walkable city with waterfront paths, rambling gardens, fascinating museums, and splendid 19th-century architecture. In some senses remote, it's roughly midway between Vancouver and Seattle and about three hours by car and ferry from either city.

9 **Vancouver Island.** The largest island on North America's west coast, Vancouver Island has a diverse landscape, with striking coastal scenery, vineyards, farms, and dense rainforests. Just outside the city of Victoria, the island's southwest coast around the town of Sooke offers remote beaches and forested hiking trails, while the Cowichan Valley to the north is the island's wine country. The Pacific Rim region, on the island's west coast, is known for its dramatically crashing waves and its fabulous wildlife-watching opportunities. Of the two west coast towns, Tofino is slightly north of Ucluelet and is a bit more established in terms of tourism, with upscale lodgings and fine-dining destinations.

10 Whistler. Just 120 km (75 miles) north of Vancouver—about a two-hour drive along the stunning Sea-to-Sky Highway—Whistler is an outdoor paradise in both winter and summer. The two mountains, Whistler and Blackcomb, are the focus of activities, and Whistler Village, at their base, is a compact mecca of lodgings, restaurants, shops, and cafés, where you can walk (or ski) to nearly all the town's attractions.

11 Okanagan Valley. About a five-hour drive east from Vancouver, the Okanagan Valley is the fruit-growing capital of Canada and a major wine-producing area—maybe you've heard it called the "Napa of the North." The sandy lakeside beaches and hot, dry climate help make it a wildly popular summer destination.

TO EDMONTON

Wells Gray Provincial Park

BRITISH COLUMBIA

24

Kamloops

Salmon Arm

97

Vernon

6

Okanagan Lake

Whistler

Garibaldi Provincial Park

Whistler Mtn.

Aspen Cove

Kelowna

Powell River

99

97

Squamish

Okanagan Wine Country

33

Golden Ears Prov. Park

Princeton

Peachland

11

Strait of Georgia

Manning Provincial Park

Hope

Penticton

2 – 7

Vancouver

Chilliwack

3

Osoyoos

Nanaimo

Richmond

3

CANADA USA

Langley

Abbotsford

Oroville

5

North Cascades National Park

Duncan

Billingham

WASHINGTON

20

8

VICTORIA

Mt. Vernon

97

Juan de Fuca Strait

Colwood

Port Angeles

112

101

Everett

TO SEATTLE

5

0   50 miles

0   50 kilometers

Olympic N.P.

VANCOUVER AND VICTORIA PLANNER

When to Go

Both Vancouver and Victoria are cosmopolitan, year-round destinations with an outdoor vibe that kicks into high gear whenever the sun shines.

Daffodils and cherry blossoms transform city streets from March to May. From June to September, it seems like the entire populace of Vancouver and Victoria migrates to the beaches, parks, and hiking trails. Despite the risk of rain, October's cool, crisp mornings almost invariably give way to marvelous sunshine sparkling through multicolored leaves. Come November through February, expect lots of hotel and restaurant bargains and an active cultural calendar, but lots of rain in Vancouver and Victoria. In contrast, this is also high season in Whistler for snow sports, and along Vancouver Island's westernmost coast, where storm-watching is a favorite activity.

Canadian money

U.S. dollars are widely accepted but usually at par, so it makes more sense to carry local cash. ATMs are in abundance. Canadian currency uses one- and two-dollar coins ("loonies" and "toonies") and colorful notes for larger denominations.

Getting Here

Air Travel. There are direct flights from most major U.S. and international cities to Vancouver International Airport (YVR), with connecting services to Victoria (YYJ). Another possibility is if you can get a great deal on a flight to Seattle, it's about a three-hour drive to Vancouver, or you can take the train or bus from Seattle to Canada.

Car Travel. Interstate highway I–5 heads straight up the U.S. coast into Vancouver. It's Highway 99 on the Canadian side of the border.

However you travel, carry a passport. Without one, even U.S. citizens might not be allowed home. That includes minors.

Getting Around

In both Victoria and Vancouver, a car can be useful for out-of-town excursions, though having one in the city can be a nuisance: parking is expensive (if it's available at your hotel, it will often be extra), and parking officers prowl the streets looking for meter violators. Vancouver is a highly walkable city, as is downtown Victoria. Bike-rental shops are numerous, public transportation is easy to use, and there are taxis for when all else fails.

What to Pack

Layering is the best solution to the region's variable weather. Men don't usually need a tie—West Coast casual means smart cotton dress pants or jeans and T-shirts. Ward off cool summer breezes with a light jacket, bring Gore-Tex for warmth in winter, and no matter what time of year it's never a bad idea to stash something waterproof. If you forget an umbrella, they're a dime a dozen at every corner store. Vancouver and Victoria are walking cities, so pack comfortable shoes.

LIKE A LOCAL

Heading out to Vancouver or Victoria? Here are a few helpful tips for appreciating this unique part of western Canada just like the locals do.

Eat Local

Supporting local producers has always been part of the West Coast lifestyle, so back in 2005 when two Vancouver writers originated the 100-mile diet, they didn't expect it to catch on across North America, let alone the world. Look for neighborhood farmers' markets, some open year-round. The renowned Granville Island Market, for example, sells such products as handcrafted island cheeses, organic meats, freshly caught fish, salmon jerky "candy," homemade jams and honey, and seasonal fresh produce.

Layer Up

Dressing for success around Vancouver and Victoria means layering to suit the sea breezes and rain. Especially the rain. Local mythology says that real natives don't carry umbrellas, they just wear a lot of Gore-Tex, but reliable insider info says the locals do use their umbrellas and we'd guess that most locals own at least one pair of rain boots.

Love Your Lattes

West Coasters have a love–hate relationship with the ubiquitous S chain, which has an outlet on almost every street corner. Locals, however, prefer the authenticity of Bean Around the World, the Italian coffee shops along Commercial Drive, or the award-winning creations of the champion baristas at the Caffè Artigiano outlets. Vancouverites like to linger over their lattes at sidewalk tables at any time of year, rain or shine.

Be Eco-Savvy

Doing your bit for the planet is integral to living like a local in Vancouver and Victoria, so rinse and recycle your cans and bottles, take a reusable bag if you're going shopping, and search out socially responsible products and companies.

Read the *Georgia Straight*

This Vancouver weekly echoes Vancouver's inner cool. Everything's in here, from opinion pieces to offbeat travel articles, insightful restaurant reviews, theater schedules, and personal ads of all genres. Online, check out Miss 604 (⊕ *www.miss604.com*), Scout Magazine (⊕ *www.scoutmagazine.ca*), and Vancouver Is Awesome (⊕ *www.vancouverisawesome.com*) for more local news and happenings.

Exercise a Passion

Keeping the body healthy is a local preoccupation, as is having the wardrobe to suit the way of life, preferably purchased along Kitsilano's 4th Avenue or on West Broadway—the meccas for sporting goods and clothing. Hike the Grouse Grind, scuba-dive Howe Sound, try out your stand-up paddling skills, sweat in Bikram yoga, or practice Pilates. Visitors can partake in all these passions, too!

VANCOUVER AND VICTORIA TOP ATTRACTIONS

(A) Museum of Anthropology, Vancouver. The city's most spectacular museum displays art from the Pacific Northwest and around the world—dramatic totem poles and canoes; exquisite carvings of gold, silver, and argillite; and masks, tools, and textiles from many cultures.

(B) The Bill Reid Gallery, Vancouver. If First Nations heritage is your thing, be sure to visit this repository of regional art.

(C) Granville Island, Vancouver. Take the foot-passenger ferry across the inlet from Downtown, and bring your appetite. This small island houses an extremely popular indoor market, a marina, theaters, restaurants, coffee shops, parks, and dozens of crafts shops and artist studios. Wander the stalls in the market, then grab a bench outside to get your fill of delicacies and the view.

(D) Dr. Sun Yat-Sen Chinese Garden, Vancouver. "Life is not measured by the number of breaths we take," according to the old saying, "but by the places and moments that take our breath away." That sentiment sums up this elegant Downtown destination. It's the first authentic Ming Dynasty–style garden outside of China to incorporate symbolism and design elements from centuries-old Chinese gardens.

(E) Stanley Park, Vancouver. An afternoon in this gorgeous 1,000-acre wilderness, just blocks from downtown Vancouver, can include beaches, the ocean, the harbor, Douglas fir and cedar forests, First Nations sculptures, and a view of the North Shore Mountains. Walk, bike, picnic, or just take the trolley tour around the perimeter, but don't miss it.

(F) **Whistler.** With two of the longest vertical ski drops on the continent, this ski-in, ski-out village at the base of Whistler and Blackcomb mountains has enough shops, restaurants, and nightlife to fill a vacation without even hitting the slopes.

(G) **Inner Harbour, Victoria.** The lovely capital of British Columbia has a remarkably intimate and pedestrian-friendly downtown that wraps around the harbor. Street entertainers and crafts vendors—and lots of people—come out to stroll the waterfront walkway in summer.

(H) **Butchart Gardens, Victoria.** Just 20 minutes from downtown Victoria, the 55-acre Butchart Gardens was planted in a limestone quarry in 1904. Highlights include the Japanese and Italian gardens, as well as the proliferation of roses and 700 other varieties of flowers. On summer nights you can enjoy a fireworks display.

(I) **Pacific Rim National Park Reserve, Vancouver Island.** This park on the island's far west coast has a seemingly endless white-sand beach and hiking trails with panoramic views of the sea and rain forest. Many visitors go in the winter to witness the dramatic storms coming off the water—and to take advantage of the off-season rates. Adventurous souls can try a kayak trip out to the Broken Group Islands.

(J) **Okanagan Valley.** East of Vancouver, the country's "fruit basket" is no longer just "beaches and peaches." It has rapidly gained a reputation as a wine region because of the many vineyards surrounding pristine Okanagan Lake. They produce a wide range of notable varietals, including ice wines made from late-harvest grapes. The bountiful resources and gifted chefs in the area also mean the food is on par with the quality of the wines.

VANCOUVER AND VICTORIA WITH KIDS

Vancouver and Victoria are great places to entertain children, especially ones who like the outdoors. Check the calendar for family-oriented special events, like the Vancouver International Children's Festival in May and the Vancouver Folk Music Festival in July.

In Downtown Vancouver

Allow a day to enjoy the kid-friendly activities in Stanley Park: the miniature train, aquarium, pool, water park, and beaches are great for all ages. And getting around this huge park—on a horse-drawn wagon or the park shuttle—is half the fun. Make sure you also plan a trip on the mini Aquabus ferry to Granville Island, home of North America's largest free public water park and the Kids' Market, a two-story complex of toy stores and play areas. The Granville Island market is a great place for lunch or snacking, and even the pickiest kids should be able to find something they like. You can check out the interactive displays at Science World, or hop a foot-passenger ferry to see one of the kid-friendly museums at Vanier Park: the Maritime Museum or the H.R. MacMillan Space Centre.

Beyond Downtown

Outside downtown Vancouver, the North Shore is a wilderness playground. Older kids will no doubt enjoy terrifying their parents by trying to wobble the Capilano Suspension Bridge (or the Lynn Canyon-Suspension Bridge). The Treetops Adventure at Capilano Suspension Bridge Park and the salmon-spawning displays at the nearby Capilano Salmon Hatchery tend to be big hits, too. Take a Skyride trip up Grouse Mountain, where you can skate or take a sleigh ride in winter, or hike and visit the bear-and-wolf refuge in summer. For a day at the beach, head west to Spanish Banks or Locarno for warm, shallow water and wide stretches of sand. Kits Beach is busier, but has a playground and a saltwater pool.

Don't underestimate the entertainment power of public transportation. For a few dollars, a SeaBus ride across Burrard Inlet (a larger ferry than the Granville Island Aquabus) provides a water-level view of the harbor; the same ticket gets you on an elevated SkyTrain ride across town.

In Victoria

Like Vancouver, Victoria has small foot-passenger ferries zigzagging across the harbor, and Fisherman's Wharf, with its houseboats, seals, and fish-and-chips stands, is popular. Preschoolers are mesmerized by the tiny displays at Miniature World and charmed by the friendly critters at the Beacon Hill Park petting zoo, while older kids enjoy the Victoria Bug Zoo, the Royal British Columbia Museum, and shopping for allowance-priced souvenirs in Chinatown. Easy hikes, bike rides, and picnics are also popular. For serious "what I did on my summer vacation" material, you can't beat a whale-watching trip. For a night out, try a movie at the IMAX theaters or the spectacular fireworks displays on summer evenings at Butchart Gardens.

At Butchart Gardens

If Victoria's Butchart Gardens is on your to-do list, you can make a full day of it by meandering through the peninsula—Sea Cider (about a 10-minute drive from the ferry and about 15 minutes from the gardens) is the place for munchies. Nearby, the Shaw Ocean Discovery Centre has amazing touchy-feely exhibits to entertain everyone from 8 to 80 years old.

FREE AND ALMOST FREE

The best things in life are free and a surprising number of them are in and around Vancouver, Victoria, and Whistler. In fact, most of what's enjoyable in this part of the world—including beaches, parks, hiking trails, interesting architecture, great views, and fun-and-funky neighborhoods—is available without charge.

Vancouver

In Vancouver, you can visit Stanley Park, Granville Island, Downtown, Gastown, Chinatown, and Yaletown and rarely have to open your wallet to pay admission fees. Granville Island's markets and galleries are all free, as are Canada Place and Stanley Park.

If that's not enough, here are a few lesser-known ways to stretch those loonies and toonies:

On Tuesday evening between 5 and 9, the Vancouver Art Gallery charges admission by donation, while the Museum of Anthropology has reduced rates. In North Vancouver, most visitors head for the fun, if pricey, Capilano Suspension Bridge, but a few miles away, the equally thrilling Lynn Canyon Suspension Bridge, in Lynn Canyon Park, is absolutely free. It might be a bit of a trek, but also free on the North Shore is the Capilano Salmon Hatchery, where you can learn about the life cycle of salmon (and, in fall, watch them struggling upstream to spawn).

Public Transit

Don't forget one of Vancouver's great unsung bargains: an off-peak, two-zone SkyTrain ticket. For just a few dollars, you can see much of the city's east side and mountains from a clean, efficient elevated train, or venture to the Asian malls and night markets in Richmond. Using the same ticket you can transfer to the SeaBus for a 15-minute ride across the harbor.

The tiny foot-passenger ferries across False Creek are great bargains, too, at just a few dollars a ticket.

Victoria

In Victoria, Beacon Hill Park or any of the city's parks and beaches are free, as are most of the city's iconic buildings. A stroll through the public areas of the venerable Fairmont Empress Hotel or a guided tour of the Parliament Buildings won't cost a dime. The Inner Harbour Walk has views of Victoria's Edwardian architecture, boats, and seaplanes, and the great people-watching is also free. If you're there on a Sunday morning, you can even watch the foot-passenger ferries perform a 10-minute water ballet (10:45 am, May through September).

Bargains in Whistler?

Even in jet-set Whistler you can find a few bargains. In the village, you can make like the glitterati for the price of a latte: start with people-watching from a café patio, enjoy the street entertainers, then move on to a stroll through the village's half dozen or so art galleries or join a free tour at the BrewHouse. Even the village shuttle buses are free, while Whistler Transit buses can get you pretty much anywhere in the valley for C$2.50.

GREAT ITINERARIES

See the Cities: 7–10 days

It's possible to see Vancouver, Whistler, and Victoria in a week to ten days, although you'll probably just have time to hit the highlights. Start with two or three days in Vancouver, seeing Stanley Park and strolling through some neighborhoods like Granville Island, Yaletown, Kitsilano, and Gastown. Add a day to explore the mountains and parks of the North Shore (Capilano, Grouse, or Lynn Canyon) or the Museum of Anthropology on the city's west side before heading north to Whistler. Be sure to make the trip in daylight because the Sea-to-Sky Highway, along Howe Sound and into the Coast Mountains, is too stunning to miss. After a day or two of biking, hiking, skiing, or just shopping and café-sitting in Whistler, head back down the Sea-to-Sky Highway to Horseshoe Bay, where you can board a car ferry to Nanaimo. From there, a two-hour drive south takes you to Victoria, BC's lovely seaside capital, where the museums, restaurants, and shopping warrant at least two or three days of browsing. A ferry from nearby Swartz Bay will have you back in Vancouver in half a day.

Wilderness and Wildlife: 7–10 days

To get in some serious outdoors time, spend a few days in Vancouver hiking in the North Shore Mountains or kayaking in Indian Arm—then head up the Sea-to-Sky Highway, one of the world's great scenic drives, to Whistler. Here, lift-accessed hiking, mountain biking, and snowshoeing are easy ways into the backcountry. If you've ever wanted to try an outdoor sport, this is the place to do it: summer options run from golf and fishing to rafting, zip-lining, and rock climbing. And in winter, skiing is just the start. From Whistler, you can retrace your steps to Horseshoe Bay, catch a ferry to Nanaimo, then make the three-hour drive across the mountains of Vancouver Island to Tofino and Ucluelet for a few days of whale-watching, bear-watching, kayaking, surfing, beachcombing, and perhaps some spa time, in and around the Pacific Rim National Park Reserve.

Food and Wine: 5–10 days

So many restaurants, so many wineries, so little time! A food-and-wine tour of British Columbia would start with a couple days of browsing Vancouver's markets and specialty shops, followed by evenings in a selection of its 3,000 or so restaurants. Then you can head to the source of the bounty you've just sampled, traveling east (at five hours, Highway 5 is the quickest) to the Okanagan Valley, where more than 125 wineries line a 200-km (120-mile) string of lakes (the largest is picturesque Okanagan Lake). The dozen vineyards around "Canada's wine capital," Oliver, make a good focus if you're short on time. Another option is a visit to BC's "Wine Island," better known as Vancouver Island. All around Victoria, southern Vancouver Island, and the offshore Gulf Islands are home to about a dozen wineries, as well as organic produce stands, farmers' markets, cider and cheese makers, and some of BC's best country inns.

FIRST NATIONS CULTURE

Home to more than 30 First Nations, each with its own language and culture, BC has the most vibrant range of aboriginal cultures in North America.

Museums and Galleries

Southern BC has several First Nations museums. In Vancouver, the Bill Reid Gallery of Northwest Coast Art has a wide range of aboriginal art. Vancouver's Museum of Anthropology and Victoria's Royal British Columbia Museum each has a renowned collection of First Nations artifacts, from archaeological finds to modern-day works. A number of Vancouver art galleries, notably the Coastal Peoples Fine Arts Gallery, Hill's Native Art, and the Douglas Reynolds Gallery, show works by contemporary and traditional BC First Nations artists.

Cultural Centers

Another way to experience aboriginal culture is to visit one of the cultural centers run by First Nations people. In Vancouver's Stanley Park, Klahowya Village is essentially an outdoor cultural center, where First Nations artisans and performers demonstrate traditional crafts, dancing, and storytelling throughout the summer. An easy day trip from Vancouver, the impressive Squamish Lil'wat Cultural Centre (⊕ www.slcc.ca) in Whistler showcases the history and culture of the two First Nations whose traditional terrirtories encompass the Whistler region. On Vancouver Island, the Quw'utsun' Cultural and Conference Centre (⊕ www.khowutzun.com) is an hour north of Victoria, in Duncan. The riverside site's cedar longhouses include the Riverwalk Café, open June to September, where you can sample traditional First Nations cuisine— perhaps salmon or stew with bannock (unleavened bread).

Powwows

Visitors are welcome at the First Nations powwows that take place in BC each August. Check out Chilliwack's Spirit of the People Pow Wow (⊕ www.tourism chilliwack.com), a huge gathering of First Nations groups with drumming circles, dancing, and exhibits; and West Vancouver's Squamish Nation Pow Wow (⊕ www.vancouversnorthshore.com), which also features dance competitions, crafts, and food. Kamloops hosts the annual Kamloopa Pow Wow (⊕ www.tourism kamloops.com), British Columbia's biggest festival of First Nations dance.

Other Special Events

Canada celebrates National Aboriginal Day during the third weekend in June with festivals and events nationwide; the Aboriginal Tourism Association of British Columbia (⊕ www.aboriginalbc.com) has details about what's going on around BC, including festivities at Canada Place in downtown Vancouver. Every winter, Vancouver hosts the Talking Stick Festival (⊕ www.fullcircle.ca), two weeks of theater, dance, music, and other performances by aboriginal artists and celebrating aboriginal culture.

Exploring with a First Nations guide

A growing number of First Nation–owned tourism operators offers everything from kayaking to hiking to jet-boat tours, typically with traditional songs, legends, historic insights, and food (think waterfront salmon barbecues) thrown in. The Aboriginal Tourism Association of British Columbia (⊕ www.aboriginalbc.com) has more details about sites, tours, and experiences. Takaya Tours *(see the Sports and Outdoors chapter)* offers kayak tours.

HOW TO SPEAK BC

"In Canada we have enough to do keeping up with two spoken languages without trying to invent slang, so we just go right ahead and use English for literature, Scotch for sermons, and American for conversation." —Stephen Leacock (1869–1944)

Canadian humorist Stephen Leacock was right: Canadians don't like to confuse visitors with obscure regional dialects. For that, there is the metric system. Still, Canadians have their eccentricities, and a brief primer may help avoid some confusion.

Terms useful in BC include the words for money: loonies for the dollar coin (because of the loon that graces the coins) and toonies for the two-dollar version. British Columbians, like other Canadians, spell many things the British way (colour instead of color, for example), pronounce the letter "z" as "zed," and occasionally (okay, more than occasionally) tack an "eh?" to the end of a sentence—to turn it into a question, to invite a response, or just out of habit.

Canadianisms like toque (woolly cap) are used here, albeit less frequently given the temperate weather. What you will hear are many words for precipitation. A Vancouverite might observe that it's drizzling, spitting, pouring, or pissing down, but will avoid saying "Yup, it's raining again." That just shows a lack of imagination. Oh, and if someone does say, "It's raining again, eh?" he's not asking a question; he's just inviting you to discuss the situation.

A few words are uniquely West Coast, including some derived from Coast Salish, a First Nations trading language. *Skookum*, for example, means big or powerful; *chuck* means water (as in a body of water); salt *chuck* is seawater. Chinook, which means a warm wind in Alberta, is a species of salmon in BC. Thus you might find: "He caught a skookum chinook then chucked it right back in the salt chuck."

Probably the best sources of confusion out in BC are geographical. The Okanagan, and anything else not on the coast, is called "the Interior" by Vancouverites— unless it's north of, say, Williams Lake, in which case it's "Up North." There are thousands of islands in BC, but "the Island" refers to Vancouver Island. (Many newcomers forget that Vancouver isn't on Vancouver Island; Victoria is.) The Lower Mainland is the term used to refer to Metro Vancouver, including the communities of Langley, Abbotsford, North Shore, Richmond, and even Maple Ridge and White Rock.

Food and drink offer more room for misunderstanding: order soda and you'll get soda water (Canadians drink pop). Homo milk? It's short for homogenized milk and it means whole milk. Bacon is bacon, but Canadian bacon is called back bacon in Canada. Fries are generally fries, but will be called chips if they come with fish, in which case they'll also come with vinegar.

And beer? You can just order "beer," but be prepared to discuss with the bartender your preference for lager, ale, porter, et cetera. You'll probably also be told that Canadian beer is stronger than American. This is a widely held belief that simply doesn't hold water. The alcohol levels are the same—they're just measured differently.

EXPLORING VANCOUVER

WELCOME TO VANCOUVER

TOP REASONS TO GO

★ **Stanley Park:** The views, the activities, and the natural wilderness beauty here are quintessential Vancouver.

★ **Granville Island:** The mini-ferry will take you across False Creek to the Granville Island Public Market where you can browse local foodstuffs; come at lunchtime and eat outside when the weather's good.

★ **Kitsilano beaches:** Options range from beaches with grass-edged shores to windswept stretches of sand to cliffside coves so private that clothing is optional.

★ **Museum of Anthropology at University of British Columbia:** The phenomenal collection of First Nations art and cultural artifacts, and the incredible backdrop, make this a must-see.

★ **Forest, trees, and suspension bridges:** There are a variety of bridges, canopies, and even zip lines at the UBC Botanical Garden and the Capilano Suspension Bridge Park to help you experience the surroundings.

1 Downtown and the West End. Vancouver's commercial heart includes most of the city's high-fashion shops, major hotels, and transit hubs. It's compact and easy to walk. Downtown borders the West End, a residential neighborhood that edges Stanley Park.

2 Stanley Park. A rainforest park with top-quality attractions, hikes, and views—all within blocks of the city skyscrapers.

3 Gastown and Chinatown. These adjoining neighborhoods have ornamental architecture and alleyways that give clues to the city's history.

4 Yaletown. This hip and happening neighborhood bordering False Creek is best known for its specialty shops and eateries.

5 Granville Island. Vancouver's most eclectic destination puts art alongside a giant produce and local food market, with floating homes and busker entertainment to boot. Nothing disappoints.

6 The West Side. This is the catchall name for the neighborhoods southwest of Downtown, including the university area of Point Grey;

busy Cambie Corridor with two of the city's loveliest gardens; trendy Kitsilano; and gallery-filled South Granville.

7 The East Side. Once the city's working-class heart, the rapidly changing areas southeast of Downtown are now home to the science museum, art galleries, eclectic shops, and multi-ethnic eateries. Main Street and Commercial Drive are two areas worth exploring.

Jericho Beach Park

W. 4th Ave.
W. Broadway
W. 10th Ave.
W. 16th Ave.

University of British Columbia

POINT GREY

Pacific Spirit Regional Park

S.W. Marine Dr.

Dunbar St.

WEST SIDE
6

W. 41st Ave.

Vancouver International Airport

0 ——— 2 mi
0 ——— 2 km

8 **North Shore.** Across Burrard Inlet, on the North Shore, are residential and scenic West Vancouver and the more bustling North Vancouver. The mountains, your constant compass-point of reference, are the backdrop.

9 **Richmond.** This is Vancouver's suburban Chinatown, with Asian malls, night markets, and hundreds of restaurants.

British Columbia

GETTING ORIENTED

Most of central Vancouver is on a peninsula, with streets laid out in a grid. It's easy to explore on foot. To get your bearings, use the mountains as north and you can't go too far wrong. All the avenues, which are numbered, have east and west designations; the higher the number, the farther away from the inlet you are.

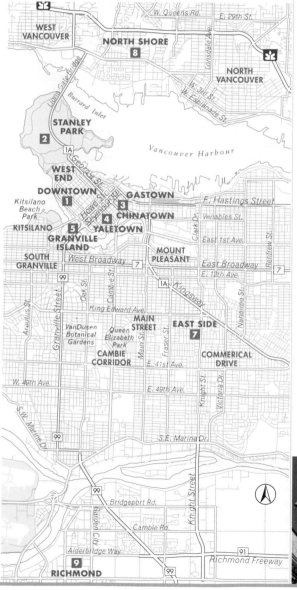

Updated By
Carolyn B.
Heller

Vancouver is a delicious juxtaposition of urban sophistication and on-your-doorstep wilderness adventure. The mountains and seascape make the city an outdoor playground for hiking, skiing, kayaking, cycling, and sailing—and so much more—while the cuisine and arts scenes are equally diverse, reflecting the makeup of Vancouver's ethnic (predominantly Asian) mosaic.

Vancouver is consistently ranked as one of the world's most livable cities, and it's easy for visitors to see why. It's beautiful, it's outdoorsy, and there's a laidback West Coast vibe. On the one hand, there's easy access to a variety of outdoor activities, a fabulous variety of beaches, and amazing parks. At the same time, the city has a multicultural vitality and cosmopolitan flair. The attraction is as much in the range of food choices—the fresh seafood and local produce are some of North America's best—as it is in the museums, shopping, and nightlife.

Vancouver's landscaping also adds to the city's walking appeal. In spring, flowerbeds spill over with tulips and daffodils while sea breezes scatter scented cherry blossoms throughout Downtown; in summer office workers take to the beaches, parks, and urban courtyards for picnic lunches and laptop meetings.

More than 8 million visitors each year come to Vancouver, Canada's third-largest metropolitan area. Because of its peninsula location, traffic flow is a contentious issue. Thankfully, Vancouver is wonderfully walkable, especially in the downtown core. The North Shore is a scoot across the harbor, and the rapid-transit system to Richmond and the airport means that staying in the more affordable 'burbs doesn't have to be synonymous with sacrificing convenience. The mild climate, exquisite natural scenery, and relaxed outdoor lifestyle keep attracting residents, and the number of visitors is increasing for the same reasons. People often get their first glimpse of Vancouver when catching an Alaskan cruise, and many return at some point to spend more time here.

CLOSE UP

Vancouver History

The city of Vancouver is integrally linked with the taming of western Canada: the trappers working for the Hudson's Bay Company (the oldest retail store still operating in North America) explored the area. Legend has it that a chatty gentleman known as "Gassy Jack" opened a saloon on the shores of Burrard Inlet in 1870 and the area became known as Gastown. The Canadian Pacific Railway, which crossed the country, chose the ramshackle town as its Pacific terminus. The coming of the railway inspired the loggers and saloon owners of Granville to incorporate as a city: on April 6, 1886, Granville Townsite, with a population of about 400, became the City of Vancouver, named after the British explorer who had toured the inlet back in 1792. On June 13, 1886, a brush fire got out of control and the fledgling community burned to the

ground in about thirty minutes, but rebuilding got underway in a matter of days.

The railway continued to thrive, and to bring people and goods across the country. The port of Vancouver also grew and, with the opening of the Panama Canal, it became internationally significant as part of an alternative shipping route to Europe. Canadian Pacific's fleet of clipper ships gave Vancouver a full week's edge over the California ports when it came to shipping tea and silk from the Orient to New York. Lumber, fish, and coal from British Columbia's hinterland—resources that are still the backbone of the provincial economy—also flowed through the port to world markets. The same ships and trains brought immigrants from all corners of the earth, helping the population grow exponentially to today's 2.5 million.

PLANNING

MAKING THE MOST OF YOUR TIME

If you don't have much time in Vancouver, you'll probably still want to spend at least a half day in Stanley Park: start out early for a walk, bike, or shuttle ride through the grounds to see the Vancouver Aquarium Marine Science Centre, enjoy the views from Prospect Point, and stroll the seawall. If you leave the park at English Bay, you can have lunch on Denman or Robson Street, then meander past the trendy shops along Robson between Jervis and Burrard streets. Another alternative is to exit the park at Coal Harbour and follow the Seawall Walk to Canada Place, stopping for lunch at a harbor-front restaurant.

A couple of hours at the Granville Island Public Market are also a must—plan to have breakfast or lunch, and, if you have time, check out the crafts stores.

Walking the downtown core is a great way to get to know the city. Start at Canada Place and head east to Gastown and Chinatown; that's a good half day. Then head north to Yaletown, perhaps for a glass of wine and dinner.

If you're traveling with children, make sure to check out Science World, Grouse Mountain, and the Capilano Suspension Bridge or Lynn Canyon.

For museums, adults and older children love the displays of Northwest Coast First Nations art at the Museum of Anthropology. The Bill Reid Gallery also has an impressive collection of aboriginal art.

RAINY-DAY ACTIVITIES

While most Vancouverites don't let a little drizzle stop them, heavier rains might inspire you to seek indoor activities. Obvious options include museums—the Museum of Anthropology at UBC is a worthwhile trek. If you're downtown, the Vancouver Art Gallery is good for an hour or two, as are the Vancouver Aquarium and Science World. Less obvious choices are the Dr. Sun Yat-Sen Classical Chinese Garden (it has covered walkways) or Granville Island Market (it's inside; you just have to get there, but then you can spend hours browsing and snacking). Lonsdale Quay is another colorful indoor market on the North Shore and getting there, via the SeaBus, is half the fun.

GETTING HERE AND AROUND

Central Vancouver is extremely walkable and the public transit system—a mix of bus, ferry, and SkyTrain (a fully automated rail system)—is efficient and easy to use. Transfer tickets enable you to travel from one mode of transport to the other. The hop-on, hop-off Vancouver Trolley buses circle the city in a continuous loop and are a great way to see the sites—especially on a rainy day; the same company runs the seasonal Stanley Park Shuttle.

One note about printed Vancouver street addresses: suite numbers often appear *before* the street number, followed by a hyphen.

Contacts Vancouver Trolley Company. ☎ 604/801–5515 ⊕ www.vancouvertrolley.com.

BUS AND RAPID-TRANSIT TRAVEL

TransLink, Metro Vancouver's public transport system, includes bus service, a rapid transit system called SkyTrain, and a 400-passenger commuter ferry (SeaBus) that connects downtown to the North Shore.

In late 2014 or early 2015 TransLink is expected to introduce a new electronic Compass Card system for single fare tickets or stored-value cards, to be purchased at station vending machines before boarding. You "tap in" your ticket or card to the electronic reader when you board the bus, SkyTrain, or SeaBus; you "tap out" when you exit, which subtracts the fare from your card. Until then you can still buy single-fare tickets; day passes (good across all zones) and discounted FareSaver tickets (sold in books of 10, at outlets such as 7-Eleven, Safeway, and London Drugs) can also be purchased. Tickets for bus travel require exact change at time of embarkation, while Sky-Train and SeaBus tickets are purchased from machines (correct change isn't necessary). Tickets, which are valid for 90 minutes and allow travel in any direction on the buses, SkyTrain, or SeaBus, must be carried with you as proof of payment. Both the ticket fares and the new Compass Card fares are based on zones: one zone (C$2.75), two zones (C$4), or three zones (C$5.50). Travel within the Vancouver city limits is a one-zone trip; traveling between Vancouver and the North Shore or from Vancouver to Richmond is two zones. The Compass Card will also have a day pass available if you're planning to use the system frequently in one day (C$9.75, good all day across all zones).

You'll be able to board a bus without a Compass Card or electronic ticket; just pay your fare as you enter (exact change required). However a Compass Card gives you free transfers between the bus and either the SkyTrain or the SeaBus; if you pay cash, your ticket is good on the bus only.

Note that when you buy a Compass Card, you also pay a C$6 refundable deposit. When you're leaving town, or if you no longer need your card, you can return it to the Compass Customer Service Centre and get your deposit back.

There are three SkyTrain lines: the Expo Line and the Millennium Line share the same stations between Downtown and Commercial Drive, so unless you're going east of Commercial Drive, you can use either line. Trains leave about every two to five minutes. The Canada Line travels to Richmond's commercial hub (for great shopping) and to Vancouver International Airport, a ride that's less than 30 minutes. Canada Line trains leave about every 6 to 10 minutes, more frequently during the morning and evening rush hours.

■ TIP➔ SkyTrain is convenient for transit between Downtown, BC Place Stadium, Pacific Central Station, Science World, and Vancouver International Airport. SeaBus is the fastest way to travel between Downtown and the North Shore (there are bus connections to Capilano Suspension Bridge and Grouse Mountain).

Contacts TransLink. ☎ *604/953–3333* ⊕ *www.translink.ca.*

CAR TRAVEL

If you're staying in the downtown core, there's really no need for a car since public transit and private tour buses—especially the hop-on/hop-off trolley bus—will take you to the major city attractions, and then some. If city adventures are too confining, car rental agencies are numerous.

FERRY TRAVEL

Twelve-passenger Aquabus Ferries and False Creek Ferries bypass busy bridges and are a key reason why you don't need a car in Vancouver. Both of these are private commercial enterprises—not part of the TransLink system—that provide passenger services between key locales on either side of False Creek. Single-ride tickets range from C$3.25 to C$5.50 depending on the route; day passes are C$15–C$16. Aquabus Ferries connections include The Village (Science World and the Olympic Village), Plaza of Nations, Granville Island, Stamp's Landing, Spyglass Place, Yaletown, David Lam Park, and the Hornby Street dock. False Creek Ferries provides service between the Aquatic Centre on Beach Avenue, Granville Island, Science World, Stamp's Landing, and Vanier Park.

The large SeaBus ferries travel between Waterfront Station and Lonsdale Quay in North Vancouver. TransLink tickets valid on the city's buses and subways are also good for the SeaBus.

Contacts Aquabus Ferries.
☎ 604/689–5858 ⊕ www.theaquabus.
com. **False Creek Ferries.** ☎ 604/684–
7781 ⊕ www.granvilleislandferries.
bc.ca. **SeaBus foot-passenger ferry**
☎ 604/953–3333 ⊕ www.translink.ca.

TAXI TRAVEL

It can be hard to hail a cab in Vancouver. Unless you're near a hotel or find a taxi rank (designated curbside parking areas), you'll have better luck calling a taxi service. Try Black Top & Checker Cabs or Yellow Cab. Both companies allow you to book online.

Contacts Black Top & Checker Cabs.
☎ 604/731–1111 ⊕ www.btccabs.ca. **Yellow Cab.** ☎ 604/681–1111
⊕ www.yellowcabonline.com.

HOLLYWOOD NORTH

It's cheaper to film movies and television shows in Canada than in the United States and as a result, Vancouver often stands in for various American cities, including New York, Seattle, Oregon, and somewhat surprisingly, various cities in California. For a list of what's shooting around town, check out the Creative BC website (⊕ www.creativebc.com), and keep a lookout for celebrities in town.

SAVING MONEY

Some attractions, like the Vancouver Art Gallery (Tuesday 5–9 pm) and the Museum of Anthropology (Tuesday 5–9 pm) have reduced rates or "by donation" evenings.

TOURS

Edible Canada. Culinary tour company Edible Canada has guided tours of Granville Island, including a food-focused exploration of the Public Market. They also run guided culinary walks around Vancouver's Chinatown, with an optional dim sum lunch. ☎ 604/558–0040 ⊕ www.
ediblecanada.com.

Tour Guys. The lively Tour Guys (and Gals) who run these urban walking tours share lots of anecdotes about the city and its history. Their tours of Downtown and the waterfront, Granville Street and Gastown, Chinatown, and Granville Island are free, although the guides work hard to earn your tips. In spring and summer, you can also book a "Beer Makes History Better" tour or an "Eat Your Cart Out" snacking tour of downtown food trucks. ☎ 604/259–7740, 800/691–9320
⊕ www.tourguys.ca.

Vancouver Foodie Tours. To explore Vancouver with your tastebuds, book one of these food-focused walking tours. The "Guilty Pleasures Gourmet Tour" includes stops at several Downtown eateries, while the "World's Best Food Truck" tour combines Downtown sightseeing with samples from several popular street-food purveyors. ☎ 604/339–0078
⊕ www.foodietours.ca.

2

DOWNTOWN AND THE WEST END

Vancouver's compact Downtown juxtaposes historic architecture with gleaming brand-new buildings. There are museums and galleries to visit, as well as top-notch shopping, most notably along Robson Street, which runs into the city's West End. The harbor front, with the green-roofed convention center, has a fabulous water's edge path all the way to Stanley Park—walk along here to get a feel for what Vancouver is all about.

DOWNTOWN

At the top of a gentle rise up from the water, the intersection of Georgia and Granville streets is considered Downtown's epicenter, and it's always bustling with activity. Georgia Street runs east–west, past Library Square and Rogers Arena (home of the NHL's Vancouver Canucks), straight through to Stanley Park and the Lions Gate Bridge (which leads to the North Shore and on to Whistler, a two-hour drive away). North–south Granville Street is a pedestrian-friendly strip of funky shops, nightclubs, and street-side cafés, with a few pockets of grunge to keep things feeling real. From this corner of Georgia and Granville, there are many key attractions within a five-minute walk, including the Vancouver Art Gallery, Robson Square, and Pacific Centre Mall.

TOP ATTRACTIONS

Fodor'sChoice
★

Bill Reid Gallery. Named after one of British Columbia's preeminent artists, Bill Reid (1920–98), this small aboriginal gallery is as much a legacy of Reid's works as it is a showcase of current First Nations artists. Displays include wood carvings, jewelry, print, and sculpture, and programs often include artist talks and themed exhibitions such as basket weaving. Reid is best known for his bronze statue *The Spirit of Haida Gwai, The Jade Canoe* —measuring 12 feet by 20 feet; the original is an iconic meeting place at the Vancouver International Airport, and its image is on the back of the Canadian $20 bill. More Bill Reid pieces are at the Museum of Anthropololgy. ✉ *639 Hornby St., Downtown* ☎ *604/682–3455* ⊕ *www.billreidgallery.ca* ⊠ *C$10* ⊙ *Wed.–Sun. 11–5.*

Canada Place. Extending four city blocks (about a mile and a half) north into Burrard Inlet, this complex mimics the style and size of a luxury ocean liner, complete with exterior esplanades and a landmark roofline that resembles five sails (it was made with NASA-invented material: a Teflon-coated fiberglass once used in astronaut space suits). Home to Vancouver's main cruise-ship terminal, Canada Place can accommodate up to four liners at once. All together, the giant building is definitely worth a look and the very cool **Flyover Canada** *(604/620–8455, www.flyovercanada.com, C$19.95, daily 10–9)* attraction, a simulated flight that takes you on a soaring and swooping virtual voyage across the country, is an excellent reason to go inside. If this dramatic journey above Niagara Falls, the Rocky Mountains, and the vast Arctic sparks your curiosity about other parts of Canada, follow the **Canadian Trail** on the west side of the building, which has displays about the country's provinces and territories. Use your smartphone or tablet to access multimedia content along the way: there's free Wi-Fi. Canada Place is also home to the posh **Pan Pacific Hotel** and the east wing of the **Vancouver Convention Centre.** A waterfront promenade winds all the way to (and around) Stanley Park, with spectacular vantage points from which to view Burrard Inlet and the North Shore Mountains; plaques posted at intervals have historical information about the city and its waterfront. At the **Port Metro Vancouver Discovery Centre** *(604/665–9179, free, weekdays 9–4),* at the north end of the Canada Place complex, you can catch a video about the workings of the port, see some historic images of Vancouver's waterfront, or try your hand at a virtual container-loading game. ✉ *999 Canada Place Way, Downtown* ☎ *604/775–7200* ⊕ *www.canadaplace.ca.*

QUICK BITES

Bella Gelateria. If you're strolling around downtown, take note of this tiny shop tucked into a corner of the Fairmont Pacific Rim Hotel building. Bella Gelateria makes its gelato the old-fashioned Italian way, changing the selection of 24 flavors every day (not the night before) from fresh natural ingredients. These treats don't come cheap, but they're delicious. ✉ *1001 W. Cordova St., Downtown* ☎ *604/569–1010* ⊕ *www.bellagelateria.com.*

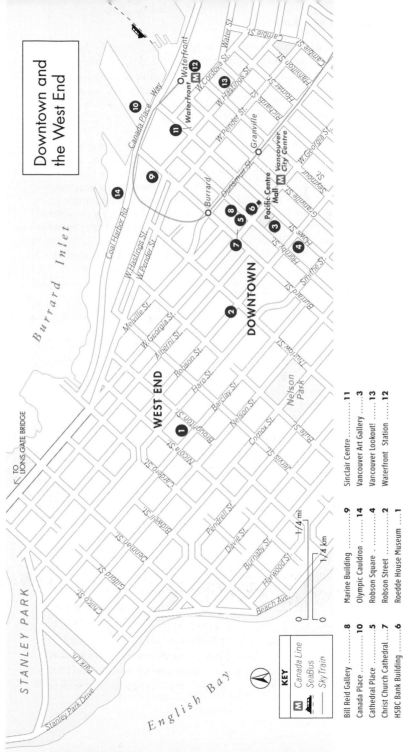

Downtown and the West End

KEY

M Canada Line
SeaBus
— Sky Train

Bill Reid Gallery **8**
Canada Place **10**
Cathedral Place **5**
Christ Church Cathedral ... **7**
HSBC Bank Building **6**

Marine Building **9**
Olympic Cauldron **14**
Robson Square **4**
Robson Street **2**
Roedde House Museum **1**

Sinclair Centre **11**
Vancouver Art Gallery **3**
Vancouver Lookout! **13**
Waterfront Station **12**

0   1/4 mi
0   1/4 km

Olympic Cauldron. A four-pronged sculpture towering more than 30 feet, the Olympic Cauldron is next to the Vancouver Convention Centre's West Building. In 2010, when Vancouver hosted the Winter Olympic and Paralympic Games, it burned with the Olympic flame and it's re-lit occasionally, for Canada Day and other special events. The Cauldron overlooks the Burrard Inlet on Jack Poole Plaza, which is named for the Canadian businessman who led the bid to bring the Olympics to Vancouver. Sadly, Poole died of cancer just one day after the flame for the Olympic torch relay was lit in Olympia, Greece, at the start of its journey to Vancouver. ⊠ *foot of Thurlow St., at Canada Pl., Downtown.*

Robson Street. Running from the Terry Fox Plaza outside BC Place Stadium down to the West End, Robson is Vancouver's busiest shopping street, where fashionistas hang out at see-and-be-seen sidewalk cafés, high-end boutiques, and chain stores. Most of the designer action takes place between Jervis and Burrard streets and that's also where you can find buskers and other entertainers in the evenings. ⊕ *www. robsonstreet.ca.*

Vancouver Art Gallery. Canadian painter Emily Carr's haunting evocations of the British Columbian hinterland are among the attractions at western Canada's largest art gallery. Carr (1871–1945), a grocer's daughter from Victoria, BC, fell in love with the wilderness around her and shocked middle-class Victorian society by running off to paint it. Her work accentuates the mysticism and danger of BC's wilderness, and records the diminishing presence of native cultures during that era (there's something of a renaissance now). The gallery, which also hosts touring historical and contemporary exhibitions, is housed in a 1911 courthouse that Canadian architect Arthur Erickson redesigned in the early 1980s as part of the Robson Square redevelopment. Stone lions guard the steps to the parklike Georgia Street side; the main entrance is accessed from Robson Square or Hornby Street. ⊠ *750 Hornby St., Downtown* ☎ *604/662–4719* ⊕ *www. vanartgallery.bc.ca* ⌫ *C$20 (with tax C$21); higher for some exhibits; by donation Tues. 5–9* ☉ *Wed.–Mon. 10–5, Tues. 10–9.*

NEED A BREAK?

Gallery Café. The culinary artists at Gallery Café (inside the Vancouver Art Gallery) make tasty homemade soups, salads, pies, and other delicious desserts. Try to avoid the noon-hour crush, though, and if the sun is shining, opt for a patio seat overlooking the square. ⊠ *750 Hornby St., Downtown* ☎ *604/688–2233* ⊕ *www.thegallerycafe.ca.*

FAMILY **Vancouver Lookout!** Resembling a flying saucer stuck atop a high-rise, the 553-foot-high Vancouver Lookout has fabulous views of Vancouver. A glass elevator whizzes you up 50 stories to the circular observation deck, where knowledgeable guides point out the sights and give a (free) tour every hour on the hour. On a clear day you can see Vancouver Island and Mt. Baker in Washington State. The top-floor restaurant (*604/669–2220, www.topofvancouver.com*) makes one complete revolution per hour; the elevator ride up is free for diners. Tickets are good all day, so you can visit in daytime and return for another look after dark. ⊠ *555 W. Hastings St., Downtown* ☎ *604/689–0421* ⊕ *www.vancouverlookout.com*

Robson Square, in front of the Vancouver Art Gallery, is a downtown focal point; there's a skating rink here in winter.

📷 *C$15.75* 🕐 *May–mid-Oct., daily 8:30 am–10:30 pm; mid-Oct.–Apr., Mon.–Thurs. 9–9, Fri.–Sun. 9 am–9:30 pm.*

WORTH NOTING

Cathedral Place. One of Vancouver's most handsome postmodern buildings, the 23-story Cathedral Place has a faux-copper roof that mimics that of the Fairmont Hotel Vancouver nearby. The three large sculptures of nurses at the building's corners are replicas of the statues that adorned the Georgia Medical–Dental Building, the art deco structure that previously occupied this site. Step into the lobby to see another interesting sculpture: Robert Studer's *Navigational Device*, suspended high up on the north wall. The small garden courtyard, which also leads to the entrance of the Bill Reid Gallery, is an unexpected respite from Downtown's bustle. ✉ *925 W. Georgia St., Downtown* ☎ *604/669–3312* ⊕ *www.925westgeorgia.com.*

Christ Church Cathedral. Built between 1889 and 1895, this is the oldest church in Vancouver. Constructed in the Gothic style, the Anglican church looks like the parish church of an English village from the outside, though underneath the sandstone-clad exterior it's made of Douglas fir from what is now south Vancouver. The 32 stained-glass windows depict Old and New Testament scenes, often set against Vancouver landmarks (St. Nicholas presiding over the Lions Gate Bridge, for example). The building's excellent acoustics enhance the choral evensong and carols frequently sung here. Gregorian chants are performed every Sunday evening at 9:30 pm. ✉ *690 Burrard St., Downtown* ☎ *604/682–3848* ⊕ *www.cathedral.vancouver.bc.ca* 🕐 *Weekdays 10–4. Services Sun. at 8 am and 10:30 am; weekdays at 12:10 pm.*

HSBC Bank Building. Kitty-corner to the Fairmont Hotel Vancouver, this building has a five-story-high public atrium with a branch of the Sciué Italian café mini-chain (⇨ *see Where to Eat*), regularly changing art exhibitions, and one of the city's more intriguing public-art installations: *Pendulum*, by BC artist Alan Storey, is a 90-foot-long hollow aluminum sculpture that arcs hypnotically overhead. ⊠ *885 W. Georgia St., Downtown* ☎ *604/525–4722.*

Marine Building. Inspired by New York's Chrysler Building, the Marine Building is worth stopping for a look. The terra-cotta bas-reliefs on this 21-story, 1930s art deco structure depict the history of transportation—airships, steamships, locomotives, and submarines—as well as Mayan and Egyptian motifs and images of marine life. Step inside for a look at the beautifully restored interior, then walk to the corner of Hastings and Hornby streets for the best view of the building. ⊠ *355 Burrard St., Downtown.*

Robson Square. Architect Arthur Erickson designed this plaza to be *the* gathering place for downtown Vancouver, although its below-street-level access makes it a bit of a secret. Landscaped walkways connect the Vancouver Art Gallery, government offices, and law courts at street level while the lower level houses a University of British Columbia satellite campus and bookstore. In winter, there's also a covered, outdoor, public ice skating rink; in summer the rink becomes a dance floor for weekly (free) salsa sessions. Political protests and impromptu demonstrations take place on the grandiose gallery stairs facing Georgia Street, a tradition that dates from the days when the building was a courthouse. ⊠ *Bordered by Howe, Hornby, Robson, and Smithe Sts., Downtown.*

Sinclair Centre. Vancouver architect Richard Henriquez knitted four buildings together into Sinclair Centre, an office–retail complex that takes up an entire city block between Cordova and Hastings, and Howe and Granville streets. Inside are high-end designer-clothing shops, federal government offices, and a number of fast-food outlets. The two Hastings Street buildings—the 1910 **Post Office**, which has an elegant clock tower, and the 1911 **Winch Building** —are linked with the 1937 **Post Office Extension** and the 1913 **Customs Examining Warehouse** to the north. As part of a meticulous restoration in the mid-1980s, the post-office facade was moved to the Granville Street side of the complex. The original clockwork from the old clock tower is on display inside, on the upper level of the arcade. ⊠ *757 W. Hastings St., Downtown* ☎ *604/488–0672* ⊕ *www.sinclaircentre.com.*

Waterfront Station. This former Canadian Pacific Railway passenger terminal was built between 1912 and 1914 as the western terminus for Canada's transcontinental railway. After Canada's two major railways shifted their focus away from passenger service, the station became obsolete, but a 1978 renovation turned it into an office–retail complex and depot for SkyTrain, SeaBus, and the West Coast Express (a suburban commuter rail). In the main concourse, murals up near the ceiling depict the scenery travelers once saw on journeys across Canada. This is where you catch the SeaBus for the 13-minute trip across the harbor to the waterfront public market at Lonsdale Quay in North Vancouver. ⊠ *601 W. Cordova St., Downtown* ☏ *604/953–3333 SeaBus and SkyTrain, 604/488–8906, 800/570–7245 West Coast Express.*

WEST END

Robson Street, Vancouver's prime shopping boulevard, runs from Downtown into the West End, a partly residential and partly commercial district. The West End has Vancouver's prettiest streetscapes and harks back to the early 1930s when it housed the affluent middle class: trees are plentiful, gardens are lushly planted, and homes and apartment buildings exude the character of that era. Vancouver's large gay community has a major presence here, too. There are lots of restaurants and cafés along the main arteries: Robson, Denman, and Davie streets.

WORTH NOTING

OFF THE
BEATEN
PATH

Roedde House Museum. On a pretty residential street, the Roedde (pronounced *roh* -dee) House Museum is an 1893 home in the Queen Anne Revival style, set among Victoriana gardens. Tours of the restored, antiques-furnished interior take about an hour. On Sunday, tours are followed by tea and cookies. Museum hours can vary, so it's a good idea to phone before visiting. The gardens (free) can be visited anytime. The museum also hosts a concert series (classical music on the second Sunday of the month at 3 pm, jazz on the second Thursday at 7 pm). ⊠ *1415 Barclay St., between Broughton and Nicola Sts., West End* ☏ *604/684–7040* ⊕ *www.roeddehouse.org* ▱ *C$5; Sun. C$8 including tea and cookies* ☽ *Mid-May–Aug., Tues.–Sat. 10–4, Sun. 1–4; Sept.–mid-May, Tues.–Fri. and Sun. 1–4.*

STANLEY PARK

Fodor's Choice
★

A 1,000-acre wilderness park, only blocks from the downtown section of a major city, is a rare treasure and Vancouverites make use of it to bike, walk, jog, in-line skate, play cricket and tennis, go the beach (⇨ *see Stanley Park Beaches in Sports and the Outdoors*), and enjoy outdoor art shows and theater performances alongside attractions such as the renowned aquarium and Klahowya Village, a summer aboriginal cultural village.

The fact that Stanley Park is so close to the city is actually sort of thanks to the Americans. In the 1860s, because of a threat of American invasion, this oceanfront peninsula was designated a military reserve, though it was never needed. When the City of Vancouver was incorporated in 1886, the council's first act was to request the land be set aside as a park. Permission was granted two years later and the grounds were named Stanley Park after Lord Stanley, then governor general of Canada.

When a storm swept across the park's shores in December 2006, it destroyed close to 10,000 trees as well as parts of the perimeter seawall. Locals contributed thousands of dollars to the clean-up and replanting effort in addition to the monies set aside by local authorities. The storm's silver lining was that it cleared some dead-wood areas, making room for the reintroduction of many of the park's original species of trees. It also gave rise to an unusual ecological arts program in which ephemeral sculptures were placed in various outdoor locations. Made of natural and organic materials, the elements are constantly changing the look of each piece which, over time, will decay and return to the earth.

In addition to **Stanley's Park Bar and Grill** and **Prospect Point Cafe**, both of which are good for a quick bite *(see the listings in this section)*, the **Teahouse in Stanley Park** and **The Fish House Restaurant** are other restaurants in the park (⇨ *see the Where to Eat chapter for full listings of these latter two*).

GETTING HERE AND AROUND

If you're driving to Stanley Park, head northwest on Georgia Street from Downtown. Parking is available at or near all the major attractions; one ticket (C$11 April–September, C$6 October–March) allows you to park all day and to move between lots. Tickets are purchased from automated dispensers in lots and should be displayed on your dashboard.

If you're taking public transit, catch Bus 19 "Stanley Park" along West Pender Street downtown; it runs to the park bus loop, which is within walking distance of the aquarium and Klahowya Village. You can also catch North Vancouver Bus 240 or 246 from anywhere on West Georgia Street to the park entrance at Georgia and Chilco streets, or a Robson Bus 5 to Robson and Denman streets, where there are a number of bicycle-rental outlets.

There is no public transit around or within the park; you can bike, walk, drive, or take the Stanley Park shuttle *(see Getting Here and Around)* to reach the main attractions.

TOURS

The Stanley Park Nature House *(see Worth Noting)* has guided two-hour nature walks in the park.

TOP ATTRACTIONS

Prospect Point. At 211 feet, Prospect Point is the highest point in the park and provides striking views of the Lions Gate Bridge (watch for cruise ships passing below), the North Shore, and Burrard Inlet. There's also a year-round souvenir shop, a snack bar with terrific ice cream, and a restaurant. From the seawall, you can see where cormorants build their seaweed nests along the cliff ledges. ⊠ *Stanley Park.*

NEED A BREAK?

Prospect Point Café. At the top of Prospect Point, this café has a deck overlooking the Lions Gate Bridge. It specializes in salmon dishes and is a good lunch stop, though it's often crowded with tour groups. ⊠ *Stanley Park* ☎ 604/669–2737 ▭ *No credit cards* ☾ *No dinner.*

Stanley Park Seawall. Vancouver's seawall path includes a 9-km (5½-mile) paved shoreline section within Stanley Park. It's one of several car-free zones in the park and it's popular with walkers and cyclists. If you have the time (about a half day) and the energy, strolling the entire seawall is an exhilarating experience. It extends an additional mile east past the marinas, cafés, and waterfront condominiums of Coal Harbour to Canada Place downtown, so you could start your walk or ride from there. From the south side of the park, the seawall continues for another 28 km (17 miles) along Vancouver's waterfront to the University of British Columbia, allowing for a pleasant, if ambitious, day's bike ride. Along the seawall, cyclists must wear helmets and stay on their side of the path. Within Stanley Park, cyclists must ride in a counterclockwise direction. The seawall can get crowded on summer weekends, but inside the park is a 28-km (17-mile) network of peaceful walking and cycling paths through old- and second-growth forest. The wheelchair-accessible Beaver Lake Interpretive Trail is a good choice if

DID YOU KNOW?

The view from Stanley Park out over the marina and Coal Harbour shows just how close this fabulous 1,000-plus-acre park is to Downtown.

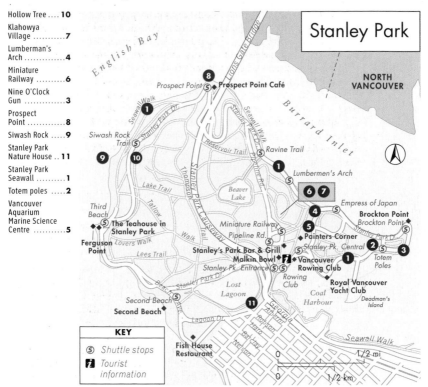

you're interested in park ecology. Take a map—they're available at the park-information booth and many of the concession stands—and don't go into the woods alone or after dusk. ⊠ *Stanley Park*.

Totem poles. Totem poles are an important art form among native peoples along British Columbia's coast. These nine poles—eight carved in the latter half of the 20th century, and one created in 2009—include replicas of poles originally brought to the park from the north coast in the 1920s, as well as poles carved specifically for the park by First Nations artists. The several styles of poles represent a cross section of BC native groups, including the Kwakwaka'wakw, Haida, and Nisga'a. The combination of carved animals, fish, birds, and mythological creatures represents clan history. An information center near the site has a snack bar, a gift shop, and information about BC's First Nations. ⊠ *Brockton Point, Stanley Park*.

Fodor's Choice   **Vancouver Aquarium Marine Science Centre.** Massive floor-to-ceiling win-
★   dows let you get face-to-face with beluga whales, sea otters, sea lions,
FAMILY   dolphins, and harbor seals at this award-winning research and educa-
tional facility. In the Amazon Gallery you walk through a rain-forest jungle populated with piranhas, caimans, and tropical birds; in summer, hundreds of free-flying butterflies add to the mix. The Tropic Zone is home to exotic freshwater and saltwater life, including clown fish,

moray eels, and black-tip reef sharks. Other displays, many with hands-on features for kids, show the underwater life of coastal British Columbia and the Canadian Arctic. Beluga whale, sea lion, and dolphin shows, as well as dive shows (where divers swim with aquatic life, including sharks) are held daily. Be sure to check out the "4-D" film experience; it's a multisensory show that puts mist, smell, and wind into the 3-D equation. For an extra fee, you can help the trainers feed and train otters, belugas, and sea lions. There's also a café and a gift shop. Be prepared for lines on weekends and school holidays. In summer, the quietest time to visit is before 11 am or after 4 pm; in other seasons, the crowds are smaller before noon or after 2 pm. ⊠ *845 Avison Way, Stanley Park* ☎ *604/659–3474* ⊕ *www.vanaqua.org* ⊠ *C$30* ☉ *July– Labor Day, daily 9:30–6; Labor Day–June, daily 10–5.*

WORTH NOTING

Hollow Tree. Near Siwash Rock, this centuries-old 56-foot-wide burnt cedar stump has shrunk over the years but still gives an idea of how large some of the old-growth trees can grow. ⊠ *Stanley Park.*

FAMILY **Klahowya Village.** Celebrating the cultures of the First Nations whose historical territory encompasses parts of Stanley Park, this aboriginal village is staffed by First Nations artisans and performers who demonstrate carving, weaving, and other crafts; perform traditional dances; and hold storytelling sessions to narrate aboriginal legends. You can take a ride on the "Spirit Catcher" train, the child-size Miniature Railway (⇨ *see separate listing*) steam train that chugs through the woods, and sample aboriginal foods in the Raven's Landing café. The village is a short walk from the Stanley Park bus loop, the terminus for Bus 19 from downtown; the park shuttle stops nearby as well. ⊠ *Off Pipeline Rd., Stanley Park* ☎ *604/921–1070* ⊕ *www.aboriginalbc.com/ Klahowya-Village* ⊠ *village free, Spirit Catcher train C$5* ☉ *Mid-June–early Sept., daily 10–6.*

NEED A BREAK?

Stanley's Park Bar and Grill. In a 1911 manor house, this seasonal bar and grill with a large patio is very family-friendly, with a menu of burgers, fish, soups, and salads. It's not cheap but the location right in Stanley Park is great, especially mid-bike-ride. It overlooks the Rose Garden and is near the Malkin Bowl, where outdoor theater and concerts are held in summer. ⊠ *610 Pipeline Rd., Stanley Park* ☎ *604/602–3088* ⊕ *www. stanleyparkpavilion.com* ☉ *June–Sept.*

FAMILY **Lumbermen's Arch.** Made of one massive log, this archway, erected in 1952, is dedicated to the workers in Vancouver's first industry. Beside the arch is an asphalt path that leads back to Lost Lagoon and the Vancouver Aquarium. There's a picnic area, a snack bar, and small beach here, too. The Variety Kids Water Park is across the road. ⊠ *Stanley Park.*

FAMILY **Miniature Railway.** This child-size steam train takes kids and adults on a ride through the woods. In summer, the railway operates as the "Spirit Catcher," a First Nations–themed excursion as part of the Klahowya

A Tour of Stanley Park

Stanley Park Drive circles the park, often parallel to the **Seawall walking/cycling path.** If you're walking or cycling, start at the foot of Alberni Street, beside Lost Lagoon. Go through the underpass and veer right, following the cycle-path markings, to the seawall.

Whichever route you travel, the old wooden structure that you pass on your right is the Vancouver Rowing Club, a private athletic club established in 1903. Ahead and to your left is a parking lot, an information booth, and a turnoff to the aquarium and Painters Circle, where artists sell their work. A Salmon Demonstration Stream near the information booth has facts about the life cycle of the fish.

Continue along past the Royal Vancouver Yacht Club, and after ½ km (¼ mile) you'll reach the causeway to Deadman's Island. The **totem poles,** a bit farther down Stanley Park Drive and on your left, are a popular photo stop. The **Nine O'Clock Gun** is ahead at the water's edge, just past the sign for Hallelujah Point. Brockton Point and its small lighthouse and foghorn are to the north. Brockton Oval, where you can often catch a rugby game in winter or cricket in summer, is on your left. On the water side, watch for the *Girl in a Wetsuit,* a sculpture that mimics Copenhagen's *Little Mermaid.* A little farther along the seashore stands a replica of the dragon-shaped

figurehead from the SS *Empress of Japan,* which plied these waters between 1891 and 1922.

Lumbermen's Arch, a log archway, is at km 3 (mile 2) of the drive. There's a picnic area, a snack bar, and a small beach. The Variety Kids Water Park, across the road, is a big draw in summer. Cyclists and walkers can turn off here for a shortcut back to the **Vancouver Aquarium, Klahowya Village,** the **Miniature Railway,** and the park entrance.

At the Lions Gate Bridge: cyclists go under the bridge, past **Prospect Point**; drivers go over the bridge to a viewpoint–café at the top of Prospect Point. Both routes continue to the English Bay side of the park and its beaches. Keep an eye open for the **Hollow Tree.** The imposing monolith offshore (not visible from the road) is **Siwash Rock,** the focus of a native legend. Continue to the swimming area and snack bar at Third Beach, then the heated pool at Second Beach. If you're walking or cycling, you can shortcut from here back to Lost Lagoon by taking the perpendicular path behind the pool that cuts into the park. Either footbridge ahead leads to a path along the south side of the lagoon that will take you to Alberni and Georgia streets. If you continue along the seawall from Second Beach, you'll emerge into a residential part of the West End.

Aboriginal Village. Halloween displays draw crowds throughout October for the annual "Ghost Train," and at Christmastime, an elaborate light display illuminates the route during "Bright Nights." The train periodically runs outside of these special events, too; call or check the website for details. ⊠ *Off Pipeline Rd., Stanley Park* ☎ *604/257–8531* ⊕ *vancouver.ca/parks-recreation-culture/stanley-park-miniature-train.aspx* 🎫 *Special events (Spirit Catcher, Ghost Train, Bright Nights): C$8–C$11* ⊙ *Spirit Catcher mid-June–early*

An underwater view of a beluga whale at the Vancouver Aquarium.

Sept., Mon.–Thurs. 11–4, Fri.–Sun. 11–5; Ghost Train Oct., Mon.–Thurs. 6–10 pm, Fri.–Sun. 11 am–11 pm; Bright Nights Dec., Mon.–Thurs. 3–10 pm, Fri.–Sat. 11 am–11 pm, Sun. 11 am–10 pm; call for off-season hours and prices.

Nine O'Clock Gun. This cannonlike apparatus by the water was installed in 1890 to alert fishermen to a curfew ending weekend fishing. Now it signals 9 o'clock every night. ✉ *Stanley Park.*

Stanley Park Nature House. Vancouver's only ecology center is a treasure trove of information and showcases Stanley Park's true natural beauty with a host of programs and guided walks. The Nature House is on the south shore of Lost Lagoon, at the foot of Alberni Street. ✉ *Stanley Park, Alberni St., north end, under the viewing platform* ☎ *604/257–8544* 🌐 *www.stanleyparkecology.ca* 🎟 *guided walks C$10* ⏲ *July and Aug., Tues.–Sun. 10–5; Sept.–June, weekends 10–4.*

Siwash Rock. According to a local First Nations legend, this 50-foot-high offshore promontory is a monument to a man who was turned into stone as a reward for his unselfishness. The rock is visible from the seawall; if you're driving, you need to park and take a short path through the woods. ✉ *Stanley Park.*

GASTOWN AND CHINATOWN

Historic Gastown and adjacent Chinatown are full of character. They're favorite destinations for visitors and residents alike, and easily explored together. Both neighborhoods are experiencing gentrifcation as historic buildings get a new lease on life.

GASTOWN

Gastown is known for its cobblestone streets and Victorian era–style streetlamps; it's also joined Yaletown as one of Vancouver's trendiest neighborhoods, as überhip stores, ad agencies, high-tech companies, and restaurants take over refurbished brick warehouses. It's a relatively small area, bordered by Hastings, Richards, and Main streets and it was nicknamed for the garrulous ("Gassy") Jack Deighton who opened his saloon where his statue now stands on Maple Tree Square. This is essentially where Vancouver originated and it's the zero point from which all Vancouver street addresses start. By the time the first transcontinental train arrived in 1887, the waterfront area was crowded with hotels, warehouses, brothels, and dozens of saloons—you can still see place names such as Gaoler's Mews and Blood Alley, which hint at those early rough-and-tumble days.

GETTING HERE AND AROUND

Getting to Gastown is easy: head for the waterfront. It's just east of Waterfront Station. Allow about an hour to explore Gastown—that's without shopping too much.

TOP ATTRACTIONS

Steam Clock. An underground steam system, which also heats many local buildings, supplies the world's first steam clock—possibly Vancouver's most-photographed attraction. On the quarter hour a steam whistle rings out the Westminster chimes, and on the hour a huge cloud of steam spews from the apparatus. The ingenious design, based on an 1875 mechanism, was built in 1977 by Ray Saunders of Landmark

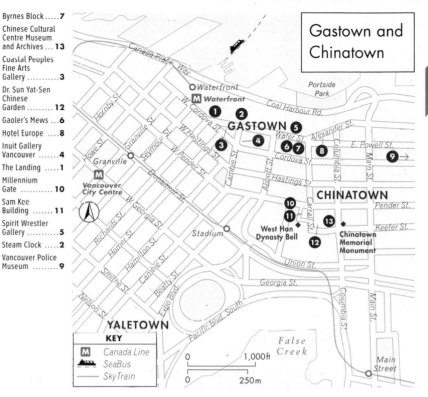

Clocks to commemorate the community effort that saved Gastown from demolition. ✉ *Gastown.*

Coastal Peoples Fine Arts Gallery. The collection of First Nations jewelry, ceremonial masks, prints, and carvings at this gallery is impressive. Check out the gorgeous books and postcards if you're looking for more affordable souvenirs. The gallery has a second location at 1024 Mainland Street in Yaletown. ✉ *312 Water St., Gastown* ☎ *604/684–9222* ⊕ *www.coastalpeoples.com.*

WORTH NOTING

Byrnes Block. After the 1886 Great Fire, which wiped out most of the fledgling settlement of Vancouver, George Byrnes built what is now Vancouver's oldest brick building. It now houses shops and offices, but for a while this two-story building was Vancouver's top luxury hotel, the Alhambra Hotel, charging a dollar a night. The site of Deighton's original saloon, east of the Byrnes Block where his statue now stands, is the starting point from which all Vancouver street addresses begin. ✉ *2 Water St., Gastown.*

Gaoler's Mews. Once the site of the city's first civic buildings—the constable's cabin and customs house, and a two-cell log jail—this atmospheric brick-paved courtyard is now home to cafés and offices. ✉ *Behind 12 Water St., Gastown.*

Inside the Coastal Peoples Fine Arts Gallery

Hotel Europe. Once billed as the best hotel in the city, this 1908 flatiron building is one of the world's finest examples of triangular architecture. Now used for government-subsidized housing and not open to the public, the building still has its original Italian tile work and lead-glass windows. The glass tiles in the sidewalk on Alexander Street were the former "skylight" for an underground saloon. ✉ *43 Powell St., Gastown.*

The Landing. Built in 1905 with gold-rush money, this elegantly renovated brick warehouse is now home to offices, shops, and Steamworks, a popular brewpub. From the oversized bay window at the rear of the lobby you can appreciate where the shoreline was 100 years ago, as well as enjoy terrific views of Burrard Inlet and the North Shore Mountains. ✉ *375 Water St., Gastown.*

Inuit Gallery of Vancouver. In addition to quality Inuit art like the signature carvings in soapstone and antler, there's also an excellent collection of Northwest Coast Native art such as baskets, totems, bentwood boxes, and masks. ✉ *206 Cambie St., Gastown* ☎ *888/615–8399, 604/688–7323* ⊕ *www.inuit.com.*

Spirit Wrestler Gallery. With exhibits that include works of the Pacific Northwest First Nations, the Inuit of the Canadian Arctic, and the New Zealand Maori, this gallery showcases an intriguing comparison of cultural styles. ✉ *47 Water St., Gastown* ☎ *604/669–8813* ⊕ *www. spiritwrestler.com.*

CHINATOWN

Although a large percentage of Vancouver's Chinese community has shifted to suburban Richmond, there's still a wonderful buzz of authenticity in the open-front markets, bakeries, and herbalist and import shops of the city's historic Chinatown. Street signs are in Chinese lettering, streetlights look like lanterns topped with decorative dragons, and much of the architecture is patterned on that of Guangzhou (Canton). Chinatown's early residents, immigrants who arrived from China in the late 1800s, came primarily to seek work in BC's emerging railroad and mining industries. More recently, hip young newcomers have been settling in the neighborhood, bringing funky shops, eclectic eateries, and even a few condominium buildings. You can still linger over a traditional dim sum lunch, but you can also settle in for a creative cocktail, a currywurst, or a slice of pie before scoping out the indie fashions.

You could easily spend an hour wandering around Chinatown, checking out the architecture and exotic wares; add at least an hour if you also want to visit the Dr. Sun Yat-Sen Classical Chinese Garden. Be aware that you might come across one or two seedy corners in Chinatown; it's all pretty safe by day, but you might prefer to cab it at night.

GETTING HERE AND AROUND

If you're heading to Chinatown from Gastown, it's about a 10 to 15 minute walk.

The #19 Metrotown and #22 Knight buses travel east to Chinatown from stops along West Pender Street; the #3 Main and #8 Fraser serve Gastown and Chinatown from Cordova and Seymour near Waterfront Station. The Stadium SkyTrain station is a five-minute walk from Chinatown. From the station head down the Keefer Street steps, and turn left at Abbott Street. This will take you to Pender Street and the Millennium Gate.

TOP ATTRACTIONS

Fodor's Choice
★

Dr. Sun Yat-Sen Chinese Garden. The first authentic Ming Dynasty–style garden outside China, this small garden was built in 1986 by 52 Chinese artisans from Suzhou. No power tools, screws, or nails were used in the construction. It incorporates design elements and traditional materials from several of Suzhou's centuries-old private gardens. Guided tours (45 minutes long), included in the ticket price, are conducted on the hour between mid-June and the end of August (call ahead or check the website for off-season tour times); these are valuable for understanding the philosophy and symbolism that are central to the garden's design. Covered walkways make this a good rainy-day choice. A concert series, including classical, Asian, world, jazz, and sacred music, plays on Friday evenings in July and August. The free public park next door is also designed as a traditional Chinese garden, though it's smaller and less elaborate—it's a pleasant place to sit but lacks the context that you get with a tour of the Sun Yat-Sen garden. ⊠ *578 Carrall St., Chinatown* ☎ *604/662–3207* ⊕ *www.vancouverchinesegarden.com* ⌑ *C$14* ⊙ *May–mid-June and Sept., daily 10–6; mid-June–Aug., daily 9:30–7; Oct., daily 10–4:30; Nov.–Apr., Tues.–Sun. 10–4:30.*

DID YOU KNOW?

Gastown's steam clock is one of the Vancouver's most famous landmarks. Rather than bells, a steam whistle sounds on the quarter hour.

WORTH NOTING

Chinese Cultural Centre Museum and Archives. The Chinese have a rich, grueling, and enduring history in British Columbia, and it's well represented in this Ming Dynasty–style facility. The art gallery upstairs hosts traveling exhibits by Chinese and Canadian artists, and an on-site military museum recalls the role of Chinese Canadians in the last two world wars. Across the street is the Chinatown Memorial Monument, commemorating the Chinese-Canadian community's contribution to the city, province, and country. The monument, shaped in the Chinese character "zhong," symbolizing moderation and harmony, is flanked by bronze statues of a railroad worker and a World War II soldier. ⊠ *555 Columbia St., Chinatown* ☎ *604/658–8880* ⊕ *www. cccvan.com* ☜ *C$3, Tues. by donation* ☯ *Tues.–Sun. 11–5.*

Millennium Gate. This four-pillar, three-story high, brightly painted arch spanning Pender Street was erected in 2002 to mark the millennium and commemorate the Chinese community's role in Vancouver's history. The gate incorporates both Eastern and Western symbols, and both traditional and modern Chinese themes. Just east of the Millennium Gate, a right turn will take you into Shanghai Alley. Also known as Chinatown Heritage Alley, this was the site of the first Chinese settlement in the Vancouver area. By 1890 Shanghai Alley and neighboring Canton Alley were home to about 1,000 Chinese residents. At the end of the alley is a replica of the West Han Dynasty Bell, a gift to Vancouver from the city of Guangzhou, China. Surrounding the bell is a series of panels relaying some of the area's early history. ⊠ *Chinatown.*

Sam Kee Building. *Ripley's Believe It or Not!* recognizes this six-foot-wide structure as the narrowest office building in the world. In 1913, after the city confiscated most of the then-owner's land to widen Pender Street, he built a store on what was left, in protest. Customers had to be served through the windows. The glass panes in the sidewalk on Pender Street once provided light for Chinatown's public baths, which, in the early 20th century, were in the basement here. The presence of this and other underground sites has fueled rumors that Chinatown and Gastown were connected by tunnels, enabling residents of the latter to anonymously enjoy the vices of the former. No such tunnels have been found, however. ⊠ *8 W. Pender St., Chinatown.*

OFF THE BEATEN PATH

Vancouver Police Museum. It's not in the best neighborhood, and its morgue and autopsy areas may be off-putting to some, but this museum on the edge of Chinatown provides an absorbing glimpse into the history of the Vancouver police and the city's criminal underside. Firearms and counterfeit money are on exhibit, as are clues from some of the region's unsolved crimes: one of the more compelling mysteries, "Babes in the Woods," is about two children whose remains were found in Stanley Park in the 1950s. ⊠ *240 E. Cordova St., Chinatown* ☎ *604/665–3346* ⊕ *www.vancouverpolicemuseum.ca* ☜ *C$10* ☯ *Tues.–Sat. 9–5.*

2

YALETOWN

Yaletown is one of Vancouver's most fashionable areas and one of the most impressive urban-redevelopment projects in North America.

Back in about 1985 the BC provincial government decided they were going to take a derelict industrial site on the north shore of False Creek, clean it up, and build a world's fair. Twenty million people showed up for Expo '86 and Yaletown, on the site of the fair, was born. The brick warehouses were turned into apartment buildings and offices, and the old loading docks are now terraces for cappuccino bars and trendy restaurants. There are brewpubs, day spas, retail and wholesale fashion outlets, and shops selling upscale home decor.

There's also a seaside walk and cycle path that completely encircles False Creek. It's hard to imagine that back in the 1880s and '90s this was probably the most lawless place in Canada: it was so far into the woods that the Royal Canadian Mounted Police complained they couldn't patrol it.

GETTING HERE AND AROUND
Parking is tight in Yaletown; your best bet is the lot at Library Square nearby. It's easy to walk here from Downtown, though, and there's a Yaletown stop on the Canada Line. You can also get here by boat: the False Creek and Aquabus ferries (☎ 604/689–5858) run every 15 minutes from 7 am to 10 pm between Granville Island, Science World, Yaletown, and the south shore of False Creek.

WORTH NOTING

FAMILY **BC Sports Hall of Fame and Museum.** Inside the BC Place Stadium complex, this museum celebrates the province's sports achievers in a series of historical displays. One gallery commemorates the 2010 Winter Olympics that were held in Vancouver; another honors the province's aboriginal artists. You can test your sprinting, climbing, and throwing prowess in the high-tech participation gallery. The Scavenger History Hunt quiz is equally engaging though not as energetic. An hour-long

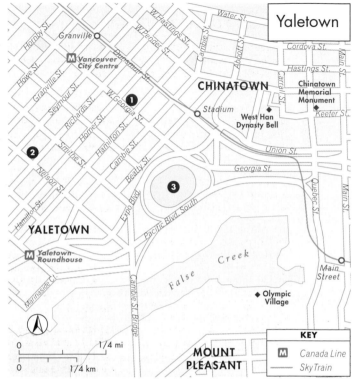

audio tour is included with admission. As you leave the museum, the **Terry Fox Memorial** is to your left. Created by artist Douglas Coupland, this series of four statues, each larger than the next, was built in honor of Terry Fox (1958–81), a local student whose cross-Canada run— after he lost his leg to cancer—raised millions of dollars for cancer research. Although Fox succumbed to the disease before he could complete his "Marathon of Hope," a memorial fund-raising run is now held annually in cities across Canada and around the world. ✉ *BC Place, 777 Pacific Blvd. S, Gate A, at Beatty and Robson Sts., Yaletown* ☎ *604/687–5520* ⊕ *www.bcsportshalloffame.com* 🖼 *C$15* ☉ *Daily 10–5.*

NEED A BREAK?

Urban Fare. Open daily 6 am–11 pm, this large and colorful grocery store is a popular destination for gastronomes, with food products from across BC and around the world. You can sample the wares at the café or purchase a take-out snack to eat at the water's edge overlooking an idyllic marina. There are additional Urban Fare outlets around town. ✉ *177 Davie St., Yaletown* ☎ *604/975–7550* ⊕ *www.urbanfare.com.*

Contemporary Art Gallery. On the lobby level of a modern apartment tower, this small nonprofit public gallery has regularly changing exhibits of contemporary local and international visual art. Events

2

TOP PLACES TO STROLL

Vancouver is a city for getting outdoors and walking around. These are some of our favorite streets for a stroll.

Robson Street: A shopaholic's dream come true, Robson has everything from finger-licking-good fudge to fashionista shopping.

Granville Island: It's always a voyage of discovery for fabulous local art, foodstuffs, boutique shops, street entertainment, and more.

West 4th Avenue: This Kitsilano strip is a prime shopping and eating destination, with funky fashions, fun gifts, and fine food.

Main Street: On the city's East Side, this is where many of Vancouver's independent fashion designers have set up shop: you'll find creative clothing and jewelry, plus several vintage and consignment boutiques.

Chinatown: Take your pick of exotic teas, sea cucumbers, dried seahorses, and nifty gifts along Keefer and East Pender streets; look

for a growing number of eclectic boutiques around the neighborhood, too.

Commercial Drive: From coffeehouses to the cantinas, "the Drive" has a healthy serving of cultural cool with an eclectic array of people and shops.

The West End: This lovely, tree-lined neighborhood is a refreshing change of pace from the urban commotion steps away.

Harborfront shoreline: With the water's edge on one side and glassy, million-dollar condo developments and commercial high-rises on the other, a walk along the harborfront epitomizes the future of this city.

Marinaside Crescent: Residents of Yaletown's intense-density condos flock to this walking and cycling path around False Creek. Combine your walk with a ride on an Aquabus ferry if time is short or your feet get weary.

include artists' talks, lectures, and tours. ⊠ *555 Nelson St., Yaletown* ☎ *604/681–2700* ⊕ *www.contemporaryartgallery.ca* 🖾 *By donation* ☉ *Tues.–Sun. noon–6.*

Library Square. The spiraling library building, open plazas, and lofty atrium of Library Square, completed in the mid-1990s, were built to evoke images of the Colosseum in Rome. A high-tech public library is the core of the structure; the outer edge of the spiral houses cafés and fast-food outlets. ⊠ *350 W. Georgia St., Yaletown* ☎ *604/331–3603* ⊕ *www.vpl.ca* ☉ *Mon.–Thurs. 10–9, Fri. and Sat. 10–6, Sun. 11–6.*

GRANVILLE ISLAND

Fodor's Choice
★

An indoor food market and a thriving diversity of artist studios as well as performing arts spaces, specialty shops (there's not a chain store or designer label in sight), and a busy marina make Granville Island one of Vancouver's top attractions.

Explore at your leisure but try to plan your expedition over a meal, since the market is an excellent place for breakfast, lunch, snacks, and shopping. The buildings behind the market are as diverse as the island's main attractions and house all sorts of crafts shops. The waterside boardwalk behind the Arts Club and around the Creekhouse building will bring you to Ocean Art Works, an open-sided longhouse-style structure where you can watch First Nations artists at work. Make time to visit the free contemporary galleries beside the covered walkway, and Sea Village, one of the few houseboat communities in Vancouver. Other nooks and alleys to note are Ron Basford Park, a natural amphitheater for outdoor performances, and Railspur Alley, home to about a dozen studios and galleries that produce everything from jewelry to leather work and sake.

Granville Island is also a venue for Vancouver's many performing arts festivals—and a great place to catch top-quality street entertainment at any time.

In the early 20th century False Creek was dredged for better access to the sawmills that lined the shore, and the sludge was heaped onto a sandbar that grew large enough to house much-needed industrial and logging-equipment plants. Although businesses thrived in the 1920s, most fell into derelict status by the '60s. In the early '70s, though, the federal government came up with a creative plan to redevelop the island with a public market, marine activities, and artisans' studios. The refurbished Granville Island opened to the public in 1979 and was an immediate hit with locals and visitors alike.

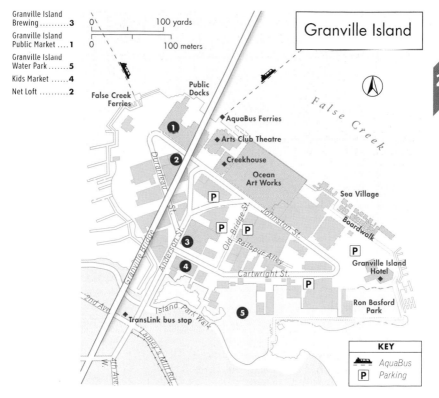

GETTING HERE AND AROUND

The mini Aquabus ferries are a favorite (and the most adorable) way to get to Granville Island (it's about a two-minute ride). They depart from the south end of Hornby Street (about a 15-minute walk from downtown Vancouver) and take passengers across False Creek to the Granville Island Public Market. The larger False Creek ferries leave every five minutes for Granville Island from a dock behind the Vancouver Aquatic Centre, on Beach Avenue. Still another option is to take a 10-minute ride on a TransLink bus: from Waterfront Station or stops on Granville Street, take #50 to the edge of the island. Several other Granville Street buses, including the #4, the #7, the #10, the #14, and #16, stop at West 5th Avenue and Granville Street, a few minutes' walk from the island. The market is a short walk from the bus or ferry stop. Come by public transit if you can, since the island's narrow roadways get clogged with traffic. If you do drive, parking is free for up to three hours (although free spots can be hard to find, particularly on busy summer days); paid parking is available in several island garages.

TIMING

If your schedule is tight, you can tour Granville Island in two to three hours. If you like to shop you could spend a full day.

TOP ATTRACTIONS

Fodor's Choice ★ **Granville Island Public Market.** The dozens of stalls in this 50,000-square-foot building sell locally grown fruits and vegetables direct from the farm and farther afield; other stalls stock crafts, chocolates, artisan cheeses and pastas, fish, meat, flowers, and exotic foods. On Thursday in summer, farmers sell fruit and vegetables from trucks outside. At the north end of the market, you can pick up a snack, lunch, or coffee from one of the many prepared-food vendors. The Market Courtyard, on the waterside, has great views of the city and is also a good place to catch street entertainers—be prepared to get roped into the action, if only to check the padlocks of an escape artist's gear. Weekends can get madly busy. ⊠ *1689 Johnston St., Granville Island* ☎ *604/666–6655* ⊕ *www. granvilleisland.com* ⊙ *Daily 9–7.*

WORTH NOTING

Granville Island Brewing. Tours of Canada's first modern microbrewery last about 45 minutes and include a four-ounce taste of three brews. You must be 19 years old and wearing close-toed shoes to take a tour. ⊠ *1441 Cartwright St., Granville Island* ☎ *604/687–2739* ⊕ *www. gib.ca* ▩ *C$9.75* ⊙ *Store open daily mid-May–early Sept. 10–9, early Sept.–mid-May 10–8. Tours mid-May–early Sept. daily at noon, 1:30 pm, 3 pm, 4:30 pm, and 5:30 pm; early Sept.–mid-May daily at noon, 2 pm, and 4 pm.*

FAMILY **Granville Island Water Park.** North America's largest, free public water park has slides, pipes, and sprinklers for children to run through. There's a grassy patch for picnics, and clean washrooms are at the adjacent community center. ⊠ *1318 Cartwright St., Granville Island* ☎ *604/257–8195* ⊕ *www.vancouver.ca/parks* ▩ *Free* ⊙ *Mid-May–Labor Day, daily 10–6; slides open mid-June.*

FAMILY **Kids Market.** A converted factory warehouse sets the stage for a slice of kids' heaven on Granville Island. The Kids Market has an indoor play area and two floors of small shops that sell all kinds of toys, magic gear, books, and other fun stuff. ⊠ *1496 Cartwright St., Granville Island* ☎ *604/689–8447* ⊕ *www.kidsmarket.ca* ⊙ *Daily 10–6.*

Net Loft. A former loft where fishermen used to dry their nets, this blue-and-red building includes a bookstore, a café, and a collection of high-quality boutiques selling imported and locally made crafts, exotic fabrics, handmade paper, and First Nations art. ⊠ *1666 Johnston St., Granville Island* ☎ ⊙ *Daily 10–7.*

THE WEST SIDE

The West Side, the set of diverse neighborhoods just south of Downtown, has some of Vancouver's best gardens and natural sights as well as some chic shopping. "Kits," as the locals refer to Kitsilano, though, is really where all the action is.

Most references to "the West Side," neighborhoods just south of Downtown, have moneyed connotations: there are South Granville's chic galleries and upscale shopping, the old-family mansions of Shaughnessy, the tony university district around Point Grey, and the revitalized area along the Cambie Street corridor. Even the once-hippie Kitsilano neighborhood has evolved into an upscale district of shops, restaurants, museums, and one of the city's best people-watching beaches. Basically, the West Side is the antithesis of the city's funkier, lower-income East Side.

Individual attractions on the West Side are easily reached by the Canada Line and TransLink buses, but a car makes things easier, especially if you want to see more than one of these sites in a day. From Downtown, you can take the Burrard, Granville, or Cambie Street bridges to get to the West Side.

KITSILANO

The beachfront district of Kitsilano (popularly known as Kits) is one of Vancouver's trendiest neighborhoods. Originally inhabited by the Squamish people, whose Chief Khahtsahlanough gave the area its name, Kitsilano has fashionable shops, popular clubs and cafés, and three museums (the Museum of Vancouver, the Vancouver Maritime Museum, and the H.R. MacMillan Space Centre), all in beachside Vanier Park. Kits has hidden treasures, too: rare boats moored at Heritage Harbour, stately mansions on forested lots, and, all along the waterfront, quiet coves and shady paths within a stone's throw of lively **Kits Beach** (⇨ *see the Beaches section of Sports and the Outdoors*), one of the city's most popular spots for sun and sand.

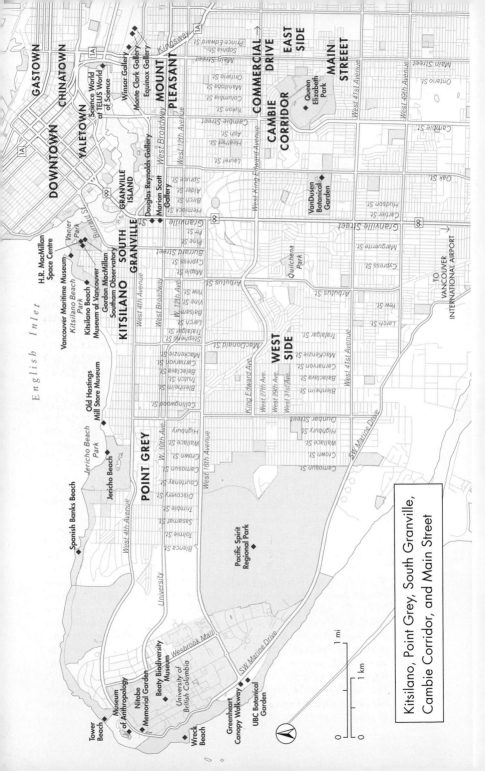

Kitsilano, Point Grey, South Granville, Cambie Corridor, and Main Street

2

GETTING HERE AND AROUND

The most enjoyable way to get to Kitsilano is by a False Creek ferry from Granville Island or from the dock behind the Vancouver Aquatic Centre, on Beach Avenue. The ferries dock at Heritage Harbour in Kitsilano, behind the Vancouver Maritime Museum. You can also walk or cycle the 1 km (½ mile) or so along the waterfront pathway from Granville Island (leave the island by Anderson Street and keep to your right along the waterfront, following the Seaside Bike Path signs). If you prefer to come by road, drive over the Burrard Street Bridge, turn right at Chestnut Street, and park in either of the museum parking lots. By public transit, take Bus #2 or #22, traveling south on Burrard Street downtown, get off at Cypress Street and Cornwall Avenue, and walk over to Vanier park; for Kits Beach, get off the bus at Arbutus or Yew streets.

WORTH NOTING

FAMILY **H.R. MacMillan Space Centre.** The interactive exhibits and high-tech learning systems at this museum include a Virtual Voyages ride, where visitors can take a simulated space journey (definitely not for those afraid of flying); GroundStation Canada, showcasing Canada's achievements in space; and the Cosmic Courtyard, full of hands-on space-oriented exhibits including a moon rock and a computer program that shows what you would look like as an alien. You can catch daytime astronomy shows or evening music-and-laser shows at the **H.R. MacMillan Planetarium.** ⊠ *Vanier Park, 1100 Chestnut St., Kitsilano* ☎ *604/738–7827* ⊕ *www.spacecentre.ca* ✉ *C$18* ⊙ *July and Aug., daily 10–5; Sept.–June, weekdays 10–3, Sat. 10–5, Sun. noon–5.*

Gordon MacMillan Southam Observatory When the sky is clear, the ½-meter telescope at the Gordon MacMillan Southam Observatory is focused on whatever stars or planets are worth watching that night. Admission to the observatory is by donation and it's open year-round Saturday evenings, from 8 to midnight, weather permitting. ⊠ *Kitsilano* ☎ *604/738–2855.*

Museum of Vancouver. Vancouver's short-but-funky history comes to life at this seaside museum. The 1930s gallery remembers some poignant episodes involving the Japanese internment during WWII, as well as local stories of the war effort. The 1950s Gallery has a 1955 Ford Fairlane Victoria and a Seeburg select-o-matic jukebox. The 1960s-theme Revolution Gallery revisits the city's days as the hippie capital of Canada: visitors can hear local bands from the '60s and poke around a re-created communal house. The museum regularly mounts intriguing temporary exhibits and hosts lectures and other public events. ⊠ *Vanier Park, 1100 Chestnut St., Kitsilano* ☎ *604/736–4431* ⊕ *www.museumofvancouver.com* ✉ *C$14* ⊙ *July and Aug., Fri.–Wed. 10–5, Thurs. 10–8; Sept.–June, Tues., Wed., and Fri.–Sun. 10–5, Thurs. 10–8.*

FAMILY **Vancouver Maritime Museum.** Sharing the seafaring history of the Pacific Northwest and Arctic regions, this family-friendly museum houses the *RCMP Arctic St. Roch*, the first ship to sail in both directions through the treacherous Northwest Passage and the first to circumnavigate North America. You can scramble around the decks and into the St.

Roch's cabins, imagining yourself as a sea captain attempting to navigate the Arctic. About a third of this museum has been turned over to kids, with touchable displays offering a chance to drive a tug, maneuver an underwater robot, or dress up as a seafarer. Toddlers and school-age children can work the hands-on displays in Pirates' Cove and the Children's Maritime Discovery Centre. The museum also has an extensive collection of model ships. While you're here, take a moment to look at the 100-foot-tall replica Kwakiutl totem pole in front of the museum. The massive white-and-yellow contraption behind the Vancouver Maritime Museum is the *Ben Franklin* submersible. It looks like something a Jules Verne character would put to sea but was actually built in 1968 as a marine research tool to, among other things, chart the Gulf Stream. A more fascinating claim to fame is that it was once the largest of its kind in America and was instructional for NASA: the information about how people lived in such close quarters for extended periods of time provided preliminary research data on the dynamics of living aboard a space station. ⊠ *Vanier Park, 1905 Ogden Ave., north end of Cypress St., Kitsilano* ☎ *604/257–8300* ⊕ *www.vancouvermaritimemuseum. com* 🖾 *C$11* ⊙ *Mid-May–Labor Day, daily 10–5; Labor Day–mid-May, Tues.–Sat. 10–5, Sun. noon–5.*

Vanier Park. Home to the **Museum of Vancouver**, the **Vancouver Maritime Museum**, and the **H.R. MacMillan Space Centre**, Vanier Park is also known as the best kite-flying venue in the city. Every summer, this is also where you'll find the Children's Festival and Bard on the Beach theater—both presented under billowing tents. ⊠ *Kitsilano* 🖾 *free.*

POINT GREY

Some of Vancouver's best gardens, natural sights, and museums, including the renowned Museum of Anthropology on the campus of the University of British Columbia, are southwest of downtown Vancouver in the Point Grey neighborhood. Established in 1908, UBC is the city's main university campus with a student population of nearly 50,000. The university is also where you'll find the Chan Centre for the Performing Arts (⇨ *see the Nightlife and Performing Arts chapter*), the Botanical Gardens, and Pacific Spirit Regional Park—the latter, although it can't compare with Stanley Park, is where the locals go for meandering forested trails that put you in touch with nature.

UBC Museums and Gardens Pass. If you're planning to visit several of the attractions at the University of British Columbia, the UBC Museums and Garden Pass can save you money. It includes admission to the Museum of Anthropology, UBC Botanical Garden, Nitobe Memorial Garden, and Beaty Biodiversity Museum. There's also a family version of the pass (C$85) that covers two adults and up to four children under 18. The pass doesn't include the Greenheart Canopy Walkway, but it does give you 10% off walkway tickets. Passes are valid for six months, so you don't need to squeeze all your sightseeing into one day. Purchase the pass at any of the participating attractions. ⊕ *www.botanicalgarden. ubc.ca/rates* 🖾 *C$33.*

GETTING HERE AND AROUND

Except during rush hour, it takes about 30 minutes to drive and 30–40 minutes to travel by bus from Downtown to the University of British Columbia.

TOP ATTRACTIONS

Fodor's Choice **Museum of Anthropology.** Part of the University of British Columbia, the
★ MOA has one of the world's leading collections of Northwest Coast First Nations art. The Great Hall has dramatic cedar poles, bentwood boxes, and canoes adorned with traditional Northwest Coast–painted designs. On clear days, the gallery's 50-foot-tall windows reveal a striking backdrop of mountains and sea. Another highlight is the work of the late Bill Reid, one of Canada's most respected Haida artists. In *The Raven and the First Men* (1980), carved in yellow cedar, he tells a Haida story of creation. Reid's gold-and-silver jewelry work is also on display, as are exquisite carvings of gold, silver, and argillite (a black shale found on Haida Gwaii, also known as the Queen Charlotte Islands) by other First Nations artists. The museum's visible storage section displays, in drawers and cases, contain thousands of examples of tools, textiles, masks, and other artifacts from around the world. The Koerner Ceramics Gallery contains 600 pieces from 15th- to 19th-century Europe. Behind the museum are two Haida houses, set on the cliff over the water. Free guided tours—given several times daily (call or check the website for times)—are immensely informative. For an extra C$5 you can rent a VUEguide—an electronic device that senses where you are in the museum and shows relevant artist interviews, archival footage, and photographs of the artifacts in their original contexts, on a hand-held screen. The MOA also has an excellent book and fine-art shop, as well as a café. To reach the museum by transit, take any UBC-bound bus from Granville Street downtown to the university bus loop, a 15-minute walk (or 10-minute ride on shuttle bus C18 or C20) from the museum. Pay parking is available in the Rose Garden parking lot, across Marine Drive from the museum. A UBC Museums and Gardens Pass will save you money if you're planning to visit several attractions at UBC. ☒ *University of British Columbia, 6393 N.W. Marine Dr., Point Grey* ☎ *604/822–5087* ⊕ *www.moa.ubc.ca* ☒ *C$16.75, Tues. 5–9 C$9;* ☉ *Late May–mid-Oct., Tues. 10–9, Wed.–Mon. 10–5; mid-Oct.–late May, Tues. 10–9, Wed.–Sun. 10–5.*

Nitobe Memorial Garden. Opened in 1960 in memory of Japanese scholar and diplomat Dr. Inazo Nitobe (1862–1933), this 2½-acre walled garden, which includes a pond, a stream with a small waterfall, and a ceremonial teahouse, is considered one of the most authentic Japanese tea and strolling gardens outside Japan. Designed by Professor Kannosuke Mori of Japan's Chiba University, the garden incorporates many native British Columbia trees and shrubs, pruned and trained Japanese style, and interplanted with Japanese maples and flowering shrubs. The circular path around the park symbolizes the cycle of life and provides a tranquil view from every direction. Cherry blossoms are the highlight in April and May, and in June the irises are magnificent.

Because the garden is so exotic, it's worth renting an audio guide. Japanese tea ceremonies are held the last Saturday of every month, May through September; call 604/939–7749 for reservations. A UBC Museums and Gardens Pass will save you money if you're planning to visit several attractions at UBC. ⊠ *University of British Columbia, 1895 Lower Mall, Point Grey* 🕾 *604/822–6038* ⊕ *www.botanicalgarden. ubc.ca/nitobe* 🖾 *C$7 Apr.–Oct.; C$13 includes admission to the UBC Botanical Garden; by donation Nov.–Mar.* ☉ *Apr.–Oct., daily 9:30–5; Nov.–Mar., weekdays 10–2.*

FAMILY **University of British Columbia Botanical Garden.** Ten thousand trees, shrubs, and rare plants from around the world thrive on this 70-acre research site on the university campus, which edges on Pacific Spirit Park. The complex feels as far away from the city as you can get, with forested walkways through an Asian garden, a garden of medicinal plants, and an alpine garden with some of the world's rarest plants. A Walk in the Woods is a 20-minute loop that takes you through more than 1,000 species of coastal plant life. The garden gift store is one of the best of its kind. One-hour guided tours, free with garden admission, are offered on certain days; call or check the website for schedule. A UBC Museums and Gardens Pass will save you money if you're planning to visit several attractions at UBC.

The 308-meter-long (1,010-foot-long) **Greenheart Canopy Walkway,** a swaying network of suspended bridges weaving a trail between gargantuan cedars and hemlocks, is a thrilling way to explore the garden. Along the way, you stop off on eight platforms in the trees, each more than 15 meters (49 feet) high, while an additional two-story viewing platform tops a free-standing tower more than 22 meters (72 feet) in the air. Visits to the walkway are by 45-minute guided tour, where you learn about the forest, local wildlife, environmental issues, and First Nations traditions; call or check the website for seasonal tour schedules. The walkway is a great adventure for kids; just note that small children must either be able to walk on their own or be carried in a child backpack or other carrier (strollers aren't permitted).

⊠ *6804 S.W. Marine Dr., Point Grey* 🕾 *604/822–4208* ⊕ *www. botanicalgarden.ubc.ca* 🖾 *C$9; C$13 includes admission to Nitobe Memorial Garden; C$20 includes Greenheart Canopy Walkway; C$24 includes Nitobe Memorial Garden and Greenheart Canopy Walkway* ☉ *Daily 9:30–5.*

WORTH NOTING

FAMILY **Beaty Biodiversity Museum.** If you can imagine a vast underground library but instead of books, the stacks are filled with bones, fossils, and preserved lizards, then you can begin to imagine this modern museum on the UBC campus that exhibits more than two million specimens from the university's natural history collections. The most striking attraction hangs in the entrance atrium: a 25-meter-long (82-foot-long) skeleton of a blue whale—the largest on view in Canada (the blue whale in New York's American Museum of Natural History is 94 feet long). On the lower level, you'll find scads of animal skulls, taxidermied birds, and other creatures displayed through glass windows (many of which

The exhibits outside the museum, on the cliffs overlooking the water, are part of the attraction of the Museum of Anthropology.

are at kids' eye level). In the interactive Discovery Lab, you can play scientist yourself; you might compare the claws of different birds or examine animal poop under a microscope. There's also a family space stocked with books, art supplies, and kid-size furniture. To find the museum from the university bus loop, walk west to the Main Mall and turn left; the museum is just south of University Boulevard. A ⇨ ⇨ *UBC Museums and Gardens Pass* will save you money if you're planning to visit several attractions at UBC. ⊠ *University of British Columbia, 2212 Main Mall, Point Grey* ☎ *604/827–4955* ⊕ *www. beatymuseum.ubc.ca* ✉ *C$12* ☾ *Mid-May–mid-Oct., daily 10–5; mid-Oct.–mid-May, Tues.–Sun. 10–5.*

EN ROUTE **Old Hastings Mill Store Museum.** Vancouver's first store and oldest building was built in 1865 at the foot of Dunlevy Street in Gastown and moved to this seaside spot near the Royal Vancouver Yacht Club in 1930. It's a little wooden structure at the corner of Point Grey Road and Alma Street– west of Kitsilano en route to UBC—and is the only building to predate the 1886 Great Fire. The site is now a museum with displays of First Nations artifacts and pioneer household goods. ⊠ *1575 Alma St., Point Grey* ☎ *604/734–1212* ⊕ *hastings-mill-museum.ca* ✉ *By donation* ☾ *Open mid-June–mid-Sept., Tues.–Sun. 1–4; mid-Sept.–mid-Dec. and Feb.–mid-June, weekends 1–4.*

Pacific Spirit Regional Park. Close to the University of British Columbia, on Vancouver's West Side, Pacific Spirit Regional Park has 73 km (45 miles) of multi-use walking, hiking, and biking trails within its 763-hectare (1,885-acre) forest. Open dawn to dusk year-round, it also has access to Spanish Banks and Wreck beaches. ⊠ *4915 W. 16th Ave., Point Grey* ☎ *604/224–5739* ⊕ *www.metrovancouver.org.*

SOUTH GRANVILLE

The section of Granville Street between 5th and 15th avenues is the city's traditional "Gallery Row." Although some showrooms have decamped to larger, less expensive quarters on the East Side, a number of high-end galleries remain, alongside furniture stores and upscale clothing boutiques.

GETTING HERE AND AROUND

If you cross the Granville Bridge from Downtown, you'll be in South Granville. Several Translink buses can take you here; Bus #10 runs the length of Granville Street, Bus #4 or #7 will drop you at West 5th and Granville, and Bus #14 or #16 stop at the corner of Broadway and Granville.

TOP ATTRACTIONS

Douglas Reynolds Gallery. In this collection of Northwest Coast First Nations art, which is particularly strong in woodwork and jewelry, some pieces date back to the 1800s, while others are strikingly contemporary. ⊠ *2335 Granville St., South Granville* ☎ *604/731–9292* ⊕ *www.douglasreynoldsgallery.com.*

WORTH NOTING

Marion Scott Gallery. Specializing in fine Inuit art from the Canadian North, exhibits here include sculpture, prints, wall hangings, and drawings. ⊠ *2423 Granville St., South Granville* ☎ *604/685–1934* ⊕ *marionscottgallery.com.*

CAMBIE CORRIDOR

Two of Vancouver's top garden attractions are over the Cambie Bridge, south of Downtown: Queen Elizabeth Park (just off Cambie at 33rd Avenue), and the VanDusen Botanical Garden, which is at Oak Street at 37th Avenue, west of Cambie. The Cambie Corridor has also become something of a shopping destination, with several big box stores clustered near the intersection of Broadway and Cambie, and more independent shops in the blocks between 18th and 20th avenues.

GETTING HERE AND AROUND

The Canada Line SkyTrain runs along Cambie Street after traversing False Creek from Downtown. Stops convenient for the area include Olympic Village (at West 2nd Avenue), Broadway/City Hall, King Edward (the closest stop to Queen Elizabeth Park), and Oakridge/41st (for the Oakridge Centre shopping mall).

TOP ATTRACTIONS

FAMILY **Queen Elizabeth Park.** Lavish sunken gardens (in a former stone quarry), a rose garden, and an abundance of grassy picnicking spots are just a few of the highlights at this 52-hectare (130-acre) park. Poised at the highest point in the city, there are 360-degree views of Downtown. Other park facilities include 18 tennis courts, pitch and putt (an 18-hole putting

2

green), and a restaurant. On summer evenings there's free outdoor dancing on the Plaza—everything from Scottish country dance to salsa, for all ages and levels. In the **Bloedel Conservatory** you can see tropical and desert plants and 100 species of free-flying tropical birds in a glass geodesic dome—the perfect place to be on a rainy day. To reach the park by public transportation, take the Canada Line to King Edward station; from there, it's a six-block walk to the edge of the park (and a hike up the hill to appreciate the views). Cambie Bus 15, which runs south along Cambie Street from the Olympic Village SkyTrain station, will drop you a little closer, at the corner of 33rd and Cambie. Park activities make for a great family excursion, and unlike Stanley Park with its acres of rain forest, Queen Elizabeth Park is all about the flowers. ⊠ *Cambie St. and 33rd Ave., Cambie Corridor* ☏ *604/257–8584* ⊕ *www.vancouver.ca/parks* ⊠ *Conservatory C$6.50* ☉ *Park daily year-round; Bloedel Conservatory May–early Sept., weekdays 9–8, weekends 10–8; early Sept.–Apr., daily 10–5.*

FAMILY **VanDusen Botanical Garden.** An Elizabethan maze, a formal rose garden, a meditation garden, and a collection of Canadian heritage plants are among the many displays at this 55-acre site. The collections include flora from every continent and many rare and endangered species. The Phyllis Bentall Garden area features hybrid water lilies and carnivorous plants (a hit with kids). From mid-May to early June the Laburnum Walk forms a canopy of gold; in August and September the wildflower meadow is in bloom. The garden is also home to five lakes, a garden shop, a library, and the Truffles Fine Foods Café (serving breakfast, lunch, and afternoon tea). Special events throughout the year include a spectacular Christmas-theme Festival of Lights every December (daily 4:30–9 pm). From Downtown, catch the Oak Bus #17 directly to the garden entrance; alternatively, ride the Canada Line to Oakridge/41st, then take the UBC Bus #41 to Oak Street, and walk four blocks north to the garden. Queen Elizabeth Park is a 1-km (½-mile) walk away, along West 37th Avenue. Because this was once a golf course, pathways make this garden extremely wheelchair accessible. ⊠ *5251 Oak St., at W. 37th Ave., Cambie Corridor* ☏ *604/257–8335 garden, 604/267–4966 restaurant* ⊕ *www.vandusengarden.org* ⊠ *C$10.75 Apr.–Sept.; C$7.75 Oct.–Mar.* ☉ *June–Aug., daily 9 am–9 pm; Apr.–May and Sept.–Oct, daily from 9 am, Nov.–Mar. daily from 10 am (call for seasonal closing times).*

THE EAST SIDE

Vancouver's East Side, which spans the area from Ontario Street east to the suburb of Burnaby, was originally a working-class district. These days, as real estate prices across the city have continued to climb, many artists, young families, and professional people have moved east, and this half of the metropolitan area now mixes multicultural residential communities, art galleries, theaters, and an eclectic assortment of restaurants.

MAIN STREET/MT. PLEASANT

Main Street bisects Vancouver, running from the Burrard Inlet and Chinatown south to the Fraser River. Science World, the city's popular science museum is just off Main, as is the rail station and the Olympic Village, a residential community that housed Olympic athletes during the 2010 Winter Games. An arts district known as "The Flats" has emerged off Main, near East 2nd Avenue and Great Northern Way, where a growing number of contemporary art galleries have set up shop. On the south end, Main Street is lined with independent boutiques that showcase local designers, as well as lots of intriguing places to eat. At the interection of Main and East 49th Avenue is the Punjabi Market, a long-established "Little India"; while many newer Indo-Canadian immigrants have settled outside Vancouver, in Surrey and other suburbs, the Punjabi Market is worth visiting for its jewelry stores, sari shops, and restaurants.

The Main Street/Science World SkyTrain station is one block from both Pacific Central Station and Science World. Plenty of buses travel around this side of town, too. From Downtown, Bus #3 goes down Main Street. Another useful route is the express Bus #99, which travels east-west along Broadway, linking the University of British Columbia with both Main Street and Commercial Drive.

2

GETTING HERE AND AROUND

The Main Street/Science World SkyTrain station is one block from both Pacific Central Station and Science World. Plenty of buses travel around this side of town, too. From Downtown, Bus #3 goes down Main Street. Another useful route is the express Bus #99, which travels east-west along Broadway, linking the University of British Columbia with both Main Street and Commercial Drive.

TOP ATTRACTIONS

FAMILY **Science World.** In a gigantic shiny dome on the False Creek waterfront, this hands-on science center encourages children to participate in interactive exhibits and demonstrations about the natural world, the human body, and other science topics. Exhibits change throughout the year, so there's always something new to see; there's an Omnimax theater, too. Adjacent to the museum, the Ken Spencer Science Park is an outdoor exhibit area focusing on environmental issues. Science World is an easy walk (or mini-ferry ride) from Yaletown; the Main Street/Science World SkyTrain station is on its doorstep, and there's plenty of parking. ⊠ *1455 Quebec St., Main St./Mt. Pleasant* ☎ *604/443–7440* ⊕ *www.scienceworld.ca* ⊠ *C$23.50 Science World, C$29 Science World and Omnimax theater* ۞ *July–Labor Day, daily 10–6; Labor Day–June, weekdays 10–5, weekends 10–6.*

WORTH NOTING

Equinox Gallery. In a bright orange former tractor company building, this 14,000-square-foot gallery exhibits works by contemporary Canadian and international artists. The Monte Clark Gallery is in the same building. ⊠ *525 Great Northern Way, Main St./Mt. Pleasant* ☎ *604/736–2405* ⊕ *www.equinoxgallery.com* ⊠ *free* ۞ *Tues.–Sat. 10–5.*

Monte Clark Gallery. Next door to the Equinox Gallery, in a former tractor company facility now painted bright orange, this two-level space showcases work by contemporary Canadian artists. ⊠ *525 Great Northern Way, Main St./Mt. Pleasant* ☎ *604/730–5000* ⊕ *www.monteclarkgallery.com* ⊠ *free* ۞ *Tues.–Sat. 10–5:30.*

Winsor Gallery. Owner Jennifer Winsor exhibits works by Canadian and international artists in her 7,000-square-foot gallery, just east of Main Street. ⊠ *258 East 1st Ave., Main St./Mt. Pleasant* ☎ *604/681–4870* ⊕ *www.winsorgallery.com* ⊠ *free* ۞ *Tues.–Fri. 10–6, Sat. 10–5.*

COMMERCIAL DRIVE AND AROUND

East of Main Street, Commercial Drive used to be the hub of Vancouver's Italian community. These days, the area is popular for its many cafés, drinking spots, and funky shops.

The SkyTrain runs through the East Side, with a stop at Broadway/Commercial. Plenty of buses travel around this side of town, too. From downtown, Bus 20 will take you to Commercial Drive. Another useful route is the express Bus 99, which travels east-west along Broadway, linking the University of British Columbia with both Main Street and Commercial Drive.

NORTH SHORE

The North Shore and its star attractions—the Capilano Suspension Bridge, Grouse Mountain, Lonsdale Quay, and, farther east, the lovely hamlet of Deep Cove—are just a short trip from downtown Vancouver. The North Shore is where people come to kayak up fjords, and hike, ski, and explore the forest and mountainous terrain. The two main communities on the North Shore are North Vancouver and West Vancouver.

NORTH VANCOUVER

North Vancouver is probably the most commercial of the North Shore communities, and it's where you'll find popular tourist destinations, including Grouse Mountain and the Capilano Suspension Bridge. It's worth noting that there's another suspension bridge in the area, at lesser-known Lynn Canyon, and that one is free. If you're trying to decide between the two, the Lynn Canyon bridge is shorter (130 feet versus 450 feet at Capilano), and it's not quite as high over the canyon. Lynn Canyon is a little harder to get to than Capilano, especially if you don't have a car. The Capilano bridge is a high-profile tourist attraction whereas Lynn Canyon is a public park with the bridge and hiking trails.

GETTING HERE AND AROUND
From downtown, drive west down Georgia Street to Stanley Park and across the Lions Gate Bridge to North Vancouver. Stay in the right lane, take the North Vancouver exit, and then turn left onto Capilano Road. In about 2 km (1 mile), you'll arrive at the Capilano Suspension Bridge. A few hundred yards up Capilano Road, on the left, is the entrance to Capilano River Regional Park. About 1½ km (1 mile) along the park access road is the Capilano Salmon Hatchery.

Returning to Capilano Road and continuing north, you'll reach Cleveland Dam (also part of the park), where you can stop for great mountain views. As you continue north, Capilano Road becomes Nancy Greene Way, which ends at the base of Grouse Mountain.

If you don't have a car, you can take the SeaBus from Waterfront Station to Lonsdale Quay and then catch a Grouse Mountain Bus #236. This stops at the Capilano Suspension Bridge and near the Salmon Hatchery on its way to the base of Grouse Mountain. It's an easy trip, but if you only have the Capilano Suspension Bridge on your agenda, take advantage of its complimentary shuttle from Downtown.

TIMING

You need at least a half day to see the sights around the North Shore; allow a full day if you want to hike at Grouse Mountain or Capilano River Regional Park, or include a meandering drive through West Vancouver. You'll literally pass the entrance of the Capilano Bridge en route to Grouse Mountain, so it makes sense to do both together. To save time, avoid crossing the Lions Gate Bridge during weekday rush hours (about 7–9 am and 3–6 pm).

TOP ATTRACTIONS

Fodor'sChoice
★
FAMILY

Capilano Suspension Bridge. At Vancouver's oldest tourist attraction (the original bridge was built in 1889), you can get a taste of rain-forest scenery and test your mettle on the swaying, 450-foot cedar-plank suspension bridge that hangs 230 feet above the rushing Capilano River. Across the bridge is the Treetops Adventure, where you can walk along 650 feet of cable bridges suspended among the trees. If you're even braver, you can follow the **Cliffwalk**, a series of narrow cantilevered bridges and walkways hanging out over the edge of the canyon. Without crossing the bridge, you can enjoy the site's viewing decks, nature trails, totem park, and carving center (where you can watch First Nations carvers at work), as well as history and forestry exhibits. There's also a massive gift shop in the original 1911 teahouse, and a restaurant. May through October, guides in 19th-century costumes conduct free tours on themes related to history, nature, or ecology, while fiddle bands, First Nations dancers, and other entertainers keep things lively. In December, more than 250,000 lights illuminate the canyon during the Canyon Lights winter celebration. Catch the attraction's free shuttle service from Canada Place; it also stops along Burrard and Robson streets. ✉ *3735 Capilano Rd., North Vancouver* ☎ *604/985–7474* ⊕ *www.capbridge.com* 💳 *C$34.95* ⊙ *Mid-May–Labor Day, daily 8:30–8; Labor Day–mid-Oct. and mid-Mar.–mid-Apr. daily 9–6; mid-Oct.–Nov. and Jan–mid-Mar., daily 9–5; Dec. daily 11–9; mid-Apr.–mid-May daily 9–7.*

Fodor'sChoice
★
FAMILY

Grouse Mountain. North America's largest aerial tramway, the **Skyride** is a great way to take in the city, sea, and mountain vistas (be sure to pick a clear day or evening). The Skyride makes the 2-km (1-mile) climb to the peak of Grouse Mountain every 15 minutes. Once at the top you can watch a half-hour video presentation at the Theatre in the Sky (it's included with your Skyride ticket). Other mountaintop activities include, in summer, lumberjack shows, chairlift rides, walking tours, hiking, falconry demonstrations, and a chance to visit the grizzly bears and gray wolves in the mountain's wildlife refuge. For an extra fee you can also try zip-lining and tandem paragliding, tour the wind turbine that tops the mountain, or take a helicopter flight. In winter you can ski, snowshoe, snowboard, ice-skate on a mountaintop pond, or take Sno-Cat-drawn sleigh rides. A stone-and-cedar lodge is home to snack shops, a pub-style bistro, and a high-end restaurant, all with expansive city views. The Grouse Grind—a hiking trail up the face of the mountain—is one of the best workouts on the North Shore. Depending on your fitness level, allow between 40 minutes and two hours to complete it (90 minutes is an average time). Then you can take the Skyride down. The BCMC Trail is a less crowded, slightly longer alternative. From late May through September, you can catch a free shuttle to Grouse Mountain from Canada Place. ⊠ *6400 Nancy Greene Way, North Vancouver* ☎ *604/980–9311* ⊕ *www.grousemountain.com* ⧉ *Skyride and many activities C$39.95* ⊙ *Daily 9 am–10 pm.*

WORTH NOTING

FAMILY **Capilano River Regional Park.** This small but spectacular park is where you'll find old-growth Douglas fir trees approaching 61 meters (200 feet). There are 26 km (16 miles) of hiking trails and footbridges over the Capilano River, which cuts through a dramatic gorge. At the park's **Capilano Salmon Hatchery** (*4500 Capilano Park Rd., 604/666–1790*), viewing areas and exhibits illustrate the life cycle of the salmon. The best time to see the salmon run is between July and November. **The Cleveland Dam** (*Capilano Rd., about 1½ km [1 mile] past main park entrance*) is at the north end of the park. Built in 1954 and named for Dr. E.A. Cleveland, a former chief commissioner of the Greater Vancouver Water District, it dams the Capilano River to create the 5½-km-long (3½-mile-long) Capilano Reservoir. A hundred yards from the parking lot, you can walk across the top of the dam to enjoy striking views of the reservoir and mountains behind it. The two sharp peaks to the west are the Lions, for which the Lions Gate Bridge is named. The park is off Capilano Road in North Vancouver, near Capilano Suspension Bridge. ⊠ *Capilano Rd., North Vancouver* ☎ *604/224–5739* ⊕ *www.metrovancouver.org/services/parks_lscr/ regionalparks/pages/capilanoriver.aspx* ⧉ *Free* ⊙ *Park daily 8–dusk. Hatchery June–Aug., daily 8–8; May and Sept., daily 8–7; Apr. and Oct., daily 8–6; Nov.–Mar., daily 8–4.*

Indian Arm Provincial Park. This remote region of rugged mountains, alpine lakes, vigorous creeks, and the roughly 50-meter (164-foot) Granite Falls lies just east of Vancouver along an 18-km (11-mile) fjord called Indian Arm. The park is ancestral home of the Tsleil-Wau-tuth Nation, who have lived here since "time out of mind." There's boating, kayaking, scuba diving, and fishing, as well as excellent hiking opportunities through old-growth forests. Most trails are steep and are not for novices. ⊠ *Shores of Indian Arm, North Vancouver* ☎ *604/990–3800* ⊕ *www.env.gov.bc.ca/bcparks.*

DID YOU KNOW?

The 450-foot-long cedar-plank Capilano Suspension Bridge hangs 230 feet above the rushing Capilano River and makes for an exhilarating walk in the woods.

FAMILY **Lonsdale Quay.** Stalls selling fresh produce and ready-to-eat food fill the lower level of this popular indoor seaside market, and upstairs there are boutiques, toy stores, and a kids' play area. Outside you can wander the quay, admire the fishing boats and tugs moored here, and enjoy the views of the Downtown skyline across the water. You'll also see a number of old dry docks and canneries finding fresh leases on life as modish condominiums. This is a great place to explore on a rainyday. ✉ *123 Carrie Cates Ct., at foot of Lonsdale Ave., North Vancouver* ☎ *604/985–6261* ⊕ *www.lonsdalequay.com* 🎫 *Free* ☉ *Daily 9–7.*

Lower Seymour Conservation Reserve. Nestled into the precipitous North Shore Mountains, this 5,668-hectare (14,000-acre) reserve includes 25 km (15½ miles) of hiking and biking trails—some that are steep and challenging. The meandering **Seymour Valley Trailway** is a 10-km (6-mile) paved pathway, suitable for cyclists, in-line skaters, strollers, and wheelchairs. There are challenging advanced mountain biking trails in the park, including Corkscrew and Salvation. ✉ *End of Lillooet Rd., North Vancouver* ☎ *604/432–6286.*

OFF THE
BEATEN
PATH

Lynn Canyon Park. With a steep canyon landscape, a temperate rain forest complete with waterfalls, and a suspension bridge (circa 1912) 166½ feet above raging Lynn Creek, this 616-acre park provides thrills to go with its scenic views. There are many hiking trails, including a popular one that ends at a waterfall where you can swim. Lynn Canyon Park's on-site Ecology Centre distributes maps of area hiking trails, waterfalls, and pools as well as information about the local flora and fauna. There's also a gift shop and a café here. To get to the park, take the Lions Gate Bridge and Capilano Road, go east on Highway 1, take the Lynn Valley Road exit, and turn right on Peters Road. From downtown Vancouver, you can take the SeaBus to Lonsdale Quay, then Bus #228 or #229 from the quay; both stop near the park. ■**TIP**➔ The suspension bridge here is shorter than the Capilano Suspension Bridge (130 feet versus 450 feet at Capilano) so the experience is less thrilling, but also less touristy. ✉ *3663 Park Rd., at end of Peters Rd., North Vancouver* ☎ *604/990–3755 Ecology Centre, 604/984–9311 café* ⊕ *www.dnv.org/ecology* 🎫 *Ecology Centre by donation, suspension bridge free* ☉ *Park daily, dawn–dusk; Ecology Centre June–Sept., daily 10–5; Oct.–May, weekdays 10–5, weekends noon–4.*

Mount Seymour Provincial Park. Just 30 minutes from downtown Vancouver, this 3,508-hectare (8,668-acre) wilderness park has hiking trails of varying length and difficulty and spectacular views of the Lower Mainland. Warm clothing—and caution—are advised. Popular routes include a scenic 1½-hour trip to Dog Mountain or a more intense four-hour climb to the three peaks of Seymour. You can also hike down to Deep Cove on Indian Arm in less than an hour. In winter, the trails are used for snowshoeing, and there's a supervised snow play area. ✉ *Mount Seymour Rd., off Seymour Pkwy., North Vancouver* ⊕ *www.env.gov.bc.ca.*

WEST VANCOUVER

Posh "West Van," as the locals call the North Shore suburb of West Vancouver, has retained its well-heeled character from the time when the Guinness family developed the area in the 1930s. It's a network of English-style winding country roads and multimillion-dollar homes. Cypress Mountain, which hosted the Olympic freestyle skiing and snowboard competitions, is in West Van. If you have a car, you can drive to the top of Cypress for spectacular vistas of Vancouver and beyond; unlike Grouse Mountain, the views here are free. West Van is also en route to the Horseshoe Bay ferry terminal for ferries to Vancouver Island and to the Sea-to-Sky Highway, which continues north to Squamish and Whistler. ⇨ *See Vancouver Outdoors and Sports for more details on West Vancouver's natural attractions.*

GETTING HERE AND AROUND

From Downtown, take the Lions Gate Bridge and bear left for the West Vancouver exit. You'll be on Marine Drive heading west. If you're going to Cypress Mountain, Horseshoe Bay, or Whistler, take the first right onto Taylor Way, go up the hill, then follow the signs for Highway 1 west; it's a left exit.

Cypress Mountain runs a winter-only shuttle bus for skiers and snow boarders. Otherwise, to explore West Vancouver, you really need a car.

WORTH NOTING

Fodor's Choice ★ **Cypress Provincial Park.** This 3,012-hectare (7,443-acre) park sprawls above Howe Sound, embracing Strachan, Black, and Hollyburn mountains. On a clear day you can see Mt. Baker (in Washington State) and Vancouver Island. While the park includes a commercial ski area, much of the terrain is a public hiking paradise (bikes are permitted on roadways and some trails). This is backcountry, though, and only experienced hikers should attempt the more remote routes, including the Baden Powell and Howe Sound Crest trails. ⊠ *Cypress Bowl Rd., off Hwy. 1, Exit 8, West Vancouver* ☎ *604/926–5612* ⊕ *www. env.gov.bc.ca.*

FAMILY **Lighthouse Park.** This 75-hectare (185-acre) wilderness wraps around the historic lighthouse at Point Atkinson, where Howe Sound meets Burrard Inlet in the municipality of West Vancouver. A bank of soaring granite (popular for picnicking) shapes the foreshore, while the interior is an undulating terrain of mostly Douglas fir, arbutus, and rich undergrowth. Fairly short interconnected trails, from easy to challenging, bring you close to the birds and other wildlife. ⊠ *Beacon La., off Marine Dr., West Vancouver* ☎ *604/925–7275* ⊕ *www.lpps.ca.*

RICHMOND

The suburban community of Richmond, south of Vancouver proper, is the region's "new Chinatown."

The main attractions here are two lively summer night markets, several Hong Kong–style shopping malls, and hundreds of Asian restaurants. It's easy to get to on the Canada Line—about a 20 or 25 minute ride. Vancouver International Airport is also in Richmond.

TOP ATTRACTIONS

MARKETS

Fodor's Choice

★ **Richmond Night Market.** About 80 food vendors, carnival rides, and a children's amuseument area are among the attractions at this night market near River Rock Casino. You can get here on the Canada Line from Downtown in about 20 minutes; the market is just a short walk from Bridgeport Station. ⊠ *8351 River Rd., Richmond* ☎ *604/244–8448* ⊕ *www.richmondnightmarket.com* ⊘ *Mid-May–mid-Oct., Fri.–Sat. 7 pm–midnight, Sun. and holiday Mon. 7 pm–11 pm.*

Summer Night Market. This market features vendors selling everything from socks to mops, but the real highlights are the food stalls offering noodle bowls, skewered meats, and bubble tea. Concerts, magic shows, and kung fu demonstrations fill out the rotating lineup of special events. To get here by public transit, take the Canada Line to Bridgeport Station and catch the free market shuttle, or change to Bus 407 or 430. ⊠ *12631 Vulcan Way, off Bridgeport Rd., Richmond* ☎ *604/278–8000* ⊕ *www. summernightmarket.com* ⊘ *mid-May–early Oct. Fri.–Sat. 7 pm–midnight, Sun. and holiday Mon. 7 pm–11pm.*

OUTDOORS
AND SPORTS

Updated By
Chloë Ernst

Blessed with a mild climate, fabulous natural setting, and excellent public-use facilities, Vancouverites, unsurprisingly, are an outdoorsy lot. It's not uncommon for locals to commute to work by foot or bike and, after hours, they're as likely to hit the water, trails, ski slopes, or beach volleyball courts as the bars or nightclubs.

Exceptional for North American cities, the downtown peninsula of Vancouver is entirely encircled by a seawall along which you can walk, in-line skate (which is still quite popular in Vancouver), cycle, or otherwise propel yourself for more than 22 km (13½ miles), with plenty of picturesque jumping on and off points. It's so popular that it qualifies as an, albeit unofficial, national treasure. There are places along the route where you can canoe, or kayak, or simply go for a swim. Top-rated skiing, snowboarding, mountain biking, fishing, diving, and golf are just minutes away by car or transit.

You'll find rental equipment and tour operators in Vancouver for every imaginable outdoor activity, from tandem bikes for Stanley Park trails to stand-up paddleboards on Granville Island. Yoga studios seem to be around every corner and hiking trails materialize just at the end of the road. Hotel concierges can recommend the best wilderness trails just as easily as they can top sushi spots. To buy or rent gear, head to the Mountain Equipment Co-op, a local institution (⇨ *see Shopping*).

PLANNER

TOP OUTDOORS EXPERIENCES
Walk or bike the Stanely Park Seawall: The 9-km (5½-mile) paved path around Stanley Park is a civilized entrée into the coastal habitat where forest meets sea. The entire 22-km (13½-mile) Seawall circles the city and is great for biking.

Hike the Grouse Grind: This intense 1½-hour climb up Grouse Mountain is a local rite of passage. The city and ocean views from the top are stunning. You can take the gondola back down, or take it both up and down and do your hiking along the trails up top such as to Goat Mountain.

White-water kayak the Capilano River: It's a serious tumble along canyons, through rain forest, and over rocks and rapids.

Play volleyball at Kits Beach: Vancouverites play a mean game of beach volleyball. Listen for the shouts of "good kill" on weekends from late spring to fall.

Kayak Indian Arm: Barely 30 minutes from Downtown, the North Shore's fjordic landscape is stunning and best appreciated under paddle power.

WHEN TO DO IT

Vancouver has a moderate climate, with temperatures rarely exceeding 30°C (86°F) or falling below freezing for sustained periods, though winter storms that blend relentless rain with 5°C (41°F) chills can feel colder than the Canadian Rockies. Whatever you're doing, wearing layers is key, as a downpour may abruptly turn into a 60-minute sun break, or marine air can bring a sudden chill to a July day.

Year-round: If Vancouverites postponed running, biking, or golfing because of a bit of rain, they'd get outside only half the time (Vancouver's annual precipitation is about 103 cm [40.6 inches], compared to Seattle's 92 cm [36.2 inches]). Visitors are encouraged to venture out in all but the worst rainstorms to participate in adventure, whether crossing the Capilano Suspension Bridge, hiking in Stanley Park, or kayaking on False Creek. Though water temps in the Georgia Strait hardly vary from summer to winter, visibility improves significantly from December to March in what Jacques Cousteau declared the second-best scuba location in the world. Sportfishing and most wilderness tours take place year-round; check with operators for peak migration periods of sea mammals and birds.

Summer: True summer weather starts late in Vancouver, around Canada Day (July 1), but warm temperatures and sunshine persist into October. The beach scene is popular whenever the weather's good.

Winter: Most cities boast plenty of parks, but how many can claim three ski areas within the city limits? Welcome to the North Shore, where Cypress Mountain hosted the 2010 Olympic snowboard and freestyle ski events. February sometimes offers so many sunny days that a T-shirt and jeans are the preferred ski gear. The winter-sports season starts in November and runs through March—in addition to skiing and snowboarding, snowshoeing and dogsledding are also popular options.

SPECIAL EVENTS

The popular 10K Vancouver Sun Run is in mid-April; the Bank of Montreal Marathon is early May; the Scotiabank Half Marathon and 5K are in June. And every New Year's Day since 1920, thousands of Vancouverites plunge into the frigid waters at English Bay beach—often in costume—for the Polar Bear Swim.

BEACHES

Greater Vancouver is well endowed with beaches—from the pebbly coves of West Vancouver to a vast tableau of sand at Spanish Banks, in Point Grey—but the waters are decidedly cool, with summer water temperatures ranging from 12 to18°C (54 to 64°F). Aside from kids and the intrepid, most stick to quick dips, sunbathing, or wearing a wetsuit for water activities. That said, the city has several exceptional outdoor pools—right on the ocean. The most spectacular is Kitsilano Pool, a heated saltwater pool where you can gaze up at the North Shore Mountains while swimming lengths or splashing in the shallows. Beaches at Kitsilano, Spanish Banks, and Locarno are popular beach-volleyball venues. At English Bay, the city's historic beach and round-the-clock social venue, you can swim, rent a kayak, or simply stroll with an ice cream cone and people-watch. Vancouver is also known for its clothing-optional beaches, the most celebrated being Wreck Beach, which reflects the city's cosmopolitan perspective.

If you're staying in the downtown core and looking for convenient beaches, English Bay is most accessible, followed by Kits, the Stanley Park beaches, then Jericho and Spanish Banks. Jericho and English Bay are good options if you want to rent kayaks.

All city beaches have lifeguards, washrooms, concession stands, and most have paid parking. Information is available through the city, ☎ *311* or ☎ *604/873–7000*. Liquor and smoking are prohibited in parks and on beaches. With a few exceptions, dogs are not permitted on beaches.

Ambleside Park and Beach. West of the Lions Gate Bridge, this long stretch of sand is West Vancouver's most popular beach. There are tennis courts, volleyball nets, and a water park in the summer. This local favorite beach area is just off Marine Drive at the foot of 13th Street. There are superb views of Stanley Park from all along the Seawall. There's also a huge off-leash area for dogs. **Amenities:** food and drink; showers; toilets. **Best for:** sunrise; swimming; walking. ✉ *Argyle Ave. and 13th St., West Vancouver* ⊕ *westvancouver.ca/parks-recreation/parks/ambleside-park.*

English Bay Beach. The city's best-known beach, English Bay, lies just to the east of Stanley Park's southern entrance. A long stretch of golden sand, a waterslide, volleyball courts, kayak rentals, and food trucks keep things interesting all summer. Known locally for being gay friendly, it draws a diverse crowd. **Amenities:** lifeguards; water sports; food and drink; toilets; parking (fee). **Best for:** fireworks; partiers; kayaking; swimming; walking; sunset. ✉ *1700 Beach Ave., between Gilford and Bidwell Sts., West End* ☎ *604/665–3424* ⊕ *www.vancouver.ca/parks-recreation-culture/english-bay-beach.aspx.*

Jericho Beach. Home to the Jericho Sailing Centre, this Point Grey beach is popular for windsurfing and kayaking (rentals are available), especially at the western end. Swimmers can use the eastern section, where the expansive sands and a grassy park invite sunbathing. **Amenities:**

food and drink; lifeguards; parking (fee); toilets; water sports. **Best for:** kayaking; swimming; Vancouver Folk Festival; walking; windsurfing. ☒ *1300 Discovery St., Point Grey* ⊕ *www.vancouver. ca/parks-recreation-culture/jericho-beach.aspx.*

Fodor's Choice
★
Kitsilano Beach. West of the southern end of the Burrard Bridge, Kits Beach is the city's busiest beach—Frisbee tossers, beach volleyball players, and sleek young people are ever present. Facilities include a playground, restaurant, concession stand, and tennis courts. **Kitsilano Pool** is here: at 137.5 meters (451 feet), it's the longest pool in Canada and one of the few heated saltwater pools in the world (open May to September). Just steps from the sand, the Boathouse on Kits Beach serves lunch, dinner, and weekend brunch inside and on its big ocean-view deck. There's also a take-out concession at the same site. Inland from the pool, the Kitsilano Showboat, an outdoor amphitheater hosts music and dance performances during the summer. **Amenities:** food and drink; lifeguards; parking (fee); toilets. **Best for:** sunrise; sunset; swimming; walking. ☒ *2305 Cornwall Ave., Kitsilano* ☏ *604/731–0011* ⊕ *www. vancouver.ca/parks-recreation-culture/kitsilano-beach.aspx.*

Spanish Banks Beaches. The **Spanish Banks** and **Locarno** beaches form a sandy chain, and have huge expanses of sunbathing sand backed by wide lawns full of picnic tables. There are also volleyball courts. The shallow water, warmed slightly by sun and sand, is good for swimming. Farther west along the coastline, toward the Spanish Banks Extension, the scene becomes less crowded. Spanish Banks West and Locarno beaches are designated "quiet beaches," which means that amplified music is prohibited. **Amenities:** water sports; food and drink; toilets; lifeguards; parking (free). **Best for:** swimming; walking; windsurfing. ☒ *Northwest Marine Drive, at Tolmie Street, Point Grey* ⊕ *www. vancouver.ca/parks-recreation-culture/spanish-bank-beach.aspx.*

Fodor's Choice
★
Stanley Park Beaches. There are two fine beaches accessed from Stanley Park, with other unnamed sandy spots dotted along the seawall. The most popular with families is **Second Beach,** which has a playground and large heated pool with slides. **Third Beach** is a little more removed than the other central beaches. It has a larger stretch of sand, fairly warm water, and unbeatable sunset views. It's a popular evening picnic spot. **Amenities:** lifeguards; toilets; food and drink; parking (fee). **Best for:** sunset; swimming; walking. ☒ *7495 Stanley Park Dr., Stanley Park* ⊕ *www. vancouver.ca/parks-recreation-culture/third-beach.aspx.*

Sunset Beach. Farther along Beach Avenue toward Burrard Bridge, Sunset Beach, between Thurlow and Broughton streets, is too close to the downtown core for clean safe swimming, but is a great spot for an evening stroll. It's also a "quiet" beach, which means no amplified music. You can catch a ferry to Granville Island here. **Amenities:** lifeguards; food and drink; toilets; parking (fee). **Best for:** walking; sunset. ☒ *1204 Beach Ave., between Broughton and Thurlow Sts., West End* ⊕ *www. vancouver.ca/parks-recreation-culture/sunset-beach.aspx.*

Trout Lake Beach. The only freshwater lake in the center of Vancouver, Trout Lake's sandy beach has a swimming raft and places to launch small kayaks (though no rentals available). Family picnics are popular here, and there's an attractive farmers' market on summer Saturdays. **Amenities:** food and drink; lifeguards; parking (free); toilets. **Best for:** walking. ⌧ *3300 Victoria Dr., between E. 14th and 19th Aves., Commercial Drive* ☏ *604/738–8535* ⊕ *www.vancouver.ca/parks-recreation-culture/trout-lake-beach.aspx.*

Whytecliff Park. West Vancouver residents are fond of leaping from the cliffs along this rocky beach for a quick, cheap thrill. This calm cove is usually good for swimming and sunset watching. Also along the north side of Burrard Inlet in West Vancouver are dozens of coveted retreats for in-the-know beach-seekers, including (from west to east) **Kew Beach, Caulfield Cove, Sandy Cove, West Bay,** and **Dundarave.** East of Marine Drive is a designated off-leash area for well-behaved dogs. **Amenities:** food and drink; parking (fee); toilets. **Best for:** swimming; walking; sunset. ⌧ *7116 Marine Dr., west of Horseshoe Bay, West Vancouver* ☏ *604/925–7275* ⊕ *www.westvancouver.ca/parks-recreation/parks/whytecliff-park.*

BIKING

Vancouver's most popular bike path is the 9-km (5½-mile) **Stanley Park Seawall,** which follows the park's perimeter, hugging the harbor along the way. The views of Lion's Gate Bridge and the mountains to the north are breathtaking. The path connects at both ends with the city's longer seawall path, if you feel like making a day of it. Rent your bike near the entrance to Stanley Park, in the West End, as there are no rentals once you're inside the park.

In North Vancouver, the **Lower Seymour Conservation Reserve** has some trails that are bike accessible, as does **Pacific Spirit Regional Park** in Point Grey, and **Cypress Provincial Park** in West Vancouver.

For biking on city streets, downtown Vancouver's "separated bike lanes" have made biking even easier—most bike lanes have a barrier between them and the traffic. Especially useful ones are along Hornby and Dunsmuir streets. These lanes are in addition to the city's many bikeways, identified by green bicycle signs.

Vancouver cycling routes connect with those in nearby communities and here most routes do share the road with cars, but they're quite safe and include cyclist-activated traffic signals and other bike-friendly measures. Many TransLink buses have bike racks, and bikes are welcome on the SeaBus and on the SkyTrain at off-peak times. Aquabus Ferries transport bikes and riders across False Creek, too. If cycling is a key component of your visit, check online with the Vancouver Area Cycling Coalition (⊕ *www.vacc.bc.ca*).

There are detailed maps and other information on the website operated by the City of Vancouver (⊕ *www.vancouver.ca/streets-transportation/biking-and-cyclists.aspx*). Cycling maps are also available from most bike shops and bike-rental outlets. Helmets are required by law, and a sturdy lock is essential.

Fodor's Choice **Seawall.** The paved bike paths of Vancouver's 22-km (13½-mile) seawall
★ start downtown at Canada Place, go around Stanley Park, and follow
False Creek to Kitsilano. ✉ *Downtown* ⊕ *www.vancouver.ca/parks-recreation-culture/seawall.aspx.*

BIKE RENTALS

Bayshore Bike Rentals. If you're starting your ride near Stanley Park, try
this friendly store. It has a wide range of bikes as well as bike trailers for
kids, and in-line skates. ✉ *745 Denman St., West End* ☎ *604/688–2453*
⊕ *www.bayshorebikerentals.ca.*

Reckless Bike Stores. This outfit rents bikes on the Yaletown section
of Vancouver's seawall route. To explore Granville Island, check out
the branch at 1810 Fir Street in Kitsilano. ✉ *110 Davie St., Yaletown*
☎ *604/648–2600* ⊕ *www.reckless.ca.*

Spokes Bicycle Rentals. Near Stanley Park, Spokes has a wide selection of
mountain bikes, tandem bikes, and children's bikes. Everything from
hourly to weekly rentals are available. Helmets, locks, and route maps
are complimentary. ✉ *1798 W. Georgia St., West End* ☎ *604/688–5141*
⊕ *www.spokesbicyclerentals.com.*

MOUNTAIN BIKING

Mountain biking may be a worldwide phenomenon, but its most radical
expression, known as free-riding, was born in the 1990s on the steep-
and-rugged North Shore Mountains. This extreme type of mountain
biking has thrill-seekers riding ultra-heavy-duty bikes through gnarly
forests, along log-strewn trails, over rocky precipices, and down stony
stream beds (not to mention along obstacles like planks and teeter-
totters). The **Lower Seymour Conservation Reserve** in nearby North Vancouver has challenging biking trails through alpine meadows, forested
slopes, and river flood plains: the Corkscrew and Salvation trails are
classified as advanced or extreme. There are also advanced mountain
biking trails on the lower slopes of **Mount Fromme** (next to Grouse Mountain) and **Mount Seymour.**

MOUNTAIN BIKE RENTALS

Endless Biking. Convenient to North Vancouver's challenging trails, this
bike shop specializes in mountain bikes including those with rugged
suspension systems. Reservations are recommended. The shop also runs
guided tours, as well as a shuttle to local trail heads. ✉ *1401 Hunter St.,
North Vancouver* ☎ *604/985–2519* ⊕ *www.endlessbiking.com.*

DIVING

The rugged coastline of southwestern British Columbia offers excellent
and varied diving with vistas of below surface sheer rock walls and thick
plots of plumose anemones. From late summer through winter, when
water clarity is best and allows visibility of up to 100 feet, the region
delivers some of the most spectacular temperate-water (average 4–8°C
[39–46°F]) diving in the world, including sightings of the North Pacific
Giant Octopus. Dry suits are imperative.

Rowand's Reef Scuba Shop. This PADI-certified scuba and snorkeling business specializes in year-round diving trips to nearby Howe Sound. Courses are also available. ⊠ *1731 West 4th Ave., Kitsilano* ☎ *604/669–3483* ⊕ *www.rowandsreef.com.*

ECOTOURS AND WILDLIFE VIEWING

Given a temperate climate and forest, mountain, and marine environments teeming with life, it's no surprise that wildlife-watching is an important pastime and growing business in and around Vancouver. Many people walk the ocean foreshores or park and mountain trails, binoculars or scopes in hand, looking for exceptional or rare birds. Others venture onto the water to see seals, sea lions, and whales—as well as the birds that inhabit the maritime world.

Fodor'sChoice
★
Sewell's Marina. This marina near the protected waters of Howe Sound runs year-round, two-hour ecotours of the surrounding marine and coastal mountain habitat. Sightings range from swimming seals to soaring eagles. High-speed rigid inflatable hulls are used. They also offer guided and self-driven salmon-fishing charters in Howe Sound and to the mouths of the Capilano and Fraser rivers. ⊠ *6409 Bay St., West Vancouver* ☎ *604/921–3474* ⊕ *www.sewellsmarina.com.*

Steveston Seabreeze Adventures. In April and early May thousands of male California sea lions settle on rocks near the mouth of the Fraser River to feed on the eulachon, a member of the smelt family. Seabreeze's sightseeing boats make the short trip into the estuary from Steveston, in Richmond—south of Vancouver. During the autumn bird migratory season, Seabreeze also ventures to the George C. Reifel Bird Sanctuary on Westham Island; summer means orca and occasional humpback whale sightings. They also operate fishing charters as far west as the Gulf Islands: the seven-passenger boats, with guides, cost C\$1,000 on weekends, C\$900 on weekdays. ⊠ *12551 No. 1 Rd., Richmond* ☎ *604/272–7200* ⊕ *www.seabreezeadventures.ca.*

BIRD- AND EAGLE-WATCHING

Brackendale Eagles Provincial Park. Between mid-November and mid-February, the world's largest concentration of bald eagles gathers to feed on salmon at Brackendale Eagles Provincial Park, near Squamish, about an hour north of Vancouver on the scenic Sea-to-Sky Highway. The Brackendale Art Gallery has a teahouse that's a good place to stop along the way. ⊠ *41950 Government Rd., off Hwy. 99, Brackendale* ⊕ *www.brackendaleartgallery.com.*

George C. Reifel Migratory Bird Sanctuary. More than 280 species of migratory and nonmigratory birds visit this nearly 350-hectare (850-acre) site on Westham Island, about an hour south of Vancouver. A seasonal highlight is the arrival of 50,000 to 100,000 Lesser Snow Geese, from early fall through winter. ⊠ *5191 Robertson Rd., Delta* ☎ *604/946–6980* ⊕ *www.reifelbirdsanctuary.com* ⊠ *C\$5* ☼ *Daily 9–4.*

Whale-watching tours from Vancouver (or Victoria) are popular. Sightings include humpbacks, minkes, and orcas.

WHALE-WATCHING

Between April and October pods of orca whales migrate through the Strait of Georgia, near Vancouver. The area is also home to year-round pods of harbor seals, elephant seals, minke whales, porpoises, and a wealth of birdlife, inlcuding bald eagles. Other migrating whales include humpbacks and grays.

Prince of Whales. This established operator runs four-hour trips from Vancouver's Coal Harbour waterfront across the Strait of Georgia to Victoria, in season. ⊠ *The Westin Bayshore, 1601 Bayshore Dr., West End* ☎ *888/383–4884* ⊕ *www.princeofwhales.com.*

Wild Whales Vancouver. Boats leave Granville Island in search of orca pods in the Strait of Georgia, often traveling as far as Victoria. Rates are C$135 for a three- to seven-hour trip in either an open or glass-domed boat (trip lengths depend on where the whales are hanging out on a particular day). Each boat leaves once daily, April through October, conditions permitting. ⊠ *1806 Mast Tower Rd., Granville Island* ☎ *604/699–2011* ⊕ *www.whalesvancouver.ca.*

FISHING

You can fish for salmon all year round in coastal British Columbia, weather and marine conditions permitting. Halibut, at 25 kilograms (55 pounds) and heavier, is the area's other trophy fish. Charters ply the waters between the mouth of the Capilano River in Burrard Inlet

CLOSE UP

Sea 'n' Ski

Given the proximity of water to mountain, and bike path to swimming pool, and the ease of getting around by bike, bus, car, and ferry, it's definitely possible to undertake two or more outdoor activities in a single day. Cross-trainers, this is the place for you. If you're going to multitask, though, it's a good idea to plan ahead, and if you need to rent equipment, do so in advance.

Whatever you're planning to do, in the interest of making the most of your time, and ensuring safety, download maps and other descriptive information you may need. If you're venturing off the beaten path, be sure you're dressed suitably, have emergency food and gear, and leave notification of where you're headed and when you'll return.

The possibilities are almost endless, but here are some pointers for combining activities:

Kayaking in False Creek: The waters are usually tranquil in early morning, which makes it a good time to savor the pleasures of traveling at sea level.

Jogging around Stanley Park: Early-morning runners have the seawall pretty much to themselves.

Swimming in Kitsilano Pool: The lanes in this heated saltwater pool are less crowded in the early morning.

Cycling the city: By midmorning, all but the city's major arterial streets should be relatively calm.

Fishing or wildlife-watching: In all but the worst weather, you can rent a boat for a few hours spent in pursuit of salmon, or join a tour in search of whales, sea lions, or eagles.

Beach volleyball: Late afternoon is a good time to head to Kitsilano Beach for a volleyball game.

Golf at Fraserview: A warm summer evening is the ideal time to golf at this celebrated public golf course.

Night skiing at Grouse: On a crisp winter night, there's no better place to be than on the slopes of Grouse Mountain. The canopy of stars will glitter, while below, the city dazzles.

and the outer Georgia Strait and Gulf Islands. A fishing license can be purchased from the boat rental or tour operator. **Sewell's Marina** (⇨ *see Ecotours*) is also known for its salmon fishing excursions.

Bonnie Lee Fishing Charters. From moorings in the Granville Island Maritime Market, this company runs five-hour fishing trips into Burrard Inlet and the Georgia Strait, year-round. Guided outings start at C$425for the boat. ✉ *104-1676 Duranleau St., Granville Island* ☎ *604/290–7447* ⊕ *www.bonnielee.com.*

GOLF

Vancouver-area golf courses offer golfing with fantastic scenery. Most are open year-round. Three championship golf courses (including serene Fraserview) are operated by the city, meaning they are more affordable. To reserve up to 30 days in advance, contact the Vancouver Board of Parks and Recreation (⊕ *www.vancouver.ca/parks/golf*). The Vancouver

Park Board operates three 18-hole pitch-and-putt sites, including one right near Stanley Park and one in Queen Elizabeth Park.

Last Minute Golf. For advance tee-time bookings at about 20 Vancouver area courses, or for a spur-of-the-moment game, call Last Minute Golf. The company matches golfers and courses, sometimes at substantial greens-fee discounts. ☎ *604/878–1833, 800/684–6344* ⊕ *www. lastminutegolfbc.com.*

Fodor's Choice **Fraserview Golf Course.** The most celebrated of Vancouver's public
★ courses, the 18-hole Fraserview Golf Course sits on 91 heavily wooded hectares (225 acres) overlooking the Fraser River. It has a tree-lined fairway, a driving range, and a lovely clubhouse. There's a golf institute staffed with instructors who teach players of all levels. Golf carts are available on a first-come, first-served basis. ⊠ *7800 Vivian Dr., South Vancouver* ☎ *604/257–6923* ⊕ *www.vancouver.ca/parks-recreation-culture/fraserview-golf-course.aspx* ☜ *C$65* 🔾 *18 holes, 6692 yards, par 72.* ☞ *Driving range, putting green, pitching area, golf carts, rental clubs, pro-shop, golf academy/lessons.*

Northview Golf and Country Club. In the rolling terrain southeast of Vancouver, this lovely golf club is home to two Arnold Palmer–designed courses. The Ridge Course crosses meandering streams, while the Canal Course has wide fairways and undulating greens. An optional cart at either course costs C$40. There's a strict dress code: no jeans or T-shirts allowed. ⊠ *6857 168th St., Surrey* ☎ *604/576–4653, 888/574–2211* ⊕ *www.northviewgolf.com* ☞ *Driving range, putting green, golf carts, pull carts, caddies, rental clubs, pro-shop, golf academy/lessons, restaurant, bar.*

University Golf Club. In Point Grey's Pacific Spirit Park, this challenging 1929 public course includes a clubhouse and restaurant and is home to the British Columbia Golf Museum. The course's narrow fairways, lined with old-growth trees, appeal to golfers of all skill levels. ⊠ *5185 University Blvd., Point Grey* ☎ *604/224–1818* ⊕ *www.universitygolf. com* ☜ *C$69* 🔾 *18 holes, 6531 yards, par 72* ☞ *Driving range, putting green, pitching area, golf carts, caddies, rental clubs, pro-shop, golf academy/lessons, restaurant, bar.*

HEALTH, FITNESS, AND YOGA

Vancouver embraces health and wellness with open arms. Public and private gyms are well patronized, and there are myriad martial arts, yoga, and Pilates classes offered around the city. If you're craving a fitness fix, you'll easily find something that suits you.

Richmond Olympic Oval. This speed-skating oval was built alongside the Fraser River, in Richmond, for the 2010 Olympic Games. The facility, with a gorgeous glass-and-steel design, contains Olympic-size ice rinks and a huge fitness center with a climbing wall. It's a 15-minute walk from the Canada Line. ⊠ *6111 River Rd., Richmond* ☎ *778/296–1400* ⊕ *www.richmondoval.ca* ☜ *Day passes C$16.50.*

The hike up Grouse Mountain is no easy feat, but the views from the top, and from Goat Mountain, slightly farther up, are breathtaking. Or you can always take the Skyride gondola.

Robert Lee YMCA. This downtown YMCA has the latest in fitness facilities, including an indoor pool, sports courts, and yoga studios. ✉ *955 Burrard St., Downtown* ☏ *604/689–9622* ⊕ *www.robertleeymca.ca.*

Semperviva Yoga Studios. The Granville Island location of Semperviva, one of Vancouver's most popular yoga studios, is called the Sea Studio, and it overlooks False Creek. The drop-in fee is C$22, including a mat. ✉ *Pier 32 Bldg., 1333 Johnston St., Granville Island* ☏ *604/739–2087* ⊕ *www.semperviva.com.*

YWCA. With aerobics and yoga classes, a six-lane indoor pool, a cardio room, three weight rooms (one reserved for women only), and a hot tub and steam room, the YWCA has it all. ✉ *535 Hornby St., Downtown* ☏ *604/895–5777* ⊕ *www.ywcahealthandfitness.com* ✉ *Day pass C$17.*

HIKING

With its expansive landscape of mountains, inlets, alpine lakes, and approachable glaciers, as well as low-lying rivers, hills, dikes, and meadows, southwestern British Columbia is a hiker's paradise. For easy walking and hiking, you can't beat Stanley Park in downtown Vancouver but for more strenuous hiking, there are fabulous parks not far away. Popular hiking desintations include **Mount Seymour Provincial Park, Lynn Canyon, Lynn Headwaters Regional Park,** and **Capilano River Regional Park** in North Vancouver; **Pacific Spirit National Park** in Point Grey; and **Cypress Provincial Park** and **Lighthouse Park** in West Vancouver. With their photoworthy profile, the North Shore Mountains may appear benign, but this is a vast and rugged territory filled with natural pitfalls and occasionally hostile wildlife. Areas and trails should be approached with physical ability and stamina in mind, and you should exercise great caution. Every year, hikers wander off clearly marked trails, or outside well-posted public areas, with tragic results. If you're heading into the mountains, hike with a companion, pack warm clothes (even in summer), bring extra food and water, and always leave word of your route and the time you expect to return. Remember, too, that weather can change quickly in the mountains.

In addition to the Mountain Equipment Co-op (⇨ *see Shopping*), there are several places around town for good books, maps, and advice.

Environment Canada. It's always a good idea to check the weather forecast with Environment Canada. ☎ *604/664–9010* ⊕ *www.weather.gc.ca.*

Wanderlust. A major supplier of goods and gear for travelers, Wanderlust also stocks maps and guidebooks. ⊠ *1929 W. 4th Ave., Kitsilano* ☎ *604/739–2182* ⊕ *www.wanderlustore.com.*

HIKING TRAILS

Baden Powell Trail. This 48-km (30-mile) trail crosses the entire length of the North Shore Mountains, from Horseshoe Bay in the west to Deep Cove in the east. On the way it passes through both Cypress Provincial Park and Mount Seymour Provincial Park, and is best completed in three or four sections. For a quick and scenic taste of the route, make the 4-km (2.5-mile) round-trip jaunt up to Quarry Rock in Deep Cove. ⊠ *North Shore Mountains, North Vancouver.*

Fodor's Choice
★
FAMILY
Capilano River Trails. About 26 km (16 miles) of hiking trails explore in and around Capilano Canyon—where the Capilano River is flanked by old-growth forest. There is also a salmon hatchery that's open to the public. Trailheads are off Capilano Road in North Vancouver (near Capilano Suspension Bridge) and near Ambleside Beach. ⊠ *4500 Capilano Park Rd., North Vancouver* ☎ *604/224–5739.*

Fodor's Choice
★
Dog Mountain Trail. One of the popular routes in Mount Seymour Provincial Park, this trail is a scenic 5-km (3-mile) return trip (about 1½ or 2 hours), with minimal elevation. It's best done June to October. For a longer, half-day trek, head to one or all three of the peaks of Mount Seymour. ⊠ *Mount Seymour Provincial Park, North Vancouver.*

Fodor's Choice
★
Garibaldi Provincial Park. About 80 km (50 miles) north of Vancouver, Garibaldi Provincial Park is a serious hiker's dream. You can't miss it: the 2,678-meter (8,786-foot) peak of Mount Garibaldi kisses the heavens just north of Squamish. Alpine meadows and wildlife viewing await you on trails leading to Black Tusk, Diamond Head, Cheakamus Lake, Elfin Lakes, and Singing Pass. Mountain goats, black bears, and bald eagles are found throughout the park. This is truly one of Canada's most spectacular wildernesses, and being easily accessible from Vancouver makes it even more appealing. A compass is mandatory, as are food and water, rain gear, a flashlight, and a first aid kit. There are also two medium to advanced mountain bike trails. Take seriously the glacier hazards and avalanche warnings. Snow tires are necessary

in winter. ⊠ *Hwy. 99, between Squamish and Pemberton, Squamish-Lillooet* ☎ *800/689–9025.*

FAMILY **Grouse Grind.** Vancouver's most famous, or infamous, hiking route, the Grind, is a 2.9-km (1.8-mile) climb straight up 853 meters (2,799 feet) to the top of Grouse Mountain. Thousands do it annually, but climbers are advised to be very experienced and in excellent physical condition. The route is open daily during daylight hours, from spring through autumn (conditions permitting). Or you can take the Grouse Mountain Skyride to the top 365 days a year; a round-trip ticket is C$41.95. Hiking trails in the adjacent Lynn Headwaters Regional Park are accessible from the gondola, including **Goat Mountain Trail.** ⊠ *Grouse Mountain, 6400 Nancy Greene Way, North Vancouver* ☎ *604/980–9311* ⊕ *www.grousemountain.com.*

Saint Mark's Summit. Though the Howe Sound Crest Trail continues north for a multiday trek, this first portion to Saint Mark's traverses old-growth forest and woodland trails to a rocky outlook. It covers about 11 km (7 miles) return. This is one of many hikes within Cypress Provincial Park. Equally lovely alternatives include the route to **Eagle Bluff** and cross-country routes near Hollyburn Lodge. ⊠ *West Vancouver.*

Sendero Diez Vistas Trail. In the most accessible section of Indian Arm Provincial Park, the lovely 13-km (8-mile) Sendero Diez Vistas is a moderate trail that reaches scenic heights at 10 or so viewpoints. The return leg follows the shores of Buntzen Lake (stop at North Beach for a swim if it's hot), and takes about 4 to 5 hours. ⊠ *At Buntzen Lake, North Vancouver.*

GUIDED HIKING TOURS

Novice hikers and serious walkers can join guided trips or do self-guided walks of varying approach and difficulty. **Grouse Mountain** hosts several daily "eco-walks" along easy, meandering paths, including a discussion of flora and fauna and a visit to the Refuge for Endangered Wildlife. They're free with admission to Grouse Mountain Skyride.

Rockwood Adventures. This company gives guided walks of rain forest or coastal terrain, in areas including Lighthouse Park, Lynn and Capilano canyons, and Bowen Island in Howe Sound. Many of the tours also include a gourmet picnic or box lunch. ⊠ *6342 Bruce St., West Vancouver* ☎ *604/913–1621, 888/236–6606* ⊕ *www.rockwoodadventures.com.*

FAMILY **Stanley Park Ecology Centre.** A calendar of guided nature walks and discovery sessions is filled with fun, kid-friendly options. Despite its urban access, Stanley Park offers incredible wildlife diversity—from the namesake rodents in Beaver Lake to a rookery of great blue herons near the tennis courts. The organizaiton also operates the Stanley Park Nature House on the shores of Lost Lagoon. ⊠ *Alberni and Chilco Sts., Stanley Park* Southeast corner of Lost Lagoon ☎ *604/257–8544, 604/718–6522* ⊕ *www.stanleyparkecology.ca* ☞ *Free.*

HOCKEY

The Canucks have sold out every game since 2004. Tickets can be purchased at legal resale outlets. Watching NHL hockey in a Canadian city is an unparalleled experience, so try and catch a game if possible at Rogers Arena. If you can't attend in person, head into any bar on game night, especially Saturday, which is "Hockey Night in Canada."

Vancouver Canucks. The city's most beloved sports team, the Vancouver Canucks, plays at Rogers Arena. ⊠ *800 Griffiths Way, Downtown* ☎ *604/899–7676* ⊕ *canucks.nhl.com.*

3

RUNNING

Vancouverites go for a run at any time of day, in almost any weather. The seawall around the downtown peninsula remains the most popular route, though the hilly byways of the North Shore are also popular with trail runners. Visitors staying downtown will be drawn to the 10-km (6-mile) route around Stanley Park, or the short 2-km (1-mile) circuit around Lost Lagoon.

Running Room. This Canada-based business is a good source for gear, advice, and downloadable route maps. There are many branches around the city and throughout British Columbia and the rest of Canada. A running club leaves from this location at 6 pm on Wednesday and 8:30 am on Sunday. ⊠ *679 Denman St., Suite 103, West End* ☎ *604/684–9771* ⊕ *www.runningroom.com.*

WATER SPORTS

From kayaking in False Creek to windsurfing in English Bay, whitewater rafting in North Vancouver rivers, or excursions farther afield, Vancouver is full of opportunities for water sport enthusiasts. There are also several spots to go stand-up paddleboarding, including right downtown in False Creek, English Bay, and Sunset Beach. Eco-marine Ocean Kayak Centre and Deep Cove Canoe & Kayak Centre rent SUP equipment, as well as kayaks and canoes.

BOATING AND SAILING

With an almost limitless number and variety of waterways—from Indian Arm near Vancouver, up Howe Sound and the Sunshine Coast, across Georgia Strait to the Gulf Islands, and on to Vancouver Island, southwestern British Columbia is a boater's paradise. And much of this territory has easy access to marine and public services. One caution: this ocean territory is vast and complex; maritime maps are required. Always consult the Environment Canada marine forecasts (☎ *604/664–9010,* ⊕ *www.weather.gc.ca*).

Blue Pacific Yacht Charters. This company rents speedboats and sailboats for cruising around Vancouver Island and Seattle, including the San Juan Islands, Southern Gulf Islands, and the Sunshine Coast. Sailboats and power boats can be rented for a day or for longer excurions.

✉ *1519 Foreshore Walk, Granville Island* ☎ *604/682–2161, 800/237–2392* ⊕ *www.bluepacificcharters.ca.*

Cooper Boating. Sailboats and cabin cruisers, either with or without skippers, can be rented at Cooper Boating. There is a two- to five-day minimum. ✉ *1815 Mast Tower Rd., Granville Island* ☎ *604/687–4110, 888/999–6419* ⊕ *www.cooperboating.com.*

CANOEING AND KAYAKING

Kayaking—seagoing and river kayaking—has become something of a lifestyle in Vancouver. Many sea kayakers start out (or remain) in Downtown's calm False Creek, while others venture into the open ocean and or head along the Pacific Coast. You can also white-water kayak or canoe down the Capilano River and several other North Vancouver rivers. Paddling in a traditional, seagoing First Nations–style canoe is an increasingly popular way to experience the maritime landscape.

FAMILY **Deep Cove Canoe and Kayak Centre.** Ocean-kayak rentals, guided excursions, and lessons for everyone in the family are available between April and October at this company's waterfront base in North Vancouver. Winter paddling tours are also available. ✉ *2156 Banbury Rd., North Vancouver* ☎ *604/929–2268* ⊕ *www.deepcovekayak.com.*

Ecomarine Ocean Kayak Centre. Lessons and rentals are offered year-round from this well-regarded company's main branch on Granville Island. There are also locations at Jericho Beach and English Bay. ✉ *1668 Duranleau St., Granville Island* ☎ *604/689–7575, 888/425–2925* ⊕ *www.ecomarine.com.*

Takaya Tours. A trip with Takaya Tours is a unique experience: you can paddle an oceangoing canoe while First Nations guides relay local legends, sing traditional songs, and point out the sites of ancient villages. The two-hour tours leave from Cates Park in North Vancouver or Belcarra Park in Port Moody. They also have kayak trips along the Burrard Inlet and up Indian Arm. Reservations are essential and trips run on a six-person minimum. ✉ *North Vancouver* ☎ *604/904–7410* ⊕ *www.takayatours.com.*

RIVER RAFTING

Snowmelt from the coastal mountains, and broad rivers that run through the Pemberton Valley, north of Squamish, provide some of the best white-water rafting in British Columbia.

FAMILY **Canadian Outback Adventure Company.** White-water rafting and scenic, family-oriented floats are offered on day trips from Vancouver. Transportation to and from Vancouver is available for an extra charge. ✉ *North Vancouver* ☎ *800/565–8735* ⊕ *www.canadianoutback.com.*

WINDSURFING

The winds aren't heavy on English Bay, making it a perfect place for learning to windsurf. If you're looking for more challenging conditions, head north to Squamish.

Windsure Windsurfing School. Sailboard and wetsuit rentals as well as lessons are available between May and September at Jericho Beach, in Point Grey. Skim boarding (a low-tech activity using a wooden board to skim along wet sand) and stand-up paddling lessons are also offered. ☒ *1300 Discovery St., Point Grey* ☏ *604/224–0615* ⊕ *www.windsure.com.*

WINTER SPORTS

Whistler-Blackcomb, just a two-hour drive from Vancouver, is the top-ranked ski destination in the region but there are plenty of winter sports and activities closer to Vancouver proper. The North Shore Mountains have three excellent ski and snowboard areas: Cypress Mountain, just 30 minutes away, is the largest of the local ski hills and was a venue for the 2010 Olympics; Grouse Mountain is particularly known for night skiing; and Mount Seymour is generally known as the most family friendly of the three. All have rentals, lessons, night skiing, and a variety of runs suitable for all skill levels. All three also offer snowshoeing and snow tubing, and Cypress Mountain has cross-country trails complete with a historic cabin, Hollyburn Lodge, that serves warm treats. Grouse Mountain can be reached using TransLink buses. Cypress and Seymour each run local shuttle buses.

Ski areas and trails are generally well marked; pay close attention to maps and signposts. The ski season generally runs from early December through early spring.

SKIING, SNOWBOARDING, SNOWSHOEING, AND SNOW-TUBING

Fodor's Choice ★ **Cypress Mountain ski resort.** Just 30 minutes from Downtown, the ski facilities at Cypress Mountain include six quad or double chairs, 53 downhill runs, and a vertical drop of 610 meters (2,001 feet). The resort has a snow-tubing area and snowshoe tours. This is also a major cross-country skiing area. Summer activities at Cypress Mountain include hiking, geocaching, wildlife viewing, and mountain biking. ☒ *Cypress Provincial Park, Cypress Bowl Rd., West Vancouver* ☏ *604/926–5612* ⊕ *www.cypressmountain.com.*

FAMILY **Grouse Mountain ski resort.** A 15-minute excursion from downtown Vancouver, the Skyride gondola takes skiers up to the ski resort on a slope overlooking the city. The views are fine on a clear day, but at night they're spectacular, and the area is known for its night skiing. Facilities include two quad chairs, 26 skiing and snowboarding runs, and several all-level freestyle-terrain parks. There's a choice of upscale and casual dining in a handsome stone-and-timber lodge. Summer activities at Grouse Mountain include hiking, disc golf, zip-lining (in winter, too), and wildlife viewing. ☒ *6400 Nancy Greene Way, North Vancouver* ☏ *604/980–9311, 604/986–6262 snow report* ⊕ *www.grousemountain.com.*

FAMILY **Mount Seymour ski resort.** A full-service winter activity area, the Mount Seymour ski resort sprawls over 81 hectares (200 acres) accessed from eastern North Vancouver. With three chairs for varying abilities; beginner's lifts, equipment rentals, and lessons; as well as toboggan and

DID YOU KNOW?

Kayaking is a popular sport in False Creek and farther out.

tubing runs, it's a favorite destination for families. Snowboarding is particularly popular, as is snowshoeing on ski hill trails and provincial park routes. The dining options aren't fancy. ⊠ *1700 Mt. Seymour Rd., North Vancouver* ☎ *604/986–2261* ⊕ *www.mountseymour.com.*

SKATING RINKS

FAMILY **Robson Square Ice Rink.** Rent skates and lace them up tight to enjoy this free ice-skating rink in the city center. It's the best of indoor and outdoor skating combined—with a triodesic glass dome covering the open-air rink. The season runs mid-November through February. ⊠ *800 Robson St., Downtown* ☎ *604/822–3333* ⊕ *www.robsonsquare.com* ⊿ *Free.*

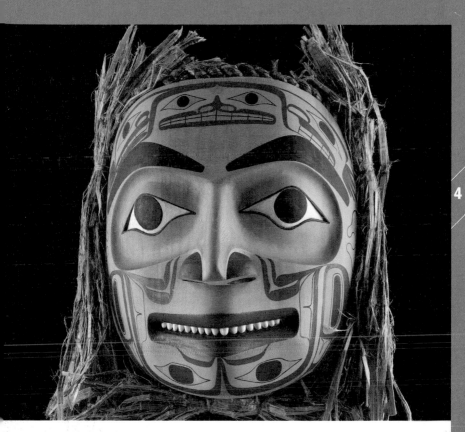

SHOPPING

Updated by
Carolyn B.
Heller

Art galleries, ethnic markets, gourmet-food shops, and high-fashion boutiques abound in Vancouver. Shopping here is more unique than in many other North American cities because of the prevalence of Asian and First Nations influences in crafts, home furnishings, and foods.

Downtown Vancouver has many of the same chain stores that you can find across North America but there is also an exciting community of budding local fashion designers whose creative clothes and accessories fill the smaller boutiques. If you're looking for interesting local shops, head beyond Downtown, especially to the Gastown and Main Street neighborhoods, and to the Portobello West Market. Keep in mind, too, that the word "mall" here can mean more than just generic shopping, particularly in suburban Richmond, where malls tend to cater to an upscale Asian community. It's almost like shopping in Hong Kong, Beijing, or Tokyo.

In the art scene, look for First Nations and other aboriginal art, from souvenir trinkets to stellar contemporary art; many galleries showcasing First Nations artists are in Gastown. Area artisans also create a variety of fine crafts, exhibiting and selling their wares at Granville Island galleries. Some local favorites are included in the listings, and the "Artists & Artisans of Granville Island" brochure, available at shops around Granville Island, has a complete listing of island galleries and studios.

Food—especially local seafood (available smoked and packed to travel), cheeses from British Columbia and across Canada, and even locally made chocolates, jams, and other goodies—makes tasty souvenirs (or delicious snacking or picnic fare). British Columbia also has a rapidly maturing wine industry, and local shops give advice about the region's offerings (and tastings, too). Remember the restrictions about taking alcohol back into your home country before you stock up.

Outdoor-oriented Vancouver is also a great place to pick up camping and hiking gear. There's a cluster of outdoor-equipment shops on West Broadway between Yukon and Manitoba streets just west of Main Street, and you'll find several snowboard and skiing outlets on West 4th Avenue, just east of Burrard Street in Kitsilano.

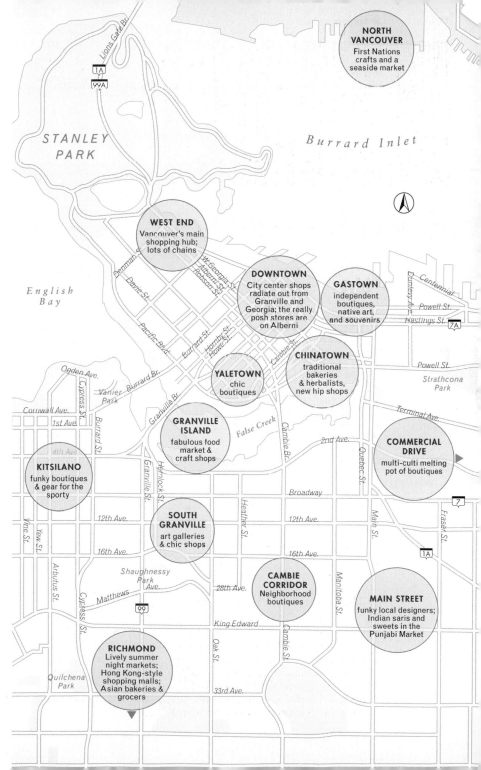

SHOPPING PLANNER

WHAT TO BRING HOME

First Nations artwork: there's always something to fit your budget

Salmon, smoked and vacuum-packed for travel

One-of-a-kind fashions from emerging local designers

Anything from Roots, the quintessential Canadian brand

Wine from a BC vineyard

STORE HOURS

Store hours vary, but are generally Monday, Tuesday, Wednesday, and Saturday 10 to 6; Thursday and Friday 10 to 9; and Sunday 11 to 5 or 11 to 6. In Gastown, along Main Street, and on Commercial Drive, many shops don't open until 11 or noon.

TAXES

Most purchases are subject to a 7% Provincial Sales Tax (PST) and 5% federal Goods and Services Tax (GST). The PST on wine, beer, and spirits is 10%, but is included in the price.

DOWNTOWN AND THE WEST END

DOWNTOWN

The main Downtown shopping streets radiate out from the intersection of Granville and West Georgia streets. In this Downtown area, shoppers will find major department stores, including the Bay and Holt Renfrew, as well as lots of North American chains and big-name European brands.

ART AND ANTIQUES

DoDa Antiques. Concentrating on mid-20th-century jewelry, ceramics, glass, paintings, and prints, this old-timey treasure box is crammed with intriguing finds. It also stocks First Nations art. ⊠ *434 Richards St., Downtown* ☎ *604/602–0559* ⊕ *www.dodaantiques.com.*

BOOKS

Chapters. These Canadian shops (most with a Starbucks attached) stock a vast selection of popular books. Check out the display tables for hot sellers, local authors, and bargain books. In addition to the Downtown location, there's a convenient South Granville branch at the corner of Broadway and Granville Street. ⊠ *788 Robson St., Downtown* ☎ *604/682–4066* ⊕ *www.chapters.indigo.ca.*

MacLeod's Books. One of the city's best antiquarian and used-book stores, this jam-packed shop is a treasure trove of titles from mainstream to wildly eclectic. ⊠ *455 W. Pender St., Downtown* ☎ *604/681–7654.*

CLOTHING: MEN'S AND WOMEN'S

Leone. Marble alcoves in an elegantly palatial store set the scene for men's and women's fashions by Versace, Alexander McQueen, Moschino, Dior, Miu Miu, and others. On the lower level is L-2 Leone, where you'll find edgier fashions and an Italian café. ⊠ *Sinclair Centre, 757 W. Hastings St., Downtown* ☎ *604/683–1133* ⊕ *www.leone.ca.*

DID YOU KNOW?

The Museum of Anthropology at the University of British Columbia has an excellent collection of Northwest Coast First Nations art, and the building and grounds are spectacular. The museum shop sells unusual art and gift items.

Fodor's Choice **Lululemon Athletica.** Power-yoga devotees, soccer moms, and anyone who
★ likes casual, comfy clothes covets the fashionable, well-constructed
workout wear with the stylized "A" insignia from this Vancouver-based
company. The stores also provide free drop-in yoga classes. In addition to this flagship location, there are several branches around town,
including one at 2113 West 4th Avenue in Kitsilano. ⊠ *970 Robson St.,
Downtown* ☎ *604/681–3118* ⊕ *www.lululemon.com.*

DEPARTMENT STORES

Fodor's Choice **Holt Renfrew.** This is Canada's ritziest department store name, a swanky
★ showcase for international high fashion and accessories for men and
women. Think Prada, Dolce & Gabbana, and other designer labels.
⊠ *Pacific Centre, 737 Dunsmuir St., Downtown* ☎ *604/681–3121*
⊕ *www.holtrenfrew.com.*

Hudson's Bay. A Canadian institution (though it's now American-owned),
the Bay was founded as part of the fur trade in the 17th century. There's
a whole department selling the signature tri-color blankets and other
Canadiana. On the lower level, the Topshop and Topman boutiques
carry imports from the trendy British retailer. ⊠ *674 Granville St., at
Georgia St., Downtown* ☎ *604/681–6211* ⊕ *www.thebay.com.*

Winners. This discount department store chain is heaven for bargain
hunters. Among the regularly changing stock, you might unearth great
deals on designer fashions, shoes, and housewares. ⊠ *798 Granville
St., at Robson St., Downtown* ☎ *604/683–1058* ⊕ *www.winners.ca.*

FOOD

Purdy's Chocolates. A chocolatier since 1907, Purdy's once made a
liqueur-filled line, which was hawked to Americans during Prohibition.
These days, Purdy's purple-foiled boxes of chocolate temptations are a
popular gift. Outlets are scattered throughout the city. ⊠ *Pacific Centre,
700 W. Georgia St., Downtown* ☎ *604/683–3467* ⊕ *www.purdys.com.*

Urban Fare. If you're a fan of Whole Foods, check out Vancouver's most
stylish supermarket. The mouthwatering food displays come from all
corners of the globe. In addition to this Downtown store, there are
also branches at 305 Bute Street (Downtown), 177 Davie Street in
Yaletown, and at 1688 Salt Street in the Olympic Village, just west of
Main Street. ⊠ *1133 Alberni St., Downtown* ☎ *604/648–2053* ⊕ *www.
urbanfare.com.*

Viti Wine and Lager Store. What this diminutive shop lacks in size it
makes up in quality. The shelves are stocked with a strong selection of
wines, beers, and liquors, with an emphasis on regional products. Wine
tastings are held Saturday; beer and spirits tastings are regularly held
on Sunday afternoons. ⊠ *Moda Hotel, 900 Seymour St., Downtown*
☎ *604/683–3806* ⊕ *www.vitiwinelagers.com.*

JEWELRY

Birks. Vancouver's link in this Canada-wide chain of high-end jewelers—
a national institution since 1879—is in a neoclassical former bank
building. An impressive staircase connects the main level to the mezzanine floor—you'll feel like royalty while descending. ⊠ *698 W. Hastings
St., Downtown* ☎ *604/669–3333* ⊕ *www.birks.com.*

Palladio. This is one of Vancouver's most stylish jewelers. Expect high-fashion pieces in gold and platinum, top-name timepieces, and distinguished accessories. ⊠ *855 W. Hastings St., Downtown* ☎ *604/685–3885* ⊕ *www.palladiocanada.com.*

OUTDOOR EQUIPMENT

Atmosphere. You can count on finding high-performance (and high-fashion) gear for hiking, camping, or just battling the rain at this chain of sporting goods stores. ⊠ *Pacific Centre, 777 Dunsmuir St., Downtown* ☎ *604/687–7668* ⊕ *www.atmosphere.ca.*

SHOPPING CENTERS

Pacific Centre. Filling three city blocks in the heart of Downtown, this mall is filled with mostly mainstream clothing shops, with some more sophisticated and pricier boutiques scattered throughout. There are several street-level entrances as well as access via Holt Renfrew and the Vancouver City Centre Station—worth knowing about on rainy days. ⊠ *701 W. Georgia St., Downtown* ☎ *604/688–7235* ⊕ *www.pacificcentre.ca.*

Sinclair Centre. Shops in and around this complex cater to sophisticated tastes with outposts such as Leone and Cartier. ⊠ *757 W. Hastings St., Downtown* ☎ *604/488–0672* ⊕ *www.sinclaircentre.com.*

WEST END

Robson Street, particularly the blocks between Burrard and Bute streets, is the city's main fashion-shopping and people-watching artery. The Gap and Banana Republic have their flagship stores here, as do Canadian fashion outlets Club Monaco and Roots. Souvenir shops, shoe stores, and cafés fill the gaps. West of Bute, the shops cater to the thousands of Asian students in town to study English: Japanese, Korean, and Chinese food shops, video outlets, and noodle bars abound, particularly near the intersection of Robson and Denman.

CLOTHING: CHILDREN'S

FAMILY **Roots Kids.** Synonymous with outdoorsy Canadian style, this Canadian company's signature casual wear is also available in children's sizes. The kids store is just down the street from the Roots flagship store on Robson Street. ⊠ *1153 Robson St., West End* ☎ *604/684–8801* ⊕ *canada.roots.com.*

CLOTHING: MEN'S AND WOMEN'S

Fodor'sChoice **Roots.** For outdoorsy clothes that double as souvenirs (many sport maple-
★ leaf logos), check out these Canadian-made sweatshirts, leather jackets, and other comfy casuals. In addition to this Downtown flagship store, there are branches on South Granville Street and on West 4th Avenue in Kitsilano. ⊠ *1001 Robson St., West End* ☎ *604/683–4305* ⊕ *canada.roots.com.*

FOOD

Ayoub's Dried Fruits and Nuts. The freshly roasted almonds, pistachios, and cashews from this pretty Persian-style shop make excellent snacks; try them with the signature lime-saffron seasoning. Boxes of nuts and sweets make excellent gifts, too. There are other locations at 2048 West 4th Avenue in Kitsilano and 1332 Lonsdale Avenue in North Vancouver. ⊠ *986 Denman St., West End* ☎ *604/732–6887* ⊕ *www.ayoubs.ca.*

GASTOWN AND CHINATOWN

GASTOWN

A hip crowd—restaurateurs, advertising gurus, photographers, and other creative types—have settled into Gastown, which has made the boutiques here correspondingly cool. Look for locally designed and one-of-a-kind clothing and accessories, First Nations art, and souvenirs—both kitschy and expensive. The best blocks for browsing are Water Street between Richards and Carrall, and West Cordova between Richards and Cambie. Also check out the ever-changing shops on Abbott and Carrall streets, between Water and Cordova.

ART AND ANTIQUES

Fodor's Choice
★

Hill's Native Art. This highly respected store has Vancouver's largest selection of First Nations art. The main floor is crammed with souvenirs, keepsakes, and high-quality pieces, including carvings, masks, and drums. If you think that's impressive, head upstairs for one-of-a-kind collector pieces and limited editions. ✉ 165 Water St., Gastown ☎ 604/685–4249 ⊕ www.hills.ca.

CLOTHING: MEN'S AND WOMEN'S

Dream Apparel & Articles for People. Come here to find a variety of wares by up-and-coming local designers. The creative selections target the hip twentysomething crowd. ✉ 356 Water St., Gastown ☎ 604/683–7326 ⊕ www.dreamvancouver.com.

Oak + Fort. Based in Vancouver, with locations elsewhere in Canada, Oak + Fort sells simple but stylish locally designed women's clothing and accessories plus a small selection of menswear at its spacious storefront. ✉ 355 Water St., Gastown ☎ 604/566–9199 ⊕ www.oakandfort.com.

One of a Few. The clothing here, from local and international makers, may not be one of a kind, but as the name of this funky little shop attests, you won't see the designs at mass-market retailers either. ✉ 354 Water St., Gastown ☎ 604/605–0685 ⊕ www.oneofafew.com.

Secret Location. If you think that Vancouverites wear nothing but T-shirts and yoga pants, find your way to this deluxe boutique, an all-white gallery of highly curated clothing, accessories, and art books. Sharing the adjacent space is a restaurant with the same name. ✉ 1 Water St., Gastown ☎ 604/685–0090 ⊕ www.secretlocation.ca.

SHOES AND ACCESSORIES

Fodor's Choice
★

John Fluevog. You might have seen John Fluevog shops in New York and Los Angeles, but did you know that these funky shoes were created by a Vancouverite? The Gastown location is worth a look for the store itself, with its striking glass facade and soaring ceilings. There's another branch downtown at 837 Granville Street. ✉ 65 Water St., Gastown ☎ 604/688–6228 ⊕ www.fluevog.com.

CHINATOWN

Bustling Chinatown—centered on Pender and Main streets—is full of Chinese bakeries, restaurants, herbalists, tea merchants, and import shops, as well as a new crop of funky boutiques, cocktail lounges, and casual eateries.

FOOD

T&T Supermarket. Check out this chain of Asian supermarkets for exotic produce, baked goods, and prepared foods. You can assemble an inexpensive lunch-to-go from the extensive hot food counter. In addition to this Chinatown location, there are branches at 2800 East 1st Avenue on the East Side and at 8181 Cambie Road in Richmond. ⊠ *179 Keefer Pl., Chinatown* ☎ *604/899–8836* ⊕ *www.tnt-supermarket.com.*

YALETOWN

Frequently described as Vancouver's SoHo, Yaletown, on the north bank of False Creek, is where you'll find boutiques, home furnishings stores, and restaurants—many in converted warehouses—that cater to a trendy, moneyed crowd.

CLOTHING: MEN'S AND WOMEN'S

Fine Finds Boutique. It's hard to predict what you'll find in this pretty little shop—it's a fun spot to browse for cute women's clothing, jewelry, and accessories. ⊠ *1014 Mainland St., Yaletown* ☎ *604/669–8325* ⊕ *www. finefindsboutique.com.*

FOOD AND WINE

Ganache Patisserie. In true Parisian style, every delicious and decadent item here is a work of art. You can buy whole cakes—perhaps a chocolate-banana cake or a coconut mango cheesecake—but just a slice will perk up your shopping day. ⊠ *1262 Homer St., Yaletown* ☎ *604/899–1098* ⊕ *www.ganacheyaletown.com.*

Long Table Distillery. Vancouver's first microdistillery brews small batches of gin and vodka, along with a changing selection of seasonal spirits. Stop in for free tastings Tuesday through Saturday. ⊠ *1451 Hornby St., Yaletown* ☎ *604/266–0177* ⊕ *www.longtabledistillery.com.*

Swirl. To learn more about British Columbia wines, or to pick up a bottle (or a few), visit the knowledgeable staff at this Yaletown store that stocks more than 650 varieties produced in the province. There are complimentary tastings offered on most days. ⊠ *1185 Mainland St., Yaletown* ☎ *604/408–9463* ⊕ *www.swirlwinestore.ca.*

MARKETS

Yaletown Farmers' Market. If you're interested in local produce, this farmers' market operates outside the Yaletown/Roundhouse Canada Line station on Thursdays from 2 to 6 pm, May to October. In addition to fresh fruits and veggies, look for locally made jams and delicious baked goods (from Whistler's Purebread Bakery). ⊠ *Mainland St., between Davie and Helmcken Sts., Yaletown* ⊕ *www.eatlocal.org.*

A Bit About—and How to Buy—Aboriginal Art

With 198 First Nations peoples in British Columbia alone, it's easy to be mesmerized, even confused, by the range and diversity of the indigenous art you'll see. Different bands have traded materials, skills, and resources for centuries, so today it's often difficult to attribute any particular style to any one group. It's this blending, though, that has created such a rich cultural mosaic. That said, there are still some groups, such as the Haida and Coast Salish, who have strong identifiable traits.

Broadly speaking, First Nations art is a language of symbols, which come together to describe the legends and stories that link one community with another. Contrary to popular belief, although these symbols may share a similar meaning, they are by no means a common language: the Coast Salish, for example, view the hummingbird differently from how the Tsimshian Tribe do.

According to Rikki Kooy, whose Shuswap name is Spirit Elk Woman, there are two heartfelt ways many people purchase First Nations art. "The first is to fall in love with a region of British Columbia, and find the First Nations group that represents that area," she says. "The second is to fall in love with a piece for its calling." Rikki has been involved with retailing aboriginal art for more than 35 years and is a former advisor to Aboriginal Tourism BC.

Once you've found yourself drawn to a particular piece, whether it's jewelry, a mask, or a print, there are three essential questions to consider in judging its integrity and authenticity.

Does the work or design have a title? Because First Nations art is highly symbolic, authentic pieces will be titled. Bear in mind that the title will usually allude to mythical lore, real-life stories, and/or the artist's ancestry.

Is the cultural group identified? Every piece holds a story, against which there is often a broader background of heritage, hierarchy, and geographic origin. For example, a Haida piece will likely have come from the Queen Charlottes, or have been made by a descendant from that region. By knowing the region, the nuances of the piece's symbolic language are more easily identifiable.

Is the artist named, or better still, is there a background sheet available? First Nations peoples hold relationships in high esteem, so dealers with integrity will have established a relationship with the artists they represent and should have a background sheet on the artist and his or her heritage. This adds to the authenticity of the work, as well as giving you some background about the artist and his or her other works.

GRANVILLE ISLAND

On the south side of False Creek, Granville Island has a lively food market and a wealth of galleries, crafts shops, and artisans' studios, many of which you'll find in the Net Loft building in the center of the island. Granville Island gets so busy, especially on summer weekends, that the crowds can detract from the pleasure of the place; you're best off getting there before 11 am or going during the week. The **Kids Market**, in a converted warehouse, has kids shops as well as an indoor play area.

ART AND ANTIQUES

Circle Craft. This artist co-op sells finely crafted textiles, wood pieces, jewelry, ceramics, and glass works. Chosen by juried selection, the artists are all local to BC and all their work must be made by hand. ✉ *Net Loft, 1–1666 Johnston St., Granville Island* ☎ *604/669-8021* ⊕ *www. circlecraft.net.*

Fodor'sChoice **Crafthouse.** Run by the Crafts Council of British Columbia, this tiny
★ structure contains a veritable smorgasbord of works by local artisans. The artworks range from jewelry and other small gift items to large investment pieces. For last-minute shopping, visit their location at the Vancouver International Airport, on the Domestic Departures level. ✉ *1386 Cartwright St., Granville Island* ☎ *604/687–7270* ⊕ *www. craftcouncilbc.ca.*

Gallery of BC Ceramics. An impressive display of functional and decorative ceramics by local artists is for sale here. Several times a year, the gallery also hosts special exhibitions of work by members of the Potters Guild of British Columbia. ✉ *1359 Cartwright St., Granville Island* ☎ *604/669-3606* ⊕ *www.bcpotters.com.*

Lattimer Gallery. Stocking native arts and crafts in all price ranges, this shop, which is designed to resemble a Pacific Northwest longhouse, is a short stroll from Granville Island. Look for masks, jewelry, bentwood boxes, carvings, and other works that reflect First Nations and Inuit designs. ✉ *1590 W. 2nd Ave., Granville Island* ☎ *604/732–4556* ⊕ *www.lattimergallery.com.*

CLOTHING: MEN'S AND WOMEN'S

Little Dream. Under the same ownership as Dream Apparel & Articles for People in Gastown, Little Dream is a smaller version of this fashion-forward shop showcasing local designers. ✉ *Net Loft, 130–1666 Johnston St., Granville Island* ☎ *604/683–6930* ⊕ *www.dreamvancouver.com.*

FOOD AND WINE

Artisan Sake Maker. You can learn all about sake (Japanese rice wine), and sample the locally made product, at Vancouver's own sake brewery. ✉ *1339 Railspur Alley, Granville Island* ☎ *604/685–7253* ⊕ *www. artisansakemaker.com.*

Edible Canada. Opposite the Granville Island Public Market, this shop sells jams, sauces, chocolates, and hundreds of other edible items from around the province. It's a great place to find gifts for foodie friends. ✉ *1596 Johnston St., Granville Island* ☎ *604/682–6675* ⊕ *www. ediblecanada.com.*

Liberty Distillery. Crafting artisanal vodka, gin, and whiskey from 100% BC grain, this distillery offers tastings in its stylish Granville Island shop. You can take a guided distillery tour (C$10) on weekends at 1 or 3 pm. ⊠ *1494 Old Bridge Rd., Granville Island* ☎ *604/558–1998* ⊕ *thelibertydistillery.com.*

Liberty Wine Merchants. The helpful employees at this local chain can assist you in selecting wines from BC or around the world. ⊠ *1660 Johnston St., Granville Island* ☎ *604/602–1120* ⊕ *www.libertywine merchants.com.*

MARKETS

Fodor's Choice
★
Granville Island Public Market. Locals and visitors alike crowd this indoor market that's part farm stand, part gourmet grocery, and part upscale food court. The stalls are packed with locally made sausages, exotic cheeses, just-caught fish, fresh produce, baked goods, and prepared foods from handmade fudge to frothy cappuccinos. This is definitely the place to come for lunch. If the sun is out, you can dine on your purchases out on the waterfront decks. The crowds can get crazy, though, so avoid weekends if possible (or come early). ⊠ *1689 Johnston St., Granville Island* ☎ *604/666–5784* ⊕ *www.granvilleisland.com/public-market.*

SPECIALTY STORES

Granville Island Hat Shop. You name the hat and somewhere on the walls, rafters, shelves, or floor you'll find it. There are fedoras, cloches, toques, sun hats, rain hats, straw hats, and pretty much any other hat you might want want. ⊠ *Net Loft, 4–1666 Johnston St., Granville Island* ☎ *604/683–4280* ⊕ *www.thehatshop.ca.*

The Umbrella Shop. Stocking good-quality umbrellas of all sizes, this little shop will help you keep stylishly dry. If you get caught in the rain Downtown, visit their location at 526 West Pender Street. ⊠ *1550 Anderson St., Granville Island* ☎ *604/697–0919* ⊕ *www.theumbrellashop.com.*

THE WEST SIDE

KITSILANO

West 4th Avenue, between Burrard and Balsam, is the main shopping strip in funky Kitsilano. There are clothing and shoe boutiques, as well as housewares and gift shops. Just east of Burrard, several stores on West 4th sell ski and snowboard gear. Look for food boutiques on West 2nd and 3rd.

BOOKS

Fodor's Choice
★
Barbara-Jo's Books to Cooks. Local-chef-turned-entrepreneur Barbara-Jo McIntosh spreads the good-food word with scores of cookbooks, including many by Vancouver- and BC–based chefs, as well as wine books, memoirs, and magazines. The store also hosts special events, recipe demos, and drop-in classes in its sparkling demonstration kitchen—they're a tasty way to explore local cuisine. ⊠ *1740 W. 2nd Ave., Kitsilano* ☎ *604/688–6755* ⊕ *www.bookstocooks.com.*

Fodor's Choice **Kidsbooks.** The helpful staff at this cheery shop is happy to make recom-
★ mendations about books appropriate for young people ranging from
FAMILY toddlers to teens. Choose from the many titles by Canadian authors—
excellent for take-home gifts or on-the-road reading. ⊠ *3083 W. Broadway, Kitsilano* ☎ *604/738–5335* ⊕ *www.kidsbooks.ca.*

Wanderlust. Travelers and armchair travelers love this shop, which feeds
everyone's wanderlust. There are thousands of travel books and maps,
as well as luggage, gear, and accessories. ⊠ *1929 W. 4th Ave., Kitsilano*
☎ *604/739–2182* ⊕ *www.wanderlustore.com.*

FOOD

Chocolate Arts. Looking for a present for a chocolate lover? Check out the
chocolates in First Nations motifs, specially designed by Robert David-
son, one of Canada's premier artists. This delicious shop and café, where
you can refuel with a hot chocolate, some bonbons, or a handmade ice-
cream bar, is a short walk from Granville Island. ⊠ *1620 W. 3rd Ave.,
Kitsilano* ☎ *604/739–0475, 877/739–0475* ⊕ *www.chocolatearts.com.*

Fodor's Choice **Les Amis du Fromage.** If you love cheese, don't miss the mind-boggling
★ array of selections from BC, the rest of Canada, and elsewhere at this
shop of delicacies. The extremely knowledgeable mother-and-daughter
owners, Alice and Allison Spurrell, and their staff encourage you to
taste before you buy. Yum. The fromagerie is located between Granville
Island and Kitsilano Beach—useful to keep in mind if you're assembling a seaside picnic. ⊠ *1752 W. 2nd Ave., Kitsilano* ☎ *604/732–4218*
⊕ *www.buycheese.com.*

MARKETS

Kitsilano Farmers' Market. This popular farmers' market sets up in the
Kitsilano Community Centre parking lot on Sunday from 10 am to 2
pm, mid-May to mid-October. It's larger than the one in Yaletown, and
you can buy cheese, baked goods, and some prepared foods here, in
addition to produce. ⊠ *2690 Larch Street, at 10th Avenue, Kitsilano*
⊕ *www.eatlocal.org.*

SHOES AND ACCESSORIES

Gravity Pope. Foot fashionistas make tracks to this Kitsilano shop that's
jam-packed with trendy choices, including Camper, Puma, Kenneth
Cole, and other international brands for men and women. ⊠ *2205 W.
4th Ave., Kitsilano* ☎ *604/731–7673* ⊕ *www.gravitypope.com.*

POINT GREY

The Point Grey neighborhood has a small shopping district along West
10th Avenue, between Discovery and Tolmie streets, but the main
reason shoppers venture this far west is the excellent gift shop at the
Museum of Anthropology.

ART AND ANTIQUES

Museum of Anthropology Gift Shop. This museum store carries an excellent selection of Northwest Coast jewelry, carvings, and prints, as well
as books on First Nations history and culture. ⊠ *University of British Columbia, 6393 N.W. Marine Dr., Point Grey* ☎ *604/827–4810*
⊕ *www.moa.ubc.ca.*

MADE IN VANCOUVER

Vancouver doesn't just produce overpriced lattes and undersized condos. The city's creative denizens have designed a range of products from shoes to yoga wear.

Happy Planet Juices: Vancouverites have been supporting this local company's mission to "turn the planet on to 100% organic juices" since the company got its start in 1994.

Holey Soles: A competitor of the ubiquitous Crocs, these brightly colored, cloglike, rubber-compound shoes are designed in the Vancouver area and sold at outdoor and garden shops around town.

John Fluevog: Yep, those outrageous shoes took their first steps in Vancouver.

Lululemon Athletica: The stylized "A" insignia is as recognizable to yoga enthusiasts as the Nike "swoosh" is to sports fans.

Rocky Mountain Bicycles: BC invented the aggressive, stunt-heavy "free-riding" or "north shore" (from the North Shore Mountains) style of riding that's taken over the sport, and Rocky Mountain makes the steeds on which the style was pioneered.

SOUTH GRANVILLE

About two dozen high-end art galleries, antiques shops, and furniture stores are packed between 5th and 15th avenues on Granville Street, in an area known as Gallery Row. *See the Exploring listings for galleries here that are worth browsing.* Granville Street between Broadway and 16th Avenue is known as Granville Rise, and it's lined with chic fashion, home-decor, and specialty-food shops.

CLOTHING: MEN'S AND WOMEN'S

Tilley Endurables. Globe-trotters search out this practical, hard-wearing line of Canadian-made travel clothing. The Tilley Hat is an icon of seasoned travelers. ⊠ *2401 Granville St., South Granville* ☎ *604/732–4287* ⊕ *www.tilleyvancouver.com.*

Turnabout. The quality of the previously owned clothing here is so good that "used" is almost a misnomer at this long-established vintage-clothing store. They sell upscale women's wear from labels like Gucci, Missoni, and Prada. A second branch, at 3112 West Broadway in Kitsilano, sells more casual clothing, as well as men's clothes. ⊠ *3109 Granville St., South Granville* ☎ *604/734–5313* ⊕ *www.turnabout.ca.*

CAMBIE CORRIDOR

CLOTHING: MEN'S AND WOMEN'S

Shop Cocoon. This is a great showcase for independent designers, who can rent a rack, shelf, or wall space to showcase their work trade show–style in this small shop. Products change frequently and include ethically manufactured clothing, accessories, and jewelry. ⊠ *3345 Cambie St., Cambie Corridor* ☎ *778/232–8532.*

Walrus. "A pleasant surprise" is the motto of this airy gallerylike shop, where you never quite know what you'll find—perhaps candle holders, jewelry, handcrafted purses, one-of-a-kind T-shirts, or original artwork. They stock a mix of local and international designers and often host small exhibitions. ✉ *3408 Cambie St., Cambie Corridor* 🕾 *604/874–9770* ⊕ *www.walrushome.com.*

OUTDOOR EQUIPMENT
Three Vets. This army surplus–style store stocks budget-priced camping equipment, outdoor clothing, and boots. They also have a native art collection worth seeing. ✉ *2200 Yukon St., Cambie Corridor* 🕾 *604/872–5475.*

SHOPPING CENTERS
Oakridge Centre. If you're intent on browsing, head to the skylighted atrium of Oakridge Centre (perhaps if the weather's bad and you want to be inside). There's a mix of trendy shops, upscale boutiques, and North American chains. It's a quick trip on the Canada Line from Downtown to the Oakridge–41st Avenue stop. ✉ *650 W. 41st Ave., at Cambie St., Cambie Corridor* 🕾 *604/261–2511* ⊕ *www.oakridgecentre.com.*

SPECIALTY STORES
City Cigar. Cuban cigars are legal and plentiful (although it's not legal to take them into the United States). Is this why Tommy Lee Jones and Arnold Schwarzenegger stop at this shop when they're in town? ✉ *888 W. 6th Ave., Cambie Corridor* 🕾 *604/879–0208* ⊕ *www.citycigarcompany.com.*

THE EAST SIDE

MAIN ST./MOUNT PLEASANT

Main Street, between 20th and 30th avenues, is a funky, ever-changing neighborhood, rich with ethnic restaurants and vintage-fashion shops. The main reason to explore here, though, is the growing number of eclectic boutiques that showcase the creations of local designers. If distinctive yet relatively economical fashion is your thing, you could easily spend a whole afternoon poking around these stores.

For outdoor gear, check out the stores on Broadway, especially along the area west of Main Street.

In the Punjabi Market area, Vancouver's "Little India," curry houses, sweets shops, grocery stores, discount jewelers, and silk shops abound. This small community centers on Main Street between 48th and 51st avenues.

ART AND ANTIQUES
Maynards Auction House. Put up your bidding paddle! Specializing in fine art, estate jewelry, and antiques, Maynards holds auctions monthly. Although you can get a quick glimpse at the goods before the auctioneer begins, serious bidders should call or check the website to find out preview times. ✉ *1837 Main St., Main St./Mt. Pleasant* 🕾 *604/876–6787* ⊕ *www.maynardsfineart.com.*

BOOKS

Y's Books. Need something to read? This well-organized shop stocks good quality used books, including many titles by BC and Canadian authors. ✉ *4307 Main St., Main St./Mt. Pleasant* ☎ *604/879–9676* ⊕ *ys-bookstore.blogspot.ca.*

CLOTHING: MEN'S AND WOMEN'S

Barefoot Contessa. This cute shop has a creative take on '40s-style glamour. Look for frilly feminine clothing (dresses, dresses, and more dresses), jewelry, and bags—some by local designers—as well as vintage linens and decorative accessories. ✉ *3715 Main St., Main St./Mt. Pleasant* ☎ *604/879–1137* ⊕ *www.thebarefootcontessa.com.*

Front and Company. Value-conscious fashionistas eagerly browse the consignment and vintage clothing in this smart shop. There's a small section of designer samples and new items, as well as eclectic gifts. ✉ *3772 Main St., Main St./Mt. Pleasant* ☎ *604/879–8431* ⊕ *www. frontandcompany.ca.*

Hazel & Jools. While many Main Street shops cater to the young and hyper fashion-conscious, this hip boutique appeals to women of all ages with fashionable labels such as Mexx, Kensie, and its own in-house line. It also carries cool clothes for moms-to-be. ✉ *4280 Main St., Main St./ Mt. Pleasant* ☎ *604/730–8689* ⊕ *www.hazelhipmoms.com.*

FodorsChoice **Portobello West.** Modeled on London's Portobello Road, Portobello
★ West showcases emerging local designers—some are students, others are more established—and their unique, stylish wares. The event is held four weekends each year in March, May, September, and November and there is a C$2 admission charge. Other events, including a home and design show, are more expensive. The Creekside Community Centre is a 15-minute walk from either the Olympic Village or Main Street Sky-Train station. ✉ *Creekside Community Centre, 1 Athletes Way, Main St./Mt. Pleasant* ⊕ *www.portobellowest.com* ⊠ *$2.*

Twigg & Hottie. Local and national designers stock this outlet with one-of-a-kind creations ranging from the edgiest of Hollywood glam to chic street-wear funk. Look for the in-house We3 label. ✉ *3671 Main St., Main St./Mt. Pleasant* ☎ *604/879–8595* ⊕ *www.twiggandhottie.com.*

FOOD

Chocolaterie de La Nouvelle France. This petite bonbon of a confectionary shop sells delectable, hand-crafted truffles and caramels, as well as rich, thick "drinking chocolate." This decadent hot cocoa is the perfect pick-me-up while browsing the nearby boutiques, especially on a chilly rainy day. ✉ *198 E. 21 Ave., Main St./Mt. Pleasant* ☎ *604/566–1065* ⊕ *www.chocolaterienouvellefrance.ca.*

HOUSEWARES

Vancouver Special. This shop carries a stylish selection of household items by local and international designers and stocks an eclectic assortment of books about art, architecture, and design. ✉ *3612 Main St., Main St./Mt. Pleasant* ☎ *604/568–3673* ⊕ *www.vanspecial.com.*

MARKETS

Vancouver Flea Market. Housed in a "big red barn," this weekend market is a five-minute walk from the Main Street SkyTrain station. You'll find all manner of treasures at all sorts of prices. ⊠ *703 Terminal Ave., Main St./Mt. Pleasant* ☎ *604/685–0666* ⊕ *www.vancouverfleamarket.com.*

OUTDOOR EQUIPMENT

Fodor'sChoice
★
MEC (Mountain Equipment Co-op). This warehouse-style store stocks a good selection of high-performance clothing and equipment for hiking, cycling, climbing, and kayaking, and for just looking good while hanging around outdoors. You can rent sports gear here, too. A onetime C$5 membership is required for purchases or rentals. ⊠ *130 W. Broadway, Main St./Mt. Pleasant* ☎ *604/872–7858* ⊕ *www.mec.ca.*

Taiga. Vancouver-based Taiga sells popular waterproof cycling gear, as well as other outdoor clothing, sleeping bags, and tents. ⊠ *301 W. Broadway, Main St./Mt. Pleasant* ☎ *604/875 8388* ⊕ *www.taigaworks.ca.*

COMMERCIAL DRIVE AND AROUND

Guatemalan crafts, Italian shoes, and espresso bars with soccer matches being broadcast live from Italy come together on Commercial Drive, Vancouver's world-beat, offbeat melting pot. You'll find the largest collection of shops between Venables Street and East 2nd Avenue, with restaurants and cafés extending south along "the Drive" to Broadway.

ART AND ANTIQUES

Doctor Vigari Gallery. In keeping with its offbeat environs on "the Drive," this gallery is home to a wildly eclectic assortment of jewelry, crafts, paintings, and household items, most by BC artists. ⊠ *1816 Commercial Dr., Commercial Drive* ☎ *604/255–9513* ⊕ *www.doctorvigarigallery.com.*

CLOTHING: CHILDREN'S

FAMILY **Dandelion Kids.** If you're shopping for style-conscious babies, toddlers, and grade-schoolers, check out this store's organic and "recycled" duds. Fair-trade toys also fill the shelves. ⊠ *1206 Commercial Dr., Commercial Drive* ☎ *604/676–1862* ⊕ *www.dandelionkids.ca.*

CLOTHING: MEN'S AND WOMEN'S

Roots 73 Outlet. You can pay top dollar downtown or head to this factory outlet, which stocks good quality off-season and closeout items at bargain prices. ⊠ *3695 Grandview Hwy., at Boundary Rd., East Side* ☎ *604/433–4337* ⊕ *www.canada.roots.com.*

MARKETS

Trout Lake Farmers' Market. Vancouver's largest farmers' market is crowded with East Side denizens on Saturday from 9 am to 2 pm, mid-May to mid-October. There is prepared food, baked goods, and often crafts to tempt shoppers, in addition to produce. The market is about a 15-minute walk from the Commercial Drive SkyTrain station. ⊠ *John Hendry Park, between Templeton and Lakewood Sts., south of E. 13th Ave., Commercial Drive* ⊕ *www.eatlocal.org.*

The Lululemon brand of yoga attire was founded in Vancouver in 1998.

SHOES AND ACCESSORIES

Dayton Boot Company. These biker boots have a cultlike following because they're durable and hip, too. Celebrities like Kurt Russell, Harry Connick Jr., Cindy Crawford, and Sharon Stone are wearers. ⊠ *2250 E. Hastings St., East Side* ☎ *604/253–6671* ⊕ *www.daytonboots.com.*

Kalena's. You'll find everything from traditional leather sandals to fanciful purple pumps at this family-run store that's been a fixture on Commercial Drive since the 1960s. Fine Italian shoes are a specialty. ⊠ *1526 Commercial Dr., Commercial Drive* ☎ *604/255–3727* ⊕ *www. kalenashoes.com.*

NORTH SHORE

NORTH VANCOUVER

Cross the Burrand Inlet to North Vancouver and you'll find the Lonsdale Quay market (a mini-mall filled with snack stalls and boutiques), as well as a one-of-a-kind First Nations shop.

ART AND ANTIQUES

Khot-la-Cha Art Gallery & Gift Shop. On the Capilano First Nations Reserve in North Vancouver, this longhouse-style gallery showcases items crafted by members of the Squamish Indian Band, as well as work by other aboriginal artists in British Columbia and western Canada. You'll find ceremonial masks, hand-knit sweaters, and jewelry made of silver, gold, porcupine quill, or bone. The store is owned by Nancy Nightingale, the daughter of Chief Simon Baker, whose traditional name, Khot-la-Cha, means "kind heart" in the Squamish language. ⊠ *270 Whonoak St., North Vancouver* ☎ *604/987–3339* ⊕ *www.khot-la-cha.com.*

FOOD

Lonsdale Quay Market. At this two-level indoor market—less frenzied than its Granville Island counterpart—vendors sell prepared foods, just-caught seafood, and fresh produce. Also look for arts and crafts, kitchenware, and delicious pastries that can be enjoyed on the terrace, which has views of the city skyline. The market is a short ride from Downtown on the SeaBus. ⊠ *123 Carrie Cates Ct., North Vancouver* ☎ *604/985–6261* ⊕ *www.lonsdalequay.com.*

4

RICHMOND

In suburban Richmond, south of downtown Vancouver, several large shopping malls—centered on and around No. 3 Road between Cambie Road and Granville Avenue—mix chain stores with small boutiques and eateries that cater to the area's upscale Asian residents. The Aberdeen Centre seems like it could just as well be in Hong Kong. There are two night markets in Richmond, the Richmond Night Market and the Summer Night Market *(see Exploring Vancouver)*, with vendors, food stalls, and entertainment. The Canada Line from Downtown makes several stops in Richmond, convenient for getting to the malls.

BOOKS

International Travel Maps & Books. The well-regarded International Travel Maps & Books publishes its own maps, and is also the local distributor for the Canada Map Office, stocking federally made topographic maps and charts of the region. The store, in Richmond, is a treasure house of travel guides and maps, but you can also browse and purchase online. ⊠ *12300 Bridgeport Rd., Richmond* ☎ *604/273–1400* ⊕ *www.itmb.ca.*

SHOPPING CENTERS

Fodor's Choice
★
Aberdeen Centre. First-rate Asian restaurants, vendors hawking everything from kimchi to cream puffs, clothing stores stocking the latest Hong Kong styles, and Daiso—a Japanese bargain-hunters' paradise where most items sell for C$2—make this swank mall a good introduction to Vancouver's Asian shopping experience. Take the Canada Line south to Aberdeen Station, about 20 minutes from Downtown. ⊠ *4151 Hazelbridge Way, Richmond* ☎ *604/270–1234* ⊕ *www. aberdeencentre.com.*

NIGHTLIFE AND PERFORMING ARTS

Updated By
Chloë Ernst

Vancouver might be best-known for its outdoors activities but this hip, young, innovative city delivers plenty of entertainment once the sun goes down.

Gone are the days of prohibition-era liquor laws (well, most, anyway) and the general loosening of regulations has helped liven up the city after dark. When you add in a surge of modern craft breweries, wine bars implementing the latest technology, a lively mix of festivals throughout the year, and the inspiration of a fantastic wine region nearby (the Okanagan), Vancouver's nightlife scene looks as fit as any seawall runner.

In nice weather, Vancouver is all about the patios—preferably waterfront. Otherwise, the younger set migrates to dance clubs while more laid-back types gather in friendly pubs (perhaps to watch the hockey game), live music venues hosting up-and-coming stars, and splashy cocktail bars where savvy mixologists cultivate city-wide followings.

Most major music acts make a stop in Vancouver when they're on tour, so international celebrity shows complement a packed calendar of rising local bands and performing arts. Vancouver has plenty of film festivals, cutting-edge theater, comedy, opera, and ballet amid its artistic offerings, with many companies resident in town. The added frisson of celebrity sightings are common thanks to the city's ever-strong film and TV industry (*aka* "Hollywood North").

NIGHTLIFE AND PERFORMING ARTS PLANNER

CULTURAL FESTIVALS

JAN.: The **PuSh International Performing Arts Festival** (☎ *604/605–8284* ⊕ *www.pushfestival.ca*) presents modern, intriguing works that often blur the boundaries of theater and dance.

FEB.: The **Vancouver International Mountain Film Festival** (⊕ *www.vimff.org*) is a great introduction to the mountain and wilderness culture of Canada.

Vancouver has one of North America's largest **Chinese New Year** (⊕ *www.tourismvancouver.com*) celebrations.

At the **Vancouver International Wine Festival** (☎ *604/872–6623* ⊕ *www. vanwinefest.ca*), wines from countries around the world are presented.

MAR.: International dance artists perform in various venues during the **Vancouver International Dance Festival** (☎ *604/662–4966* ⊕ *www.vidf.ca*).

APR.: About 40,000 cherry trees bloom from late March into May, and the **Vancouver Cherry Blossom Festival** (☎ *604/257–8120* ⊕ *www.vcbf.ca*) marks the occasion with a variety of programs and a haiku invitational.

MAY: The **Vancouver International Children's Festival** (☎ *604/708–5655* ⊕ *www.childrensfestival.ca*) is a week of storytelling, puppetry, circus arts, music, and theater.

JUNE: The Vancouver International Jazz Festival (☎ *888/438–5200* ⊕ *www. vanjazzfest.ca*) takes place the last week in June, in dozens of venues throughout the city.

Bard on the Beach Shakespeare Festival (☎ *604/739–0559 or 877/739– 0559* ⊕ *www.bardonthebeach.org*) takes place on the waterfront in Vanier Park. Performances continue until September.

JULY: Vancouver Pride Week (☎ *604/687–0955* ⊕ *www.vancouverpride.ca*) is a celebration of the gay community, with dances, cruises, and parties.

The **Vancouver Folk Music Festival** (☎ *604/602–9798* ⊕ *www.thefestival. bc.ca*) welcomes singers and storytellers for three days of performances and children's programs.

Canada Day, on July 1, is celebrated with fireworks at Canada Place, a Downtown parade, and interactive games and displays on Granville Island.

AUG.: The **Vancouver Queer Film Festival** (☎ *604/844–1615* ⊕ *www. queerfilmfestival.ca*) is an 11-day showcase of drama, comedy, documentaries, and musicals. There are also plenty of parties around town.

SEPT.: The **Vancouver Fringe Festival** (☎ *604/257–0350* ⊕ *www.vancouverfringe.com*) is an eclectic mix of about 800 theatrical performances.

SEPT.–OCT.: The **Vancouver International Film Festival** (☎ *604/685–0260* ⊕ *www.viff.org*) draws 140,000 people to view films from 70 countries.

HOURS

Don't expect New York City hours on a night out in Vancouver. Although the city's bars, pubs, and lounges are usually open seven nights a week, they do close at a respectable 1 or 2 am. Dance clubs get lively at about 10 or 11 pm and, depending on the Vancouver Police Department's ever-changing regulations, stay open until 3 or even 4 am on weekends; many are closed on Sunday and Monday.

INFORMATION

For event information, pick up a copy of the free *Georgia Straight* (available at cafés, bookstores, and from street boxes around town) or look in the entertainment section of the *Vancouver Sun*: Thursday's paper has listings in the "Scene" section. Check the online Scout (⊕ *www.scoutmagazine.ca*) or Vancouver is Awesome (⊕ *www. vancouverisawesome.com*) for cheekier looks at the city. Web-surf over to Gay Vancouver (⊕ *www.gayvancouver.net*) for an insider's look at the gay-friendly scene.

JAZZ

Vancouver is home to one of the most sophisticated and accessible jazz scenes in Canada, with clubs, bars, and restaurants hosting local and international talent—though a number have closed in recent years. Two local groups will make sure you're in the know.

Coastal Jazz and Blues Society. Coastal Jazz and Blues Society provides details about upcoming concerts and clubs. The society also runs the Vancouver International Jazz Festival, which lights up dozens of venues around town the last week in June. ☎ 888/438–5200 ⊕ www. coastaljazz.ca.

Rogue Folk Club. This nonprofit organization presents folk, roots, and traditional Celtic concerts at various venues around town. ☎ 604/736–3022 ⊕ www.roguefolk.bc.ca.

PRICES

Painting the town red in Vancouver costs money. Perhaps not as much as it would in New York, Paris, or London, but don't leave your credit cards at home. If you're hitting the clubs, expect to pay a cover charge of around C$15 (usually waived for women before 11 pm). To see a name band or DJ perform at a club, you'll need to buy tickets well in advance—and expect to pay anywhere from C$25 to C$60. A beer will set you back around C$6, while a glass of wine or a cocktail can cost between C$9 and C$15. Don't forget the 10% liquor tax added to the price of any alcoholic beverage, whether you're ordering at a bar, club, or restaurant.

WHAT TO WEAR

During the day, the Vancouver dress code usually falls somewhere between the fleece-pragmatism of Seattle, the cosmopolitan flair of San Francisco, and the lumberjacks of the Canadian Rockies. Especially during the drizzly winter days, people dress for warm comfort first—and you probably should, too—saving the skimpy for the summer months. But when it comes to nightlife, Vancouverites get serious. They love to dress up, so expect to see clubs and lounges filled with women in dresses and heels and lots of smartly dressed men.

WHERE TO GET TICKETS

Ticketmaster. ☎ 855/985–5000 ⊕ www.ticketmaster.ca.

Tickets Tonight. ✉ 200 Burrard St., Downtown ☎ 604/684–2787 ⊕ www. ticketstonight.ca.

NIGHTLIFE

DOWNTOWN AND THE WEST END

DOWNTOWN

Granville Street is the flashy entertainment drag at the center of Downtown and in general the area bars fill up after work. Music venues and chic hotel bars get busy around the business district, and a posh crowd of glitterati flocks to chic bars and stylish lounges on the Coal Harbour waterfront. There are usually crowds of young, scantily clad clubbers to be found when the clock nears midnight.

BARS

Bacchus. Always an elegant choice, the lounge at Bacchus, in the Wedgewood Hotel, is a gathering place for Vancouver's movers and shakers. There's music every evening, as well as classic cocktails. ⊠ *Wedgewood Hotel, 845 Hornby St., Downtown* ☎ *604/608–5319* ⊕ *www. wedgewoodhotel.com.*

Hawksworth Bar and Lounge. You'll find quality cocktails blended with house-made bitters, fresh herbs, and other local ingredients at this Vancouver hotspot which, although it's leather-paneled and clubby, is surprisingly unstuffy. Also in the Rosewood Hotel Georgia are the narrow, mahogany-paneled 1927 Lobby Lounge and the open-air rooftop oasis of Reflections, if you're looking for something different. ⊠ *Rosewood Hotel Georgia, 801 W. Georgia St., Downtown* ☎ *604/673–7000* ⊕ *www.hawksworthrestaurant.com.*

Johnnie Foxs Irish Snug. This wee sliver of a pub pulls pints of Guinness and other Emerald Isle beers. It's a cozy nook, where expats find a home-away-from-home and locals come for a casual drink amid the Granville Street glam. ⊠ *1033 Granville St., Downtown* ☎ *604/685–4946* ⊕ *www.johnniefox.ca.*

Mill Marine Bistro. This waterfront pub and restaurant has one of the best views of Stanley Park and the North Shore Mountains from its expansive patio. ⊠ *1199 W. Cordova St., Downtown* ☎ *604/687–6455* ⊕ *www.millbistro.ca.*

Fodor's Choice ★ **Tap & Barrel.** The 360-degree views from this convention center patio take in Stanley Park, the seaplane terminal, and the North Shore Mountains. You can sit inside, amid the wooden casks of wine, but waiting for a seat on the deck is worth it if the weather even hints at sunshine. There's another location—and similarly large patio—on False Creek (1 Athlete's Way). ⊠ *1055 Canada Place, Downtown* ☎ *604/235–9827* ⊕ *www.tapandbarrel.com.*

Uva Wine Bar. At street level in the century-old Moda Hotel, Uva puts a modern spin on the Italian wine bar concept, with bold decor and sleek furnishings. The well-dressed crowd comes for the not-too-wild atmosphere, often for a drink before heading to one of nearby Granville Street's performance venues. ⊠ *Moda Hotel, 900 Seymour St., Downtown* ☎ *604/632–9560* ⊕ *www.uvavancouver.com.*

Xi Shi Lounge. In the Shangri-La Hotel, the Xi Shi Lounge has Asian-inspired cocktails served by waitresses in dresses reminiscent of 1920s Shanghai. The signature Iron Lotus blends sparkling wine with vodka, elderflower, and ginger. Have a drink here and you might feel like you're on a different continent entirely. ⊠ *Shangri-La Hotel, 1128 W. Georgia St., Downtown* ☎ *604/695–1115* ⊕ *www.shangri-la.com/vancouver/ shangrila/dining/bars-lounges/xi-shi-lounge.*

Wine Room. The Wine Room is devoted to nurturing the inner oenophile in all of us by offering wines usually only available by the bottle—this is one of a growing number of bars offering by-the-glass service, thanks to cutting-edge, wine-dispensing technology. It's part of the Joey Bentall One restaurant but has its own dedicated entrance. ⊠ *507 Burrard St., Downtown* ☎ *604/915–5639* ⊕ *www.joeyrestaurants.com/bentall-one.*

5

Yew. The high-ceilinged bar at the Four Seasons is a diverse environment of glass, wood, and granite, reflecting British Columbia's stunning natural environment. Happy hour attracts business executives, and at other times you'll see Canucks fans before or after the game. There are hundreds of wines to choose from, with many available by the glass (you can peruse the full list on the restaurant iPads) plus a perpetually changing creative cocktail list. Stop by on Sunday or Monday for half-price bottles of wine. ⊠ *Four Seasons Vancouver, 791 W. Georgia St., Downtown* ☎ *604/692–4939* ⊕ *www. yewrestaurant.com.*

DANCE CLUBS
AuBAR. A fixture of the city's nightlife scene for as long as most people can remember, this dimly lit space pleases a diverse crowd of clubbers. The music ranges from reggae to hip-hop to Top 40. It's open Thursday to Saturday, with the emphasis on latter—and the later. ⊠ *674 Seymour St., Downtown* ☎ *604/648–2227* ⊕ *www.aubarnightclub.com.*

Caprice. Wannabe movie stars and young hipsters queue up at this former movie theater that's been transformed into a two-level dance bar and lounge. The much-hyped LED bar, with backlit ceilings and walls resembling mirror balls, is at street level. As flash as it is, the dress is fairly casual, meaning hoodies will likely get past the doormen, although you can usually expect to wait in line. ⊠ *967 Granville St., Downtown* ☎ *604/685–3288* ⊕ *www.capricenightclub.com.*

Commodore Ballroom. This 1929 dance hall has been restored to its art-deco glory, complete with massive dance floor and state-of-the-art sound system. Indie rock bands and renowned DJs play here most nights. ⊠ *868 Granville St., Downtown* ☎ *604/739–4550, 855/985–5000 Tickets* ⊕ *www.commodoreballroom.com.*

MUSIC: ROCK AND BLUES
Fanclub. This sultry, two-level nightclub brings a little New Orleans funk and moody atmosphere to Vancouver, presenting nightly live music in an area that's otherwise lacking in casual performance venues. There are several beverage choices on tap (wine, beer, and cider) plus a menu of nibbles with Creole and southern twists. ⊠ *1050 Granville St., Downtown* ☎ *604/689–7720* ⊕ *www.vancouverfanclub.ca.*

Railway Club. In the early evening, this spot attracts film and media types to its pub-style rooms; after 8 or so it becomes a venue for local bands. Technically it's a private social club but everyone of age is welcome. A dart board offers distraction while you enjoy a cold lager. ⊠ *579 Dunsmuir St., Downtown* ☎ *604/681–1625* ⊕ *www.therailwayclub.com.*

Vogue Theatre. A former art-deco movie palace, the Vogue hosts a variety of concerts by local and visiting performers. ⊠ *918 Granville St., Downtown* ☎ *604/569–1144* ⊕ *www.voguetheatre.com.*

WEST END

The West End—that's Denman, Davie (gay-friendly), and Robson streets—tends to be all about bumping and grinding in retro bars and clubs.

BARS

Fountainhead Pub. With one of the largest street-side patios on Davie Street, you can do as the locals do here: sit back, down a few beers, and watch the beautiful people pass by. ⊠ *1025 Davie St., West End* ☎ *604/687–2222* ⊕ *www.thefountainheadpub.com.*

GAY NIGHTLIFE

1181. This place is all about sleek interior design—plush sofas, glass coffee tables, wood-paneled ceiling—and standard cocktails (think caipirinhas and mojitos). It gets crowded on weekends, when a DJ spins behind the bar. ⊠ *1181 Davie St., West End* ☎ *604/787–7130* ⊕ *www.1181.ca.*

Celebrities. True to its name, this gay hotspot has celeb cred. Expect to find a young, scantily clad crowd bumping and grinding to Top 40 hits, hip-hop, and R&B on a huge dance floor equipped with the latest in sound, lighting, and visuals. Men and women are welcome. ⊠ *1022 Davie St., West End* ☎ *604/681–6180* ⊕ *www.celebritiesnightclub.com.*

Numbers. This veteran of the Davie Street strip features five levels of furious fun, from live music and nightly DJs to karaoke and pool. ⊠ *1042 Davie St., West End* ☎ *604/685–4077* ⊕ *www.numbers.ca.*

GASTOWN AND CHINATOWN

GASTOWN

Hipster Gastown is famed for its clusters of late-night establishments and is now the place to go for relaxed pubs and trendy wine bars.

BARS

Alibi Room. If beer is your thing, head to Alibi, which specializes in pairing beer with your meal. Kegs of microbrews from around BC and beyond are the pride and joy here and it's known for having one of the best selections of craft beers in Vancouver. There are also organic wines and a few fun cocktails if you're not feeling beer-inclined. ⊠ *157 Alexander St., Gastown* ☎ *604/623–3383* ⊕ *www.alibi.ca.*

Chill Winston. Decked out with black-leather sofas, exposed brick, warm lighting, and a view of Gastown's lively Maple Tree Square, this restaurant and lounge attracts a well-heeled crowd of urban locals. The large patio is perfect for people-watching and after-work drinks. ⊠ *3 Alexander St., Gastown* ☎ *604/288–9575* ⊕ *www.chillwinston.com.*

Fodor's Choice ★ The Diamond. At the top of a narrow staircase above Maple Tree Square, the Diamond occupies the second floor of one of the city's oldest buildings. A cool hangout and cocktail lounge, the venue serves a mix of historic tipples and inventive house concoctions. You can choose among "boozy," "proper," or "overlooked" cocktails. Many are one-of-a-kind: a Colin's Lawn mixes sake and mint; the Buck Buck Mule is a refreshing mix of gin, sherry, cucumber juice, cilantro, lime juice, and ginger beer; and the Tequila Martinez features tequila, vermouth, Lillet, peach bitters, and an orange twist. ⊠ *6 Powell St., at Carrall St., Gastown* ☎ *604/568–8272* ⊕ *www.di6mond.com.*

The Irish Heather. Expect a mixed crowd of local hipsters and out-of-towners enjoying properly poured pints of Guinness, mixed beer drinks (try a shandy, which is lager and lemonade), wine, and live Irish music some nights. The food menu focuses on pub favorites. Out back in an atmospheric coach house is the Shebeen, or whiskey house, where you can try any of 200-plus whiskeys. Reserve ahead for Sunday or Monday evening's Long Table Series, where you can make 40 or so new friends as you enjoys ales and tasty food. ⊠ *210 Carrall St., Gastown* ☎ *604/688–9779* ⊕ *www.irishheather.com.*

Fodor's Choice
★
The Portside Pub. Nautical kitsch and a friendly maritimer bent woo many a landlover to the Portside Pub. Live bands, weekend DJs, and whiskey on tap handily turn the two-level bar into a packed venue. Pub eats are above par, but line-ups start early. ⊠ *7 Alexander St., Gastown* ☎ *604/559–6333* ⊕ *www.theportsidepub.com.*

Fodor's Choice
★
Pourhouse Vancouver. The brick-and-beam 1910 architecture, antiques, and a 38-foot bar are in keeping with the menu of classic cocktails. Most are inspired by the 1862 bartending bible *How to Mix Drinks* by Jerry Thomas, the first bartending manual ever to put oral traditions to print with recipes for mint juleps, sloe gin fizzes, and more. Book ahead for one of the family-style dinners: everything is set in the center of the kitchen table, and it's a help-yourself affair, just like at home. ⊠ *162 Water St., Gastown* ☎ *604/568–7022* ⊕ *www.pourhousevancouver.com.*

Revel Room. A slightly older Gastown crowd comes to indulge at this two-story bar and eatery. The southern style means bourbon-focused cocktails and an overall welcoming charm. There's live music some nights. ⊠ *238 Abbott St., Gastown* ☎ *604/687–4088* ⊕ *www.revelroom.ca.*

Salt Tasting Room. The allure here is the selection of local and international wines, beers, and sherries that can be paired with a rotating selection of cured meats and artisanal cheeses. You can choose your own tasting menu or leave it to the professionals. Legend has it that the address, Blood Alley, is so called because this used to be the city's meat-packing district and the name comes from the buckets of blood butchers threw down the cobblestone street. ⊠ *45 Blood Alley, Gastown* ☎ *604/633–1912* ⊕ *www.salttastingroom.com.*

Steamworks. This multilevel brewpub welcomes urban professionals with a selection of traditional ales and lagers brewed in-house, in small batches, using the neighborhood's steam heat. There is patio seating with harbor views, as well, when the weather permits. ⊠ *375 Water St., Gastown* ☎ *604/689–2739* ⊕ *www.steamworks.com.*

DANCE CLUBS
Guilt & Co. The menu at this Gastown favorite features lagers, pale ales, pilsners, stouts, and ciders, and then there's what's on tap, a wine list, and a cocktail menu—in short, the thirsty have many ways to imbibe. There are a half-dozen different ways to say cheese plate, too, including "chunk of cheese." Rock bands (plus jazz, folk, and blues artists) aren't all the basement music club hosts—there are also burlesque and cabaret nights. ⊠ *1 Alexander St., Gastown* ☎ *604/288–1704* ⊕ *www.guiltandcompany.com.*

CHINATOWN

Development is expanding east in the city, and venues in the newly cool Chinatown are emerging as strong competition for those in adjacent Gastown.

BARS

The Emerald. This second-floor venue on the eastern fringes of Vancouver's changing Chinatown includes a bar area, a supper-club lounge, and a private room, all with a clubby, 1960s Las Vegas feel. There are excellent cocktails, and the occasional jazz, dance, or comedy show. ⊠ *555 Gore St., Chinatown* ☎ *604/559–8477* ⊕ *www.emeraldsupperclub.com.*

Fodor's Choice **The Keefer Bar.** The Keefer Bar has fully capitalized on its Chinatown ★ connection, using ingredients sourced from local herbalists (seahorse tincture anyone?), kombucha, oolong tea syrup, or lychee, for example. Small plates of Asian dishes make good nibbling. The decor is dark and red, with hanging cylindrical neon lights. There's usually a well-attended, weekly burlesque night. ⊠ *135 Keefer St., Chinatown* ☎ *604/688–1961* ⊕ *www.thekeeferbar.com.*

DANCE CLUBS

Fortune Sound Club. This sound-system-centric dance club and performance venue keeps the audience guessing with a mix of shows (often with hip-hop leanings). The second-floor space has red oak flooring and manages to incorporate local and eco-friendly elements into the design—so Vancouver! ⊠ *147 E. Pender St., Chinatown* ☎ *604/569–1758* ⊕ *www.fortunesoundclub.com.*

YALETOWN

Restaurants become cocktail lounges after dark in Yaletown. Once warehouse loading docks, the brick-lined patios are prime for people-watching (and fancy-car-spotting: luxury vehicles are a common sight on Mainland and Hamilton streets). This area gets busy early and continues to late night.

BARS

AFTERglow. The backroom of the Glowbal Grill restaurant, the AFTERglow lounge is a great place to sink into a comfy sofa with a colorful martini. A varied crowd comes to practice the art of see-and-be-seen, so enjoy the people-watching. ⊠ *1079 Mainland St., Yaletown* ☎ *604/602–0835* ⊕ *www.glowbalgrill.com.*

George. One of Vancouver's swankiest cocktail bars, George is dedicated to classic cocktails and the people who drink them, from local glitterati to executives in Armani suits. The wine cellar includes a choice sampling of Okanagan vintages as well as French, Chilean, and Australian wines by the bottle or by the glass. ⊠ *1137 Hamilton St., Yaletown* ☎ *604/628–5555* ⊕ *www.georgelounge.com.*

Opus Bar. Traveling executives in suits and film industry creatives sip martinis (or perhaps a cocktail made with bourbon and blood oranges) while scoping out the room, on the ground floor of the Opus Hotel. ⊠ *Opus Hotel, 350 Davie St., Yaletown* ☎ *604/642–0557* ⊕ *www.opusbar.ca.*

5

DID YOU KNOW?

The Opus Bar in Yaletown's Opus Vancouver Hotel serves handcrafted, top-of-the-line cocktails. Yaletown as a whole is great for dining and people-watching.

Yaletown Brewing Company. In a renovated warehouse with a glassed-in brewery turning out several tasty beers, this always-crowded gastropub and patio has a lively singles scene. Even though it's super popular it still feels like a neighborhood place. ⊠ *1111 Mainland St., Yaletown* ☎ *604/681–2739* ⊕ *www.mjg.ca/yaletown.*

CASINOS

Edgewater Casino. This casino has 500 slot machines, a poker room, and 60 table games. It's open around the clock. ⊠ *311–750 Pacific Blvd. S, Yaletown* ☎ *604/687–3343* ⊕ *www.edgewatercasino.ca.*

DANCE CLUBS

Bar None. Once you hit Bar None you never really have to leave Yaletown. This long-time favorite is the place to get your groove on after dinner and drinks. They like to call the vibe "NYC," but it's really Yaletown through and through. Celebrated Vancouver DJs spin house and electronica on weekend nights, and international stars sometimes take over as well. ⊠ *1222 Hamilton St., Yaletown* ☎ *604/689–7000* ⊕ *donnellygroup.ca/locations/night-clubs/bar-none.*

5

GRANVILLE ISLAND

Dockside patios are the thing here, especially before or after a performance at one of the area's many theaters.

BARS

Bridges. This bright yellow landmark near the Granville Public Market has a cozy nautical-theme pub and the city's biggest marina-side deck. In warm weather the outdoor seating has breathtaking views of the harbor, mountains, and city. ⊠ *1696 Duranleau St., Granville Island* ☎ *604/687–4400* ⊕ *www.bridgesrestaurant.com.*

Dockside Restaurant. Overlooking False Creek, Yaletown, and the North Shore Mountains, the Dockside's patio is the big draw, especially for owners of chic yachts moored alongside. Because it faces east, sunsets are behind the building and cool shadows come early, so grab a table beneath a heater. Floor-to-ceiling windows make the inside feel like the outside with decor that exudes a modern vibe and includes a 50-foot aquarium. House-brewed ales and lagers are served from the adjoining casual brewpub. ⊠ *Granville Island Hotel, 1253 Johnston St., Granville Island* ☎ *604/685–7070* ⊕ *www.docksidevancouver.com.*

The Sandbar. With a seafood restaurant, a wine bar, and live music nightly (piano Sunday to Thursday) in the Teredo Lounge, this venue has something for everyone. There are televised sports on game days. For dramatic views over False Creek, reserve a table on the rooftop patio in the summer. ⊠ *1535 Johnson St., Granville Island* ☎ *604/669–9030* ⊕ *www.vancouverdine.com/sandbar.*

COMEDY CLUBS

Vancouver TheatreSports League. A hilarious improv troupe performs Wednesday to Saturday before an enthusiastic crowd at the Improv Centre on Granville Island. The rookie showcase on Sunday can be entertaining. ⊠ *1502 Duranleau St., Granville Island* ☎ *604/738–7013* ⊕ *www.vtsl.com.*

MUSIC: ROCK AND BLUES

Backstage Lounge. Local bands of unpredictable talent perform most nights. Even though the music is hit or miss, the drink specials are cheap and reliable. ✉ *1585 Johnston St., Granville Island* ☎ *604/687–1354* ⊕ *www.thebackstagelounge.com.*

THE WEST SIDE

KITSILANO

Known as the Venice Beach of Vancouver, Kitsilano attracts a laid-back crowd that enjoys sipping beer and cocktails on outdoor patios, especially in the summer.

BARS

Abigail's Party. Curated wine and cheese menus change weekly at this friendly establishment. There are also inventive cocktails like the Abigail's Boulevardier (a twist on the classic Negroni, with bourbon, vermouth, and aperol) and the Wicca (elderflower and peach syrup with a dash of Sauvignon Blanc). ✉ *1685 Yew St., Kitsilano* ☎ *604/739–4677* ⊕ *www.abigailsparty.ca.*

Kits Beach Boathouse. A summer visit to Vancouver isn't complete without an afternoon enjoying cocktails on this rooftop patio overlooking sandcourt volleyball matches at Kits Beach. At other times of the year, the views of the vivid sunsets and dramatic winter storms are exceptional, though you may want to retreat behind the floor-to-ceiling windows to sip in comfort. ✉ *1305 Arbutus St., Kitsilano* ☎ *604/738–5487* ⊕ *www.boathouserestaurants.ca/locations/#kitsilano.*

Local Public Eatery. It won't win awards for service, but this large, sports-inclined bar has its gimmick: an enviable proximity to Kits Beach. The spacious but usually packed patio is across from a grassy park and Kitsilano Pool. Inside, multiple televisions show whatever sports game is happening while the kitchen serves inexpensive pub grub. ✉ *2210 Cornwall Ave., Kitsilano* ☎ *604/734–3589* ⊕ *www.localpubliceatery.com.*

CAMBIE CORRIDOR

COMEDY CLUBS

Yuk Yuk's. This is the place to go Wednesday to Saturday evenings for some of Canada's best professional stand-up comedians and up-and-coming amateurs. ✉ *2837 Cambie St., at 12th Ave., Cambie Corridor* ☎ *604/696–9857* ⊕ *www.yukyuks.com.*

EAST SIDE

MAIN STREET/MT. PLEASANT

The up-and-coming Main Street neighborhood is great for local beer and live jams by emerging Canadian musicians.

BARS

Cascade Room. Named after the signature beer the Vancouver Brewery once produced on this very spot, the Cascade Room is a usually busy Main Street lounge. The cocktail menu is lengthy, with a focus on classics. ⊠ *2616 Main St., at Broadway, Main St./Mt. Pleasant* ☎ *604/709–8650* ⊕ *www.thecascade.ca.*

Craft Beer Market. The stats at this beer hall in the historic Salt Building are impressive: 140 draft beer taps, more than 10,000 feet of beer lines, 3500 BTUs of chilling power, and space for 450 kegs in the keg room (that's up to 26,000 litres or 6900 gallons). And the food is good, too. It's now the flagship of Vancouver's new waterfront neighborhood that's risen from infrastructure built for the 2010 Winter Olympics. ⊠ *85 West 1st Ave., Main St./Mt. Pleasant* ☎ *604/709–2337* ⊕ *vancouver craftbeermarket.ca.*

The Main. This local favorite draws a crowd for drinks and live music in a huge warehouse venue. There's food, too, if you want to make a night of it. ⊠ *4210 Main St., Main St./Mt. Pleasant* ☎ *604/709–8555* ⊕ *www.themainonmain.ca.*

Whip Restaurant Gallery. It's a bit out of the way, but this lofty space with Douglas fir–beamed ceilings and exposed brick attracts a hip, beer-drinking Main Street crowd. There's a bar, an atrium, and a mezzanine, as well as a selection of artwork by the featured artist of the moment. There are always several offerings on tap as well as house-made sangria, and a respectable whiskey menu. ⊠ *209 E. 6th Ave., at Main St., Main St./Mt. Pleasant* ☎ *604/874–4687* ⊕ *www. thewhiprestaurant.com.*

MUSIC: ROCK AND BLUES
Biltmore Cabaret. A favorite hangout for live music, the Biltmore Cabaret hosts a mix of local bands, international performers, and burlesque. There's also a monthly ice-cream social where you can dance to '60s rock-and-roll. ⊠ *2755 Prince Edward St., Main St./Mt. Pleasant* ☎ *604/676–0541* ⊕ *www.biltmorecabaret.com.*

COMMERCIAL DRIVE AND AROUND
Commercial Drive is the center of Vancouver's offbeat rhythm. Local pubs, small music venues, and patios can be found amid shops stocked with international goods and restaurants serving world-reaching cuisines. The options are limited, but the people-watching is superb.

BARS
Biercraft. With more than 100 Belgian, craft, and draft beers, the drinks menu here verges on a novel, and there are wine and cocktails as well. A street-side patio is perfect for watching life pass by on eclectic Commercial Drive when the weather's good. ⊠ *1191 Commercial Dr., Commercial Drive* ☎ *604/254–2437* ⊕ *www.biercraft.com.*

Falconetti's East Side Grill. The second-floor patio at Falconetti's has the best neighborhood views, and it's where a diverse crowd of locals-in-the-know take in the laid-back Drive vibe. Downstairs, you're likely to catch an indie folk singer or experimental group performing. There are pleny of food options, too; a gourmet sausage from the adjoining butcher shop is a good bet. ⊠ *1812 Commercial Dr., Commercial Drive* ☎ *604/251–7287* ⊕ *www.falconettis.com.*

PERFORMING ARTS

Vancouver is a well-rounded cultural destination, with plenty of theater, classical music, and dance options to occupy arts lovers. Granville Island is the city's hub for arts and culture, and there are many stages here. Companies small and large take the platform with improv comedy, musicals, and Canadian originals.

CLASSICAL MUSIC

OPERA

Vancouver Opera. From October through May, the city's opera company stages four productions a year at the Queen Elizabeth Theatre in downtown Vancouver. ⊠ *Queen Elizabeth Theatre, 650 Hamilton St., Downtown* ☎ *604/683–0222* ⊕ *www.vancouveropera.ca.*

ORCHESTRAS

Vancouver Symphony Orchestra. The resident company at the Orpheum Theatre presents classical and popular music. Some of their performances are at the *Chan Centre* (6265 Crescent Rd., Point Grey). ⊠ *601 Smithe St., at Seymour St., Downtown* ☎ *604/876–3434* ⊕ *www. vancouversymphony.ca.*

DANCE

If you're interested in dance, some of the best modern-dance performances take place during PuSh International Performing Arts Festival (mid-January) and the Vancouver International Dance Festival (mid-March). Key venues for dance during the year are the Scotiabank Dance Centre, the Firehall Arts Centre, and the "Cultch" (Vancouver East Cultural Centre). For consistently interesting local productions, watch for the **Dances for a Small Stage** series (⊕ *www.movent.ca*), which hosts many of the city's most revered performers on a platform measuring 3 meters by 4 meters (10 feet by 13 feet). The results can be surprisingly magical.

Ballet British Columbia. Innovative dances and timeless classics by internationally acclaimed choreographers are presented by Ballet BC. Most performances are at the *Queen Elizabeth Theatre* (650 Hamilton St.). ⊠ *677 Davie St., Downtown* ☎ *604/732–5003* ⊕ *www. balletbc.com.*

The Dance Centre. The hub for dance in British Columbia, this striking building with an art-deco facade hosts full-scale performances by national and international artists, informal showcases, and also classes and workshops. There are often informal noon performances as part of the Discover Dance! series. ⊠ *677 Davie St., Scotiabank Dance Centre, Downtown* ☎ *604/606–6400* ⊕ *www.thedancecentre.ca.*

FILM

Locals sometimes refer to Vancouver as Hollywood North, mostly because of the frequent film and television shoots around town. Movie theaters featuring first- and second-run, underground, experimental, alternative, and classic films make up the urban fabric. Here's a tip from the locals: tickets are half-price on Tuesday at most chain-owned movie theaters.

Fifth Avenue Cinemas. This small multiplex shows foreign and independent films. ⊠ *2110 Burrard St., Kitsilano* ☎ *604/734–/469* ⊕ *www. cineplex.com/Theatre/fifth-avenue-cinemas.*

FAMILY **Pacific Cinémathèque.** This not-for-profit society is dedicated to all things celluloid, from exhibitions and lectures to independent and international features. The occasional Cinema Sundays are especially good for families, with discussions, games, and activities following the all-ages movies. ⊠ *1131 Howe St., Downtown* ☎ *604/688–3456* ⊕ *www.the cinematheque.ca.*

5

THEATER

Vancouver has a sophisticated theater scene, with performances by local and touring companies.

Arts Club Theatre Company. The Arts Club Theatre Company stages productions (a few by local playwrights) on three principal stages: the Stanley Industrial Alliance Stage, the Revue Stage, and the Granville Island Stage. ⊠ *1585 Johnston St., Granville Island* ☎ *604/687–1644* ⊕ *www.artsclub.com.*

FAMILY **Carousel Theatre for Young People.** Children's theater is the focus here, with most performances at the Waterfront Theatre, though some are elsewhere in the city. ⊠ *Waterfront Theatre, 1412 Cartwright St., Granville Island* ☎ *604/685–6217* ⊕ *www.carouseltheatre.ca.*

Chan Centre for the Performing Arts. This vast arts complex on the campus of the University of British Columbia includes a 1,200-seat concert hall, a theater, and a cinema. ⊠ *University of British Columbia, 6265 Crescent Rd., Point Grey* ☎ *604/822–9197* ⊕ *www.chancentre.com.*

The Cultch. The Vancouver East Cultural Centre, often just referred to as the Cultch (short for "culture"), is a multipurpose performance space that hosts music concerts, theater productions, dance shows, and more. ⊠ *1895 Venables St., East Vancouver* ☎ *604/251–1363* ⊕ *www. thecultch.com.*

Firehall Arts Centre. Innovative theater and modern dance are showcased at this intimate Downtown space on the border of trendy Gastown. ⊠ *280 E. Cordova St., Downtown* ☎ *604/689–0926* ⊕ *www. firehallartscentre.ca.*

Queen Elizabeth Theatre. Ballet, opera, touring Broadway musicals, and other large-scale events take place at the Queen Elizabeth. It seats more than 2,700 people, making it one of the largest theaters in Canada. ⊠ *650 Hamilton St., Downtown* ☎ *604/665–3050* ⊕ *www.vancouver. ca/parks-recreation-culture/queen-elizabeth-theatre.aspx.*

FAMILY **Theatre Under the Stars.** In summer, family-friendly musicals like *The Music Man* and *Shrek* are the main draw at Malkin Bowl, an outdoor amphitheater in Stanley Park. You can watch the show from the lawn and bring a picnic to make it dinner theater. Ask about the Family Package Deal when buying tickets. ⊠ *Stanley Park, Malkin Bowl, 610 Pipeline Rd.* ☎ *604/696–4295* ⊕ *www.tuts.ca/tickets.*

Waterfront Theatre. Next door to Granville Island's Kids Market, this theater often hosts children and youth-oriented performances. ⊠ *1412 Cartwright St., Granville Island* ☎ *604/685–1731* ⊕ *www.waterfront theatre.ca.*

WHERE TO EAT

Updated By
Carolyn B.
Heller

From inventive neighborhood bistros to glamorous down-town dining rooms to ethnic restaurants that rival those in the world capitals, Vancouver has a diverse array of gastro-nomic options.

Many cutting-edge establishments are perfecting what we call Modern Canadian fare, which—at the western end of the country—incorporates regional seafood (notably salmon, halibut, and spot prawns) and locally grown produce. Vancouver is all about "localism," with many restaurants emphasizing the provenance of their ingredients and embracing products that hail from within a 100-mile-or-so radius of the city, or at least from within BC.

With at least 40 percent of the region's population of Asian heritage, it's no surprise that Asian eateries abound in Vancouver. From mom-and-pop noodle shops, curry houses, and corner sushi bars to elegant and upscale dining rooms, cuisine from China, Taiwan, Hong Kong, Japan, and India (and to a lesser extent, from Korea, Thailand, Vietnam, and Malaysia) can be found all over town. Look for restaurants emphasizing Chinese regional cuisine (particularly in Vancouver's Richmond suburb), contemporary Indian-influenced fare, and different styles of Japanese cooking, from casual ramen shops to lively *izakayas* (Japanese tapas bars) that serve an eclectic array of small plates. Even restaurants that are not specifically "Asian" have long adopted abundant Asian influences—your grilled salmon may be served with *gai lan* (Chinese broccoli), black rice, or a coconut-milk curry.

VANCOUVER DINING PLANNER

DRESS
Dining in Vancouver is informal. Neat casual dress is appropriate everywhere; nice jeans are fine, though you might want something dressier than sneakers in the evening.

HOURS

Most restaurants that serve lunch are open from 11:30 until 2 or 2:30. Downtown spots that serve a business clientele may not open for lunch on weekends. Dinner is usually served from 5:30 until at least 10; some restaurants are open later on weekends, but in general, Vancouver isn't a late-night eating city. Some restaurants are closed on Sunday or Monday.

RESERVATIONS

Except in cafés and casual eateries, reservations are always a good idea, particularly for weekend evenings.

SMOKING

Smoking is prohibited by law in all Vancouver restaurants.

TIPPING AND TAXES

A 15–18% tip is expected. Restaurant meals are subject to a 5% Goods and Services Tax (GST) and there's an additional 10% liquor tax charged on wine, beer, and spirits.

WINE

Many restaurants serve excellent British Columbia wines. Sometimes the most interesting ones are from small producers, so ask for recommendations.

WHAT IT COSTS

Vancouver's top tables can be as pricey as the best restaurants in major American cities but there is generally something for every budget. In addition, some restaurants have reasonably priced prix-fixe menus, and at certain times of the year, including the midwinter Dine Out Vancouver promotion, even top dining rooms offer these fixed-price options. Check the website for Tourism Vancouver (⊕ *www.tourismvancouver. com*) for details. Family-style Asian restaurants and noodle shops are generally a good value year-round, too.

Prices in the reviews are the average cost of a main course at dinner or, if dinner is not served, at lunch.

WHAT IT COSTS IN CANADIAN DOLLARS			
$	$$	$$$	$$$$
AT DINNER	under C$12	C$13–C$20	C$21–C$30	over C$30

Prices are for an average main course or equivalent combination of smaller dishes, at dinner.

EAT LIKE A LOCAL

Like many cities, Vancouver and Victoria have embraced local eating and drinking. Yet even as "locavore" remains the rallying cry, both cities look for culinary inspiration beyond their borders, especially toward Asia and the Pacific Rim. This is what's popular with the locals.

VEGETABLES GO GLAM

With this regional bounty, you'd expect that Vancouver would be a veggie-friendly city, but until recently, its vegetarian restaurants tended to be relegated to crunchy-granola Buddha-bowl varieties. Things have changed recently, and there are more vegetarian dining rooms that offer chic and sophisticated green cuisine. Trendy non-vegetarian restaurants are increasingly "vegetable-forward," too, offering plenty of imaginative plant-based fare.

DRINKING LOCAL

British Columbia's wine industry is concentrated in the sunny Okanagan Valley and on Vancouver Island, which supply many of the region's dining rooms and wine bars. Vancouver and Victoria are now also home to several distilleries brewing spirits from local grains, as well as numerous craft breweries, too, so you can drink locally, no matter what your taste.

SIDE TRIP TO CHINA FOR DINNER

Vancouver has one of the largest Asian populations of any city outside of Asia, and the area's Chinese cuisine ranks among the best in North America. The go-to destination for Chinese food fans is Richmond, the suburban "new" Chinatown, less than 30 minutes on the

Canada Line from Downtown. Here, stylish Chinese restaurants, vast dim sum parlors, and even grab-and-go food courts cater to the well-to-do Asian community and rival the best of Hong Kong, Shanghai, or Taipei.

BEYOND THE SUSHI BAR

Vancouverites joke that they could eat sushi every day for months and never visit the same restaurant twice. While sushi bars are plentiful, though, Japanese food in Vancouver means far more than maki and nigiri. Vancouverites have fallen hard for *izakayas* (Japanese tapas bars), which combine the casual West Coast vibe with easy-to-share small plates. Ramen shops are also popular; witness the line-ups at the numerous noodle purveyors in the ramen-central West End.

A PASSAGE TO INDIA

Vancouver's Indian restaurants reflect the increasingly varied nature of the region's South Asian population, offering regional specialties from across the sub-continent. The long-established "Little India," the Punjabi Market neighborhood on Main Street, is where you'll find traditional Indian fare, but local chefs in both Indian and non-Indian eateries increasingly pair classic South Asian flavors with local Canadian ingredients, thanks, in part, to Vikram Vij, who shook up the Vancouver food

scene in the mid-1990s with his still-popular modern Indian restaurant.

FUELLED BY CAFFEINE

"Fuelled by Caffeine" is the slogan of the Bean Around the World Vancouver-based minichain of coffeehouses, but it's also an apt description of the city. Although the Starbucks invasion is extensive, there are plenty of more colorful places—from sleek and modern to comfortably bohemian. You'll find the same variety of coffee drinks that you can get across North America, though some spots refer to an "americano" (an espresso made with extra hot water) as a "canadiano." Many—but not all—provide free Wi-Fi, too.

LUNCH ON THE MOVE

Food trucks have become an important part of Vancouver's culinary scene, with mobile vendors offering quick, convenient lunches downtown and beyond. Many street carts celebrate the city's unique Asian fusion, while others, champion the locavore ethic. Most trucks operate downtown during lunch (about 11 or 11:30 til 2:30 or 3).

RESTAURANT REVIEWS

Listed alphabetically within neighborhoods.

Use the coordinate at the end of each listing (✛ B2) to locate a property on the Where to Eat in Vancouver map.

DOWNTOWN AND THE WEST END

DOWNTOWN

Downtown dining is a little bit of everything, from food trucks, cafés, and old-style diners to lively local bistros, upscale contermporary restaurants, and luxe hotel dining rooms.

$$$$
SEAFOOD

✕ **Boulevard Kitchen & Oyster Bar.** Settle into a deep cream-toned banquette or nab a sidewalk table for a seafood-centric meal at this stylish spot in the Sutton Place Hotel that manages to feel both trendy and warm. Start straight up with fresh local oysters paired with a frosty gazpacho granité, or add some drama to your dinner by ordering the tuna tartare, which the servers blend tableside with sesame oil, scallions, and shredded nori. Mains swim through the sea, too— perhaps caramelized jumbo scallops served atop a delicate broth of oven-dried tomatoes; spaghetti with clams and wild shrimp; or roasted sablefish paired with *gai lan* flan—but heartier appetites can dig into a steak or a 14-ounce pork chop sauced with a rich apple vinegar jus. The wine list is strong on BC labels. ⓢ *Average main: ✉ Sutton Place Hotel, 845 Burrard St., Downtown* ☎ *604/642–2900* ⊕ *www. boulevardvancouver.ca* ✛ *E3.*

$
CAFÉ

✕ **Bel Café.** Run by the same team that oversees the adjacent Hawksworth Restaurant, this upscale little café at the Rosewood Hotel Georgia serves fine coffee, a few salads and sandwiches, and exquisite pastries, from colorful macaroons to beautifully crafted fruit tarts. Downtown business types like to meet up here, and both shoppers and sightseers stop in to recharge; it's opposite the Vancouver Art Gallery and just a short stroll from Robson Street's boutiques. ⓢ *Average main: ✉ Rosewood Hotel Georgia, 801 W. Georgia St., Downtown* ☎ *604/673–7000* ⊕ *www.belcafe.com* ✛ *E3.*

$
CAFÉ

✕ **Caffè Artigiano.** Some of Vancouver's best coffee is served at the several locations of Caffè Artigiano, where the baristas have won prizes for their latte art—making patterns in the froth. Come for the java, although you can assuage your hunger with a pastry or sandwich, too. There are other locations Downtown at 574 Granville Street, 740 West Hastings Street, 763 Hornby Street, and in Yaletown at 302 Davie Street (adjacent to the Opus Hotel). ⓢ *Average main: C$6 ✉ 1101 W. Pender, Downtown* ☎ *604/685–5333* ⊕ *www.caffeartigiano.com* ▭ *No credit cards* ✛ *E2.*

$$
MEDITERRANEAN

✕ **Café Medina.** For Mediterranean-inspired breakfast and lunch fare, from skillets piled high with eggs, roasted potatoes, and caramelized onions to Moroccan *tagine* stews, try this casually chic (and always busy) Downtown café just off Robson Street. Look for interesting innovations like the *poisson curé*—a salad of wild salmon, crunchy sprouted farro, pistachios, and parsley—but don't leave without sampling their

BEST BETS FOR VANCOUVER DINING

With so many restaurants, how will you decide where to eat? Fodor's writers and editors have chosen their favorites by price, cuisine, and experience:

Fodor's Choice★

Bishop's, p. 152
Farmer's Apprentice, p. 154
Hawksworth Restaurant, p. 141
Maenam, p. 154
Pidgin, p. 149
Tojo's, p. 156
West, p. 155

By Price

$

Go Fish, p. 154
Kintaro Ramen, p. 146
Legendary Noodle, p. 147
Nuba, p. 148

$$

The Acorn, p. 156
Burdock & Co., p. 157
Maenam, p. 154

$$$

Chambar, p. 140
Cibo Trattoria, p. 140
L'Abbatoir, p. 148
Vij's, p. 155

$$$$

Bishop's, p. 152
Blue Water Cafe, p. 150
Hawksworth Restaurant, p. 141
Le Crocodile, p. 144
Tojo's, p. 156
West, p. 155

By Cuisine

CHINESE

Bao Bei, p. 149
Sea Harbour Seafood Restaurant, p. 159
Sun Sui Wah Seafood Restaurant, p. 158

FRENCH

Jules, p. 148
Le Crocodile, p. 144

INDIAN

Rangoli, p. 155
Vij's, p. 155

ITALIAN

Cibo Trattoria, p. 140
CinCin, p. 140
La Pentola della Quercia, p. 151

JAPANESE

Kingyo, p. 145
Tojo's, p. 156

MODERN CANADIAN

Bishop's, p. 152
Farmer's Apprentice, p. 154
Hawksworth Restaurant, p. 141
L'Abbatoir, p. 148
West, p. 155

SEAFOOD

Blue Water Cafe, p. 150
Boulevard Kitchen & Oyster Bar, p. 138
Coast Restaurant, p. 140
Sea Harbour Seafood Restaurant, p. 159
Tojo's, p. 156

VEGETARIAN

The Acorn, p. 156
Nuba, p. 148
Rangoli, p. 155
Vij's, p. 155

By Experience

DISTINCTIVELY VANCOUVER

Hapa Izakaya, p. 145
Japadog, p. 141
Maenam, p. 154
Pidgin, p. 149
Vij's, p. 155

GREAT VIEW

Salmon House on the Hill, p. 159
The Teahouse in Stanley Park, p. 147

HOT SPOTS

Boulevard Kitchen & Oyster Bar, p. 138
Chambar, p. 140
Coast Restaurant, p. 140
Hawksworth Restaurant, p. 141
Homer St. Cafe & Bar, p. 151

LOTS OF LOCALS

Bob Likes Thai Food, p. 157
Campagnolo, p. 157
Chicha, p. 158
Rodney's Oyster House, p. 151
The Union, p. 150

ROMANTIC

Le Crocodile, p. 144

specialty: Belgian waffles, with toppings like dark chocolate or salted caramel. As of this writing, dinner service is planned for the future so check if you're in the neighborhood. [$] *Average main: C$14* ✉ *780 Richards St., Downtown* ☎ *604/879–3114* 🌐 *www.medinacafe.com* 🕓 *No dinner* ✥ *G4.*

$$$ BELGIAN 🍴 **Chambar.** A smartly dressed crowd hangs out at the bar of this hip Belgian eatery sipping imported beer or delicious cocktails like the Blue Fig (gin infused with oven-roasted figs and served with a side of blue cheese). But this long-admired restaurant is not just a pretty (and prettily populated) space. Classic Belgian dishes are reinvented with flavors from North Africa and beyond. The *moules* (mussels) are justifiably popular, either steamed in white wine or sauced with exotic smoked chilies, cilantro, and coconut cream. Pan-seared salmon might be topped with a tamarind and tomato curry and served with shishito peppers and a tomatillo salsa, while another plate might combine veal tenderloin and calamari with cassava, radishes, and citrus aioli. Unusual, perhaps, but definitely delicious. [$] *Average main: C$30* ✉ *568 Beatty St., Downtown* ☎ *604/879–7119* 🌐 *www.chambar.com* ✥ *G4.*

$$$ ITALIAN 🍴 **Cibo Trattoria.** The space is fun and funky—a mix of early-1900s architectural details, modern furnishings, and oversize pop art—and the seasonally changing menu of updated Italian fare is creative and delicious. To start, consider the grilled octopus with fava bean tips, or, for more adventurous tastes, the shaved ox tongue with olives and horseradish crème fraiche. For a meat/fish course, how about ling cod with wilted spinach and ramp butter, or duck breast paired with soft polenta and grappa-soaked cherries? The lengthy wine list emphasizes Italian labels, but BC is ably represented. A three-course pre-theater fixed-price menu is available till 7 pm (C$39). For a light bite, join the local crowd at ⇨ **Uva Wine Bar** inside the same hotel, which stays open till the wee hours. [$] *Average main: C$26* ✉ *Moda Hotel, 900 Seymour St., Downtown* ☎ *604/602–9570* 🌐 *www.cibotrattoria.com* ✥ *E4.*

$$$$ ITALIAN 🍴 **CinCin.** Gold walls, terra-cotta tiles, and a crowd-pleasing modern Italian menu make this Tuscan-inspired restaurant appropriate for a business meal, a romantic tête-à-tête, or a relaxing dinner after a long day. The heated terrace, shielded with greenery, feels a long way from busy Robson Street. Inside there's a lively scene around the hand-carved marble bar. The food, from the open kitchen and the wood-fire grill, changes seasonally, but might include sablefish from BC's Haida Gwaii islands paired with a risotto of clams and sea asparagus, rack of lamb with farro and artichokes, and potato and parmesan ravioli with arugula, roasted walnuts, and pesto. [$] *Average main: C$35* ✉ *1154 Robson St., Downtown* ☎ *604/688–7338* 🌐 *www.cincin.net* 🕓 *No lunch.* ✥ *D3.*

$$$$ SEAFOOD 🍴 **Coast Restaurant.** If a fish house makes you think of lobster traps and buoys, you'll be pleasantly surprised when you come by this see-and-be-seen seafood palace. There's plenty of bling to be found here, from the shimmering lights to the sparkle-sporting patrons. What to eat? Why, seafood, of course—from oysters to sushi to fish-and-chips to any of the day's fresh catches. (The kitchen also serves excellent steak, if you must.) The Coast does a swimmingly good business,

so reservations are recommended. $ *Average main: C$32* ✉ *1054 Alberni St., Downtown* ☎ *604/685–5010* ⊕ *www.coastrestaurant.ca* ☾ *No lunch weekends* ✛ *E3.*

$$$ ✕ **Diva at the Met.** Regional cuisine shines at this comfortable and rather
MODERN traditional restaurant in the Metropolitan Hotel. The menu changes
CANADIAN frequently but focuses on freshly caught seafood, local produce, and wine. You might order herb-crusted tuna tataki with yuzu mayonnaise and cherry marmalade, smoked black cod with a potato puree, or fillet of Angus beef paired with seasonal vegetables. If you want a lighter meal, a lounge menu is available all evening. The suits meet up over breakfast or lunch. $ *Average main: C$28* ✉ *Metropolitan Hotel, 645 Howe St., Downtown* ☎ *604/602–7788* ⊕ *www.metropolitan. com/diva* ✛ *E3.*

$$ ✕ **The Elbow Room.** Known for the good-natured, sometimes raunchy,
AMERICAN abuse the staff dishes out, this entertaining diner, where the walls are
FAMILY decorated with celebrity photos, is a Vancouver institution. This is a great spot for hearty comfort food if you're downtown. Breakfast is served all day—the omelets are fluffy, the bacon is crisp, and the portions are generous. Lunchtime brings burgers, hearty sandwiches, and a few quesadillas and burritos. They're open from 8 am to 3:30 every day. $ *Average main: C$13* ✉ *560 Davie St., Downtown* ☎ *604/685– 3628* ⊕ *www.theelbowroomcafe.com* ☾ *No dinner* ⚠ *Reservations not accepted* ✛ *D5.*

$$$$ ✕ **Hawksworth Restaurant.** With sleek white tables and sparkling chan-
MODERN deliers, chef David Hawksworth's stylish restaurant welcomes locals
CANADIAN toasting new clients or celebrating a romantic anniversary. The food
Fodor's Choice (and the crowd) is suave and swanky, too. You might start with hama-
★ chi sashimi dressed with passion fruit, jalapeño, and coconut, or a simpler roasted carrot salad with avocado, crème fraîche, and dill. Although the menu changes frequently, mains might include slow-cooked wild salmon with salt-roasted beets, roasted elk sauced with a gin-barberry jus and served with savoy cabbage, or the Parmesan-crusted chicken with potato gnocchi. Look out, yoga-pants-wearing Vancouver—fine dining is back. $ *Average main: C$40* ✉ *Rosewood Hotel Georgia, 801 W. Georgia St., Downtown* ☎ *604/673–7000* ⊕ *www.hawksworthrestaurant.com* ✛ *E3.*

$ ✕ **Japadog.** There might be other places in the world that sell Japanese-
ECLECTIC style hot dogs but the phenomenon is so very multi-culti Vancouver and this storefront is the sit-down spin-off of a wildly successful food cart with a loyal following. Bratwurst and wieners are topped with teriyaki sauce, nori, and other Asian condiments. You can still find the carts at two Burrard Street locations—between Robson Street and Smithe Street and at the corner of West Pender Street—and another one near Waterfront Station on West Cordova Street at Granville. $ *Average main: C$6* ✉ *530 Robson St., Downtown* ☎ *604/569–1158* ⊕ *www. japadog.com* ▭ *No credit cards* ✛ *E4.*

$$$$ ✕ **Joe Fortes Seafood and Chop House.** Named for a much-loved English
SEAFOOD Bay bartender and lifeguard from the city's early days (he arrived in Vancouver in 1885), this lively brasserie has a piano bar, bistro, oyster bar, and a delightful covered rooftop patio. The menu is wide ranging,

6

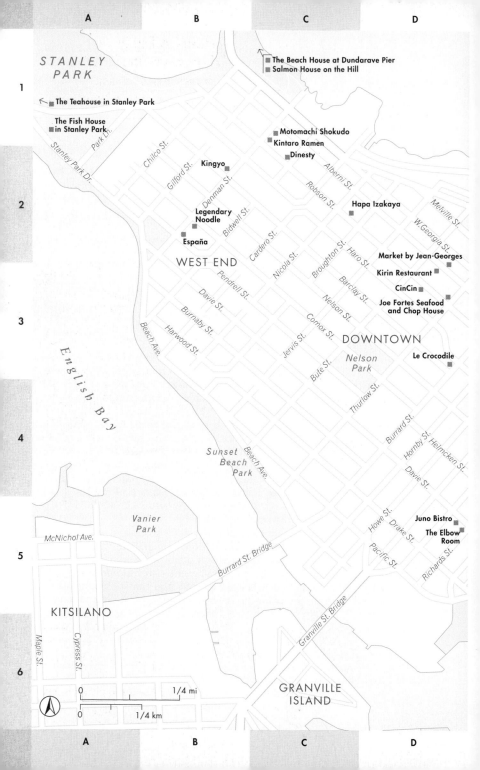

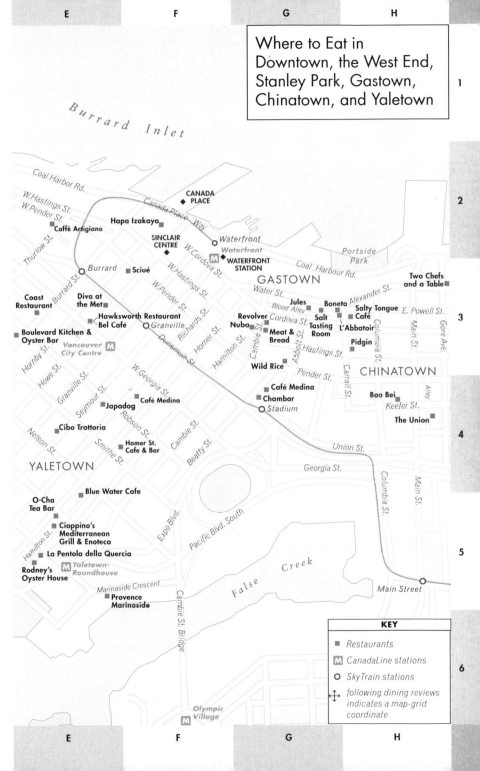

but steaks, chops, and generous portions of fresh seafood are the main draw. Select some fresh oysters from the lengthy list, then try the wild salmon, the *cioppino* (a seafood stew), or the Seafood Tower on Ice—a lavish assortment that's meant to be shared. Locals and visitors alike recommend Joe's for the great food matched with excellent service. [$] *Average main: C$35* ✉ *777 Thurlow St., at Robson St., Downtown* ☎ *604/669–1940* 🌐 *www.joefortes.ca* ✥ *D3.*

$ JAPANESE 🍴 **Juno Bistro.** In a city known for its Japanese food, this tiny storefront restaurant is a good choice for classic sushi and sashimi, and contemporary izakaya-style small plates. The yam poutine is a cross-cultural mash-up of sweet potato fries topped with mozzarella cheese and teriyaki gravy, while the fish used in the salmon gyozas is wild, and the birds used for the crispy chicken kara-age are free range. Sushi fans should ask about the specials; it's usually an interesting raw fish option. [$] *Average main: C$12* ✉ *572 Davie St., Downtown* ☎ *604/568–8805* 🌐 *www.junobistro.ca* 💳 *No credit cards* 🕒 *No lunch weekends* ✥ *D5.*

$$$ CHINESE 🍴 **Kirin Restaurant Downtown.** A striking silver mural of a *kirin* (a mythical dragonlike creature) presides over this elegant two-tier restaurant, one of the best choices for Chinese food downtown. Specialties here are northern Chinese and Szechuan dishes, which tend to be richer and spicier than the Cantonese cuisine served at Kirin's other locations. If you're adventurous, start with the spicy jellyfish, redolent with sesame oil. Then try the Peking duck or a fresh seafood dish. Dim sum is served daily at midday. [$] *Average main: C$21* ✉ *1172 Alberni St., Downtown* ☎ *604/682–8833* 🌐 *www.kirinrestaurants.com* ✥ *D3.*

$$$$ FRENCH 🍴 **Le Crocodile.** Chefs prepare classic Alsatian-inspired food—including the signature onion tart—at this long-established Downtown restaurant. Despite the white-tablecloth sophistication, the breezy curtains, golden yellow walls, and burgundy banquettes keep things cozy. Favorite dishes include lobster with beurre blanc, veal medallions with morel sauce, and sautéed Dover sole. Many lunch options, including a black truffle omelet and a mixed grill of halibut, prawns, and wild salmon, are more moderately priced. Service is attentive and professional. [$] *Average main: C$35* ✉ *100–909 Burrard St., Downtown* ☎ *604/669–4298* 🌐 *www.lecrocodilerestaurant.com* 🕒 *Closed Sun. No lunch Sat.* ✥ *D3.*

$$$$ ASIAN FUSION 🍴 **Market by Jean-Georges.** Although globetrotting celebrity chef Jean-Georges Vongerichten is rarely spotted at this contemporary dining room, his signature Asian influences abound, as in the rice cracker–crusted tuna with a citrus and chili emulsion, the roasted sablefish with scallion-chili compote and Thai basil, or the soy-glazed short ribs. If you don't fancy a full meal, you can dine lightly (and less expensively) on stylish salads or creative appetizers. Either way, you'll want to dress up a bit to match the sleek space. [$] *Average main: C$33* ✉ *Shangri-La Hotel, 1115 Alberni St., 3rd floor, Downtown* ☎ *604/695–1115* 🌐 *www.marketbyjgvancouver.com* ✥ *D2.*

$ CAFÉ 🍴 **Sciué.** Inspired by the street foods of Rome, this cafeteria-style Italian bakery–café (Sciué is pronounced "Shoe-eh") starts the day serving espresso and pastries, then moves to panini, soups, and pastas. One specialty is the *pane romano,* essentially a thick-crust pizza, sold by weight. There can be lines out the door at lunch, so try to visit early or late. (Not *too* late, though, as it's only open until 6 pm on weekdays, 4 pm on Saturday, and 3 pm Sunday.) There are two additional Downtown branches open weekdays only till 5 pm (1115 Melville and 885 West Georgia), and if you're in Yaletown, look for the location at 126 Davie Street. [$] *Average main: C$10* ✉ *110–800 W. Pender St., Downtown* ☎ *604/602–7263* 🌐 *www.sciue.ca* ⏲ *No dinner* ✍ *Reservations not accepted* ✥ *F3.*

WEST END

Storefronts full of savories line Robson, Denman, and Davie streets, making the West End a multicultural stew of Asian, European, and other cuisines. Particularly notable are the Japanese choices, from lively *izakayas* (Japanese tapas bars) to comfort-in-a-bowl ramen noodle shops.

$$ CHINESE FAMILY 🍴 **Dinesty.** Watch the dumpling makers at work in the open kitchen and you'll know what to order at this bustling Chinese eatery. From *xiao long bao* (delicate pork-and-crab-filled soup dumplings) to freshly steamed vegetable buns, you'll find plenty of doughy deliciousness here. Handmade Shanghai-style noodles, fresh greens quickly stir-fried with garlic, and salted vegetables with pork and green beans are tasty options, too. Their original location in Richmond (8111 Ackroyd Road) is larger and more upscale. [$] *Average main:* ✉ *1719 Robson St., West End* ☎ *604/669–7769* 🌐 *www.dinesty.ca* 💳 *No credit cards* ✥ *C2.*

$$ SPANISH 🍴 **España.** Relax, you're in Spain—or at least you'll feel like it when you enter this narrow West End nook, a traditional Spanish tapas bar that serves classic (and not so classic) small bites. Order a sherry or a glass of Spanish bubbly, then graze on fried local anchovies with smoked paprika aioli, grilled kale with manchego cheese and soft-boiled quail eggs, or croquettes of potato and salt cod. As in the best Iberian tapas joints, you can come in for a nibble or three, or keep ordering more dishes as you linger into the evening. [$] *Average main:* ✉ *1118 Denman St., West End* ☎ *604/558–4040* 🌐 *www.espanarestaurant.ca* 💳 *No credit cards* ⏲ *No lunch* ✍ *Reservations not accepted* ✥ *B2.*

$$ JAPANESE 🍴 **Hapa Izakaya.** Serving small plates designed for sharing, this spirited Japanese tapas bar is known for the mackerel dish, cooked table-side with a blowtorch. Also worth trying are the *ebi mayo* (tempura shrimp with spicy mayonnaise), the *ishi yaki* (a Korean-style stone bowl filled with rice, pork, and vegetables), and anything on the daily fresh sheet. Sake and Japanese beer are the drinks of choice. If you're looking for Japanese fare elsewhere around town, Hapa has branches downtown at 909 West Cordova (which is also open for lunch), at 1193 Hamilton Street in Yaletown, and at 1516 Yew Street in Kitsilano, one block from Kits Beach. [$] *Average main: C$14* ✉ *1479 Robson St., West End* ☎ *604/689–4272* 🌐 *www.hapaizakaya.com* ⏲ *No lunch* ✥ *C2.*

$$ JAPANESE 🍴 **Kingyo.** Behind its ornate wooden door, this izakaya occupies the stylish end of the spectrum, with a carved wood bar, lots of greenery, and sexy mood lighting, though the vibe is still casual. The intriguing Japanese small plates, from salmon carpaccio to grilled miso-marinated pork cheeks to the spicy *tako-wasabi* (octopus), are delicious, and the

CLOSE UP

Vancouver's Best Food Trucks

The food truck phenomenon has taken up wheels in Vancouver and a growing number of mobile kitchens have taken to the streets, selling fresh juices, spicy tacos, downhome barbecue, freshly caught seafood, and more. Needless to say, the assortment is as eclectic as the region's multicultural mix. Most trucks operate downtown during the lunch hours, generally from 11 or 11:30 until 2:30 or 3, although when they sell out, they close up for the day. Some trucks roll into town only on weekdays. The best way to find what truck is where is to check the local street food app (🌐 *www.streetfoodapp.com/vancouver*). These are some top hits.

Feastro. This purple "rolling bistro" serves local seafood (salmon or halibut tacos, Fanny Bay oysters, fish-and-chips), sweet-potato fries, soups, and other options. It's usually found at two Downtown locations: one on West Cordova Street at Thurlow Street, near the Vancouver Convention Centre; the other on Howe Street outside the Vancouver Art Gallery (🌐 *www.feastro.ca*).

The Juice Truck. Freshly squeezed juices and fruit smoothies are available at the corner of Abbott Street and Water Street in Gastown (🌐 *www.thejuicetruck.ca*).

Mogu. For Japanese street eats like spicy *karaage* (Japanese boneless fried chicken), pork *katsu* (cutlet) sandwiches, or vegetarian *kabocha korokke* (pumpkin croquette), look for this truck Downtown on Howe Street at West Dunsmuir Street and at the summertime Richmond Night Market (🌐 *www.eatmogu.com*).

Mom's Grilled Cheese Truck. Triple-decker grilled cheese sandwiches (made with love, of course) can be had at Howe Street at West Georgia Street Downtown (🌐 *www.momsgrilledcheesetruck.com*).

Soho Road Naan Kebab. Dishing up Indian butter chicken and vegetable *sabji* (a vegetarian curry served in a naan wrap), this truck parks Downtown at the corner of Granville and West Georgia streets, perfect for a shopping break (🌐 *www.facebook.com/EatSohoRoad*).

Yolk's Breakfast. While most trucks cater to the lunch crowd, this baby blue food cart serves gourmet breakfast to go, including egg sandwiches topped with tempura avocado and freshly made beignets. You can find the truck most days Downtown outside the Stadium/Chinatown SkyTrain station, at Beatty Street and West Dunsmuir (🌐 *www.yolks.ca*).

vibe is bustling and fun. To drink, choose from several varieties of *shochu* (Japanese vodka) or sake. [$] *Average main: C$13* ✉ *871 Denman St., West End* ☎ *604/608–1677* 🌐 *www.kingyo-izakaya.ca* 💳 *No credit cards* ✥ *B2.*

$ JAPANESE ✕ **Kintaro Ramen.** If your only experience with ramen is instant noodles, get thee to this authentic Japanese soup joint. With thin, fresh egg noodles and homemade broth (it's a meat stock, so vegetarians won't find much on the menu), a bowl of noodle soup here is cheap, filling, and ever so tasty. Expect long lines, but you can use the wait to decide between lean or fatty pork and miso or soy stock. Once you're inside the bare-bones storefront, the harried staff doesn't tolerate any dithering. Kintaro is owned by the same people as Motomachi: they're both top-notch ramen shops but this one is more of a quick eat-and-run stop—not the place for a leisurely meal. [$] *Average main: C$10* ✉ *788 Denman St., West End* ☎ *604/682–7568* ▭ *No credit cards* ⏲ *Closed Mon.* ✍ *Reservations not accepted* ✥ *C2.*

$ CHINESE 🍴 **Legendary Noodle.** As you'd expect from the name, this compact storefront specializes in noodles, and they're made by hand in the open kitchen, so you can watch. The choices are simple—noodles in soup or in straight-up stir-fries—but you can also order a plate of garlicky pea shoots or a steamer of dumplings to accompany your meal. The restaurant is just a short stroll from English Bay. [$] *Average main: C$10* ✉ *1074 Denman St., West End* ☎ *604/669–8551* 🌐 *www.legendarynoodle.ca* ✍ *Reservations not accepted* ✥ *B2.*

$ JAPANESE 🍴 **Motomachi Shokudo.** This small, casual neighborhood ramen shop is handy for a noodle fix en route to Stanley Park. The Japanese-style wooden furnishings reveal some flair, and the menu offers noodle soup choices for patrons who don't eat pork. A popular specialty here is smoky charcoal ramen (trust us, it tastes better than it sounds); the *gyoza* (dumplings) are a good choice for appetizer. Under the same ownership as the Kintaro ramen shop, Motomachi is also small and not great for lingering, but it's a bit more stylish. Motomachi also has chicken and vegetarian options, while Kintaro only has pork-based broth. [$] *Average main: C$10* ✉ *740 Denman St., West End* ☎ *604/609–0310* ▭ *No credit cards* ⏲ *Closed Wed.* ✥ *C1.*

6

STANLEY PARK

$$$$ SEAFOOD FAMILY 🍴 **The Fish House in Stanley Park.** Surrounded by gardens, this 1930s former sports pavilion turned fish restaurant, with a fireplace and two verandas, is an institution in the park, and the fabulous setting makes it a destination for special occasions. The food, including fresh oysters, a mixed grill of salmons, prawns, and scallops, and smoked black cod with roasted mushrooms and spinach, is flavorful and unpretentious, but the real draw is the location. Check the board for the day's catch. Traditional English afternoon tea is served daily (May–September) between 2 and 4. [$] *Average main: C$31* ✉ *8901 Stanley Park Dr., Stanley Park* ☎ *604/681–7275* 🌐 *www.fishhousestanleypark.com* ✥ *A1.*

$$$ CANADIAN 🍴 **The Teahouse in Stanley Park.** The former officers' mess at Ferguson Point in Stanley Park is a prime location for water views by day, and for watching sunsets at dusk. The Pacific Northwest menu is not especially innovative but its broad appeal will please those looking for Haida Gwaii halibut, rack of lamb, steaks, and a host of other options, including gluten-free pasta. Lunch menus include burgers, pizzas, and salads. Various tasting boards—charcuterie, cheese, seafood, and vegetarian options—make for good grazing in the afternoon. In summer you can dine on the patio. [$] *Average main: C$25* ✉ *7501 Stanley Park Dr., Stanley Park* ☎ *604/669–3281* 🌐 *www.vancouverdine.com* ✥ *A1.*

GASTOWN AND CHINATOWN

GASTOWN

Gastown has become a hub for dining and drinking, with lively bars (many with good food) and innovative restaurants.

$$$
FRENCH

✕ **Jules.** From garlicky escargots and steak frites to duck confit and crème caramel, traditional French bistro fare is alive and well at this intimate Gastown spot. You won't find many funky fusion creations or east-meets-west innovations—just the classic dishes you might find at a neighborhood bistro in Paris. It's cozy (some might say cramped), but that's part of the charm. Need a mid-afternoon pick-me-up? Light meals are served from 2:30 to 5:30. $ *Average main: C$22* ✉ *216 Abbott St., Gastown* ☎ *604/669–0033* ⊕ *www.julesbistro.ca* ✛ *G3.*

$$$
MODERN
CANADIAN

✕ **L'Abbatoir.** On the site of Vancouver's first jail, this two-level restaurant with exposed brick walls and classic black-and-white floor tiles has a bold collection of cocktails and an intriguing modern menu. From the restaurant's name—French for "slaughterhouse" (the surrounding neighborhood was once a meat-packing district)—you'd expect a meat-focused menu, and although you'll find veal sweetbreads on toast or grilled pork belly with an herbaceous salsa verde, seafood shines as well, in dishes like the crunchy potato salad with poached steelhead or roasted halibut with grapes and capers, served with thick-cut fries. Before plotting your escape into the night, dally over the Champagne sabayon with fresh berries or the white chocolate mousse with lemon curd and salted shortbread. $ *Average main: C$27* ✉ *217 Carrall St., Gastown* ☎ *604/568–1701* ⊕ *www.labattoir. ca* ⊘ *No lunch* ✛ *G3.*

$
DELI

✕ **Meat & Bread.** Like the name, the concept at this trendy sandwich shop is simple. You wait in line (there's nearly always a queue) and choose from the short daily menu of sandwiches. The rich and crispy housemade porcetta (Italian-style roast pork) with salsa verde on a freshly baked ciabatta bun is a must-try. Add a cup of soup, if you want, and a drink, then find a spot at the counter or the long communal table. Who knew simplicity could taste so good? A second weekday-only location at 1033 West Pender Street satiates sandwich enthusiasts Downtown. Neither location is open for dinner. $ *Average main: C$8* ✉ *370 Cambie St., Gastown* ☎ *604/566–9003* ⊘ *Closed Sun. No dinner* ⟡ *Reservations not accepted* ✛ *G3.*

$
MIDDLE EASTERN

✕ **Nuba.** You can make a meal of *meze* —appetizers like falafel, tabbouleh, or crispy cauliflower served with tahini—at this subterranean Lebanese restaurant. But if you're looking for something heartier, try a plate of *mjadra*, a spicy mix of lentils and rice. The kitchen serves roast chicken glazed with honey and red pepper, lamb kebabs, and other meat dishes but much of the menu is vegetarian friendly. The Kitsilano branch (3116 West Broadway) is a full-service restaurant, while other locations—1206 Seymour Street Downtown and 146 East 3rd Avenue in the Main Street neighborhood—just have a smaller, quickserve menu. $ *Average main: C$11* ✉ *207B W. Hastings St., Gastown* ☎ *604/668–1655* ⊕ *www.nuba.ca* ⊘ *No lunch Sun.* ⟡ *Reservations not accepted* ✛ *G3.*

$$ ASIAN FUSION Fodor's Choice ★ 🍴 **Pidgin.** Enter this glossy white space with an appetite for adventure. Chef Makoto Ono draws inspiration from Asia for his inventive sharing plates that are some of Vancouver's most exciting eating options. From the ever-changing menu, you might choose spicy shishito peppers topped with Parmesan and pine nuts, raw scallops, and daikon radish sauced with pomegranate red curry oil, or a Chinese-style "dan dan" noodle salad with shaved rutabega or turnip standing in for the pasta. Sake or one of the house-made cocktails—perhaps the Idle Hands, which blends pisco, lime juice, vanilla sugar, and kaffir lime leaf, or the De Capo Negroni (gin, vermouth, and campari, with a coffee ice ball)—stand up well to the bold food flavors. [$] *Average main:* ✉ *350 Carrall St., Gastown* ☎ *604/620–9400* 🌐 *www.pidginvancouver.com* ⏲ *No lunch* ✥ *H3.*

$ CAFÉ 🍴 **Revolver.** If your world revolves around your java, this hip Gastown café is a must visit. They offer a changing selection of coffees from roasters across North America, brewing coffee by the cup at the long bar (made of reclaimed BC fir) when you place your order. A small selection of cookies and pastries is available, too. [$] *Average main:* ✉ *325 Cambie St., Gastown* ☎ *604/558–4444* 🌐 *www.revolvercoffee.ca* 💳 *No credit cards* ⏲ *Closed Sun.* ✥ *G3.*

$$ ECLECTIC 🍴 **Salt Tasting Room.** If your idea of a perfect light meal revolves around fine cured meats, artisanal cheeses, and a glass of wine from a wide-ranging list, find your way to this sleek space in a decidedly unsleek Gastown location. The restaurant has no kitchen and simply assembles the selection of top-quality provisions—perhaps smoked beef tenderloin or British Columbian–made Camembert, with accompanying condiments—into artfully composed delights. The whole shebang is more like an upscale picnic than a full meal. There's no sign out front, so look for the saltshaker flag. [$] *Average main: C$16* ✉ *45 Blood Alley, off Abbott St., Gastown* ☎ *604/633–1912* 🌐 *www.salttastingroom.com* ⏲ *No lunch Mon.–Thurs.* ✥ *G3.*

$ CAFÉ 🍴 **Salty Tongue Café.** Tongues are always wagging at this deli-café's long communal table—a cheerful spot for a quick bite in Gastown. In the morning, you can pop in for coffee, muffins, or a full Irish breakfast, while at midday you can build your own sandwich or choose bangers-and-mash, quiche, or a potpie. They're only open until 4 pm. [$] *Average main: C$10* ✉ *212 Carrall St., Gastown* ☎ *604/688–9779* 🌐 *www.saltytongue.ca* ⏲ *No dinner* ✍ *Reservations not accepted* ✥ *H3.*

CHINATOWN

A growing number of hip eateries have moved into Chinatown, alongside the more traditional Chinese restaurants.

$$ CHINESE 🍴 **Bao Bei.** Start with an eclectic Chinatown storefront, stir in funky Asian-flavored cocktails, then add a creative take on traditional Chinese dishes, and the result is this hip and happening hangout. Start with a drink—perhaps a Guizhou Donkey (lemongrass-infused shochu, almond syrup, lime, and ginger beer) or a Cheung Po the Kid (rum, Dubonnet, pomegranate molasses, and housemade Chinese plum bitters). Then load up your table with nibbles like Chinese pickles and truffled pork dumplings or tapas-size dishes like *shao bing* (sesame flatbread with cumin-scented lamb, pickled red onion, cilantro, and chilies),

mantou (steamed buns stuffed with pork belly and preserved turnip), or a salad of wok-charred octopus, mustard root gnocchi, greens, and pickled butternut squash. Old Chinatown may have been tasty, but it never cooked up anything this fun. [$] *Average main: C$15* ✉ *163 Keefer St., Chinatown* ☎ *604/688–0876* 🌐 *www.bao-bei.ca* 💳 *No credit cards* 🕑 *Closed Mon. No lunch* ✍ *Reservations not accepted* ✥ *H4.*

$$ ECLECTIC 🍴 **The Union.** At this casually cool restaurant and lounge whose tag line could be "Asia's greatest hits," the sharing plates and fun cocktails have elements from Japan to India and everywhere in between. Start with a Banga, a cocktail in a jar; Banga #2 blends tequila, mandarin, lime, agave syrup, and galangal, while #3 is a mix of bourbon, mirin, mint, calamansi, and ginger beer. Nonalcoholic drinks like the Typhoon Jimi—carbonated jasmine tea, honey ginger syrup, lime leaf, and orange chili water—are also delightful. Foodwise, you can go Thai with papaya salad or sweet-and-spicy chicken wings, Vietnamese with a *banh mi* (sandwich) or the Cha Ca Hanoi (snapper, rice vermicelli, and greens in a turmeric-herb-coconut milk broth), or Indonesian with gingery peanut noodles, spicy sambal green beans, or *nasi goreng* (fried rice). [$] *Average main:* ✉ *219 Union St., Chinatown* ☎ *604/568–3230* 🌐 *www.theunionvancouver.ca* 💳 *No credit cards* 🕑 *No lunch weekdays* ✍ *Reservations not accepted* ✥ *H4.*

YALETOWN

Stylish restaurants have taken up space in the old warehouse buildings and nearby spaces in this now-trendy neighborhood.

$$$$ SEAFOOD 🍴 **Blue Water Cafe & Raw Bar.** Executive chef Frank Pabst focuses his menu on both popular and lesser-known local seafood (including frequently overlooked varieties like mackerel or herring) at his fashionable fish restaurant. You might start with Gulf Island swimming scallops in a tomato and caper relish; Dungeness crab salad with baby shrimps, mango, and jicama; or a seafood tower, ideal for sharing. Main dishes are seafood-centric, too—perhaps sturgeon with a cauliflower puree and golden beets, or Arctic char with trout caviar and pearl couscous. Ask the staff to recommend wine pairings from the BC–focused list. You can dine in the warmly lit interior or outside on the former loading dock that's now a lovely terrace. The sushi chef turns out both classic and new creations—they're pricey but among the city's best. [$] *Average main: C$35* ✉ *1095 Hamilton St., Yaletown* ☎ *604/688–8078* 🌐 *www.bluewatercafe.net* 🕑 *No lunch* ✥ *E5.*

$$$$ ITALIAN 🍴 **Cioppino's Mediterranean Grill & Enoteca.** Cioppino, the eponymous seafood stew, is the signature dish at this lofty candlelit room. Chef Pino Posteraro impresses with homemade pastas and such Italian-Mediterranean dishes as Dover sole with fresh tomatoes and basil, and roasted rack of lamb with a candied garlic-lemon reduction. More rustic Italian fare, such as veal osso buco and braised beef short ribs, is also on offer. In good weather, you can dine on the street-side patio. Note to oenophiles: the wine list runs more than 60 pages. [$] *Average main: C$35* ✉ *1133 Hamilton St., Yaletown* ☎ *604/688–7466* 🌐 *www.cioppinosyaletown.com* 🕑 *Closed Sun. No lunch* ✥ *E5.*

$$$ MODERN CANADIAN 🍴 **Homer St. Cafe and Bar.** Like chicken? That's the specialty at this classy bistro where the juicy rotisserie-roasted birds are served with peewee potatoes and (optionally) an extra portion of crispy skin. It's not just a poultry paradise, though. Plenty of other creative comfort foods are on the menu, from grilled calamari with olive bruschetta, to lemon baked halibut with spelt berries, to grilled steak served with sweet corn, eggplant, and kale. Be sure to check the daily fresh sheet for dinner specials and save room for the chewy peanut butter cookies with nutella cream. The space is interesting, too; half of the restaurant is in a restored historic structure (with details like mosaic tiles and a tin ceiling), while the other side of the dining room is set in a new condo building. [$] *Average main:* ✉ *898 Homer St., Yaletown* ☎ *604/428–4299* 🌐 *www.homerstreetcafebar.com* 🕒 *No lunch Sat. No dinner Sun.* ✥ *E4.*

$$$ ITALIAN 🍴 **La Pentola della Quercia.** This chic dining room at the Opus, Yaletown's most stylish hotel, serves innovative interpretations of Italian classics. The pastas are homemade, the fish is freshly grilled, and dishes like prosciutto-wrapped rabbit loin paired with grilled polenta or the 22-ounce bone-in rib eye would do any *nonna* proud. The best way to dine here is to choose the family-style chef's tasting menu, a multicourse parade of the kitchen's greatest hits (C$60 per person for seven courses, C$75 for ten courses). Breakfast is a delicious option, too, particularly the *kaiserschmarrn*, a puffy Northern Italian pancake served with housemade jam and whipped cream. [$] *Average main:* ✉ *Opus Hotel Vancouver, 350 Davie St., Yaletown* ☎ *604/642–0557* 🌐 *www.lapentola.ca* 💳 *No credit cards* ✥ *E5.*

$ CAFÉ 🍴 **O-Cha Tea Bar.** Because Vancouverites don't live by coffee alone—they're also tea drinkers—look for this tiny Yaletown tea bar that serves 60 of its own blends, including rich, milky "Lat-Teas." If you're feeling under the weather, order the "Cold Blaster," a rejuvinating blend of tea, orange juice, honey, ginger, and cayenne pepper. [$] *Average main: C$4* ✉ *1116 Homer St., Yaletown* ☎ *604/633–3929* 💳 *No credit cards* 🕒 *Closed Sun.* ✥ *E5.*

$$$$ MEDITERRANEAN 🍴 **Provence Marinaside.** You can imagine yourself on the Provençal seaside at this airy, modern, Mediterranean-style bistro on Yaletown's waterfront, where the focus is on French and Italian takes on seafood. Among the specialties are a delicious bouillabaisse, grilled halibut, curry-salted BC sturgeon, and lush, garlicky wild prawns. The rack of lamb and an extensive antipasti selection are also popular. The sunny marina-view patio makes this a lovely spot for breakfast, lunch, or a summertime dinner while watching the neighborhood's denizens meander along the seawall. You can enjoy the views over a glass of wine (with both BC and European choices) and a light bite at The Wine Bar next door. [$] *Average main: C$32* ✉ *1177 Marinaside Crescent, at Davie St., Yaletown* ☎ *604/681–4144* 🌐 *www.provencevancouver.com* ✥ *E5.*

$$ SEAFOOD 🍴 **Rodney's Oyster House.** This faux fishing shack in Yaletown has one of the city's widest selections of oysters (up to 18 varieties), from locally harvested bivalves to exotic Japanese Kumamotos—they're all laid out on ice behind the bar—or try the clams, scallops, mussels, and other

mollusks from the steamer kettles. If you're fishing for an afternoon snack, swim in between 3 and 6 (except Sunday) when a light menu of raw oysters, steamed clams, garlic prawns, and a few additional seafood nibbles are served. There's a second location in Gastown (52 Powell Street). [$] *Average main: C$18* ✉ *1228 Hamilton St., Yaletown* ☎ *604/609–0080* 🌐 *www.rohvan.com* 🕒 *No lunch Sun.* ✥ *E5.*

GRANVILLE ISLAND

Most visitors to Granville Island assemble a picnic or a light meal from the public market but the island has a few sit-down bistros, too.

$ CAFÉ

🍴 **Blue Parrot Coffee.** Granville Island has several coffee places, but only the Blue Parrot provides sweeping views of False Creek. If you haven't eaten your fill elsewhere in the market, accompany your espresso with a sticky cinnamon bun. Early birds, take note: you can perch at the Parrot starting at 7 am, before the rest of the Market stalls open. [$] *Average main: C$5* ✉ *Granville Island Public Market, 1689 Johnston St., Granville Island* ☎ *604/688–5127* 🌐 *www.blueparrotcoffee.com* 💳 *No credit cards* ✥ *A3.*

$$$ MODERN CANADIAN

🍴 **Edible Canada Bistro.** Looking for a sit-down meal while exploring Granville Island? At this contemporary bistro with a patio for people-watching, you can sample foods from BC and across Canada. Smaller appetites might gravitate toward the kale salad with lentils and summer vegetables, or the heirloom tomato gazpacho served with halibut ceviche. Hungrier travelers can sup on pea and ricotta ravioli with wild greens, Haida Gwaii salmon with fried artichoke, or steak with duck-fat fries. The adjacent retail store sells regional jams, chocolates, and other treats to take home. [$] *Average main: C$24* ✉ *1596 Johnston St., Granville Island* ☎ *604/682–6681* ✥ *A3.*

THE WEST SIDE

KITSILANO

Kits has it all, from easy-going neighborhood bistros to grab-a-bite sandwich shops to higher-end dining rooms.

$ CAFÉ

🍴 **Bean Around the World.** This local minichain, of the "Fuelled by Caffeine" slogan, runs a number of comfortable coffeehouses around town. If you like your cappuccino with no pretension (and perhaps with a muffin or slice of banana bread), head for "The Bean." In addition to this branch near Kitsilano Beach, their many Vancouver locations include 175 West Hastings Street (at Cambie) in Gastown, 1002 Mainland Street in Yaletown, 2977 Granville Street in South Granville, and on Main Street at #2528 and #3598. [$] *Average main: C$4* ✉ *1945 Cornwall Ave., Kitsilano* ☎ *604/739–1069* 🌐 *www.batw.ca* 💳 *No credit cards* ✥ *A2.*

$$$$ MODERN CANADIAN Fodor's Choice ★

🍴 **Bishop's.** Before "local" and "seasonal" were all the rage, this highly regarded restaurant was serving West Coast cuisine with an emphasis on organic regional produce. Menu highlights include starters like smoked salmon with chickpea blini and horseradish crème fraîche, while BC ling cod with bacon, kale, and black truffle sabayon, and locally raised

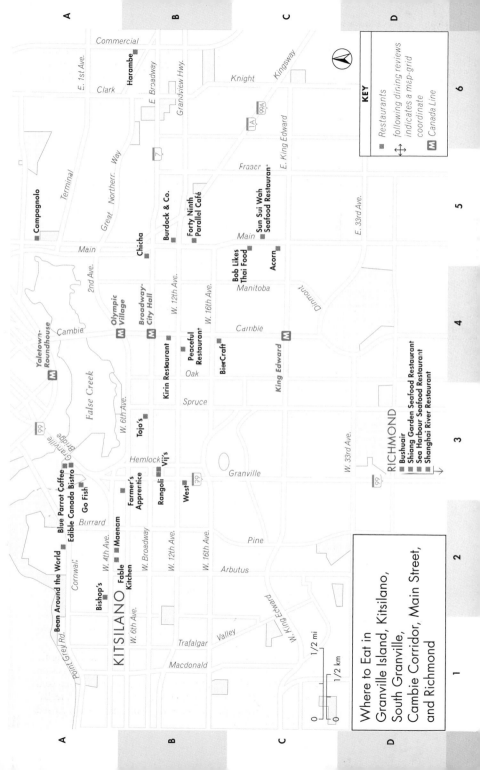

Where to Eat in
Granville Island, Kitsilano,
South Granville,
Cambie Corridor, Main Street,
and Richmond

KEY

■ Restaurants

↔ following dining reviews
indicates a map-grid
coordinate

Ⓜ Canada Line

RICHMOND
■ Bushuair
■ Shiang Garden Seafood Restaurant
■ Sea Harbour Seafood Restaurant
■ Shanghai River Restaurant

■ Campagnolo
■ Harambe
■ Chicha
■ Burdock & Co.
■ Forty Ninth Parallel Café
■ Sun Sui Wah Seafood Restaurant
■ Bob Likes Thai Food
■ Acorn
■ Olympic Village
■ Broadway–City Hall
■ Kirin Restaurant
■ Peaceful Restaurant
■ BierCraft
■ King Edward
■ Blue Parrot Coffee
■ Edible Canada Bistro
■ Go Fish
■ Bean Around the World
■ Tojo's
■ Farmer's Apprentice
■ Vij's
■ Rangoli
■ West
■ Bishop's
■ Fable Kitchen
■ Maenam
■ Yaletown–Roundhouse

KITSILANO

rack of lamb are among the tasty main dishes. All are expertly presented and impeccably served with suggestions from Bishop's extensive local wine list. The split-level room displays elaborate flower arrangements and selections from owner John Bishop's art collection. ⓢ *Average main: C$38* ✉ *2183 W. 4th Ave., Kitsilano* ☎ *604/738-2025* ⊕ *www. bishopsonline.com* ☽ *Closed Mon. No lunch* ✛ *A2.*

$$$
MODERN
CANADIAN

✕ **Fable.** The name doesn't have to do with fairy tales: it's about "farm to table," which encapsulates the philosophy of this bustling Kitsilano bistro. The idea is creative comfort food, and while the menu looks straightforward—steelhead trout, roast chicken, steak frites—it's full of surprising plot twists. The "Spaghetti and Meat Balls" turns out to be tagliatelle topped with a single oversized duck meatball that spills out the sauce when you cut into it, while pork loin might come with cracklings and a black pudding sauce. The moral? Don't judge this always-entertaining book by its cover (and order dessert when the lemon meringue parfait is on offer). ⓢ *Average main:* ✉ *1944 W. 4th St., Kitsilano* ☎ *604/732-1322* ⊕ *www.fablekitchen.ca* ✛ *B2.*

$
SEAFOOD

✕ **Go Fish.** If the weather's fine, head for this seafood stand on the seawall overlooking the docks beside Granville Island. The menu is short—highlights include fish-and-chips, grilled salmon or tuna sandwiches, and fish tacos—but the quality is first-rate. It's hugely popular, and on sunny summer days the waits can be maddening, so try to avoid the busiest times: noon to 2 pm and 5 pm to closing (which is at dusk). Since there are just a few outdoor tables, be prepared to take your food to go. ⓢ *Average main: C$10* ✉ *Fisherman's Wharf, 1505 W. 1st Ave., Kitsilano* ☎ *604/730-5040* ⊕ *www.bin941.com* ☽ *Closed Mon. No dinner* ✛ *A3.*

$$
THAI
Fodor's Choice
★

✕ **Maenam.** Chef Angus An's modern Thai menu brings this Asian cuisine to a new level. Although some of his dishes may sound familiar—green papaya salad, pad thai, curries—they're amped up with local ingredients, fresh herbs, and vibrant seasonings. Look for delicious innovations, too: perhaps crispy BC oysters, a duck confit salad with fried shallots and lychees, or the "eight-spice fish" that balances sweet, salty, and sour flavors. The bar sends out equally exotic cocktails, such as the Rumgari Geng (dark rum infused with coriander seed and mace, tamarind, Thai tea and Drambuie). The sleek dining room is stylish enough that you could dress up a bit, but you wouldn't be out of place in jeans. ⓢ *Average main: C$18* ✉ *1938 W. 4th Ave., Kitsilano* ☎ *604/730-5579* ⊕ *www.maenam.ca* ☽ *No lunch Sun. and Mon.* ✛ *B2.*

SOUTH GRANVILLE

In this sophisticated district just across the Granville Bridge from Downtown, you'll find equally sophisticated dining rooms.

$$$
MODERN
CANADIAN
Fodor's Choice
★

✕ **Farmer's Apprentice.** Book ahead to nab one of the 30 or so seats in this cozy bistro, where chef-owner David Gunawan and his team in the open kitchen craft wildly creative "vegetable forward" small plates. It's not a vegetarian restaurant, but fresh local produce plays starring roles in such dishes as heirloom tomatoes paired with shiso, shinjuku flower, and pistachios, or zucchini with blackberries, ricotta, and granola. Seafood stars, too; look for creations like smoked octopus with cherries and puffed quinoa, or a Dungeness crab, kohlrabi, and tomatillo gazpacho. Once these exotic sharing plates hit your table, you'll forget all about the cramped seating. If you don't fancy a glass of wine or a cocktail like the Smoked Martinez (smoked gin, vermouth, maraschino, and orange bitters), opt for a glass of their house-brewed kombucha. Reservations aren't accepted for lunch or brunch, but they're essential for dinner. Ⓢ *Average main:* ✉ *1535 W. 6th Ave., South Granville* ☎ *604/620–2070* ⊕ *www.farmersapprentice.ca* ☾ *Closed Mon.* ✛ *B3.*

$$ ✕ **Rangoli.** Under the same ownership as Vij's next door, this storefront
INDIAN bistro serves innovative Indian fare in a relaxed environment. Nab a table on the sidewalk or in the small but modern interior and order grilled chicken marinated in tamarind and yogurt, pulled pork with sautéed greens, or a curry of kale, jackfruit, cauliflower, and potato. Wash it all down with ginger lemonade or the Bollywood 411, a cocktail of Prosecco, pomegranate, and mango juice. It's more casual and less expensive than Vij's, with a smaller menu. Ⓢ *Average main: C$14* ✉ *1488 W. 11th Ave., South Granville* ☎ *604/736–5711* ⊕ *www.vijsrangoli.ca* ⟨⟩ *Reservations not accepted* ✛ *B3.*

$$$ ✕ **Vij's.** Long lauded as Vancouver's most innovative Indian restaurant,
INDIAN this South Granville dining destination, run by genial proprietor Vikram Vij and his wife Meeru Dhalwala, uses local ingredients to create exciting takes on South Asian cuisine. Dishes such as lamb "popsicles" in a creamy curry, BC ruby trout served with a wheat berry pilaf, or vegetables sauteed with *kalonji* (nigella seeds, also known as black cumin) and black chickpeas are far from traditional but are beautifully executed. Mr. Vij frequently circulates through the room, which is decorated with Indian antiques and whimsical elephant-pattern lanterns, greeting guests and suggesting dishes or cocktail pairings. Expect to cool your heels at the bar sipping chai or a cold beer while you wait an hour or more for a table, but if you like creative Indian fare, it's worth it. At this writing, the restaurant is expected to move to a new location at 3128 Cambie St., keeping the same general concept and menu. Check before you go. Ⓢ *Average main: C$27* ✉ *1480 W. 11th Ave., South Granville* ☎ *604/736–6664* ⊕ *www.vijs.ca* ☾ *No lunch* ⟨⟩ *Reservations not accepted* ✛ *B3.*

$$$$ ✕ **West.** Contemporary regional cuisine is the theme at this chic res-
MODERN taurant, one of the city's most splurge-worthy dining rooms. Among
CANADIAN executive chef Quang Dang's creations are butter-poached lobster
Fodor's Choice and potato gnocchi in a thyme emulsion, Haida Gwaii sablefish in a
★ three-vinegar glaze, and venison roasted in brown butter and served with an arugula bread salad. If you can't decide, opt for one of the elaborate multicourse tasting menus (C$68–C$95), which include vegetarian, seafood, and meat options. The decadent desserts might include a chocolate-caramel ice-cream cake with salty-sweet almonds or a blueberry crepe filled with lemon pound cake and topped with apricot-elderflower sorbet. Marble floors, high ceilings, and a wall of wine make the space feel simultaneously energetic and cozy. Ⓢ *Average main: C$36* ✉ *2881 Granville St., South Granville* ☎ *604/738–8938* ⊕ *www.westrestaurant.com* ✛ *B3.*

6

CAMBIE CORRIDOR

Lots of small neighborhood restaurants are clustered around the intersection of Broadway and Cambie Street, near the Broadway/City Hall Canada Line station, including two excellent Chinese restaurants.

$$$ CHINESE

🍴 **Kirin Restaurant West.** You can take in the city skyline and the surrounding mountains from the giant windows at this spacious dining room, where the focus is on Cantonese-style seafood, including fish, crab, and lobster fresh from the tanks. The kitchen does an excellent job with vegetables, too; ask for whatever's fresh that day. Dim sum is served daily at midday. It's an easy ride on the Canada Line from Downtown to the Broadway/City Hall station, two blocks from the restaurant. There's an additional location in Richmond. [$] *Average main: C$21* ✉ *City Square Shopping Centre, 555 W. 12th Ave., 2nd fl., Cambie Corridor* ☎ *604/879–8038* 🌐 *www.kirinrestaurants.com* ✣ *B4.*

$$ CHINESE

🍴 **Peaceful Restaurant.** Northern Chinese dishes are the specialty at this friendly storefront restaurant. Particularly good are the hand-pulled noodles that the cooks knead and stretch in the open kitchen; other good choices include the mustard-seed vegetable salad (crisp shredded vegetables fired up with hot mustard), Szechuan green beans, and cumin-scented lamb. Vegetarians have plenty of options, including many of the dumplings. Beef with broccoli and kung pao chicken are on the menu, but the helpful staff is happy to guide you to more authentic Mandarin fare. There are additional locations at 2394 West 4th Avenue in Kitsilano and at 43 East 5th Avenue in the Main Street neighborhood. [$] *Average main: C$13* ✉ *532 W. Broadway, Cambie Corridor* ☎ *604/879–9878* 🌐 *www.peacefulrestaurant.com* ✣ *D5.*

$$$$ JAPANESE Fodor's Choice ★

🍴 **Tojo's.** Hidekazu Tojo is a sushi-making legend in Vancouver, with thousands of special preparations stored in his creative mind. In this bright modern, high-ceilinged space, complete with a separate sake lounge, the prime perch is at the sushi bar, a convivial ringside seat for watching the creation of edible art. The best way to experience Tojo's creativity is to order *omakase* (chef's choice); the chef will keep offering you wildly adventurous fare, both raw and cooked, until you cry uncle. Budget a minimum of C$80 per person (before drinks) for five courses; tabs topping C$120 per person for six courses or more are routine. [$] *Average main: C$35* ✉ *1133 W. Broadway, Cambie Corridor* ☎ *604/872–8050* 🌐 *www.tojos.com* ⏲ *Closed Sun. No lunch* ✍ *Reservations essential* ✣ *B3.*

THE EAST SIDE

MAIN STREET/MT. PLEASANT

Do as the locals do and head for trendy but casual Main Street, where you'll find a mix of happening neighborhood bistros and interesting ethnic eateries.

$$ VEGETARIAN

🍴 **The Acorn.** Vancouver's first upscale vegetarian dining room, this barely-bigger-than-an-acorn restaurant serves imaginative plant-based fare that does its vegetables proud. Look for dishes like "linguini" made from raw zucchini and dressed with a mint-walnut pesto; kale Caesar salad with tempeh, olives, and smoked paprika croutons; and pickled beech mushrooms with a cashew herb mousse. Many menu items are vegan, raw, or gluten-free. If you have to wait for a table, pass the time with one of their signature cocktails; the Anniversaire blends gin and cava with a lemon verbena and lavender syrup, while the Old Norse combines Akvavit (from Vancouver's Long Table Distillery) with elderflower liqueur, a house-made tonic syrup, lime juice, and salt bitters. [$] *Average main:* ✉ *3995 Main St., Main St./Mt. Pleasant* ☎ *604/566–9001* 🌐 *www.theacornrestaurant.ca* 🕙 *Closed Mon. No lunch* ✍ *Reservations not accepted* ✥ *C5.*

$ THAI 🍴 **Bob Likes Thai Food.** Who's Bob? The staff at this no-frills storefront explains that he's just an average guy, and if he likes the authentically prepared Thai fare, then so will you. The menu includes all the classics, from green payaya salad to *laab* (minced pork with roasted rice, mint, fish sauce, and lime) to *pad si ew* (fried rice noodles with pork and vegetables). There's an assortment of curries, including fish with a creamy yellow curry. Some dishes are on the small side, so if you're hungry ask your server to recommend the right number of plates to share. There's a second location at 1521 West Broadway in the South Granville neighborhood. [$] *Average main: C$12* ✉ *3755 Main St., Main St./Mt. Pleasant* ☎ *604/568–8538* 🌐 *www.boblikesthaifood.com* ✥ *C5.*

$$ MODERN CANADIAN 🍴 **Burdock & Co.** Chef Andrea Carlson previously manned the stoves at locavore destinations Bishop's and Raincity Grill, and she's kept her focus on seasonal local ingredients at her own cheerful storefront bistro. Though she changes up the menu regularly, about half of her inventive sharing plates are vegetarian, like the *gomae* (typically greens with sesame sauce) made with hazelnuts, fiddleheads, pea tips, and asparagus, or the fried collards with grits and smoked ricotta. She doesn't neglect meat eaters, though, who tuck into her popular fried chicken with housemade pickles, or the slow-roasted bison ribs with spicy tomato glaze. And who can resist a salted chocolate chunk cookie, baked to order? [$] *Average main:* ✉ *2702 Main St., Main St./Mt. Pleasant* ☎ *604/879–0077* 🌐 *www.burdockandco.com* 🕙 *No lunch weekdays* ✥ *B5.*

$$ ITALIAN 🍴 **Campagnolo.** On a dark block near the Main St./Science World SkyTrain station, this relaxed trattoria lights up the neighborhood with its welcoming vibe and casually contemporary Italian fare. The kitchen cures its own *salumi*, including soppressata, capicola, and various sausages—these make good starters, as do the addictive *ceci* (crispy chickpeas with chili and mint). House-made pastas include a simple tagliatelle with pork ragú and basil, and a more unusual ricotta gnudi, made with nettles, zucchini, tomato, and black olives, while the pizzas also start straightforward with the Margherita (mozzarella, tomato, and basil) and get interesting with the Baconne, topped with cured salmon, creamed spinach, mizuna, chili, and red onion. After dinner, check out the extensive selection of grappa. [$] *Average main: C$18* ✉ *1020 Main St., Main St./Mt. Pleasant* ☎ *604/484–6018* 🌐 *www.campagnolorestaurant.ca* 🕙 *No lunch weekends* ✥ *A5.*

$$ PERUVIAN 🍴 **Chicha.** Ceviches, causas, and other classic Peruvian dishes get a West Coast spin at this lively, relaxed bistro just off Main Street. Your ceviche may include local whitefish or BC salmon, while your *causa* (whipped potatoes topped with seafood or vegetables) may feature local tuna with wasabi cream and passion fruit ponzu. Other dishes to try? The Locra de Zapallo, an empanada stuffed with butternut squash, kale, corn, and cheese, or any of the Antichuchos, skewers of grilled meat or veggies. The beverage of choice is the classic Pisco Sour but you might also sip the housemade sangria or the Chicha Morada, a nonalcoholic brew made from purple corn. [$] *Average main:* ✉ *136 E. Broadway, Main St./Mt. Pleasant* ☎ *604/620–3963* 🌐 *www.chicharestaurant.com* ⏲ *No lunch Mon.–Thurs.* ✣ *B5.*

$ CAFÉ 🍴 **Forty Ninth Parallel Café.** Locally run 49th Parallel Coffee Roasters sources and roasts their own coffees, which they feature at their flagship café on Main Street. Centered around a wood-framed counter, this large airy space has walls of windows on two sides. It's always packed with neighborhood denizens and shoppers enjoying the top-notch brews and the house-made Lucky Doughnuts, which come in flavors from simple vanilla-glazed to salted caramel to decadent triple chocolate. A second location at 2198 West 4th Avenue keeps Kitsilano caffeinated, too. [$] *Average main:* ✉ *2902 Main St., Main St./Mt. Pleasant* ☎ *604/872–4901* 🌐 *www.49thparallelroasters.com* ✣ *B5.*

$$ CHINESE FAMILY 🍴 **Sun Sui Wah Seafood Restaurant.** This bustling Cantonese restaurant is best known for its excellent dim sum (served 10:30 to 3 weekdays and 10 to 3 weekends), which ranges from traditional handmade dumplings to some highly adventurous fare. Dinner specialties include roasted squab marinated in the restaurant's secret spice blend and king crab plucked live from the tanks, then steamed with garlic. Come with a group if you can, so you can sample more dishes. There's an additional location in Richmond. [$] *Average main: C$18* ✉ *3888 Main St., Main St./Mt. Pleasant* ☎ *604/872–8822, 866/872–8822* 🌐 *www.sunsuiwah.com* ✣ *C5.*

COMMERCIAL DRIVE

Restaurants serving fare from Asia, Africa, and Latin America, as well as local pubs, pizzerias, and coffeehouses line this East Side strip that rumbas to a world beat.

$$ ETHIOPIAN 🍴 **Harambe.** The name means "working together" in Swahili, and the family that owns this welcoming restaurant does just that as it introduces guests to traditional Ethiopian fare. Savory stews are served atop platter-size pancakes of *injera,* a tangy, almost spongy flatbread used to scoop up every morsel. Order a combination platter to sample a range of flavors; the vegetarian version, which includes spinach, lentils, peas, assorted vegetables, and salad, is especially tasty. The space is colorful and the walls are hung with Ethiopian artwork. Unlike some Ethiopian restaurants with traditional low seating, there are regular tables and chairs here. [$] *Average main: C$14* ✉ *2149 Commercial Dr., Commercial Drive* ☎ *604/216–1060* 🌐 *www.harambes.com* ✣ *B6.*

NORTH SHORE

WEST VANCOUVER

There are some lovely views at the upscale destination restaurants out here, but you'll need a car.

$$$ MODERN CANADIAN 🍴 **The Beach House at Dundarave Pier.** It's worth the drive over the Lions Gate Bridge to West Vancouver for a lunch or dinner at this 1912 seaside house. Whether inside the terraced dining room or on the heated beachside patio, almost every table has views over Burrard Inlet and Stanley Park. The Pacific Northwest menu focuses on unpretentious food like Haida Gwaii halibut and chips, fish tacos, seasonal fish preparations, and a few steak and chicken dishes. Lunch is a particularly good option here, followed by a stroll along the pier or the seaside walkway. [$] *Average main: C$27* ✉ *150 25th St., off Marine Dr., West Vancouver* ☎ *604/922–1414* 🌐 *www.thebeachhouserestaurant.ca* ✣ *C1.*

$$$$ SEAFOOD 🍴 **Salmon House on the Hill.** Perched halfway up a mountain, this restaurant has stunning water and city views by day and expansive vistas of city lights by night. It's best known for its alder-grilled salmon, though the halibut from Haida Gwaii is also tempting. The seafood tower, prepared for two, gives you both chilled and grilled fish, along with a "seafood bowl"—halibut, salmon, clams, mussels, and prawns in a lemongrass coconut broth, served with grilled bannock, a traditional First Nations bread. With a good selection by the glass, the wine list emphasizes BC labels. The Northwest Coast interior is tastefully done, though it can hardly compete with what's outside the windows. The Salmon House is about 30 minutes from Vancouver by car. Head over the Lions Gate Bridge, follow Highway 1 west, then take the Folkestone Way exit. [$] *Average main: C$32* ✉ *2229 Folkestone Way, West Vancouver* ☎ *604/926–3212* 🌐 *www.salmonhouse.com* 🕓 *No lunch weekdays* ✣ *C1.*

6

RICHMOND

It's easy to get to the Vancouver suburb of Richmond on the Canada Line, for some of the best Chinese food outside of China.

$$ HUNAN 🍴 **Bushuair Restaurant.** Attention, spicy-food lovers and adventurous eaters! A portrait of Chairman Mao welcomes you to this modest but bright storefront in a strip mall—very appropriate, as the restaurant serves the fiery (and we mean, fiery!) food of Hunan, Mao's home province. The extensive picture menu (with some endearingly quirky translations) can help you order; try a whole fish buried in chilies or anything with the smoky Chinese bacon. Make sure to include some plain steamed buns or a rice dish to tone down the heat. [$] *Average main: C$18* ✉ *4600 No. 3 Rd., Richmond* ☎ *604/285–3668* ✣ *D3.*

$$$ CANTONESE 🍴 **Sea Harbour Seafood Restaurant.** Conveniently located at the entrance to Bridgeport Station on the Canada Line, this upscale Chinese restaurant serves first-rate Hong Kong–style seafood, often plucked live from the tanks and cooked to the specifications of its well-heeled clientele. Ask for whatever fish is freshest, and try the distinctive pork with chayote squash. This is also a popular spot for lunchtime dim sum, both

traditional and more contemporary. Although you won't be out of place in jeans, you could dress up a bit, particularly in the evening; reservations are recommended. $ *Average main: C$22* ✉ *8888 River Road, Richmond* ☎ *604/232–0816* ⊕ *www.seaharbour.com* ✛ *D3.*

$$

SHANGHAINESE

✕ **Shanghai River Restaurant.** A brigade of chefs is at work in the open kitchen of this popular restaurant that specializes in Shanghai-style fare, which is richer and slightly sweeter than more delicate Cantonese dishes. They're prepping the handmade dumplings, including the soup-filled *xiao long bao* and the pan-fried pork buns that are among the specialities here. Hand-pulled noodles, saucy braised eggplant, and fresh stir-fried greens are other good options. Book in advance or prepare to wait. $ *Average main: C$14* ✉ *7831 Westminster Hwy., Richmond* ☎ *604/233–8885* ▭ *No credit cards* ✛ *D3.*

$$

CHINESE

✕ **Shiang Garden Seafood Restaurant.** Dim sum aficionados make the trek to this upscale Cantonese restaurant in suburban Richmond for some of the tastiest tidbits in town, served daily for brunch or lunch. Order from the menu (there are no carts circling the dining rooms), or just point at what the other tables are having. In the evenings, Hong Kong–style seafood (plucked from tanks in the restaurant), and other subtly seasoned southern Chinese dishes are the specialties. The multilevel restaurant, which is popular with Asian families, is in a shopping plaza, set back from No. 3 Road at Leslie Road. $ *Average main: C$15* ✉ *4540 No. 3 Rd., Richmond* ☎ *604/273–8858* ✛ *D3.*

WHERE TO STAY

Updated By
Chris McBeath

Vancouver is a pretty compact city, but each neighborhood has a distinct character and its own style of accommodation options. From hip boutique hotels to historic bed-and-breakfasts to sharp-angled glass-and-mirror towers, there are lodging choices for every style and budget. You can choose to be in the center of the shopping action on Robson Street, among the gracious tree-lined boulevards near Stanley Park, or in close proximity to the pulsing heart of the city's core.

Vancouver is an extremely outdoorsy community, so hotel amenities can sometimes include free bicycles and free ski storage, and many concierges can put you in contact with hiking and running groups that welcome visitors. Some properties even offer complimentary limo service, usually to the theater, or for picking you up after shopping, which comes in especially handy if you have lots of bags.

The city is extremely pet-friendly, especially when it comes to dogs. Not only can you bring your pooch with you to many Vancouver properties, some even let you borrow *their* dog for a walk (check out the Fairmont Hotel Vancouver, for instance).

With its goal to become the greenest city in the world by 2020 (as in eco-wise, not with respect to the already abundant natural greenery), recycling and sustainability are essential parts of life in Vancouver. Many hoteliers have also made eco-friendly practices an integral part of the guest experience. For example, Fairmont Waterfront was among the first in the world to adopt a green roof concept—the garden and apiary supply the hotel with herbs and honey—and it has electric vehicle charging stations. The hotel also initiated ground-breaking water conservation and waste management systems. Supporting the community and protecting the surrounding landscapes have become good business practices, and the Westin Bayshore followed the trend by financially assisting in the creation of Cardero Park, on the east side of the property.

Be forewarned though: Environmental awareness and community building are top of mind for most Vancouverites. That means hotels with a water view or exemplary environmental report cards are coveted and book up well in advance. Some of the historic B&Bs you'll find in the more homey residential neighborhoods like the West End and near Stanley Park are also extremely popular.

PLANNING

APARTMENT RENTALS

The trend toward self-catered apartments for families or business executives has continued to increase in recent years. Vancouver has a number of hotels that offer lower rates or separate wings for longer-term residents. Options often include housekeeping, parking, satellite TV, or Wi-Fi access. Make Yourself at Home (☎ *604/874–7817* ⊕ *www.makeyourselfathome.com*) provides a terrific range of private homes and apartments for short-term rentals; this site is especially good for last-minute bookings. On the higher end of the spectrum, Dream Rentals (⊕ *www.vancouverdreamrentals.com*) lists many luxury condominiums and executive homes.

WHAT DOES IT COST?

Most hotels let children under 18 stay free in their parents' room, though you may be charged extra for more than two adults. Parking runs about C$25 to C$40 per day at downtown hotels, and can be free outside the downtown core. Watch out for phone and Internet charges, which can add up. You'll also be charged a 1.5% accommodations tax, a 10% Provincial Sales Tax (PST), and a 5% Goods and Services Tax (GST) for a total levy of 16.5%.

Prices in the reviews are the lowest cost of a standard double room in high season.

WHAT IT COSTS IN CANADIAN DOLLARS				
	$	$$	$$$	$$$$
Hotels	under C$125	C$125–C$195	C$196–C$300	over C$300

HOTEL REVIEWS

Hotels are listed alphabetically within neighborhoods. Use the coordinate at the end of each listing (✣ B2) to locate a property on the Where to Stay in Vancouver map.

For expanded hotel reviews, visit Fodors.com.

DOWNTOWN AND THE WEST END

DOWNTOWN

$$ HOTEL **The Burrard.** Freebies abound at the fun and funky Burrard, including water in recyclable bottles, biodegradable bath products, and movie channels on the huge flat-screen TVs. **Pros:** doesn't take itself too seriously; laid-back atmosphere; complimentary bicycles and umbrellas. **Cons:** cool decor is dressing for what is fundamentally a motel with so-so amenities; opposite a hospital so occasional ambulance sirens might be disturbing. [$] *Rooms from: C$189* ✉ *1100 Burrard St., Downtown* ☎ *604/681–2331* 🌐 *www.theburrard.com* 🛏 *72 rooms* 🍴 *No meals* ✣ *D4.*

$$$ HOTEL FAMILY **Century Plaza Hotel & Spa.** Full kitchens and an indoor pool make this 30-story Downtown high-rise a good family choice. **Pros:** pampering spa; on-site entertainment; large rooms. **Cons:** staff not always helpful; next to hospital with the occasional noisy ambulance siren. [$] *Rooms from: C$215* ✉ *1015 Burrard St., Downtown* ☎ *604/687–0575* 🌐 *www.century-plaza.com* 🛏 *240 rooms* 🍴 *No meals* ✣ *D4.*

$$$ HOTEL **Delta Vancouver Suites.** Exuding a swanky 5th Avenue vibe with suavely dressed doormen and a lobby that feels like a sophisticated nightclub, this upscale, all-suites business hotel is centrally located in Downtown Vancouver. **Pros:** fitness center open 24 hours; friendly service; windows that actually open. **Cons:** one-way roads make getting here a bit of a headache; expensive parking. [$] *Rooms from: C$269* ✉ *550 W. Hastings St., Downtown* ☎ *604/689–8188* 🌐 *www.deltavancouversuites.ca* 🛏 *225 suites* 🍴 *No meals* ✣ *F3.*

$$$ HOTEL **Executive Hotel Le Soleil.** The staff prides itself on attentive service at this classy, old-world-style boutique hotel with luxurious touches. **Pros:** chic and romantic; central location. **Cons:** no on-site spa or health club. [$] *Rooms from: C$299* ✉ *567 Hornby St., Downtown* ☎ *604/632–3000, 877/632–3030* 🌐 *www.lesoleilhotels.com* 🛏 *8 rooms, 105 suites* ✣ *F2.*

$$$$ HOTEL **Fairmont Hotel Vancouver.** The copper roof of this 1939 château-style hotel dominates Vancouver's skyline, and the elegantly restored hotel is considered the city's gracious grande dame. **Pros:** full-service spa; great location for shopping; stunning architecture. **Cons:** "standard" room sizes vary greatly; pricey parking. [$] *Rooms from: C$365* ✉ *900 W. Georgia St., Downtown* ☎ *604/684–3131* 🌐 *www.fairmont.com/hotelvancouver* 🛏 *556 rooms, 37 suites* 🍴 *No meals* ✣ *E3.*

$$$$ HOTEL **Fairmont Pacific Rim.** Overlooking the Downtown waterfront, and across from the impressive convention center, this luxurious 47-story tower represents the Fairmont's first foray into the condominium-hotel format, where residential sales finance the hotel development. **Pros:** prime location; Fairmont high quality all round. **Cons:** pricey;

WHERE SHOULD I STAY?

	VIBE	PROS	CONS
Downtown	Central commercial/financial district hotels are mostly mid- to high-end, catering to tourists and business travelers. Low to moderately priced hotels are on Granville Street, south of Robson.	Within walking distance of nearly all Downtown sights and handy to the Canada Place cruise-ship terminal.	A little dull come evening as few people live in the area, but Granville Street, south of Robson, is lined with bars, clubs, and movie theaters.
West End	A lovely tree-filled, gay-friendly residential neighborhood close to Downtown. Hotels in all price ranges are on the main arteries; historic hotels and B&Bs are on the side streets.	A pleasant alternative to the central business district. Stanley Park is on the doorstep, and the beach at English Bay is the West End's hot spot for people-watching and casual dining.	Could be too quiet for some folks. Parking can be difficult to find.
Gastown	Busy with a bit of a gritty city vibe.	Convenient to Downtown.	Not the cleanest part of town.
Yaletown	Also on the downtown peninsula, this is where urban chic translates into New York–style loft apartments, beneath which lie trendy restaurants and boutique shops.	Hip shopping, bars, and restaurants are nearby, as are the city's sports stadiums (Rogers Arena and BC Place). It's a short ferry ride to Granville Island.	Sidewalks can be noisy; this is one of the most densely populated, high-rise areas of the city. Parking can be difficult.
Granville Island	Lots going on; local vibe, especially in the morning before the visitors arrive.	At the center of the action, with theater and street performers, and the Granville Island Market right there.	Gets very busy with tourists.
West Side	South of downtown Vancouver, the West Side is made up of tony residential neighborhoods. Hotels here include heritage mansions and gentrified beach homes.	Near beaches, the UBC campus, parks, and gardens. Great shopping and local eats along West 4th Avenue and South Granville. Gardens and beachside walks.	You may feel "out of the action" since these are residential areas. Although bus transit is excellent, having a car makes navigation easier.

attracts a lot of business- and convention-goers. $\boxed{\$}$ *Rooms from: C$579* ✉ *1038 Canada Pl., Downtown* ☎ *877/900–5350* ⊕ *www.fairmont. com/pacificrim* ↪ *37 suites, 340 rooms* ⦿ *No meals* ✛ *F2.*

$$$$ ⬚ **Fairmont Waterfront.** Stunning views of the harbor, mountains, and
HOTEL Stanley Park from the floor-to-ceiling windows of the guest rooms are
Fodor'sChoice one of the highlights of this luxuriously modern 23-story hotel across
★ the street from Vancouver's cruise-ship terminal. **Pros:** harbor views;
proximity to the waterfront; inviting pool terrace. **Cons:** long elevator
queues; busy lobby lounge. $\boxed{\$}$ *Rooms from: C$499* ✉ *900 Canada Pl.
Way, Downtown* ☎ *604/540–4509* ⊕ *www.fairmont.com/waterfront*
↪ *489 rooms, 29 suites* ⦿ *No meals* ✛ *F2.*

BEST BETS FOR VANCOUVER LODGING

Fodor's offers a selective listing of quality lodging experiences in every price range, from the city's best budget beds to its most sophisticated luxury hotels. Here, we've compiled our top recommendations by price and experience. The very best properties—in other words, those that provide a particularly remarkable experience in their price range—are designated in the listings with the Fodor's Choice logo.

Fodor's Choice★

Corkscrew Inn, p. 174

Opus Vancouver Hotel, p. 173

Pan Pacific Vancouver, p. 167

Rosewood Hotel Georgia, p. 170

Shangri-La Hotel, p. 170

Sylvia Hotel, p. 172

Times Square Suites Hotel, p. 173

Wedgewood Hotel and Spa, p. 171

By Price

$

Barclay Hotel, p. 171

YWCA Hotel, p. 171

$$

Barclay House, p. 172

Sylvia Hotel, p. 172

Victorian Hotel, p. 171

$$$

L'Hermitage Hotel, p. 167

Opus Vancouver Hotel, p. 173

$$$$

Fairmont Pacific Rim, p. 164

Fairmount Waterfront, p. 164

Pan Pacific Vancouver, p. 167

Shangri-La Hotel, p. 170

Wedgewood Hotel and Spa, p. 171

By Experience

FOR FAMILIES

Century Plaza Hotel & Spa, p. 164

Lord Stanley Suites on the Park, p. 172

Renaissance Vancouver Harbourside Hotel, p. 170

MOST CENTRAL

Fairmont Hotel Vancouver, p. 164

Four Seasons Hotel Vancouver, p. 167

Wedgewood Hotel and Spa, p. 171

BEST HISTORIC CONVERSION

Rosewood Hotel Georgia, p. 170

St. Regis Hotel, p. 170

MOST DOG-FRIENDLY

Fairmont Hotel Vancouver, p. 164

Fairmont Waterfront, p. 164

Sheraton Vancouver Wall Centre, p. 170

MOST ROMANTIC

Barclay House, p. 172

L'Hermitage Hotel, p. 167

Wedgewood Hotel and Spa, p. 171

BEST SPA

Century Plaza Hotel & Spa (Spa at the Century), p. 164

Pan Pacific Vancouver (Spa Utopia), p. 167

Shangri-La Hotel (Chi Spa), p. 170

Sheraton Vancouver Wall Centre (Vida Spa), p. 170

BEST B&B

Corkscrew Inn, p. 174

Granville House B&B, p. 174

$$$$ HOTEL FAMILY 🏨 **Four Seasons Hotel Vancouver.** This 30-story luxury hotel is famous for pampering guests, and the service is indeed top-notch. **Pros:** great location for shopping; you're treated like royalty; indoor-outdoor heated pool. **Cons:** a hang out for business types; expensive. [$] *Rooms from: C$425* ✉ *791 W. Georgia St., Downtown* ☎ *604/689–9333* 🌐 *www.fourseasons.com/vancouver* 🛏 *306 rooms, 66 suites* 🍴 *No meals* ✥ *E3.*

$$ B&B/INN 🏨 **Kingston Hotel.** Convenient to shopping and nightlife, the budget-friendly, family-run Kingston occupies a four-story elevator building dating back to 1910 this is the type of lodging you'd expect to find in Europe. **Pros:** great location; breakfast included; single rooms available. **Cons:** some shared bathrooms; limited amenities; early checkout. [$] *Rooms from: C$155* ✉ *757 Richards St., Downtown* ☎ *604/684–9024, 604/684–9024* 🌐 *www.kingstonhotelvancouver.com* 🛏 *52 rooms, 13 with bath* 🍴 *Breakfast* ✥ *F3.*

$$$ HOTEL 🏨 **L'Hermitage Hotel.** Get beyond the marble floors, silk and velvet walls, and gold-cushion benches in the lobby and you'll discover a warm residential character at this boutique hotel. **Pros:** uptown hotel with a refreshingly residential vibe; excellent concierge; valet parking. **Cons:** in the heart of Downtown bustle; one-way streets can make driving to the hotel frustrating. [$] *Rooms from: C$255* ✉ *788 Richards St., Downtown* ☎ *778/327–4100, 888/855–1050* 🌐 *www.lhermitagevancouver.com* 🛏 *40 rooms, 20 suites* 🍴 *No meals* ✥ *F4.*

$$$$ HOTEL 🏨 **Loden Hotel.** This chic, designer boutique hotel has all manner of perks to enhance your stay, including in-room WiiFit, TVs with oversize LCD screens, a state-of-the-art gym, helpful staff, and free bicycles to explore the city. **Pros:** quiet, central location; free Downtown car service for shopping and theater pick ups. **Cons:** locals tend to snag best lounge and restaurant seats; no pool. [$] *Rooms from: C$385* ✉ *1177 Melville St., Downtown* ☎ *604/669–5060, 877/225–6336* 🌐 *www.theloden.com* 🛏 *70 rooms, 7 suites* 🍴 *No meals* ✥ *E2.*

$$$ HOTEL 🏨 **Metropolitan Hotel Vancouver.** "The Met," as the locals call it, is one of the city's top business-district hotels, with design elements that follow the principles of feng shui, from the two lions guarding the entrance to the spacious, luxurious rooms. **Pros:** top-line luxury; excellent restaurant. **Cons:** a bit pretentious; very business oriented. [$] *Rooms from: C$295* ✉ *645 Howe St., Downtown* ☎ *604/687–1122, 800/667–2300* 🌐 *www.metropolitan.com* 🛏 *104 rooms, 18 suites* 🍴 *No meals* ✥ *E3.*

$$ HOTEL 🏨 **Moda Hotel.** This century-old boutique hotel is stylish and good-value. **Pros:** good value for location; near night clubs and entertainment; discounted parking. **Cons:** some rooms are noisy; old building. [$] *Rooms from: C$190* ✉ *900 Seymour St., Downtown* ☎ *604/683–4251* 🌐 *www.modahotel.ca* 🛏 *67 rooms* 🍴 *No meals* ✥ *E4.*

$$$$ HOTEL Fodor's Choice ★ 🏨 **Pan Pacific Vancouver.** Located in the waterfront Canada Place complex, the sophisticated Pan Pacific has easy access to the city's convention center and the main cruise-ship terminal. **Pros:** lovely harbor views; staff has a "go the extra mile" attitude. **Cons:** atrium is open to the convention center, so it's often full of business executives talking shop; lobby ambience not very welcoming. [$] *Rooms from: C$369* ✉ *999*

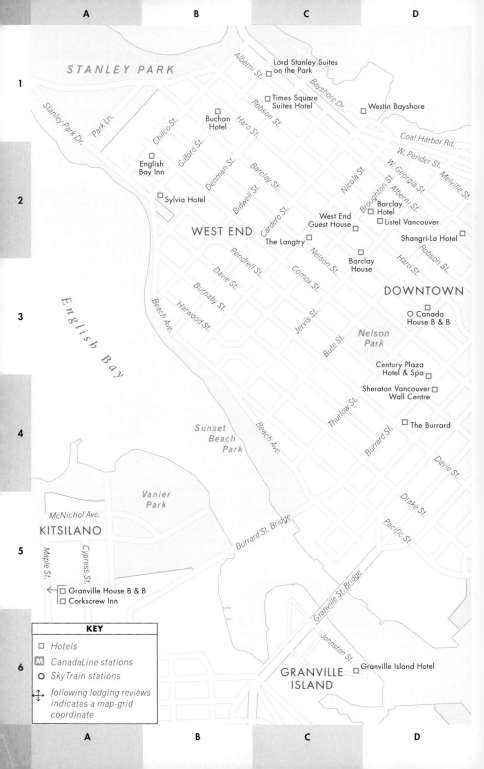

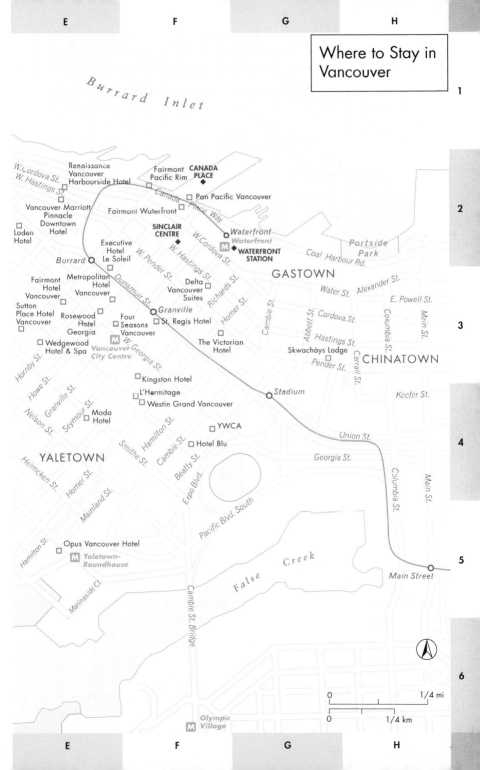

E   F   G   H

1

Burrard   Inlet

W. Cordova St.   Renaissance   Fairmont   CANADA
W. Hastings St.   Vancouver   Pacific Rim   PLACE
                 Harbourside Hotel
                          Canada   ☐ Pan Pacific Vancouver
Vancouver Marriott   Fairmont Waterfront   Place Way
Pinnacle
☐ Downtown
Loden   Hotel   SINCLAIR   Waterfront
Hotel   CENTRE   W. Cordova St.   Ⓜ Waterfront
          Executive   ◆   WATERFRONT
Burrard Ⓞ   Hotel   STATION
          Le Soleil   W. Pender St.   GASTOWN   Portside
Fairmont   Metropolitan   Coal Harbour Rd.   Park
Hotel   Hotel   Delta
Vancouver   Vancouver   ☐ Vancouver   Water St.   Alexander St.
Sutton   Suites
Place Hotel   Rosewood   Four   ☐ Granville   E. Powell St.
Vancouver   Hotel   Seasons   ☐ St. Regis Hotel   Cordova St.
          Georgia   Vancouver   Hastings St.
☐ Wedgewood   Ⓜ   The Victorian   Skwachàys Lodge   CHINATOWN
Hotel & Spa   Vancouver   Hotel   ☐
          City Centre   Pender St.   Keefer St.
          ☐ Kingston Hotel
          ☐ L'Hermitage   ☐ Stadium
          ☐ Westin Grand Vancouver   Union St.
          ☐ Moda   ☐ YWCA   Georgia St.
          Hotel   ☐ Hotel Blu
          YALETOWN
                                   Pacific Blvd. South
          ☐ Opus Vancouver Hotel
          Ⓜ Yaletown-
          Roundhouse   False   Creek
                                        ☐ Main Street
                          Cambie St. Bridge

2

3

4

5

6

0   1/4 mi
0   1/4 km

Olympic
Ⓜ Village

E   F   G   H

Canada Pl., Downtown ☎ *604/662–8111, 800/663–1515 in Canada, 800/937–1515 in U.S.* ⊕ *www.panpacificvancouver.com* ⤳ *465 rooms, 39 suites* |◯| *No meals* ✛ *F2.*

$$$
HOTEL
FAMILY

🖭 **Renaissance Vancouver Harbourside Hotel.** A good quality hotel with large rooms, the Vancouver Harbourside Hotel is a good base for exploring Downtown without being in the thick of noisy action. **Pros:** surrounding financial district is quiet at night; near the waterfront. **Cons:** a five-block walk to shopping and theaters; a five-block walk to Stanley Park. Ⓢ *Rooms from: C$275* ✉ *1133 W. Hastings St., Downtown* ☎ *604/689–9211, 888/236–2427* ⊕ *www.renaissancevancouver. com* ⤳ *434 rooms, 8 suites* |◯| *No meals* ✛ *E2.*

$$$$
HOTEL
Fodor'sChoice
★

🖭 **Rosewood Hotel Georgia.** One of Vancouver's newest hotels, the classy Rosewood is also one of the city's most historic properties: the 1927 Georgian Revival building once welcomed such prestigious guests as Elvis Presley and Katharine Hepburn. **Pros:** at the center of the city's action; top-rated spa; iconic restaurant. **Cons:** expensive valet parking; restaurant can get very busy. Ⓢ *Rooms from: C$425* ✉ *801 W. Georgia St., Downtown* ☎ *604/682–5566* ⊕ *www.rosewoodhotels.com/en/ hotelgeorgia* ⤳ *156 rooms* |◯| *No meals* ✛ *E3.*

$$$$
HOTEL
Fodor'sChoice
★

🖭 **Shangri-La Hotel.** On the first 15 floors of the tallest building in Vancouver—a 61-story tower of angled glass studded with gold squares that glint in the sunshine—is this upscale Asian chain's first hotel in North America (the second is in Toronto). **Pros:** first-rate concierge service; not as expensive as you might think; central location. **Cons:** public areas could be more inviting; on the city's busiest thoroughfare. Ⓢ *Rooms from: C$395* ✉ *1128 W. Georgia St., Downtown* ☎ *604/689–1120* ⊕ *www.shangri-la.com* ⤳ *81 rooms, 38 suites* |◯| *No meals* ✛ *D2.*

$$$
HOTEL

🖭 **Sheraton Vancouver Wall Centre.** This stunning pair of ultramodern glass high-rises is on Downtown's highest ground, which means that the top floors of both towers have unrivaled views of the water, mountains, and city skyline. **Pros:** amazing views from higher floors; extensive spa; dog-friendly packages with beds and treats. **Cons:** "cool" can feel a bit cold; although Downtown, far from the action. Ⓢ *Rooms from: C$275* ✉ *1088 Burrard St., Downtown* ☎ *604/331–1000, 800/663–9255* ⊕ *www.sheratonwallcentre.com* ⤳ *669 rooms, 64 suites* |◯| *No meals* ✛ *D4.*

$$$
HOTEL

🖭 **St. Regis Hotel.** It's the oldest continuously operating hotel in the city, but edgy, modern decor livens up the 1916 boutique property and Canadian artwork and select heritage furnishings gives it a unique sense of place. **Pros:** hot location; in-room wine delivery service; full breakfast and other perks. **Cons:** no views; slow elevator can mean the stairs are faster (plus there is original artwork in the stairwell). Ⓢ *Rooms from: C$239* ✉ *602 Dunsmuir St., Downtown* ☎ *604/681– 1135, 800/770–7929* ⊕ *www.stregishotel.com* ⤳ *50 rooms, 15 suites* |◯| *Breakfast* ✛ *F3.*

$$$
HOTEL

🖭 **Sutton Place Hotel Vancouver.** This refined, European-style hotel has gracious service, elegantly furnished rooms, and a location close to Downtown. **Pros:** terrific lounge bar for romantic trysts; wonderful spa. **Cons:** spa gets booked quickly; expensive parking. Ⓢ *Rooms from:*

C$289 ✉ 845 Burrard St., Downtown ☎ 604/682–5511, 800/961–7555 🌐 www.vancouver.suttonplace.com 🛏 350 rooms, 46 suites, 164 apartments 🍴 No meals ✥ E3.

$$$ HOTEL 🏨 **Vancouver Marriott Pinnacle Downtown Hotel.** Close to the cruise ship terminal and midway between the central business district and Stanley Park, the Marriott Pinnacle is an appealing large-scale hotel with stunning views—once you get past the rather jumbled welcome of the atrium lobby trying to be all things from sports lounge to registration area. **Pros:** accessible to financial and shopping districts; walking distance to Stanley Park. **Cons:** rooms sometimes not available until 4 pm; generic decor; pricey parking. [$] *Rooms from: C$299 ✉ 1128 W. Hastings St., Downtown ☎ 604/684–1128, 800/207–4150 🌐 www.vancouvermarriottpinnacle.com 🛏 432 rooms, 6 suites 🍴 No meals ✥ E2.*

$$ B&B/INN 🏨 **Victorian Hotel.** This handsome boutique hotel, on the edge of Downtown and historic Gastown, is one of Vancouver's best values—note that some rooms have shared bathrooms. **Pros:** nice small-hotel feel; complimentary breakfast; historic atmosphere. **Cons:** take a cab after midnight in this area; some shared bathrooms. [$] *Rooms from: C$179 ✉ 514 Homer St., Downtown ☎ 604/681–6369, 877/681–6369 🌐 www.victorianhotel.ca 🛏 39 rooms, 18 with bath 🍴 Breakfast ✥ F3.*

$$$$ HOTEL Fodor's Choice ★ 🏨 **Wedgewood Hotel and Spa.** A member of the exclusive Relais & Châteaux Group, the lavish, family-owned Wedgewood is all about pampering. **Pros:** personalized service; great location close to shops; Bacchus lounge is a destination in its own right. **Cons:** small size means it books up quickly. [$] *Rooms from: C$365 ✉ 845 Hornby St., Downtown ☎ 604/689–7777, 800/663–0666 🌐 www.wedgewoodhotel.com 🛏 41 rooms, 43 suites 🍴 No meals ✥ E3.*

$$$$ HOTEL 🏨 **Westin Grand Vancouver.** With its dramatic modern design and all-suites layout, the Westin Grand is one of Vancouver's most stylish hotels. **Pros:** walking distance to major theater and stadium events; within three blocks of designer shopping district. **Cons:** escalator access to reception; smallish rooms. [$] *Rooms from: C$315 ✉ 433 Robson St., Downtown ☎ 604/602–1999, 604/602–1999 🌐 www.westingrandvancouver.com 🛏 23 rooms, 184 suites 🍴 No meals ✥ F4.*

$ HOTEL FAMILY 🏨 **YWCA Hotel.** A secure, modern high-rise in the heart of the entertainment district, the YWCA has bright, comfortable rooms—a few big enough to sleep five. **Pros:** clean and friendly; access to fitness center; a terrific alternative to hostels. **Cons:** some shared bathrooms; no on-site restaurant. [$] *Rooms from: C$115 ✉ 733 Beatty St., Downtown ☎ 604/895–5830, 800/663–1424 🌐 www.ywcahotel.com 🛏 155 rooms, 40 with bath 🍴 No meals ✥ F4.*

WEST END

$ HOTEL 🏨 **Barclay Hotel.** The location just steps from great shopping and affordable rates make this three-story building one of the city's best-value pensione-style hotels. **Pros:** great location; spacious rooms. **Cons:** can be noisy; books up quickly. [$] *Rooms from: C$119 ✉ 1348 Robson St., West End ☎ 604/688–8850 🌐 www.barclayhotel.com 🛏 76 rooms, 10 suites 🍴 No meals ✥ D2.*

7

$$ B&B/INN **Barclay House.** If you want to get a feel for living in Vancouver's upscale West End neighborhood, just a few blocks from Stanley Park, book a room at this comfortable B&B. **Pros:** lovely historic building; residential neighborhood; helpful staff. **Cons:** there are a number of steps to climb; not wheelchair accessible. [$] *Rooms from: C$190* ✉ *1351 Barclay St., West End* ☎ *604/605–1351, 800/971–1351* 🌐 *www.barclayhouse.com* 🛏 *6 rooms* 🍴 *Breakfast* ✥ *D2.*

$$ HOTEL **Buchan Hotel.** On a tree-lined residential street a block from Stanley Park, this rather plain looking, 1926 pensione-style hotel is one of Vancouver's best values. **Pros:** quiet neighborhood; close to the beach; airport shuttle a five-minute walk away. **Cons:** parking is limited; some rooms share a bath; no elevator. [$] *Rooms from: C$139* ✉ *1906 Haro St., West End* ☎ *604/685–5354, 800/668–6654* 🌐 *www.buchanhotel.com* 🛏 *60 rooms, 34 with bath* 🍴 *No meals* ✥ *B1.*

$$$ B&B/INN **English Bay Inn.** Close to Downtown and Stanley Park, this elegantly furnished B&B serves excellent four-course breakfasts. **Pros:** elegant atmosphere; knowledgeable concierge. **Cons:** one too many gilt-edged mirrors; leaded-glass windows make rooms a bit dark. [$] *Rooms from: C$225* ✉ *1968 Comox St., West End* ☎ *604/683–8002, 866/683–8002* 🌐 *www.englishbayinn.com* 🛏 *4 rooms, 2 suites* 🍴 *Breakfast* ✥ *B2.*

$$$ HOTEL **Listel Hotel Vancouver.** Art gallery and accommodations come together in this eco-friendly hotel on one of Vancouver's most vibrant streets. **Pros:** eclectic decor; green attitude; access to Steve Nash Fitness Center. **Cons:** on a busy thoroughfare; art-oriented but not a "design hotel". [$] *Rooms from: C$229* ✉ *1300 Robson St., West End* ☎ *800/663–5491, 800/663–5491* 🌐 *www.thelistelhotel.com* 🛏 *119 rooms, 10 suites* 🍴 *No meals* ✥ *D2.*

$$$ HOTEL FAMILY **Lord Stanley Suites on the Park.** For longer stays, these small but fully equipped suites, in a modern high-rise building at the edge of Stanley Park, are good value. **Pros:** residential neighborhood; good views. **Cons:** small (but bright) fitness room; furnishings bright but a bit plain. [$] *Rooms from: C$205* ✉ *1889 Alberni St., Stanley Park* ☎ *604/688–9299, 888/767–7829* 🌐 *www.lordstanley.com* 🛏 *100 suites* 🍴 *Breakfast* ✥ *C1.*

$$$ B&B/INN **O Canada House B&B.** This beautifully restored 1897 Victorian is home to an elegant but comfortable B&B with fun historical significance: it's where the first version of "O Canada," the country's national anthem, was penned in 1909. **Pros:** gracious service; fantastic breakfast; within walking distance of Downtown. **Cons:** many rooms on the small side; no elevator to the upper rooms. [$] *Rooms from: C$205* ✉ *1114 Barclay St., West End* ☎ *604/688–0555, 877/688–1114* 🌐 *www.ocanadahouse.com* 🛏 *7 rooms* 🍴 *Breakfast* ✥ *D3.*

$$ HOTEL Fodor's Choice ★ **Sylvia Hotel.** This Virginia-creeper-covered 1912 heritage building is continually popular because of its affordable rates and near-perfect location: a stone's throw from the beach on scenic English Bay, two blocks from Stanley Park, and a 20-minute walk from Robson Street. **Pros:** beachfront location; close to restaurants; a good place to mingle with the locals. **Cons:** older building; parking can be difficult; walk to Downtown is slightly uphill. [$] *Rooms from: C$199* ✉ *1154 Gilford*

St., West End ☎ *604/681–9321* 🌐 *www.sylviahotel.com* 🛏 *97 rooms, 22 suites* 🍴 *No meals* ✥ *B2.*

$$$ HOTEL Fodor's Choice ★ 🏨 **Times Square Suites Hotel.** You can't get much closer to Stanley Park than this chic but understated all-suites hotel near plenty of restaurants. **Pros:** next to Stanley Park; good location for restaurants; roof deck for guest use. **Cons:** no concierge; on a very busy intersection. [$] *Rooms from: C$279* ✉ *1821 Robson St., West End* ☎ *604/684–2223, 877/684–2223* 🌐 *www.timessquaresuites.com* 🛏 *42 rooms* 🍴 *No meals* ✥ *C1.*

$$$ B&B/INN 🏨 **West End Guest House.** Built in 1906, this antique-filled Victorian B&B is ideally located a two-minute walk from Robson Street and five minutes from Stanley Park. **Pros:** historic interior; quiet residential location; free use of mountain bikes. **Cons:** furnishings a bit precious; no one-night reservations for some high season dates. [$] *Rooms from: C$205* ✉ *1362 Haro St., West End* ☎ *604/681–2889, 888/546–3327* 🌐 *www.westendguesthouse.com* 🛏 *8 rooms* 🍴 *Breakfast* ✥ *C2.*

$$$$ RESORT 🏨 **Westin Bayshore.** Next to Stanley Park and with the marina on its doorstep, the Westin Bayshore has impressive harbor and mountain views. **Pros:** resort amenities; fabulous water views; great waterside walkways. **Cons:** away from Downtown; conference center draws many business travelers; tower rooms are a long walk from registration. [$] *Rooms from: C$349* ✉ *1601 Bayshore Dr., off Cardero St., West End* ☎ *604/682–3377, 800/627–8634* 🌐 *www.westinbayshore.com* 🛏 *482 rooms, 28 suites* 🍴 *No meals* ✥ *D1.*

7

YALETOWN

$$$ HOTEL 🏨 **Hotel Blu.** A designer blend of comfort, high tech, and, especially, eco-friendly features, Hotel Blu could almost be called "Hotel Green" because of the focus on sustainability. **Pros:** close to theatres and sports arenas; free guest laundry; indoor pool and sauna. **Cons:** only suites and lofts have bathtubs; sports crowds swarm the neighborhood on event days. [$] *Rooms from: C$275* ✉ *177 Robson St., Yaletown* ☎ *604/620-6200* 🌐 *www.hotelbluvancouver.com* 🛏 *75 rooms* 🍴 *No meals* ✥ *F4.*

$$$$ HOTEL Fodor's Choice ★ 🏨 **Opus Vancouver Hotel.** Groundbreakingly trendy when it opened in 2002, the Opus continues to reinvent itself and live up to the motto of being a "place to be not just a place to stay." The design team created a set of on-line fictitious characters, then decorated the rooms to suit each "persona." Guests are matched with room styles using the Lifestyle Concierge. **Pros:** great Yaletown location, right by rapid transit; funky and hip vibe; the lobby bar is a fashionable meeting spot. **Cons:** trendy nightspots nearby can be noisy at night; expensive and limited parking. [$] *Rooms from: C$359* ✉ *322 Davie St., Yaletown* ☎ *604/642–6787, 866/642–6787* 🌐 *www.opushotel.com* 🛏 *85 rooms, 11 suites* 🍴 *No meals* ✥ *E5.*

GRANVILLE ISLAND

$$$ HOTEL 🏨 **Granville Island Hotel.** Granville Island is one of Vancouver's most popular destintaions, for locals and visitors, but unless you've moored up in a houseboat, the only overnight option is the Granville Island Hotel. **Pros:** unique island location; within steps of great dining and theater. **Cons:** island gets crush-busy on weekends; walk or use ferry transit to get here. [$] *Rooms from: C$285* ✉ *1253 Johnston St., Granville Island* ☎ *604/683–7373, 800/663–1840* 🌐 *www.granvilleislandhotel.com* 🛏 *74 rooms, 8 suites* 🍴 *No meals* ✥ *C6.*

GASTOWN

$$ HOTEL 🏨 **Skwachàys Lodge.** Everything about Skwàchays Lodge (pronounced skwatch-eyes), Canada's first Aboriginal arts hotel, celebrates First Nations heritage. **Pros:** unique property; gracious service. **Cons:** showers but no tubs; 10-minute walk to downtown; the neighborhood sometimes attracts transients. [$] *Rooms from: C$189* ✉ *31 Pender St., Gastown* ☎ *604/687–3589* 🌐 *www.skwachays.com* 🛏 *18 rooms* 🍴 *No meals* ✥ *G3.*

WEST SIDE

KITSILANO

$$ B&B/INN Fodor's Choice ★ 🏨 **Corkscrew Inn.** This restored 1912 craftsman-style house near the beach in Kitsilano combines the comforts of a B&B with a quirky tribute to the humble corkscrew: guests are encouraged to explore the small wine paraphernalia museum. **Pros:** great local neighborhood; delicious breakfast. **Cons:** not downtown; a 15-minute bus ride to the Canada Line airport connection. [$] *Rooms from: C$180* ✉ *2735 West 2nd Ave., Kitsilano* ☎ *604/733–7276, 877/737–7276* 🌐 *www.corkscrewinn.com* 🛏 *5 rooms* 🍴 *Breakfast* ✥ *A5.*

SOUTH GRANVILLE

$$$ B&B/INN 🏨 **Granville House B&B.** With its elegant but austere furnishings and individual breakfast tables, this Tudor-revival house feels more like a small hotel than a B&B. **Pros:** top-notch service; hot breakfasts. **Cons:** on the neighborhood's main drag; everything is so pristine that you might feel hesitant to muss the linens. [$] *Rooms from: C$235* ✉ *5050 Granville St., South Granville* ☎ *866/739–9002* 🌐 *www.granvillebb.com* 🛏 *4 rooms* 🍴 *Breakfast* ✥ *A5.*

VICTORIA

with Butchart Gardens

WELCOME TO VICTORIA

TOP REASONS TO GO

★ **The journey here:**
Yup, getting here is one of the best things about Victoria. Whether by ferry meandering past the Gulf or San Juan islands, by floatplane (try to travel at least one leg this way), or on a whale-watching boat, getting to Victoria is a memorable experience.

★ **Spend an afternoon at the Butchart Gardens:** Nearly a million annual visitors can't be wrong—these lavish gardens north of town truly live up to the hype.

★ **Tour the Royal British Columbia Museum:** One of Canada's best regional museums warrants repeat visits just to take in the myriad displays and exhibits.

★ **Embark on a whale-watching cruise:** It's an amazing way to view these magnificent animals in the wild.

★ **Traverse the Inner Harbour via a ferry boat:** The tiny foot-passenger ferries zipping across the Inner Harbour afford passengers a new perspective of the city center.

1 **Downtown.** Most of Victoria's shopping and sightseeing are in and around the Inner Harbour and along Government Street.

2 **Vic West.** Vic West is just across the bridge from Downtown.

3 **Fernwood.** This charming urban village is northeast of Downtown.

4 **Oak Bay.** East of Downtown, it's the oldest village in Victoria.

5 **Rockland.** With B&Bs and Craigdarroch Castle, this shaded village is also a tourist magnet.

6 **Fairfield.** This quiet residential area is home to the popular Abkhazi Garden.

7 **Saanich.** The southernmost town on the Saanich Peninsula is at the base of Mount Douglas.

8 **Brentwood Bay.** BC ferries sail from this tiny village that is also home to Butchart Gardens.

9 **Sidney.** The pleasant town filled with bookshops is home to the Washington State Ferry Terminal, and the airport is just to the west.

10 **The West Shore.** Wilderness parks, viewpoints, and historic sites—including Hatley Castle and Fort Rodd Hill—encourage exploration.

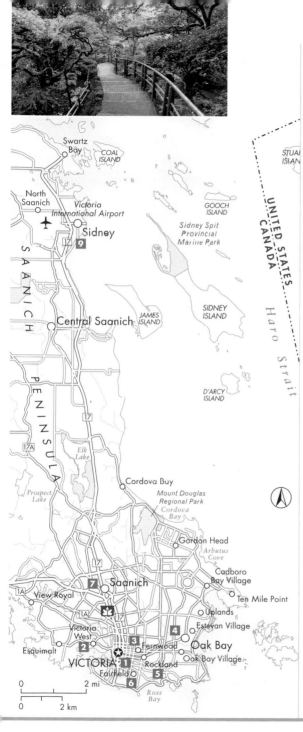

British
Columbia

GETTING ORIENTED

Victoria's iconic buildings are clustered around the Inner Harbour. To the south is Dallas Road, which runs along the shore of Juan de Fuca Strait. A short walk north along shop-lined Government Street leads to several historic neighbor-hoods, which are collec-tively called Old Town. The Johnson Street Bridge, which separates the Inner Harbour from the Upper Harbour, leads to the waterfront walk-ways of Vic West. About a mile east of Downtown are the gardens and mansions of Rockland, Fairfield, and Oak Bay, the city's older residential districts. Running parallel to Government Street are Blanshard Street, which becomes Highway 17 and leads to the Saanich Peninsula, and Douglas Street, which leads to Highway 1 and the rest of Vancouver Island.

8

Updated
By Sue
Kernaghan

Victoria, British Columbia's photogenic capital, is a walkable, livable seaside city of fragrant gardens, waterfront paths, engaging museums, and beautifully restored 19th-century architecture. In summer, the Inner Harbour—Victoria's social and cultural center—buzzes with visiting yachts, horse-and-carriage rides, street entertainers, and excursion boats heading out to visit pods of friendly local whales. Yes, it might be a bit touristy, but Victoria's good looks, gracious pace, and manageable size are instantly beguiling, especially if you stand back to admire the mountains and ocean beyond.

At the southern tip of Vancouver Island, Victoria dips slightly below the 49th parallel. That puts it farther south than most of Canada, giving it the mildest climate in the country, with virtually no snow and less than half the rain of Vancouver.

The city's geography, or at least its place names, can cause confusion. Just to clarify: the city of Victoria is on Vancouver Island (not Victoria Island). The city of Vancouver is on the British Columbia mainland, not on Vancouver Island. At any rate, the city of Vancouver didn't even exist in 1843 when Victoria, then called Fort Victoria, was founded as the westernmost trading post of the British-owned Hudson's Bay Company.

Victoria was the first European settlement on Vancouver Island, and in 1868 it became the capital of British Columbia. The British weren't here alone, of course. The local First Nations people—the Songhees, the Saanich, and the Sooke—had already lived in the area for thousands of years before anyone else arrived. Their art and culture are visible throughout southern Vancouver Island. You can see this in private and public galleries, in the totems at Thunderbird Park, and in the striking collections at the Royal British Columbia Museum. Spanish explorers were the first foreigners to explore the area, although they left little more than place names (Galiano Island and Cordova Bay, for example). The thousands of Chinese immigrants drawn by the gold rushes of the late 19th century had a much greater impact, founding Canada's oldest Chinatown and adding an Asian influence that's still quite pronounced in Victoria's multicultural mix.

Despite its role as the provincial capital, Victoria was largely eclipsed, economically, by Vancouver throughout the 20th century. This, as it turns out, was all to the good, helping to preserve Victoria's historic downtown and keeping the city largely free of skyscrapers and highways. For much of the 20th century, Victoria was marketed to tourists as "The Most British City in Canada," and it still has more than its share of Anglo-themed pubs, tea shops, and double-decker buses. These days, however, Victorians prefer to celebrate their combined indigenous, Asian, and European heritage, and the city's stunning wilderness backdrop. Locals do often venture out for afternoon tea, but they're just as likely to nosh on dim sum or tapas. Decades-old shops sell imported linens and tweeds, but newer upstarts offer local designs in hemp and organic cotton. And let's not forget that fabric prevalent among locals: Gore-Tex. The outdoors is ever present here. You can hike, bike, kayak, sail, or whale-watch straight from the city center, and forests, beaches, offshore islands, and wilderness parklands lie just minutes away. A little farther afield, there's surfing near Sooke, wine touring in the Cowichan Valley, and kayaking among the Gulf Islands. ⇨ *For more information, see the Vancouver Island chapter.*

PLANNING

WHEN TO GO

Victoria has the warmest, mildest climate in Canada: snow is rare and flowers bloom in February. Summers are mild, too, rarely topping 75°F. If you're here for dining, shopping, and museums, winter is a perfectly nice time for a visit: it's gray and wet, and some minor attractions are closed, but hotel deals abound. If your focus is the outdoors—biking, hiking, gardens, and whale-watching—you need to come with everyone else, between May and October. That's when the streets come to life with crafts stalls, street entertainers, blooming gardens, and the inevitable tour buses. It's fun and busy but Victoria never gets unbearably crowded.

MAKING THE MOST OF YOUR TIME

You can see most of the sights in Downtown Victoria's compact core in a day, although there's enough to see at the main museums to easily fill two days. You can save time by pre-booking tea at the Empress Hotel and buying tickets online for the Royal British Columbia Museum.

You should also save at least half a day or a full evening to visit Butchart Gardens. The least busy times are first thing in the morning, or on weekdays in the late afternoon and early evening; the busiest but most entertaining time is during the Saturday-evening fireworks shows. If you have a car, you can make a day of it visiting the nearby town of Sidney and some of the Saanich Peninsula wineries.

An extra day allows for some time on the water, either on a whale-watching trip—it's fairly easy to spot orcas in the area during summer—or on a Harbour Ferries tour, with stops for tea at Point Ellice House, a microbrew at Spinnakers Brewpub, or fish-and-chips at Fisherman's Wharf. You can also explore the shoreline on foot, following all, or part, of the 7-mile waterfront walkway.

With more time, you can explore some of the outlying neighborhoods; visit the Art Gallery of Greater Victoria, Craigdarroch Castle, or the delightful Abkhazi Gardens in the Oak Bay and Rockland areas; or head west to see Hatley Park and Fort Rodd Hill.

Although Victoria gets less rain than Vancouver, you still see a fair amount of moisture, so if you get a fine day, set it aside for garden touring, whale-watching, kayaking, or cycling. Car-free bike paths run north to Sidney and west to Sooke.

If you're here for a while and have a car (or really enjoy cycling), the wineries of the Cowichan Valley and the beaches past Sooke warrant a full day each, although it is possible to see both the Southwest Coast and the Cowichan Valley in a one-day circle tour from Victoria. Salt Spring Island can be done as a day trip (market Saturdays are a highlight), though ferry schedules mean that the other islands usually require an overnight. Be warned, though: many people have planned day trips to the islands and ended up staying for years. ⇨ *See Vancouver Island for details about these trips, and more.*

FESTIVALS

Victoria's top festivals take place in summer, when you're also apt to encounter the best weather. For 10 nights in late June, international musicians perform during JazzFest International. July brings the week-long International Buskers Festival, and in early August, during Symphony Splash, the Victoria Symphony plays a free outdoor concert from a barge moored in the middle of Victoria's Inner Harbour. August and September is the time for the Victoria Fringe Theatre Festival, when you can feast from a vast menu of offbeat, original, and intriguing performances around town.

Art of the Cocktail Festival. It's not only wine drinkers who can enjoy festival fun. Victoria's annual cocktail party includes tastings, workshops, and other sipping and supping events every October. ☎ *250/389–0444* ⊕ *www.artofthecocktail.ca.*

Taste: Victoria's Festival of Food and Wine. Victoria's annual food and wine fest brings a wealth of local food and wine producers, tastings, and events to town every July. ⊕ *www.victoriataste.com.*

GETTING HERE AND AROUND

It's easy to visit Victoria without a car. Most sights, restaurants, and hotels are in the compact walkable core, with bikes, ferries, horse-drawn carriages, double-decker buses, step-on tour buses, taxis, and pedicabs on hand to fill the gaps. For sights outside the core—Butchart Gardens, Hatley Castle, Scenic Marine Drive—tour buses are your best bet if you don't have your own vehicle.

Bike paths lace Downtown and run along much of Victoria's waterfront, and long-haul car-free paths run to the ferry terminals and as far west as Sooke. Most buses and ferries carry bikes.

AIR TRAVEL

Air Canada, Pacific Coastal Airlines, and WestJet fly to Victoria from Vancouver International Airport. Alaska Airlines (under its Horizon Air division) flies between Seattle and Victoria.

Victoria International Airport is 25 km (15 miles) north of downtown Victoria. The flight from Vancouver to Victoria takes about 25 minutes. To make the 30-minute drive from the airport to Downtown, take Highway 17 south. A taxi is about C$55. The YYJ Airport Shuttle bus service drops off passengers at most major hotels. The one-way fare is C$24. By public transit, take BC Transit Bus #83, #86, or #88 to the McTavish Exchange, where you transfer to Bus #70, which will take you to downtown Victoria. The one-way fare is C$2.50.

There is floatplane service to Victoria's Inner Harbour in downtown Victoria with Harbour Air Seaplanes. Harbour Air also flies from Whistler to downtown Victoria, May–September. Kenmore Air has daily floatplane service from Seattle to Victoria's Inner Harbour. Helijet has helicopter service from downtown Vancouver and Vancouver International Airport to downtown Victoria. ⇨ *See Air Travel in Travel Smart for contact information for all of these companies.*

Contacts YYJ Airport Shuttle. ☎ *778/351-1995, 855/351-4995* ⊕ *www.yyjairportshuttle.com.*

BOAT AND FERRY TRAVEL

BC Ferries has daily service between Tsawwassen, about an hour south of Vancouver, and Swartz Bay, at the end of Highway 17 (the Patricia Bay Highway), about 30 minutes north of Victoria. Sailing time is about 1½ hours. Fares are C$16.25 per adult passenger and C$53.25 per vehicle each way. Vehicle reservations on Vancouver–Victoria and Nanaimo routes are optional and cost an additional C$15 to C$22. Foot passengers and cyclists don't need reservations.

To reach the Tsawwassen ferry terminal from downtown Vancouver, take the Canada Line south to Bridgeport Station and change to Bus #620. In Swartz Bay, BC Transit buses #70 (express) and #72 (local) meet the ferries. However, if you're traveling without a car, it's easier to just take a Pacific Coach Lines bus between downtown Vancouver and downtown Victoria; the bus travels on the ferry.

BC Ferries also sails from Horseshoe Bay, north of Vancouver, to Nanaimo, about two hours north of Victoria—convenient if you're traveling by car from Whistler or Vancouver's north shore to Vancouver Island.

An excellent option combines four hours of whale-watching with travel between Vancouver and Victoria, offered by the Prince of Whales. The 74-passenger boat leaves the Westin Bayshore Hotel in downtown Vancouver daily at 9 am (June–mid-September), arriving in Victoria at 1 pm; there are also departures from Victoria's Inner Harbour at 1:45 pm (one-way C$200). ⇨ *For more information, see Whale Watching in Sports and the Outdoors.*

⇨ *See Boat and Ferry Travel in Travel Smart for full contact details for BC Ferries.*

The Victoria Harbour Ferry serves the Inner Harbour; stops include the Fairmont Empress, Chinatown, Point Ellice House, the Delta Victoria Ocean Pointe Resort, and Fisherman's Wharf. Fares start at C$5. Boats make the rounds every 15 to 20 minutes. They run 10 to 9 from mid-May through mid-September and 11 to 5 from March through mid-May and mid-September to late October. The ferries don't run from November through February. The 45-minute harbor tours cost C$22, and gorge cruises cost C$26. At 10:45 am on summer Sundays, the little ferries perform a water ballet set to classical music in the Inner Harbour.

Contacts Victoria Harbour Ferry. ☏ *250/708–0201* ⊕ *www.victoriaharbourferry.com.*

BUS TRAVEL
Pacific Coach Lines has frequent daily service between Vancouver and Victoria; the bus travels on the ferry. One-way fares are C$40 plus the ferry fare, and reservations are required. BC Transit serves Victoria and around, including the Swartz Bay ferry terminal, Victoria International Airport, the Butchart Gardens, Sidney, and Sooke. A one-way fare is C$2.50 (exact change); an all-day pass is C$5.

TAXI TRAVEL
In Victoria, call Bluebird, Victoria Taxi, or Yellow Cab. Taxi rates in Victoria begin at C$3.40 at pickup and cost about C$1.97 for each kilometer traveled.

Contacts Bluebird Cabs. ☏ *250/382–2222* ⊕ *www.taxicab.com.* **Victoria Taxi.** ☏ *250/383–7111* ⊕ *www.victoriataxi.com.* **Yellow Cab.** ☏ *250/381–2222* ⊕ *www.yellowcabvictoria.com.*

TOUR OPTIONS
AIR TOURS
Harbour Air Seaplanes. In addition to providing air service to the surrounding area, Harbour Air Seaplanes has 20-minute flightseeing tours of Victoria and beyond, starting at C$104. ☏ *250/385–9131, 800/665–0212* ⊕ *www.harbourair.com.*

BOAT TOURS
The best way to see the sights of the Inner and Upper Harbour, and beyond, is by Victoria Harbour Ferry; 45- and 50-minute tours cost C$22 to C$26. Pickle Pub Crawls, at C$15 for stops at four harborside pubs, are a fun option.

BUS TOURS
Big Bus Victoria. Big Bus has narrated tours on open-top and trolley-style buses between April and October; you can get on and off at any of the 22 stops. You can buy a two-day ticket on board for C$37, but buy online and you get a third day free. ☏ *250/389–2229, 888/434–2229* ⊕ *www.victoria.bigbusinternational.com.*

CVS Cruise Victoria. CVS Cruise Victoria runs a shuttle to Butchart Gardens, with departures from the Fairmont Empress (there's a ticket office in front of the hotel) and from several other Downtown hotels; the

C$55 round-trip fare includes entrance to the gardens. ☎ *250/386–8652, 877/578-5552* ⊕ *www.cvscruisevictoria.com.*

Gray Line. Gray Line's hop on, hop off double decker bus tours run May to mid-October and make 14 stops around town; tickets are C$32 for one day, C$40 for two. From mid-June through September, Gray Line's Butchart Gardens Express shuttle runs several times a day from the Coho ferry terminal and the Fairmont Empress. Round-trip fare is C$58, including admission to the gardens. ☎ *250/385–6553* ⊕ *www.sightseeingvictoria.com.*

FAMILY **Victoria Hippo Tours.** These 40-passenger amphibious vehicles tour the city, then slip into the harbor for a water-borne tour. Ninety-minute tours run daily from May to September. They leave on the hour from 11 to 5 from just outside the Black Ball Ferry Line Terminal. ✉ *Black Ball Ferry Line Terminal, 470 Belleville St.* ☎ *250/590–5290, 855/884-4776* ⊕ *www.victoriahippotours.com* ⌨ *From C$43.*

CARRIAGE TOURS
Tally-Ho Carriage Tours. See Victoria from a horse-drawn carriage. Tours range from a 15-minute ride for C$55 to a 100-minute romance tour for C$250. Carriages seat up to six people and prices are per carriage. Tours leave from the corner of Belleville and Menzies streets, next to the Parliament buildings. ☎ *250/514–9257, 866/383–5067* ⊕ *www.tallyhotours.com.*

Victoria Carriage Tours. Horse-drawn carriage rides for up to six people range from a half-hour seaside tour for C$100 to a 90-minute city tour for C$225; prices are per carriage. You can find them parked at Belleville and Menzies streets next to the Parliament buildings. ☎ *250/383–2207, 877/663–2207* ⊕ *www.victoriacarriage.com.*

FOOD AND WINE TOURS
Travel With Taste. On the first and third Saturdays of the month (June–September), Travel with Taste leads culinary tours of Victoria with a tea tasting, a wine tasting, and a chance to try artisanal delicacies. The company also runs day and multiday trips to the Cowichan Valley, Saanich Peninsula, Sooke, and Salt Spring Island. ☎ *250/385–1527* ⊕ *www.travelwithtaste.com.*

Vancouver Island Wine Tours. Vancouver Island Wine Tours will take you to the Cowichan Valley or Saanich Peninsula. ☎ *250/661–8844* ⊕ *www.vancouverislandwinetours.com.*

WALKING TOURS
Discover the Past Tours. Discover the Past Tours offers historic walking tours, Ghostly Walks, and Chinatown Tours. ☎ *250/384–6698* ⊕ *www.discoverthepast.com.*

Victorian Garden Tours. Victorian Garden Tours takes you to private and public gardens. ☎ *250/380–2797* ⊕ *www.victoriangardentours.com.*

VISITOR INFORMATION
Contacts Tourism Victoria Visitor Centre. ☎ *250/953–2033, 800/663–3883* ⊕ *www.tourismvictoria.com.*

8

EXPLORING

Victoria is small and easily explored. A walk around Downtown, starting with the museums and architectural sights of the Inner Harbour, followed by a stroll up Government Street to the historic areas of Chinatown and Old Town, covers most of the key attractions, though seeing every little interesting thing along the way could easily take two days. Passenger ferries dart across the Inner and Upper harbors to Point Ellice House and Fisherman's Wharf, while more attractions, including Craigdarroch Castle and the Art Gallery of Greater Victoria, lie about a mile east of Downtown in the residential areas of Rockland and Oak Bay. Most visitors also make time for the Butchart Gardens, a stunning exhibition garden 20 minutes by car north on the Saanich Peninsula. Free time is also well spent strolling or biking through Beacon Hill Park and along the Dallas Road waterfront, heading out to such less-visited sights as Hatley Castle and Fort Rodd Hill, or checking out any of the area's beaches, wilderness parks, or wineries.

DOWNTOWN

Home to the vast majority of Victoria's sights, hotels, and eateries, Downtown *is* Victoria for most visitors. At its heart is the Inner Harbour. Busy with yachts, passenger ferries, whale-watching boats, and floatplanes, and framed by such iconic buildings as the Fairmont Empress hotel, this pedestrian-friendly area is busy with horse-and-carriage rides, street entertainers, tour buses, and, yes, tourists—all summer long. The south shore of the harbor, extending to the Dallas Road waterfront and Beacon Hill Park, is known as James Bay. Two key sites, the Parliament Buildings and the Robert Bateman Centre, are here, but if you stroll just a block south, you'll find a peaceful residential district of modest historic homes, and such interesting historic sites as Emily Carr House. North of the Inner Harbour, a straight shot up Government Street leads to some great shopping and to more historic areas: Bastion Square, Market Square, and Chinatown. Founded in 1858, Victoria's Chinatown, along Fisgard Street between Government and Store streets, is the oldest such district in Canada. At just two square blocks, it's much smaller than Vancouver's but still pleasant to stroll through, particularly as hip boutiques and eateries have moved into the district. If you enter from Government Street, you'll pass under the elaborate Gate of Harmonious Interest, made of Taiwanese ceramic tiles and decorative panels.

TOP ATTRACTIONS

Fairmont Empress. Opened in 1908 by the Canadian Pacific Railway, the Empress is one of the grand château-style railroad hotels that grace many Canadian cities. Designed by Francis Rattenbury, who also designed the Parliament Buildings across the way, the solid Edwardian grandeur of the Empress has made it a symbol of the city. The elements that made the hotel an attraction for travelers in the past—old-world architecture, ornate decor, and a commanding view of the Inner Harbour—are still here. Nonguests can reserve ahead for afternoon tea (the dress code is smart casual) in the chandelier-draped Tea Lobby, meet for a curry under

The grand Fairmont Empress Hotel has a commanding position on Victoria's Inner Harbour.

the tiger skin in the Bengal Lounge, enjoy a treatment at the hotel's Willow Stream spa, or sample the superb Pacific Northwest cuisine in the Empress Room. In summer, lunch, snacks, and cocktails are served on the Verandah overlooking the Inner Harbour. ✉ *721 Government St., Downtown* ☎ *250/384–8111, 250/389–2727 tea reservations* ⊕ *www.fairmont.com/empress* ✉ *Free; afternoon tea C$59.95.*

Parliament Buildings. Officially the British Columbia Provincial Legislative Assembly Buildings, these massive stone structures are more popularly referred to as the Parliament Buildings. Designed by Francis Rattenbury (who also designed the Fairmont Empress Hotel) when he was just 25 years old, and completed in 1897, they dominate the Inner Harbour. Atop the central dome is a gilded statue of Captain George Vancouver (1757–98), the first European to sail around Vancouver Island. A statue of Queen Victoria (1819–1901) reigns over the front of the complex. More than 3,300 lights outline the buildings at night. The interior is lavishly done with stained-glass windows, gilt moldings, and historic photographs, and in summer actors play historic figures from BC's past. When the legislature is in session, you can sit in the public gallery and watch British Columbia's democracy at work (custom has the opposing parties sitting 2½ sword lengths apart). Free, informative, 30- to 45-minute tours run every 20 to 30 minutes in summer and several times a day in the off-season (less frequently if school groups or private tours are coming through). Tours are obligatory on summer weekends (mid-May until Labor Day) and optional the rest of the time. ✉ *501 Belleville St., James Bay, Downtown* ☎ *250/387–3046* ⊕ *www.leg.bc.ca* ✉ *Free* ☉ *Mid-May–early Sept., daily 9–5; early Sept.–mid-May, weekdays 9–5.*

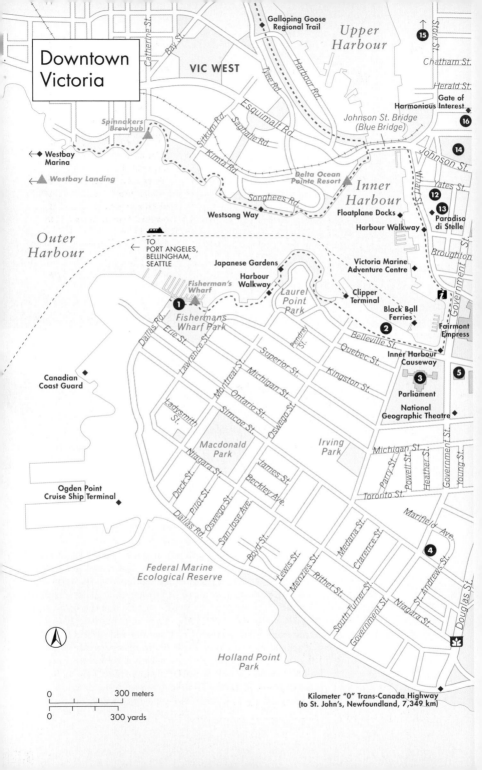

Downtown Victoria

VIC WEST

Upper Harbour

Store St.

Chatham St.

Herald St.

Gate of Harmonious Interest

15

16

Galloping Goose Regional Trail

Catherine St.

Bay St.

Tyee Rd.

Harbour Rd.

Esquimalt Rd.

Sitkum Rd.

Saghalie Rd.

Kimta Rd.

Spinnakers Brewpub

← ◆ Westbay Marina

← ▲ Westbay Landing

Delta Ocean Pointe Resort

Songhees Rd.

Westsong Way

Johnson St. Bridge (Blue Bridge)

Johnson St.

Wharf St.

Yates St.

Inner Harbour

Floatplane Docks ◆

Harbour Walkway

14

12

13

Paradiso di Stelle

Broughton St.

Outer Harbour

TO PORT ANGELES, BELLINGHAM, SEATTLE

Japanese Gardens

Harbour Walkway

Fisherman's Wharf

1

Fishermans Wharf Park

Laurel Point Park

Victoria Marine Adventure Centre

Clipper Terminal

Black Ball Ferries

2

Fairmont Empress

Inner Harbour Causeway

Government St.

Dallas Rd.

Erie St.

Lawrence St.

Montreal St.

Superior St.

Pendray St.

Belleville St.

Quebec St.

Kingston St.

3

Parliament

5

National Geographic Theatre

Canadian Coast Guard

Michigan St.

Ontario St.

Oswego St.

Simcoe St.

Ladysmith St.

Macdonald Park

Niagara St.

James St.

Beckley Ave.

Irving Park

Michigan St.

Parry St.

Powell St.

Heather St.

Government St.

Young St.

Ogden Point Cruise Ship Terminal

Dock St.

Pilot St.

Oswego St.

San Jose Ave.

Toronto St.

Marifield Ave.

Boyd St.

Lewis St.

Menzies St.

Rithet St.

Medana St.

Clarence St.

South Turner St.

Government St.

Niagara St.

Andrews St.

Douglas St.

4

Federal Marine Ecological Reserve

Holland Point Park

0 ——— 300 meters

0 ——— 300 yards

Kilometer "0" Trans-Canada Highway (to St. John's, Newfoundland, 7,349 km)

KEY

🛈 *Visitor Information Centre*

🍁 *Trans-Canada Hwy.*

⛴ *Ferry*

- - - - *Pedestrian trail*

▲ *Harbour Ferries*

The Robert Bateman Centre. Opened in 2013 in a historic waterfront structure, this gallery displays more than 100 works—from etchings to paintings—spanning seven decades in the career of Canada's best-known wildlife artist. The building, Victoria's original steamship terminal, is also home to a waterfront restaurant and a shop selling high-end local art. Proceeds from gallery admissions go to support the Bateman Foundation's conservation work. ⊠ *470 Belleville St., James Bay, Downtown* ☎ *250/940–3630* ⊕ *batemancentre.org* ☞ *C$12.50* ☾ *Tues.–Sun. 10–5.*

Fodor's Choice   **Royal British Columbia Museum.** This excellent museum, one of Victoria's
★   leading attractions, traces several thousand years of British Columbian
FAMILY   history. Especially strong is its First Peoples Gallery, home to a genuine Kwakwaka'wakw big house and a dramatically displayed collection of masks and other artifacts. A new exhibit about First Nations languages opened in 2014. The Natural History Gallery traces BC's landscapes, from prehistory to modern-day climate change, in realistic dioramas. An Ocean Station exhibit gets kids involved in running a Jules Verne–style submarine. In the History Gallery, a replica of Captain Vancouver's HMS *Discovery* creaks convincingly, and a re-created frontier town comes to life with cobbled streets, silent movies, and the rumble of an arriving train. An IMAX theater presents films on a six-story-tall screen. Optional one-hour tours, included in the admission price, run roughly twice a day in summer and less frequently in winter. Most focus on a particular gallery, though the 90-minute Highlights Tour touches on all galleries. Special exhibits, usually held between mid-May and mid-November, attract crowds despite the higher admission prices. You can skip (sometimes very long) ticket lines by booking online. The museum complex has several more interesting sights, beyond the expected gift shop and café. In front of the museum, at Government and Belleville streets, is the **Netherlands Centennial Carillon.** With 62 bells, it's the largest bell tower in Canada; the Westminster chimes ring out every hour, and free recitals are occasionally held on Sunday afternoons. Behind the main building, bordering Douglas Street, are the grassy lawns of **Thunderbird Park**, home to 10 totem poles (carved replicas of originals that are preserved in the museum). One of the oldest houses in BC, **Helmcken House** (*open late May–early Sept., daily noon–4*) was built in 1852 for pioneer doctor and statesman John Sebastian Helmcken. Inside are displays of the family's belongings, including the doctor's medical tools. Behind it is **St. Ann's School House,** built in 1858. One of British Columbia's oldest schools, it is thought to be Victoria's oldest building still standing. Both buildings are part of the Royal British Columbia Museum. ⊠ *675 Belleville St., Downtown* ☎ *250/356–7226, 888/447–7977 Museum, 877/480–4887 IMAX Theater* ⊕ *www.royalbcmuseum.bc.ca* ☞ *C$21.60, IMAX theater C$11.80; combination ticket C$31.40* ☾ *Daily 9–5.*

WORTH NOTING

Bastion Square. James Douglas, the former colonial governor for whom Douglas Street was named, chose this spot for the original Fort Victoria and Hudson's Bay Company trading post in 1843. In summer the square comes alive with street performers, crafts vendors, and a

The wooly mammoth at the Royal British Columbia Museum

weekly farmers' market. The former courthouse houses the Maritime Museum of British Columbia. ⊠ *Off Wharf St., at View St., Downtown* ☎ *250/885–1387* ⊕ *www.bastionsquare.ca.*

NEED A BREAK?

Paradiso di Stelle. You might be tempted to dismiss Paradiso di Stelle, with its busy patio and prime Bastion Square location, as a bit of a tourist trap. True, it's popular, but the service is quick and friendly, and the authentic Italian coffee, house-made gelato, paninis, and pastas are excellent. A water-view and people-watching table right in the action of Bastion Square is irresistible on a summer day. ⊠ *10 Bastion Sq., Downtown* ☎ *250/920–7266.*

FAMILY **Beacon Hill Park.** This 154-acre park links downtown Victoria to the waterfront. Its rambling lawns overlook the Pacific Ocean, the Olympic Mountains, and the Strait of Juan de Fuca. Kite-fliers, hang gliders, and dog walkers are numerous. Take your photo at the Mile 0 marker of the Trans-Canada Highway, at the foot of Douglas Street. Beacon Hill includes ponds where you can feed ducks, jogging and walking paths, flowers and gardens, a cricket pitch, and a petting zoo (open daily 10–4). There's live music in the bandshell on summer evenings, and on Saturday nights in August the Victoria Film Festival screens free movies. ⊠ *Bordered by Douglas St., Southgate St., and Cook St., Downtown* ☎ *250/361–0600* ⊕ *www.victoria.ca* ⊡ *Free.*

Emily Carr House. One of Canada's most celebrated artists and a respected writer, Emily Carr (1871–1945) lived in this extremely proper, wooden Victorian house before she abandoned her middle-class life to live in the

CLOSE UP

Victoria Waterfront on Foot

You can walk most of the way around Victoria's waterfront from Westbay Marina on the Outer Harbour's north shore, to Ross Bay on the Strait of Juan de Fuca. The entire 7-mile route takes several hours, but it passes many of the city's sights and great scenery. Waterfront pubs and cafés supply sustenance; ferries and buses offer transport as needed. A new bridge should replace the Johnson Street Bridge by late 2015.

Begin with a ride on Harbour Ferries to Westbay Marina, the start of Westsong Way. This 2-mile pedestrian path follows the Vic West waterfront to the Johnson Street Bridge. The views across the harbor are rewarding, as is a stop at the waterfront Spinnakers Brewpub. Harbour Ferries stop at Spinnakers and at the Delta Ocean Pointe Resort, so you can choose to start from either point.

Once across the bridge, you can detour to Chinatown and Market Square, turn right and head south on Wharf Street towards the Inner Harbour, or turn right again at Yates (a "Downtown Walk" sign shows the way) and follow the waterfront. The route runs past floatplane docks and whale-watching outfitters to the Inner Harbour Causeway. Snack options en route include fish tacos at Red Fish, Blue Fish—a waterfront take-out spot—or burgers and fish-and-chips at The Flying Otter—a café floating at the seaplane dock. Starting from the Visitor Information Centre, this waterfront walkway—busy all summer with street entertainers and crafts and snack vendors—curves around the Inner Harbour. It's only about a quarter-mile around, but the walk could take a while if you stop to watch all the torch jugglers and caricature artists. The Fairmont Empress, the Royal BC Museum, and the Parliament Buildings are all here—just across the road from the water.

Detour along Belleville Street past the ferry terminals and pick the path up where it enters Laurel Point Park just past the Clipper terminal. From here, the route leads through the pretty waterfront park and past a marina to Fisherman's Wharf, where you can stop for fish-and-chips on the dock or grab a ferry back downtown. To keep going, follow Dallas Road to the Ogden Point Cruise Ship terminal, where you can walk out on the breakwater for a view of the ships or grab a snack on the ocean-view deck at the Ogden Point Café.

You're now on the shore of Juan de Fuca Strait, where a footpath—the Dallas Road Waterfront Trail—runs another four miles along clifftops past Beacon Hill Park to the historic cemetery at Ross Bay. Dog walkers, joggers, and kite flyers are usually out in force on the grassy clifftop; stairways lead down to pebbly beaches. A hike north through Beacon Hill Park will get you back downtown. You can also do this route by bike, though you'll have to follow the streets running parallel to the waterfront, as most of the pathway is pedestrian-only. The ride along Dallas Road and through Beacon Hill Park has the least traffic.

wilds of British Columbia. Carr's own descriptions, from her autobiography *Book of Small*, were used to restore the house. Art on display includes reproductions of Carr's work—visit the Art Gallery of Greater Victoria or the Vancouver Art Gallery to see the originals. ⊠ *207 Government St., James Bay, Downtown* ☎ *250/383–5843* ⊕ *www.emilycarr. com* ✉ *C$6.75* ⊘ *May–Sept., Tues.–Sat. 11–4.*

Fan Tan Alley. Mah-jongg, fan-tan, and dominoes were games of chance played on Fan Tan Alley, said to be the narrowest street in Canada. Once the gambling and opium center of Chinatown, it's now lined with offbeat shops (few of which sell authentic Chinese goods). Look for the alley on the south side of Fisgard Street between nos. 545½ and 549½. ⊠ *South side of Fisgard St., Chinatown, Downtown.*

FAMILY **Fisherman's Wharf.** Victoria Harbour Ferries stops at this fun nautical spot just west of the Inner Harbour. You can watch fishers unload their catches and admire the various vessels, or picnic in the shoreside park. If you stroll the docks and walk among the colorful houseboats, you'll come across several floating shacks where you can buy ice cream, fish tacos, and live crabs, take kayak tours, buy tickets for whale-watching cruises, or join a pirate-themed boat tour. Other booths sell fish to feed the harbor seals who often visit the quay (you can even watch them on the underwater "seal cam"). The busiest vendor is Barb's, an esteemed fish-and-chips spot that is open only in the summer, from May through October. ⊠ *Corner of Dallas Rd. and Erie St., James Bay, Downtown* ⊕ *fishermanswharfvictoria.com.*

Legacy Art Gallery Downtown. Rotating exhibits from the University of Victoria's vast art collection, as well as contemporary installations, are displayed in this airy Downtown space. Shows in the 3,000-square-foot space focus on mostly Canadian works, including many by First Nations artists, but international painters are represented, too. ⊠ *630 Yates St., Downtown* ☎ *250/721–6562* ⊕ *uvac.uvic.ca* ✉ *Free* ⊘ *Wed.–Sat. 10–4.*

FAMILY **Maritime Museum of British Columbia.** In Victoria's original courthouse, these two floors of model ships, weaponry, ships' wheels, and photographs chronicle the province's seafaring history, from its early explorers to whale hunters to pirates. The place isn't as interactive as some museums, but if you have any interest in maritime stuff, it's pretty cool. Among the hand-built boats on display is the *Tilikum*, a dugout canoe that sailed from Victoria to England between 1901 and 1904. On the third floor, the original 1888 vice-admiralty courtroom looks ready for a court-martial. Oh yes, and check out the gilded elevator. ⊠ *28 Bastion Sq., Downtown* ☎ *250/385–4222* ⊕ *www.mmbc.bc.ca* ✉ *C$12* ⊘ *Daily 10–5.*

Market Square. During the late 19th century, this three-level square provided everything a sailor, miner, or lumberjack could want. Restored to its original brick-and-beam architectural character, it's now a pedestrian-only hangout lined with cafés and boutiques. Shops sell gifts, jewelry, and local art. In the summer, watch for open-air art shows, a flea market, and street entertainers. ⊠ *560 Johnson St., Downtown* ☎ *250/386–2441* ⊕ *www.marketsquare.ca* ✉ *Free* ⊘ *Mon.–Sat. 10–5, Sun. 11–4.*

8

FAMILY   **Miniature World.** At this charmingly retro attraction, more than 85 miniature dioramas—including space, castle, and fairy-tale scenes, and one of the world's largest model railways—are housed in kid-height glass cases with recorded narration. The level of detail is impressive in the models, some of which date to the site's 1969 opening. Some of the models are animated, and you can start and stop trains and turn dollhouse lights on and off with push buttons. Most people walk through in 30 minutes, but dollhouse collectors, model-train builders, and preschoolers can be absorbed for hours. ⊠ *Fairmont Empress Hotel, 649 Humboldt St., Downtown* ☎ *250/385–9731* ⊕ *www.miniatureworld.com* ⊠ *C$12* ⊙ *Mid-May–mid-Sept., daily 9–9; mid-Sept.–mid-May, daily 9–5.*

Point Ellice House. The O'Reilly family home, an 1861 Italianate cottage overlooking the Selkirk Waterway, has been restored to its original splendor, with the largest collection of Victorian furnishings in western Canada. You can take a half-hour audio tour of the house (presented from a servant's point of view) and stroll in the English country garden. Point Ellice House is only a few minutes' drive north of downtown Victoria, but it's in an industrial area, so it's more fun to come by sea. Victoria Harbour Ferries leave from a dock in front of the Fairmont Empress; the trip lasts about 15 minutes and takes in the sights of the harbor. Tea and fresh-baked goodies are served under an awning on the lawn daily from 11 to 2:30 when the house is open. ⊠ *2616 Pleasant St., Downtown* ☎ *250/380–6506* ⊕ *www.pointellicehouse.ca* ⊠ *C$6* ⊙ *Early May–early Sept., Thurs.–Mon. 11–4.*

St. Ann's Academy National Historic Site. This former convent and school, founded in 1858, played a central role in British Columbia's pioneer life. The academy's little chapel—the first Roman Catholic cathedral in Victoria—has been restored to look just as it did in the 1920s. The 6-acre grounds, with their fruit trees and herb and flower gardens, have also been restored as historic landscapes. ⊠ *835 Humboldt St., Downtown* ☎ *250/953–8829* ⊕ *www.stannsacademy.com* ⊠ *By donation* ⊙ *Mid-May–early Sept., daily 10–4; early Sept.–mid-May, Thurs.–Sun. 1–4.*

FAMILY   **Victoria Bug Zoo.** Local kids clamor to visit this offbeat minizoo, home to the largest collection in North America of live tropical insects. You can even hold many of the 70 or so varieties, which include walking sticks, scorpions, millipedes, and a pharnacia—at 22 inches, the world's longest insect. The staff members know their bug lore and are happy to dispense scientific information and fun entomological anecdotes. ⊠ *631 Courtney St., Downtown* ☎ *250/384–2847* ⊕ *www.bugzoo.com* ⊠ *C$10* ⊙ *Mon.–Sat. 10:30–5:30, Sun. 11–5.*

Victoria Public Market at the Hudson. Planning a picnic? Stop here first. Bakers and butchers, pie makers, green grocers, cheesemakers, spice mongers, and other artisanal producers from across Vancouver Island sell their wares in this lofty, century-old indoor space that was once a department store. Ready-to-eat treats abound here, from homemade pies and fresh baked bread to tacos, sandwiches, and fish-and-chips. For even more organic, home-grown goodies, time your visit for a Wednesday, when a farmers' market runs from 11 to 3. ⊠ *1701 Douglas St., #6, Downtown* ☎ *778/433–2787* ⊕ *www.victoriapublicmarket.com* ⊠ *Free* ⊙ *Tues.–Sat. 9:30–6:30, Sun. 9:30–5.*

VIC WEST

Close to Downtown—just across the Johnson Street Bridge—lies the residential neighborhood of Victoria West, or Vic West. Bordered by the Outer and Upper harbors, it's home to the Westsong Way seaside walking path, the Galloping Goose Trail (a long-distance hiking and biking path), and a brace of waterfront eateries warranting a trip across the bridge.

GETTING HERE AND AROUND

The main attractions in Vic West are a short stroll across the Johnson Street Bridge, or you could take Bus #6 from the corner of Government and Johnson.

FERNWOOD

Fernwood Square, at Gladstone and Fernwood roads, is framed by historic buildings housing independent galleries and cafés, as well as the Belfry Theatre, a contemporary theater housed in an 1891 church. The square lies at the heart of one of Victoria's most charming urban villages, popular with artists and young families.

GETTING HERE AND AROUND

To get here, catch the #22 bus from Fort and Douglas streets downtown, or enjoy the pleasant 1½-mile walk along Pandora and up Fernwood Road.

OAK BAY

One of several urban villages around greater Victoria, Oak Bay is probably the oldest and best-known. Described as a place "behind the tweed Curtain" for its adherence to Tudor facades, pubs, and tea shops, this historically British area (with its own mayor and municipal hall) is home to the Penny Farthing Pub, as well as sweet shops, bookstores, galleries, and antiques stores. Several more contemporary boutiques and eateries have moved in, too.

GETTING HERE AND AROUND

Oak Bay Village is oriented around Oak Bay Avenue, between Foul Bay Road and Monterey Avenue. A car or a bike is handy, but not essential, for exploring this area. Big Bus, Gray Line, and other tour companies offer Oak Bay and Marine Drive tours.

By public transit, take Bus #2 to Oak Bay Village (or Bus #2A, which continues to Willows Beach) from Johnson and Douglas streets downtown.

WORTH NOTING

Willows Beach Park. This neighborhood park has a nice sandy beach, a grassy park with a playground, and, this being Oak Bay, a teahouse. ⊠ *Foot of Dalhousie St., Oak Bay.*

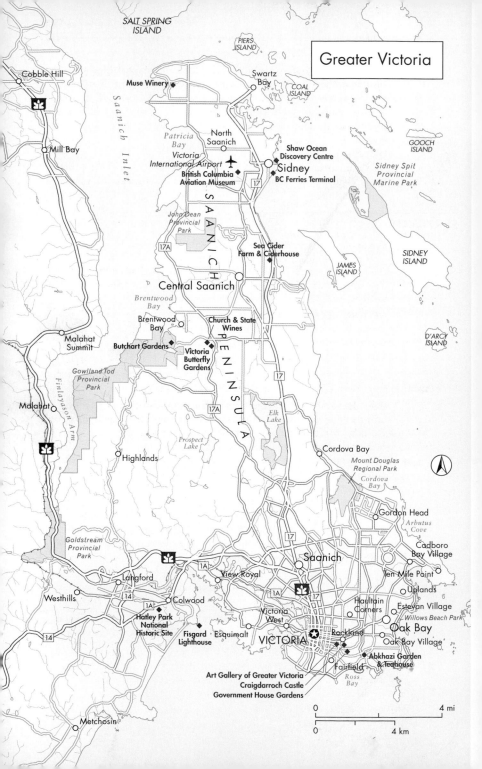

ROCKLAND

The winding, shady streets of Rockland—roughly bordered by Fort Street, Richmond Avenue, Fairfield Road, and the Strait of Juan de Fuca—are lined with beautifully preserved Victorian and Edwardian homes. These include many stunning old mansions now operating as bed-and-breakfasts, and Victoria's most elaborate folly: Craigdarroch Castle. With mansions come gardens, and several of the city's best are found here.

GETTING HERE AND AROUND

By public transit, take Bus #11 or #14 from the corner of Fort and Douglas streets to Moss Street (for the Art Gallery of Greater Victoria), or to Joan Crescent (for Craigdarroch Castle). Government House is a few blocks south. The walk, about a mile past the antiques shops of Fort Street, is also interesting.

TOP ATTRACTIONS

Art Gallery of Greater Victoria. Attached to an 1889 mansion, this modern building houses one of Canada's largest collections of Asian art. The Japanese garden between the buildings is home to the only authentic Shinto shrine in North America. The gallery, a few blocks west of Craigdarroch Castle, displays a permanent exhibition of works by well-known Canadian artist Emily Carr and regularly changing exhibits of Asian and Western art. ⊠ *1040 Moss St., at Fort St., Rockland* ☎ *250/384–4171* ⊕ *www.aggv.ca* ✉ *C$13* ☉ *May–Sept., Mon.–Wed. and Fri.–Sat. 10–5, Thurs. 10–9, Sun. noon–5; Oct.–Apr., Tues.–Wed. and Fri.–Sat. 10–5, Thurs. 10–9, Sun. noon–5.*

Craigdarroch Castle. This resplendent mansion complete with turrets and Gothic rooflines was built as the home of one of British Columbia's wealthiest men, coal baron Robert Dunsmuir, who died in 1889, just a few months before the castle's completion. It's now a museum depicting life in the late 1800s. The castle's 39 rooms have ornate Victorian furnishings, stained-glass windows, carved woodwork, and a beautifully restored painted ceiling in the drawing room. A winding staircase climbs four floors to a tower overlooking Victoria. Castles run in the family: son James went on to build the more lavish Hatley Castle west of Victoria. The castle is not wheelchair accessible and has no elevators. ⊠ *1050 Joan Crescent, Rockland* ☎ *250/592–5323* ⊕ *www.thecastle.ca* ✉ *C$13.95* ☉ *Mid-June–early Sept., daily 9–7; early Sept.–mid-June, daily 10–4:30.*

WORTH NOTING

Government House Gardens. Take a stroll through the walled grounds and 35 acres of formal gardens at Government House, residence of British Columbia's Lieutenant Governor, the Queen's representative in BC. The 19th-century Cary Castle Mews on-site are home to an interpretive center, a costume museum, and a tearoom. The main house is open for guided tours one Saturday a month. ⊠ *1401 Rockland Ave., Rockland* ⊕ *www.ltgov.bc.ca* ✉ *Free* ☉ *Gardens: Daily dawn–dusk. Cary Castle Mews: Mid-May–Sept. Tues.–Sat. 10–4.*

8

FAIRFIELD

Bordered by Beacon Hill Park to the west and Dallas Road, a winding seaside drive to the south, this quiet residential district is home to heritage homes and seaside walks, bike paths, parkland, and Cook Street Village, a tree-lined stretch of cafés, restaurants, and independent shops on the edge of Beacon Hill Park. Moss Street Market is a popular summer weekend event, and Ross Bay Cemetery is a fount of historic information. A seaside path follows the waterfront from Beacon Hill Park to Clover Point Park, offering views across Juan de Fuca Strait to the Olympic Mountains.

GETTING HERE AND AROUND
A useful route is Bus #7: from Johnson and Douglas streets, it travels to Ross Bay Cemetery, Abkhazi Garden, and on to Oak Bay Village. Winding seaside Dallas Road also makes a great bike ride.

TOP ATTRACTIONS
Abkhazi Garden and Teahouse. Called "the garden that love built," this once-private garden is as fascinating for its history as for its innovative design. The seeds were planted, figuratively, in Paris in the 1920s, when Englishwoman Peggy Pemberton-Carter met exiled Georgian Prince Nicholas Abkhazi. World War II internment camps (his in Germany, hers near Shanghai) interrupted their romance, but they reunited and married in Victoria in 1946. They spent the next 40 years together cultivating their garden. Rescued from developers and now operated by the Land Conservancy of British Columbia, the 1-acre site is recognized as a leading example of West Coast horticultural design, resplendent with native Garry Oak trees, Japanese maples, and mature rhododendrons. The teahouse (*www.abkhaziteahouse.com*), in the parlor of the modernist home, serves lunch and afternoon tea until 4 pm. ☒ *1964 Fairfield Rd., Fairfield* ☏ *778/265–6466* ⊕ *www.conservancy.bc.ca* ☒ *C$10* ☺ *May–Sept., daily 11–5; Oct.–Apr., Wed.–Sun., 11–5.*

SAANICH

Saanich is 7 km (4½ miles) north of Victoria on Hwy. 17.

Home to the BC and Washington State ferry terminals as well as the Victoria International Airport is the Saanich Peninsula, with its rolling green hills and small family farms, and its southernmost community is called, simply, Saanich. This is the first part of Vancouver Island that most visitors see. Although it's tempting to head straight for downtown Victoria, 25 minutes to the south, there are many reasons to linger here, including Mt. Douglas, which offers magnificent views of Victoria and the rest of the peninsula on a clear day.

GETTING HERE AND AROUND
To reach the area by car from downtown Victoria, follow the signs for the ferries straight up Highway 17, or take the Scenic Marine Drive starting at Dallas Road and following the coast north. It joins Highway 17 at Royal Oak Drive. Victoria transit buses serve the area, though not frequently. Cyclists can take the Lochside Trail, which runs from Victoria to Sidney, detouring, perhaps, to visit some wineries along the way.

TOP ATTRACTIONS

FAMILY **Mount Douglas Regional Park.** A footpath and a road lead to the 213-meter (758-foot) summit of Mt. Douglas, offering a 360-degree view of Victoria and the Saanich Peninsula. On a clear day, you can even see the Gulf and San Juan islands and the mountains of Washington. The park, known locally as Mt. Doug, is also home to a long sandy beach, evergreen forests, hiking trails, and wildflower meadows. ⊠ *Off Cedar Hill Rd., Saanich* ☎ *250/475–5522* ⊕ *www.saanich.ca* ☑ *Free.*

Sea Cider Farm & Ciderhouse. Traditional ciders, made with apples grown on-site and nearby, are paired with local cheeses, preserves, and other delectables at this Saanich Peninsula ciderhouse. It's open year-round for tours and tastings. ⊠ *2487 Mt. Saint Michael Rd., off Central Saanich Rd.* ☎ *250/544–4824* ⊕ *www.seacider.ca* ☑ *Samples C$3* ⊗ *June–Sept., daily 11–4; Oct.–May, Wed.–Sun. 11–4.*

BRENTWOOD BAY

20 km (12 miles) north of Victoria on Hwy. 17A.

The tiny seaside village of Brentwood Bay is best known as the home of the famous Butchart Gardens. From Brentwood Bay, BC Ferries sail to Mill Bay in the Cowichan Valley, so you don't have to backtrack to Victoria if you're touring the island.

GETTING HERE AND AROUND

If you're not driving, the easiest way to get to Brentwood Bay is on a bus tour. These range from direct shuttles offered by Gray Line and CVS Cruise Victoria, to day trips taking in other Saanich Peninsula sights. Several companies also offer winery tours.

TOP ATTRACTIONS

Fodor'sChoice **Butchart Gardens.** This stunning 55-acre garden and National Historic
★ Site has been drawing visitors since it was started in a limestone quarry in 1904. Highlights include the dramatic 70-foot Ross Fountain, the formal Japanese garden, and the intricate Italian garden complete with a gelato stand. Kids will love the old-fashioned carousel and will likely enjoy the 45-minute mini-boat tours around Tod Inlet. From mid-June to mid-September the gardens are illuminated at night with hundreds of hidden lights. In July and August, jazz, blues, and classical musicians play at an outdoor stage each evening and fireworks draw crowds every Saturday night. The wheelchair- and stroller-accessible site is also home to a seed-and-gift shop, a plant identification center, two restaurants (one offering traditional afternoon tea), and a coffee shop; you can even call ahead for a picnic basket on fireworks nights. To avoid crowds, come at opening time, in the late afternoon or evening (except ultrabusy fireworks Saturday evenings), or between September and June, when the gardens are still stunning and admission rates are reduced. The grounds are especially magical at Christmas, with themed lighting and an ice rink. The gardens are a 20-minute drive north of Downtown; parking is free but fills up on fireworks Saturdays. You can get here by city Bus 75 from Douglas Street in downtown Victoria, but service is slow and infrequent. CVS Cruise Victoria (⊕ *www.cvscruisevictoria.com*; 877/578–5552) runs shuttles

8

from downtown Victoria. ✉ *800 Benvenuto Ave.* ☎ *250/652–5256,
866/652–4422* ⊕ *www.butchartgardens.com* ✑ *C$30.80* ☒ *Mid-
June–Aug., daily 9 am–10 pm; Sept.–mid-June, daily 9 am–dusk*
✑ *Rates are lower between Sept. and mid-June.*

WORTH NOTING

Church and State Wines. A vineyard-view bistro and tasting bar make
this expansive winery a popular stop en route to nearby Butchart Gardens. Pinot Gris and Pinot Noir are grown on-site; several Bordeaux
blends from a sister winery in the Okanagan Valley are also worth
a try. ✉ *1445 Benvenuto Ave.* ☎ *250/652–2671* ⊕ *churchandstatew-
ines.com* ✑ *C$8 for tastings* ☒ *Winery: May–Oct., daily 11–6. Bistro:
Wed.–Sun. 11–3.*

FAMILY **Victoria Butterfly Gardens.** Thousands of butterflies—of up to 70 different species—flutter freely in an indoor tropical garden that's also home
to orchids and carnivorous plants, tropical fish, flamingos, tortoises,
geckos, poison dart frogs, and 30 kinds of free-flying tropical birds.
The butterflies are sourced from a sustainable farm or bred in house
(displays show the whole life cycle) and all the birds, fish, and animals
have been donated or rescued. The site is a popular stop en route to the
Butchart Gardens. Be prepared for tropical temperatures year-round.
✉ *1461 Benvenuto Ave., corner of West Saanich Rd. and Keating
Cross Rd., Brentwood Bay* ☎ *250/652–3822, 877/722–0272* ⊕ *www.
butterflygardens.com* ✑ *C$16* ☒ *Jan.–mid-June and Sept.–Nov., daily
10–5; mid-June–Aug., daily 10–7; Dec., daily 10–6* ✑ *Last admission
1 hr before closing.*

SIDNEY

23 km (14 miles) north of Victoria on Hwy. 17.

Sidney, short for Sidney-by-the-Sea, is an inviting seaside town just 30
minutes north of Victoria. Home to the Washington State Ferry terminal and just five minutes south of the BC Ferries terminal, it's worth
a stop or even a weekend visit. The streets are lined with independent
shops, including a wealth of bookstores—so many, in fact, that Sidney has earned a place as Canada's only official Booktown (⊕ *www.
sidneybooktown.ca*). Sidney's parklike waterfront, which houses a
marine ecology center as well as cafés, restaurants, and a wheelchair-
accessible waterfront path, is a launching point for kayakers, whale-
watchers, and eco-tour boats heading out to explore the Gulf Islands
National Park Reserve offshore.

GETTING HERE AND AROUND

Bus #72, usually a double-decker, serves Sidney and the Swartz Bay
ferry terminal from downtown Victoria. Sidney itself is easily explored
on foot.

TOP ATTRACTIONS

FAMILY **Shaw Ocean Discovery Centre.** A simulated ride underwater in a deep-
sea elevator is just the beginning of a visit to this fun and educational
marine interpretive center. Devoted entirely to the aquatic life and
conservation needs of the Salish Sea—the waters south and east of

Vancouver Island—the small but modern center displays local sea life, including luminous jellyfish, bright purple starfish, wolf eels, rockfish, and octopi. Hands-on activities and touch tanks delight kids, who also love the high-tech effects, including a floor projection that ripples when stepped on and a pop-up tank you can poke your head into. ⊠ *9811 Seaport Pl., Sidney* 🕿 *250/665–7511* ⊕ *www.oceandiscovery. ca* ⌷ *C$15* ⊙ *July–Aug., daily 10–5; Sept.–June daily 10–4.*

NEED A BREAK? **Stonehouse Restaurant.** Not everyone loves ferry food. An option, if you're heading to or from a ferry at the Swartz Bay terminal, is to duck into the Stonehouse for a pint or a home-cooked meal. The tiny stone pub with garden looks like something you'd find in rural England. To find it, follow the signs for Canoe Cove Marina. ⊠ *2215 Canoe Cove Rd.* 🕿 *778/426–1200* ⊕ *www.stonehouserestaurant.ca.*

WORTH NOTING

FAMILY **British Columbia Aviation Museum.** Volunteers passionate about the history of flight have lovingly restored several dozen historic military and civilian airplanes, and even a 1910-era flying machine, at this museum near Victoria's International Airport. A 1957 Vickers Viscount, one of the world's first commercial turbo-prop airliners, a 1970s kit-built helicopter, and a model of Leonardo da Vinci's Ornithopter are among the many aircraft displayed in the museum's two hangars. Tours take about an hour. ⊠ *1910 Norseman Rd., Sidney* 🕿 *250/655–3300* ⊕ *www.bcam.net* ⌷ *C$10* ⊙ *May–Sept., daily 10–4; Oct.–Apr., daily 11–3.*

Muse Winery. At the northern tip of the Saanich Peninsula, Muse Winery specializes in estate-grown Ortega and Pinot Gris varieties; a patio bistro serves lunch on summer weekends. ⊠ *11195 Chalet Rd.* 🕿 *250/656–2552* ⊕ *www.musewinery.ca* ⌷ *Tastings: C$6* ⊙ *Tues.–Sun. 11–5.*

FAMILY **Sidney Spit.** In summer, a passenger ferry, run by Alpine Sidney Spit Ferry (⊕ www.alpinegroup.ca), makes the half-hour trip several times a day to this long stretch of beach on Sidney Island, part of the Gulf Islands National Park Reserve. Hiking trails and picnic sites make for a pleasant day on the island. ⊠ *Sidney* 🕿 *250/474–5145 ferry information, 250/654–4000 park information* ⊕ *www.pc.gc.ca/gulf* ⌷ *Park: free. Ferry: C$19* ⊙ *Ferry: Mid-May–June, weekends; July–early Sept., daily.*

THE WEST SHORE

View Royal is 6.8 km (4.2 miles) west of Victoria on Hwy. 1A; Metchosin is 22 km (13.6 miles) west of Victoria on Hwy. 1A.

West of downtown Victoria, along highways 1 and 14, are the rapidly growing communities of View Royal, Colwood, the Highlands, Langford, and Metchosin, collectively known as the West Shore Communities. Although its rural nature is quickly giving way to suburban development, the area is worth a visit for its wilderness parks and national historic sites.

TOP ATTRACTIONS

FAMILY **Fort Rodd Hill and Fisgard Lighthouse National Historic Sites of Canada.** The world's best-preserved coastal artillery fort (it dates to 1895) and Canada's oldest West Coast lighthouse occupy a parklike backdrop 13 km (8 miles) west of Victoria. You can walk through most of the buildings, including the lighthouse keeper's house, guard houses, and the delightfully named fortress-plotting room. Interactive exhibits in the lighthouse let you navigate a 19th-century schooner. Wandering deer, forest trails, an interpretive nature trail, and historic military hardware share the rolling seaside site, and the views from the gun emplacements over the entrance to Esquimalt Harbour are fabulous. Between mid-May and mid-October you can stay the night in one of five oTENTiks (a cross between a tent and cabin) on-site. Each sleeps six and must be reserved in advance. To get here, take Highway 1A west to Ocean Boulevard. ⊠ *603 Fort Rodd Hill Rd., off Ocean Blvd., West Shore* ☎ *250/478– 5849, 877/737–3783 Cabin reservations* ⊕ *www.pc.gc.ca* ⊠ *Fort C$4; tent cabins C$120 per night* ☉ *Grounds: Daily year-round. Fort and Lighthouse: Mar.–mid-May, Wed.–Sun. 10–5:30; mid-May–mid-Oct., daily 10–5:30; mid-Oct.–Feb., weekends 10–4:30.*

FAMILY **Goldstream Provincial Park.** Eagles, bears, and three species of salmon thrive in this 477-hectare (1,180-acre) wilderness park 16 km (10 miles) north of downtown Victoria. Picnic areas, easy riverside walks, and challenging hikes draw visitors in summer. In winter, a spotting scope is set up in the Goldstream Nature House to watch hundreds of bald eagles gather to feed on salmon. Naturalists provide guidance at the Nature House, a year-round visitor center that's a 10-minute walk from the parking lot. ⊠ *Hwy. 1, at Finlayson Arm Rd., Langford, West Shore* ☎ *250/478–9414* ⊕ *www.env.gov.bc.ca/bcparks* ⊠ *Donations accepted* ☉ *Nature House daily 9–4:30.*

OFF THE
BEATEN
PATH

Hatley Park National Historic Site. Envisioned by James Dunsmuir, a former premier of British Columbia and son of the man who built Craigdarroch Castle, this ivy-draped 40-room manor and its 565 acres of oceanfront grounds make up one of the finest intact Edwardian estates in Canada. Started in 1908 and built in just 18 months, the manor mixes Norman and Renaissance styles, which are meant to suggest a house that had stood for centuries. It's now part of Royal Roads University and the interior of the castle can be seen only by guided tour. The tours are informative, although almost none of the original furnishings—except a billiard table that was too big to remove—remain. You don't need to join a tour to see the beautifully preserved Italian, Japanese, and English rose gardens. To get here, take Highway 1A west from Victoria. Royal Roads University is on your left about half a mile past the turnoff to Fort Rodd Hill. ⊠ *2005 Sooke Rd., Colwood, West Shore* ☎ *250/391–2666, 866/241–0674* ⊕ *www. royalroads.ca/about/explore-hatley-park-castle* ⊠ *Gardens C$9.75; house tours C$18.50* ☉ *Gardens daily 10–5. House tours mid-Apr.– mid-Sept., daily at 10:30, 11:45, 1:30, and 2:45; mid-Sept.–mid-Apr., tour hrs vary and are less frequent.*

Hatley Park's 40-room castle is one of Canada's finest intact Edwardian estates; the gardens are quite spectacular, too.

WHERE TO EAT

Victoria has a tremendous number and variety of restaurants for such a small city; this fact, and the glorious pantry that is Vancouver Island—think local fish, seafood, cheese, and organic fruits and veggies—keeps prices down (at least compared to Vancouver) and standards up. Restaurants in the region are generally casual. Smoking is banned in all public places, including restaurant patios, in Greater Victoria and on the Southern Gulf Islands. Victorians tend to dine early—restaurants get busy at 6 and many kitchens close by 9. Pubs, lounges, and the few open-late places mentioned here are your best options for an after-hours nosh.

Wild salmon, locally made cheeses, Pacific oysters, organic vegetables, local microbrews, and wines from the island's farm-gate wineries (really small wineries are allowed to sell their wines "at the farm gate") are tastes to watch for. Vegetarians and vegans are well catered to in this health-conscious town, and seafood choices go well beyond traditional fish-and-chips. You may notice an "Ocean Wise" symbol on a growing number of menus: this indicates that the restaurant is committed to serving only sustainably harvested fish and seafood.

Some of the city's best casual (and sometimes not-so-casual) fare is served in pubs—particularly in brewpubs; most have an all-ages restaurant as well as an adults-only bar area.

Afternoon tea is a Victoria tradition, as is good coffee—despite the Starbucks invasion, there are plenty of fun and funky local caffeine purveyors around town.

WHAT IT COSTS IN CANADIAN DOLLARS				
	$	**$$**	**$$$**	**$$$$**
Restaurants	under C$13	C$13–C$20	C$21–C$30	over C$30

Prices in the restaurants reviews are the average cost of a main course or equivalent combination of small dishes at dinner or, if dinner is not served, at lunch.

DOWNTOWN

Use the coordinate (⊕ B2) at the end of each listing to locate a site on the corresponding map.

$$$
PACIFIC
NORTHWEST
Fodor'sChoice
★

✕ **Aura.** When an award-winning chef names "imagination" as his most treasured possession, you know the food here is likely to be creative, if not exquisite. The seasonal menu uses primarily local ingredients, revealing Asian influences. Think poached BC salmon paired with barbecued eel and a Japanese rice-cabbage roll; or free-range chicken with a wasabi-pea crust. The wine cellar is full of hard-to-find Vancouver Island wines and Okanagan labels. Sleek lines, warm colors, and waterview windows create a room that's both stylish and cozy. Plus, Aura has the city's best waterfront patio when the weather is cooperative. $ *Average main: C$26* ⊠ *Inn at Laurel Point, 680 Montreal St., James Bay, Downtown* ☎ *250/414–6739* ⊕ *www.aurarestaurant.ca* ⊕ *C4.*

$$
SEAFOOD
FAMILY

✕ **Barb's Fish & Chips.** Funky Barb's, a tin-roofed take-out shack, floats on the quay at Fisherman's Wharf, west of the Inner Harbour off St. Lawrence Street. Halibut, salmon, oysters, mussels, crab, burgers, and chowder are all prepared fresh. The picnic tables on the wharf provide a front-row view of the brightly colored houseboats moored here, or you can carry your food to the grassy park nearby. Ferries sail to Fisherman's Wharf from the Inner Harbour, or you can work up an appetite with a leisurely stroll along the waterfront. $ *Average main: C$13* ⊠ *Fisherman's Wharf, St. Lawrence St., James Bay, Downtown* ☎ *250/384–6515* ⊕ *www.barbsplace.ca* ☉ *Closed Nov.–early Mar.* ⊕ *B4.*

$$
VEGETARIAN

✕ **be love.** A stylish crowd of locals tucks into black bean burgers, sweet potato sandwiches, pad thai, asparagus risotto, and plates piled high with farm-to-fork salads at this chic, bustling Downtown spot. Everything here, from the spring rolls and yam chips to the long list of power juices and smoothies, is free of wheat, gluten, dairy, meat, additives, and processed sugar—but delicious nonetheless. Most ingredients are organic and locally sourced as well, and everything is made from scratch. This is no 1960s throwback, though: the lofty white room and creative cocktails keeps be love firmly rooted in the 21st century. $ *Average main:* ⊠ *1019 Blanshard St., Downtown* ☎ *778/433–7181* ⊕ *beloverestaurant.ca* ⊕ *G4.*

$$
BURGER
FAMILY

✕ **Bin 4 Burger Lounge.** This hip little burger joint elevates the humble patty with local ingredients and naturally raised meats, serving up intriguing burger combos like beef with chipotle-bourbon barbecue

BEST BETS FOR VICTORIA DINING

Fodor's Choice★	Spinnakers Gastro Brewpub, p. 211	**By Experience**
Aura, p. 204		GREAT VIEW
Brasserie l'École , p. 205	**$$$**	**Aura**, p. 204
Café Brio, p. 206	Aura, p. 204	**LURE Restaurant & Bar,** p. 211
Ulla, p. 210	Brasserie L'École , p. 205	**Ulla Restaurant**, p. 210
	Café Brio , p. 206	
By Price	Il Terrazzo, p. 207	
	Ulla Restaurant , p. 210	LOTS OF LOCALS
$		**be love**, p. 204
Pig BBQ Joint, p. 208	**$$$$**	**Mo:Lé**, p. 207
Red Fish Blue Fish, p. 208	Empress Room, p. 206	
	Restaurant Matisse, p. 210	ROMANTIC
$$		**Camille's**, p. 206
be love, p. 204		**Empress Room**, p. 206
Bin 4 Burger Lounge, p. 204		**Il Terrazzo**, p. 207
		Restaurant Matisse, p. 210

sauce, BC–raised bison with aged cheddar and fried onions, or chicken with bacon, Brie, and balsamic red onion jam. Vegetarians can substitute crispy tofu on any sandwich or opt for the "Mr. Bean," a chickpea, black bean, and goat cheese burger. Sandwiches come with excellent fries or salad; ask for half and half, and make sure to sample one of the housemade dips, perhaps roasted garlic aioli or lime-and-tomatillo hot sauce. Kids are welcome, but this fun, lounge-y room, where drink choices include creative cocktails, beer from island microbreweries, and house-made berry iced tea, serves up happy meals for grownups. [$] *Average main: C$14* ✉ *911 Yates St., Downtown* ☎ *250/590–4154* ⊕ *www.bin4burgerlounge.com* ✣ *H3.*

$$$ ✕ **Blue Crab Seafood House.** Fresh-daily seafood and expansive harbor

SEAFOOD views make this airy James Bay hotel restaurant a popular lunch and dinner spot. Signature dishes include a crab cake starter, a scallop-and-prawn sauté, and bouillabaisse in coconut green curry, but check the tempting daily specials on the blackboard as well. Desserts made in-house and a wine list highlighting British Columbia and Pacific Northwest labels round out the menu. The lounge area and patio, serving until 11 pm nightly, has equally impressive views and a more casual menu. [$] *Average main:* ✉ *Coast Harbourside Hotel and Marina, 146 Kingston St., James Bay, Downtown* ☎ *250/480–1999* ⊕ *www.bluecrab.ca* ✣ *C5.*

$$$ ✕ **Brasserie L'École.** French-country cooking shines at this informal Chi-

FRENCH natown bistro, and the historic room—once a schoolhouse for the Chi-

Fodor's Choice nese community—evokes a timeless brasserie, from the patina-rich fir

★ floors to the chalkboards above the slate bar listing the day's oyster, mussel, and steak options. Sean Brennan, one of the city's better-known

8

chefs, works with local farmers and fishers to source the best seasonal, local, and organic ingredients. The menu changes daily but lists such contemporary spins on classic bistro fare as duck confit with house-made sausage, steak frites, or spring salmon with beets, shallots, and *pommes rissolées*. Be prepared for lines as this petite spot does not take reservations. [$] *Average main: C$24* ✉ *1715 Government St., Downtown* ☎ *250/475–6260* 🌐 *www.lecole.ca* ⏲ *Closed Sun. and Mon. No lunch* ✍ *Reservations not accepted* ✥ *F2.*

$$$ MODERN CANADIAN Fodor's Choice ★

🍴 **Café Brio.** This intimate yet bustling Italian villa–style room has long been a Victoria favorite, mainly because of its Mediterranean-influence atmosphere and cuisine, which is prepared primarily with locally raised ingredients. The menu changes almost daily, but you might find local rockfish pan-roasted and paired with heirloom beans and grilled scallions, or roast duck breast with semolina polenta. Most dishes come in full or half sizes, which are ideal for smaller appetites or for those who want to sample the menu more widely. However, the Family Meal (priced per person) is the choice for sharing, comprising six chef's choice-of-the-day dishes. Virtually everything, including the bread, most pastas, charcuterie, and desserts, is made in-house. The 400-label wine list has a top selection of BC choices. [$] *Average main: C$27* ✉ *944 Fort St., Downtown* ☎ *250/383–0009, 866/270–5461* 🌐 *www.cafe-brio.com* ⏲ *No lunch* ✥ *H4.*

$$$ MODERN CANADIAN

🍴 **Camille's.** Working closely with independent farmers, the chef at this long-established favorite concentrates on such locally sourced products as lamb, duck, and seafood; quail and venison often make an appearance, too. The menu is based on what's fresh but might include seafood bisque with lemon and ginger; Hecate Strait ling cod; or organic beef striploin. The wine cellar–like backdrop, on the lower floor of a historic building on Bastion Square, is candlelit and romantic, with exposed brick, soft jazz and blues, and lots of intimate nooks and crannies hung with local art. The wine list is well selected. [$] *Average main: C$28* ✉ *45 Bastion Sq., Downtown* ☎ *250/381–3433* 🌐 *www.camillesrestaurant.com* ⏲ *Closed Sun. and Mon. No lunch* ✥ *E3.*

$$ CANADIAN

🍴 **Canoe Brewpub.** The lofty windows of this power station–turned–brewpub open onto one of Victoria's best waterfront patios, overlooking the kayaking and ferry action on the gorge. The casual, locally sourced menu runs from such high-end pub snacks as chickpea fritters, mussels with chorizo, steelhead trout, and crispy duck confit, to flatbread pizzas and good old fish-and-chips. Choose from the adults-only brewpub or the all-ages restaurant—both have water-view patios. And try the beer—the Dark Ale, Pale Ale, India Pale Ale, and other signature creations are brewed the old-fashioned way. You can even see the vats from the pub. Reservations are accepted in the restaurant section only. [$] *Average main: C$19* ✉ *450 Swift St., Downtown* ☎ *250/361–1940* 🌐 *www.canoebrewpub.com* ✥ *E2.*

$$$$ CANADIAN

🍴 **Empress Room.** Candlelight dances beneath a carved mahogany ceiling at the Fairmont Empress hotel's flagship restaurant, where one of the two gracious rooms has expansive harbor views. The classically influenced Pacific Northwest menu changes seasonally but might feature such appetizers as Angus beef tartare or caramelized scallops and pork. Mains, featuring sustainably sourced meat and seafood, might include roasted Haida Gwaii halibut or butter-poached venison tenderloin. Simply grilled proteins with a choice of sides and sauces are also an option. The service is discreet and attentive and there are more than 800 labels on the wine list. If the weather is fine, the summer-only Veranda serves lunch, cocktails, and early-evening snacks. [$] *Average main: C$35* ✉ *Fairmont Empress, 721 Government St., Downtown* ☎ *250/389–2727* 🌐 *www.fairmont.com/empress* ⏲ *No lunch* ✣ *E5.*

$$ ECLECTIC FAMILY 🍴 **Ferris' Grill.** The wooden booths at the back of this dim, narrow room look just the place for an illicit meeting; it's certainly as close as you'll get to an underworld haunt in fresh-faced Victoria. Most of the arty-looking clientele are here for the oysters (served shucked, smoked, baked, breaded, or as shooters) and large portions of updated comfort food (try the sweet-potato fries; lamb, beef, or halibut burgers; or chicken-penne soup). The service is snappy, there's a small patio out back, and even the kids' menu portions would feed a linebacker. The evening-only, upstairs oyster bar with its black-granite bar and inviting sofas is even more intimate, and mains like prosciutto-wrapped ling cod are included on the pricier, more upscale menu. [$] *Average main:* ✉ *536 Yates St., at street level, Downtown* ☎ *250/360–1824 Grill, 250/382–2344 Oyster Bar* 🌐 *www.ferrisoysterbar.com* ✣ *F3.*

$$$ ITALIAN 🍴 **Il Terrazzo.** A cute redbrick terrace edged with potted greenery and warmed by fireplaces and overhead heaters makes Il Terrazzo—tucked away off Waddington Alley near Market Square and not visible from the street—the locals' choice for romantic alfresco dining. Starters might include steamed mussels with sundried tomatoes and spicy banana peppers, while mains range from such traditional northern Italian favorites as breaded scaloppini of pork tenderloin to a more local-leaning halibut with blackberries. Thin-crust pizzas come piping hot from the restaurant's open-flame stone oven. [$] *Average main: C$24* ✉ *555 Johnson St., off Waddington Alley, Downtown* ☎ *250/361–0028* 🌐 *www.ilterrazzo.com* ⏲ *No lunch weekends* ✣ *E3.*

$$ CHINESE 🍴 **J & J Wonton Noodle House.** Fresh house-made noodles and wontons draw local office workers to this long-standing Chinese spot. Szechuan and Shanghai specialties, from shrimp noodle soup to beef with hot-chili bean sauce, dominate the long menu, but Singapore-style noodles and Indonesian chow mein appear, too. The diner-style eatery is low on character, but the crowds of locals and an open kitchen keep things buzzing. Reservations are accepted only for groups of four or more. [$] *Average main: C$15* ✉ *1012 Fort St., Downtown* ☎ *250/383–0680* 🌐 *www.jjnoodlehouse.ca* ⏲ *Closed Sun. and Mon.* ✣ *H4.*

$$ CANADIAN FAMILY 🍴 **Mo:Lé.** A good choice for vegans, this brick-lined Chinatown café has plenty of wholesome, organic, local fare for meat eaters, too. All-day breakfasts of free-range eggs, locally made sausages, and organic spelt griddle cakes fuel a post-party, pre-yoga crowd. At lunch, locals might pop in for an avocado, seaweed, and sprout sandwich, a yam wrap, or an organic beef burger. The place is popular, so expect to wait on weekends. [$] *Average main: C$13* ✉ *554 Pandora St., Downtown* ☎ *250/385–6653* 🌐 *www.molerestaurant.ca* ⏲ *No dinner* ✍ *Reservations not accepted* ✣ *F2.*

8

$ ASIAN 🍴 **The Noodle Box.** Noodles, whether Indonesian style with peanut sauce, thick hokkien in teriyaki, or Thai-style chow mein, are scooped straight from the open kitchen's steaming woks into bowls or cardboard take-out boxes. Malaysian-, Singapore-, and Thai-style curries tempt those who like it hot. Gluten-free, vegan, and kid-friendly options are all available. There are half a dozen "boxes" around town. The Douglas Street outlet is a loud and busy spot near the Inner Harbour; the branch at 626 Fisgard Street is a tiny hole-in-the-wall near Chinatown. [$] *Average main: C$12* ✉ *818 Douglas St., Downtown* ☎ *250/384–1314* 🌐 *www.thenoodlebox.net* ✍ *Reservations not accepted* ✥ *F4.*

$$$ ITALIAN 🍴 **Pagliacci's.** Expect long lines at this lively New York–meets–Victoria trattoria, where the tables are tightly packed to accommodate the crowds. Opened by Brooklyn's Siegel brothers in 1979, Pagliacci's is all showbiz, from the signed photos of the owners' movie-star friends plastering the walls to the live jazz playing several nights a week. The menu runs from the "Mae West" (veal with artichoke hearts) to the "Prawns Al Capone" (shell-on butterfly shrimp sautéed in butter and white wine). Pag's is crowded, frenetic, and buckets of fun. [$] *Average main: C$24* ✉ *1011 Broad St., Downtown* ☎ *250/386–1662* 🌐 *www.pagliaccis.ca* ✍ *Reservations not accepted* ✥ *F4.*

$ BARBECUE 🍴 **Pig BBQ Joint.** The food's as no-nonsense as the name at this funky little Downtown barbecue corner that dispenses with such niceties as table service and plates. No matter—the overflowing pulled pork, brisket, or smoked chicken sandwiches served on butcher paper are hearty and delicious. Add a side of beans or cole slaw, or, for a heart-stopping mashup of southern 'cue and Canadian homestyle cuisine, there's also pulled pork *poutine*. Beer, cider, and iced tea help wash it all down. If you're headed to the West Shore, stop at the second location (2955 Phipps Road in the Westshore Village Shopping Centre) or watch for the mobile Pigmobile at events around town. [$] *Average main: C$10* ✉ *1325 Blanshard St., Downtown* ☎ *250/590–5193* 🌐 *pigbbqjoint.com* ✍ *Reservations not accepted* ✥ *G3.*

$$ VEGETARIAN FAMILY 🍴 **ReBar Modern Food.** Bright and casual, with lime-green walls and a splashy Bollywood poster, this kid-friendly café in Bastion Square is *the* place for vegetarians in Victoria. But don't worry, the almond burgers, decadent baked goodies, and wild salmon tacos keep omnivores happy, too. Try the yam and pumpkin-seed quesadillas or the vegan Monk's Curry, or join locals for the popular weekend-only brunches. An extensive selection of teas, fresh juices, and wheat-grass concoctions shares space on the drinks list with espresso, microbrews, and BC wines. [$] *Average main: C$16* ✉ *50 Bastion Sq., Downtown* ☎ *250/361–9223* 🌐 *www.rebarmodernfood.com* ⏲ *No breakfast weekdays* ✥ *E3.*

$ SEAFOOD 🍴 **Red Fish Blue Fish.** If you like your fish both yummy *and* ecologically friendly, look no further than this former shipping container on the pier at the foot of Broughton Street. From the soil-topped roof and biodegradable packaging to the sustainably harvested local seafood, this waterfront take-out shop minimizes its ecological footprint. The chef offers a choice of local wild salmon, tuna, and oysters from the barbecue. Portuguese buns are baked daily for the seafood sandwiches,

Afternoon Tea in Victoria

Maybe it's the city's British heritage, but afternoon tea—a snack of tea, cakes, and sandwiches taken mid-afternoon and not to be confused with "high tea," a hot meal eaten at dinnertime—lives on in Victoria. Several of Victoria's gardens and historic homes also make atmospheric settings for tea. The most authentic places are near the Inner Harbour and in the very British Oak Bay district, often described as being "behind the tweed curtain."

Fairmont Empress Hotel Tea Lobby. Victoria's most elaborate and most expensive afternoon tea is served, as it has been since 1908, in the ornate lobby of the Fairmont Empress Hotel. The tea is the hotel's own blend, and the cakes, scones, and crustless sandwiches are prepared by some of Victoria's finest pastry chefs. As you face the bill of C$60 per person in high season, remember that tea here is more than a snack; it was, historically, a way to keep civilization alive in this farthest outpost of the empire. Seatings start daily at noon. The price drops to C$50 per person from October to April. Children under 12 pay half-price year-round. ⊠ 721 Government St., Downtown ☎ 250/389-2727 ⊕ www.fairmont. com/empress ☉ Afternoon tea daily noon–3:45; Evening tea May–Aug., Thurs.–Sat. 7–9 pm.

Pacific Restaurant. For a Pacific Rim twist on the tea tradition, try this window-lined restaurant in the Hotel Grand Pacific. You can choose from an assortment of Asian-style teas, like the cherry haiku or dragon tears (green tea with jasmine), while you nibble on Dungeness crab cakes, tuna tataki, scones with clotted cream, and lemon meringue tarts. Tea is served from 2 to 4:30 daily, for C$42 per person. Reservations must be made 24 hours in advance. ⊠ Hotel Grand Pacific, 463 Belleville St., Downtown ☎ 250/380-4458 ⚓ Reservations essential.

Point Ellice House. Wicker armchairs under an awning on the lawn of the Victorian Point Ellice House are a lovely setting for afternoon tea with home-baked goodies. Harbour Ferries from the Inner Harbour deliver you directly to the garden. From early May to early September, tea is served daily 11 to 2:30. The C$25 cost includes admission to the house. ⊠ 2616 Pleasant St., Downtown ☎ 250/380-6506 ⊕ www.pointellicehouse.ca.

The Teahouse at Abkhazi Garden. Afternoon teas, with fresh-baked scones and cream, mini-quiches, cucumber sandwiches, and seasonal treats featuring produce from the garden, are served in the sun-drenched living room of the Abkhazi Garden. Late morning snacks (called "elevenses") and light lunches are also available at this romantic garden setting. ⊠ 1964 Fairfield Rd., Fairfield ☎ 778/265-6466 ⊕ www. abkhaziteahouse.com ☉ May.–Sept., daily 11–5; Oct.–Apr., Wed.–Sun. 11–5.

White Heather Tea Room. Everything, including the jam, is homemade for the Scottish-style teas served in the White Heather Tea Room, a lovely place with big windows. Tuesday to Saturday, lunch and afternoon tea are served 10 to 5. ⊠ 1885 Oak Bay Ave., Oak Bay ☎ 250/595-8020 ⊕ www. whiteheather-tearoom.com ☉ Closed Sun. and Mon.

8

fish tacos come in grilled tortilla cones, and even plain old fish-and-chips are taken up a notch with a choice of wild salmon, halibut, or cod in tempura batter with hand-cut fries. Be prepared for queues on sunny days and for variable closures during the winter months. [$] *Average main: C$12* ✉ *1006 Wharf St., Downtown* ☎ *250/298–6877* 🌐 *www.redfish-bluefish.com* 🕒 *No dinner. Call for winter closures* ✍ *Reservations not accepted* ✥ *E4.*

$$$$ FRENCH 🍴 **Restaurant Matisse.** The gracious owner greets each guest personally at this tiny gem of a traditional French restaurant, where white linens, fresh flowers, and candlelight on the dozen or so tables set the stage for meals of seasonally changing, well-executed bistro classics like crepes, rack of lamb, and poached sable fish. The primarily French wine list has plenty of affordable options, and the bread pudding, crème brûlée, and house-made sorbets are much-loved finales. Piaf *chansons* on the speakers and Matisse originals on the wall add to the pleasing ambience. [$] *Average main: C$31* ✉ *512 Yates St., Downtown* ☎ *250/480–0883* 🌐 *www.restaurantmatisse.com* 🕒 *Closed Jan. Closed Mon. and Tues. No lunch* ✥ *E3.*

$$ SPANISH 🍴 **The Tapa Bar.** Chef-owner Danno Lee has re-created the fun and flavors of a Spanish tapas bar in this little pedestrian-only lane off Government Street. Small, flavorful dishes run from simple-but-tasty grilled vegetables to prawns in white wine, spicy mussels, thin-crust pizzas, pastas, and a multitude of vegetarian options. One specialty is the Pollo Armanda: charbroiled boneless chicken with artichokes, sun-dried tomatoes, capers, lemon, and white wine. Almond-stuffed dates are a particular hit. Rich colors and lively artwork create a casual interior; the patio is a choice spot on a sunny day. Just need a snack? Tapas are served all afternoon and late into the evening. A wine bar next door is run by the same owners. [$] *Average main: C$18* ✉ *620 Trounce Alley, Downtown* ☎ *250/383–0013* 🌐 *tapabar.ca* ✥ *F3.*

$$$ MODERN CANADIAN Fodor's Choice ★ 🍴 **Ulla Restaurant.** Victoria's foodies are buzzing about this Chinatown restaurant that's serving up some of the city's most innovative fare. From the frequently changing, locally sourced menu, you could choose starters like grass-fed beef carpaccio, giant Pacific octopus, or perhaps pea soup with cauliflower and an "egg" made from cheddar and carrot. Mains might include chicken with cheddar pierogies, butter radish and cabbage shoots, short-rib steak from a local organic farm, or coho salmon with birch syrup. The high-arched windows, solid fir tables, and art-filled walls make the room feel both airy and relaxed. [$] *Average main: C$27* ✉ *509 Fisgard St., Downtown* ☎ *250/590–8795* 🌐 *www.ulla.ca* 🕒 *Closed Sun. and Mon. No lunch* ✥ *E2.*

$ CAFÉ FAMILY 🍴 **Willie's Bakery & Café.** Housed in a handsome Victorian building near Market Square, this eatery goes free-range and local in its omelets, French toast, and homemade granola all-day breakfasts and its lunches of homemade soups, thick sandwiches, and tasty baked treats. A brick patio with an outdoor fireplace is partially glassed-in so you can lunch alfresco even on chilly days. [$] *Average main: C$12* ✉ *537 Johnson St., Downtown* ☎ *250/381–8414* 🌐 *www.williesbakery.com* 🕒 *No dinner* ✍ *Reservations not accepted* ✥ *E3.*

$$$ ✕**Zambri's.** This lively trattoria, in a glam space with floor-to-ceiling
ITALIAN windows and eclectic chandeliers, has a setting to match the top-notch
Italian food. The kitchen uses local and organic ingredients to turn out
contemporary versions of traditional dishes. During the always-busy
lunch service, choose from pizzas, pastas, and hot sandwiches, or in the
evening, opt for tagliatelle with gorgonzola cream, leeks, and candied
walnuts, or crispy pork shoulder served on a bed of greens, potatoes,
and grapes. The mostly Italian wine list includes lesser-known labels,
with many available by the glass. $ *Average main: C$22* ✉ *820 Yates
St., Downtown* ☎ *250/360–1171* ⊕ *www.zambris.ca* ✛ *G3.*

VIC WEST

$$ ✕**LURE Restaurant & Bar.** A sunny patio, intimate balconies, and a wall
MODERN of windows take in sweeping views across the Inner Harbour at this
CANADIAN seaside spot in the Delta Victoria Ocean Pointe Resort. Casual mains
and share plates, such as local-brew battered halibut and spiced-
grilled Angus beef striploin, along with elaborate desserts (try the ice
cream sandwich with whiskey caramel and sweet pickled cherries) are
served all day and into the evening. Creative cocktails, wines by the
glass, sunset views, and a lively bar scene make this a great choice for
a casual night out. $ *Average main: C$20* ✉ *Delta Victoria Ocean
Pointe Resort, 45 Songhees Rd., Vic West* ☎ *250/360–5873* ⊕ *www.
lurevictoria.com* ✛ *D3.*

$$ ✕**Spinnakers Gastro Brewpub.** Victoria's longest list of handcrafted beers
CANADIAN is just one reason to trek over the Johnson Street Bridge or hop a Har-
bour Ferry to this Vic West waterfront pub. Canada's oldest licensed
brewpub, Spinnakers relies almost exclusively on locally sourced ingre-
dients for its top-notch casual fare. Opt for the pubby adults-only tap-
room, with its covered waterfront deck, double-sided fireplace, and
wood-beamed ceilings, or dine in the all-ages waterfront restaurant.
Either way you can enjoy such high-end pub grub as mussels steamed
in ale, fish-and-chips with thick-cut fries, or brick oven pizzas (try the
house-smoked wild salmon or the mushroom and beer). You can also
stop by for breakfast, served from 8 am to 2 pm daily, or grab some
house-made picnic fixings at the take-away deli and bakery. $ *Average
main: C$20* ✉ *308 Catherine St., Vic West* ☎ *250/386–2739, 877/838–
2739* ⊕ *www.spinnakers.com* ✛ *A2.*

OAK BAY

$$$ ✕**Marina Restaurant.** This circular room with art-deco rosewood booths
SEAFOOD and a 180-degree view over the sailboats of Oak Bay Marina has a chef
with a flair for seafood. Sustainably sourced wild salmon, white sturgeon, miso-cured sablefish, and Dungeness crab are teamed with local
organic vegetables. Starters include spot prawn bisque or Salt Spring
Island mussels and fresh shucked oysters. A lunch menu of salads, burgers, and fish, and an evening-only sushi bar also favor local ingredients.
An attached marina-side coffee bar makes a handy stop for a seaside
drive or cycle tour. $ *Average main: C$27* ✉ *1327 Beach Dr., Oak Bay*
☎ *250/598–8555* ⊕ *www.marinarestaurant.com.*

BRENTWOOD BAY

$$$ CANADIAN 🍴 **Seagrille Restaurant.** Local seafood paired with wines from neighboring vineyards shine at this lofty ocean-view restaurant in the Brentwood Bay Resort. Start with some tuna and salmon sashimi or oysters on the half shell, then opt for coconut-crusted lingcod or wild Pacific salmon. Beef, lamb, poultry, and vegetarian dishes appear as well: duck in an orange-pomegranate glaze or braised lamb shank, for example. A big fireplace, two-story-high windows, and a wonderful array of Canadian art warm the interior; outside, a heated patio takes in views of Saanich Inlet. A more casual marina-view pub offers burgers, pizzas, and craft beers at lunch and dinner. [$] *Average main: C$27* ✉ *Brentwood Bay Resort, 849 Verdier Ave.* ☎ *250/544–5100* 🌐 *www.brentwoodbayresort.com* ⏲ *No lunch.*

WHERE TO STAY

Victoria has a vast range of accommodations, with what seems like whole neighborhoods dedicated to hotels. Options range from city resorts and full-service business hotels to mid-priced tour-group haunts and family-friendly motels, but the city is especially known for its lavish B&Bs in beautifully restored Victorian and Edwardian mansions. Outlying areas, such as Sooke and Saanich, pride themselves on destination spa resorts and luxurious country inns, though affordable lodgings can be found there, too.

British Columbia law prohibits smoking inside any public building or within 3 meters (20 feet) of an entrance. As a result, all Victoria hotels are completely smoke-free, including on patios and balconies, and in public areas. Only the larger modern hotels have air-conditioning, but it rarely gets hot enough to need it. Advance reservations are always a good idea, especially in July and August. Watch for discounts of up to 50% in the off-season (roughly November to February), though even then you'll need to book, as many rooms fill with retirees escaping prairie winters. Most downtown hotels also charge at least C$15 per day for parking. Ask about phone and Internet charges (these can range from free to excessive) and have a look at the hotel breakfast menu; nearby cafés are almost always cheaper.

Downtown hotels are clustered in three main areas. James Bay, on the south side of the Inner Harbour near the Parliament Buildings, is basically a residential and hotel neighborhood. Bordered by the waterfront and Beacon Hill Park, the area is quiet at night and handy for sightseeing by day. It is, however, thin on restaurants and a bit of a hike from the main shopping areas. Hotels in the downtown core, particularly along Government and Douglas streets, are right in the thick of shopping, dining, and nightlife, but they get more traffic noise. If you're willing to walk a few blocks east of the harbor, several quieter hotels and small inns are clustered amid the condominium towers. Vic West, across the Johnson Street Bridge on the harbor's north shore, is another quiet option, but it's a 15-minute walk or ferry ride to the bulk of shopping, dining, and sightseeing. Even so, you won't need a car to stay in any of these areas, and, given parking charges, you may be better off without one.

Outside of Downtown, Rockland and Oak Bay are lush, peaceful, tree-lined residential districts; the mile or so walk into town is pleasant, but you won't want to do it every day. The resorts and inns that we've listed farther afield, in Saanich, the West Shore, and Sooke, are, for the most part, self-contained resorts with restaurants and spas. Each is about 30 minutes from downtown Victoria, and you'll need a car if you want to make day trips into town.

	WHAT IT COSTS IN CANADIAN DOLLARS			
	$	$$	$$$	$$$$
Hotels	under C$126	C$126–C$195	C$196–C$300	over C$300

Prices in the hotel reviews are the lowest cost of a standard double room in high season, including taxes. For expanded reviews, please visit 🌐 *www.fodors.com*

Use the coordinate (✣ B2) at the end of each listing to locate a site on the corresponding map.

DOWNTOWN

$$$ B&B/INN **Abigail's Hotel.** A Tudor-style inn built in 1930, this adult-oriented boutique hotel is four blocks from the Inner Harbour. **Pros:** luxurious comforts; free parking and free Wi-Fi; only older kids (over 13) allowed. **Cons:** no pool, gym, or elevator; not family-friendly. [$] *Rooms from: C$250* ✉ *906 McClure St., Downtown* ☎ *250/388–5363, 800/561–6565* 🌐 *www.abigailshotel.com* 🛏 *23 rooms* 🍴 *Breakfast* ✣ *H5.*

$$ B&B/INN **Beaconsfield Inn.** This 1905 building four blocks from the Inner Harbour is one of Victoria's most faithfully restored, antiques-filled mansions. **Pros:** luxurious; opportunities to mingle over breakfast or sherry. **Cons:** romantic ambience is not suited for kids; several blocks from shopping and dining. [$] *Rooms from: C$159* ✉ *998 Humboldt St., Downtown* ☎ *250/384–4044, 888/884–4044* 🌐 *www.beaconsfieldinn.com* 🛏 *9 rooms* 🍴 *Breakfast* ✣ *H6.*

$$ HOTEL FAMILY **Chateau Victoria Hotel & Suites.** Far-reaching views from the upper-floor suites are a plus at this good-value, centrally located, independent hotel. **Pros:** indoor pool, gym, and hot tub; free Wi-Fi and local calls in rooms; great rates and location. **Cons:** standard rooms lack views. [$] *Rooms from: C$159* ✉ *740 Burdett Ave., Downtown* ☎ *250/382–4221, 800/663–5891* 🌐 *www.chateauvictoria.com* 🛏 *59 rooms, 118 suites* 🍴 *No meals* ✣ *F5.*

$$$$ HOTEL Fodor's Choice ★ **Fairmont Empress.** Opened in 1908, this ivy-draped harborside château and city landmark has aged gracefully, with top-notch service and sympathetically restored Edwardian furnishings. **Pros:** central location; professional service; great spa and restaurant. **Cons:** small- to average-size rooms and bathrooms; pricey. [$] *Rooms from: C$349* ✉ *721 Government St., Downtown* ☎ *250/384–8111, 866/540–4429 Central reservations* 🌐 *www.fairmont.com/empress* 🛏 *436 rooms, 41 suites* 🍴 *No meals* ✣ *E5.*

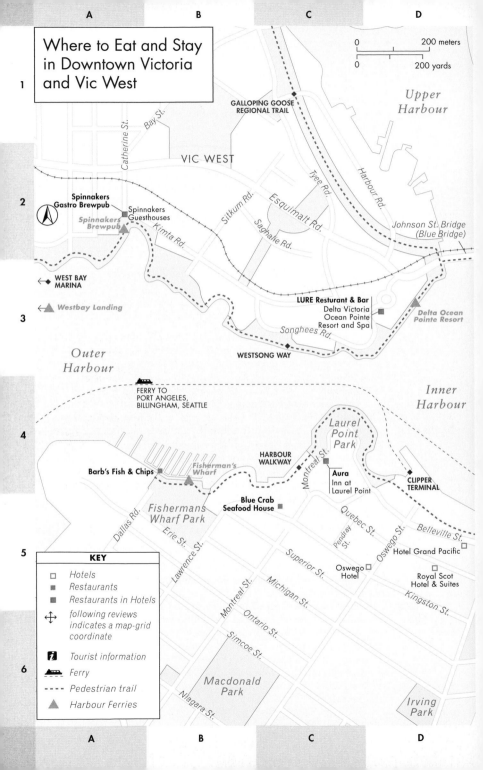

Where to Eat and Stay in Downtown Victoria and Vic West

| | **A** | **B** | **C** | **D** |

1

0   200 meters
0   200 yards

Upper Harbour

GALLOPING GOOSE
REGIONAL TRAIL

Bay St.

Catherine St.

VIC WEST

2

**Spinnakers
Gastro Brewpub**

*Spinnakers
Brewpub*

Spinnakers
Guesthouses

Kimta Rd.

Sitkum Rd.

Saghalie Rd.

Esquimalt Rd.

Tyee Rd.

Harbour Rd.

*Johnson St. Bridge
(Blue Bridge)*

← **WEST BAY
MARINA**

← ▲ *Westbay Landing*

3

LURE Resturant & Bar
Delta Victoria
Ocean Pointe
Resort and Spa

▲ *Delta Ocean
Pointe Resort*

Songhees Rd.

WESTSONG WAY

*Outer
Harbour*

FERRY TO
PORT ANGELES,
BILLINGHAM, SEATTLE

*Inner
Harbour*

*Laurel
Point
Park*

4

Barb's Fish & Chips

*Fisherman's
Wharf*

HARBOUR
WALKWAY

Montreal St.

Aura
Inn at
Laurel Point

◆ **CLIPPER
TERMINAL**

*Fishermans
Wharf Park*

**Blue Crab
Seafood House**

Dallas Rd.

Erie St.

Lawrence St.

Quebec St.

Pendray St.

Oswego St.

Belleville St.

□ Hotel Grand Pacific

5

KEY

□   *Hotels*

■   *Restaurants*

■   *Restaurants in Hotels*

✛   *following reviews
indicates a map-grid
coordinate*

🛈   *Tourist information*

🚢   *Ferry*

---   *Pedestrian trail*

▲   *Harbour Ferries*

Superior St.

Michigan St.

Montreal St.

Ontario St.

Simcoe St.

Oswego
Hotel

Royal Scot
Hotel & Suites

Kingston St.

6

*Macdonald
Park*

Niagara St.

*Irving
Park*

| | **A** | **B** | **C** | **D** |

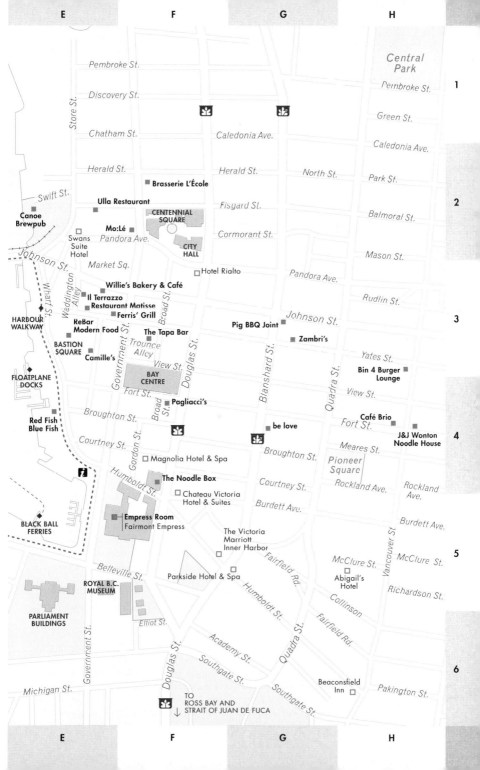

BEST BETS FOR VICTORIA LODGING

Fodor's Choice★

Abbeymoore Manor, p. 218
Brentwood Bay Resort & Spa, p. 219
Fairholme Manor, p. 218
Fairmont Empress, p. 213
Oak Bay Beach Hotel, p. 218

By Price

$$

Beaconsfield Inn, p. 213
Sidney Pier Hotel & Spa, p. 219

$$$

Abbeymoore Manor, p. 218
Brentwood Bay Resort & Spa, p. 219
Hotel Grand Pacific, p. 216
Inn at Laurel Point, p. 216
Oak Bay Beach Hotel, p. 218

$$$$

Fairmont Empress, p. 213

By Experience

FOR FAMILIES

Chateau Victoria Hotel & Suites, p. 213
Parkside Hotel & Spa, p. 217
Royal Scot Hotel & Suites, p. 217

MOST CENTRAL

Fairmont Empress, p. 213
Magnolia Hotel & Spa, p. 217

HISTORIC

Beaconsfield Inn, p. 213
Fairmont Empress, p. 213

ROMANTIC

Abigail's Hotel, p. 213
Fairholme Manor, p. 218

BEST SPA

Fairmont Empress, p. 213
Oak Bay Beach Hotel, p. 218

$$$ HOTEL **Hotel Grand Pacific.** The city's biggest and best health club (with an indoor lap pool, yoga classes, squash courts, and state-of-the-art equipment), a great spa, and a prime Inner Harbour location appeal to savvy regulars, including Seattleites stepping off the ferry across the street. **Pros:** great health club and spa; concierge; complimentary Wi-Fi. **Cons:** standard hotel decor in some rooms. [$] *Rooms from: C$229* ✉ *463 Belleville St., James Bay, Downtown* ☎ *250/386–0450, 800/663–7550* 🌐 *www.hotelgrandpacific.com* 🛏 *258 rooms, 46 suites* 🍴 *No meals* ✣ *D5.*

$$ HOTEL **Hotel Rialto.** This historic Downtown landmark has been transformed into a 21st-century boutique hotel. **Pros:** great location; friendly, helpful staff; free Wi-Fi and local calls; historic ambience. **Cons:** no on-site parking; no pool or fitness room (though patrons can get a pass to a nearby fitness club). [$] *Rooms from: C$160* ✉ *653 Pandora Ave., Downtown* ☎ *250/383–4157, 800/332–9981* 🌐 *www.hotelrialto.ca* 🛏 *40 rooms, 11 suites* 🍴 *Breakfast* ✣ *F3.*

$$$ HOTEL **Inn at Laurel Point.** A seaside Japanese garden, a museum-quality art collection, and water views from every room make this Asian-inspired independent hotel on the Inner Harbour's quiet south shore a favorite among Victoria regulars. **Pros:** views; quiet, parklike setting. **Cons:** 10-minute walk from downtown. [$] *Rooms from: C$199* ✉ *680 Montreal St., James Bay, Downtown* ☎ *250/386–8721, 800/663–7667* 🌐 *www.laurelpoint.com* 🛏 *135 rooms, 65 suites* 🍴 *No meals* ✣ *C4.*

$$$ HOTEL **Magnolia Hotel & Spa.** From the on-site spa to the soaker tubs, sauna, and herb tea, this locallyowned boutique hotel, without actually saying so, caters beautifully to the female traveler—though the attention to detail, hop-to-it staff, and central location won't be lost on men either. **Pros:** great location; friendly and helpful service; welcoming lobby with fireplace, tea, and coffee. **Cons:** no on-site pool or hot tub. [$] *Rooms from: C$249* ✉ *623 Courtney St., Downtown* ☎ *250/381–0999, 877/624–6654* 🌐 *www.magnoliahotel.com* 🛏 *64 rooms* 🍴 *No meals* ✥ *F4.*

$$ HOTEL **Oswego Hotel.** In quiet-but-handy James Bay, this chic all-suites boutique property has 80 sleek studio, one-, and two-bedroom units. **Pros:** stylish design; friendly staff; free local calls and Wi-Fi. **Cons:** 10-minute walk to town center; no pool. [$] *Rooms from: C$175* ✉ *500 Oswego St., James Bay, Downtown* ☎ *250/294–7500, 877/767 9346* 🌐 *www.oswegovictoria.com* 🛏 *21 studios, 44 one-bedroom suites, 15 two-bedroom suites* 🍴 *No meals* ✥ *C5.*

$$$ HOTEL **Parkside Hotel & Spa.** From the three-story glass atrium with babbling fountains to the rooftop terrace and on-site spa, this downtown condo-hotel feels like an escape from the city. **Pros:** spacious accommodations; family-friendly vibe; close to downtown attractions. **Cons:** no doors on en-suite bathrooms creates a lack of privacy. [$] *Rooms from: C$249* ✉ *810 Humboldt St., Downtown* ☎ *250/940–1200, 855/616-3557* 🌐 *www.parksidevictoria.com* 🛏 *126 suites* 🍴 *No meals* ✥ *G5.*

$$ HOTEL FAMILY **Royal Scot Hotel & Suites.** Large suites, great rates, a handy location, and a friendly staff keep couples, families, and bus tours coming back to this well-run James Bay hotel. **Pros:** great for kids; quiet neighborhood; free Wi-Fi and local calls. **Cons:** lots of kids and tour groups. [$] *Rooms from: C$179* ✉ *425 Quebec St., James Bay, Downtown* ☎ *250/388–5463, 800/663–7515* 🌐 *www.royalscot.com* 🛏 *30 rooms, 146 suites* 🍴 *No meals* ✥ *D5.*

$$ HOTEL FAMILY **Swans Suite Hotel.** This 1913 former warehouse in Victoria's old town is one of the city's most enticing small inns and is further enhanced by the all-suites accommodations. **Pros:** handsome suites with kitchens; great for families; handy to shopping and restaurants. **Cons:** tiny lobby; pub noise on the lower floors; parking is off-site. [$] *Rooms from: C$185* ✉ *506 Pandora Ave., Downtown* ☎ *250/361–3310, 800/668–7926* 🌐 *www.swanshotel.com* 🛏 *30 suites* 🍴 *No meals* ✥ *E2.*

$$$ HOTEL **Victoria Marriott Inner Harbour.** Film people, business travelers, and tourists like this full-service hotel located two blocks east of the Inner Harbour. **Pros:** great service; work-friendly rooms; indoor pool, hot tub, and large modern gym. **Cons:** local calls cost C$1 each. [$] *Rooms from: C$199* ✉ *728 Humboldt St., Downtown* ☎ *250/480–3800, 877/333–8338* 🌐 *www.marriottvictoria.com* 🛏 *228 rooms, 8 suites* 🍴 *No meals* ✥ *G5.*

8

VIC WEST

$$$ HOTEL
Delta Victoria Ocean Pointe Resort and Spa. Across the Johnson Street Bridge from downtown Victoria, this waterfront resort has all sorts of amenities, from tennis and squash courts to an indoor pool, popular spa, around-the-clock gym, and a waterfront walking path. **Pros:** water views; free Wi-Fi; downtown shuttle and harbor ferry service. **Cons:** not right downtown; gets busy with conferences. [$] *Rooms from: C$229* ✉ *45 Songhees Rd., Vic West* ☎ *250/360–2999, 800/667–4677* 🌐 *www.deltavictoria.com* 🛏 *229 rooms, 11 suites* 🍴 *No meals* ✥ *D3.*

$$ B&B/INN FAMILY
Spinnakers Guesthouses. Three houses make up the accommodations at this B&B, run by the owner of the popular Spinnakers Gastro Brewpub. **Pros:** nice breakfast included in rates; free parking. **Cons:** 15-minute walk to Downtown; little else in the neighborhood. [$] *Rooms from: C$179* ✉ *308 Catherine St., Vic West* ☎ *250/386–2739, 877/838–2739* 🌐 *www.spinnakers.com* 🛏 *5 rooms, 4 suites, 1 cottage* 🍴 *Breakfast* ✥ *A2.*

OAK BAY

$$$ HOTEL Fodor's Choice ★
Oak Bay Beach Hotel. This lavish waterfront hotel, complete with a seaside spa, ocean-view restaurant, and even an on-site theater, offers a resort ambience within a few miles of downtown Victoria. **Pros:** luxurious surroundings; lavish spa. **Cons:** Not central, but shuttles run the three miles to downtown Victoria. [$] *Rooms from: C$229* ✉ *1175 Beach Drive, Oak Bay* ☎ *250/598–4556, 800/668–7758* 🌐 *www.oakbaybeachhotel.com* 🛏 *100 rooms, 19 suites* 🍴 *No meals.*

ROCKLAND

$$$ B&B/INN Fodor's Choice ★
Abbeymoore Manor. This 1912 mansion has the wide verandas, dark wainscoting, and high ceilings of its era, but the attitude is informal and welcoming, from the super-helpful hosts to the free snacks to the coffee on tap all day. **Pros:** good value; friendly hosts; excellent service. **Cons:** a mile from the Inner Harbour; often booked in advance. [$] *Rooms from: C$219* ✉ *1470 Rockland Ave., Rockland* ☎ *250/370–1470, 888/801–1811* 🌐 *www.abbeymoore.com* 🛏 *5 rooms, 2 suites* 🍴 *Breakfast.*

$$ B&B/INN FAMILY
Craigmyle Bed & Breakfast. Affordable and historic, this four-story manor near Craigdarroch Castle has been a guesthouse since 1913. **Pros:** free local calls and Wi-Fi; guest laundry (also free); homey atmosphere. **Cons:** a mile from downtown; no elevator; street parking only. [$] *Rooms from: C$135* ✉ *1037 Craigdarroch Rd., Rockland* ☎ *250/595–5411, 844/595–5411* 🌐 *www. thecraigmyle.com* 🛏 *15 rooms* 🍴 *Breakfast.*

$$ B&B/INN Fodor's Choice ★
Fairholme Manor. Original art, Viennese antiques, and dramatic furnishings shine in this lavish, 1885 Italianate mansion. **Pros:** peaceful setting; stunning decor; welcoming hostess. **Cons:** a mile from Downtown; no elevator. [$] *Rooms from: C$175* ✉ *638 Rockland Pl., off Rockland Ave., Rockland* ☎ *250/598–3240, 877/511–3322* 🌐 *www.fairholmemanor.com* 🛏 *1 room, 5 suites* 🍴 *Breakfast.*

$$$ B&B/INN **Villa Marco Polo Inn.** A classical European garden with a stone terrace, reflecting pool, and fountains is all part of the Tuscan-hideaway feel at this 1923 Italian Renaissance–style manor. **Pros:** lots of comfy common areas; gracious hosts; full concierge services. **Cons:** a mile from Downtown; no elevator. [$] *Rooms from: C$245* ✉ *1524 Shasta Place, Rockland* ✣ *Off St. Charles St.* ☎ *250/370–1524, 877/601–1524* 🌐 *www.villamarcopolo.com* 🛏 *4 rooms* 🍴 *Breakfast.*

BRENTWOOD BAY

$$$ RESORT Fodor's Choice ★ **Brentwood Bay Resort & Spa.** Every room has a private ocean-view patio or balcony at this adult-oriented boutique resort in a tiny seaside village. **Pros:** magnificent setting; close to Butchart Gardens; free Wi-Fi. **Cons:** pricey rates; 30-minute drive from Downtown. [$] *Rooms from: C$289* ✉ *849 Verdier Ave.* ☎ *250/544–2079, 888/544–2079* 🌐 *www.brentwoodbayresort.com* 🛏 *30 rooms, 3 suites, 2 villas* 🍴 *No meals.*

SIDNEY

$$ HOTEL **Sidney Pier Hotel & Spa.** Stylish and ecologically friendly, this glass-and-stone boutique hotel on the parklike waterfront has helped introduce Sidney to more travelers. **Pros:** lovely views; eco-friendly vibe; free airport and ferry shuttle in summer. **Cons:** 30 minutes from Downtown; no pool. [$] *Rooms from: C$179* ✉ *9805 Seaport Pl.* ☎ *250/655–9445, 866/659–9445* 🌐 *www.sidneypier.com* 🛏 *46 rooms, 9 suites* 🍴 *No meals.*

WEST SHORE

$$$ RESORT **Westin Bear Mountain Golf Resort & Spa.** Two Nicklaus Design golf courses are the draw at this resort about 30 minutes northwest of the city center. **Pros:** challenging golf; great spa and health club. **Cons:** a car is essential; C$20 nightly resort fee. [$] *Rooms from: C$199* ✉ *1999 Country Club Way, West Shore* ☎ *250/391–7160, 888/533–2327* 🌐 *www.bearmountain.ca* 🛏 *78 rooms, 78 suites* 🍴 *No meals.*

NIGHTLIFE AND PERFORMING ARTS

Victoria isn't the busiest destination after dark. But there are two important local sources to help visitors keep on top of the happenings, whether they're looking for a quiet pint, a music festival, or a night on the town. One is a monthly digest of arts and nightlife; the other is the local tourist office, which also sells tickets.

Monday Magazine. For entertainment listings, pick up a free copy of this monthly arts magazine, or check out listings online. 🌐 *www.mondaymag.com.*

Victoria Visitor Information Centre. Tourism Victoria also has event listings, and you can buy tickets for many events at the Victoria Visitor Information Centre. ✉ *812 Wharf St.* ☎ *250/953–2033, 800/663–3883* 🌐 *www.tourismvictoria.com.*

8

NIGHTLIFE

Victoria's nightlife is low-key and casual, with many wonderful pubs, but a limited choice of other nightlife. Pubs offer a casual vibe for lunch, dinner, or an afternoon pint, often with a view and an excellent selection of beer. The pubs listed here all serve food, and many brew their own beer. Patrons must be 19 or older to enter a bar or pub in British Columbia, but many pubs have a separate restaurant section open to all ages. The city is enjoying a resurgence of cocktail culture, with several of Victoria's trendier restaurants doubling as lounges, offering cocktails and small plates well into the night. Dance clubs attract a young crowd and most close by 2 am. A dress code (no jeans or sneakers) may be enforced, but otherwise, attire is casual. Smoking is not allowed in Victoria's pubs, bars, and nightclubs—this applies both indoors and on patios.

DOWNTOWN

BARS AND LOUNGES

Bengal Lounge. Deep leather sofas and a tiger skin help to re-create the days of the British Raj at this iconic lounge in the Fairmont Empress Hotel. Martinis and a curry buffet are the draws through the week. On Friday and Saturday nights a jazz combo takes the stage. ⊠ *Fairmont Empress Hotel, 721 Government St., Downtown* ☎ *250/384–8111* ⊕ *www.fairmont.com/empress.*

Clive's Classic Lounge. Leading Victoria's cocktail renaissance, the bartenders at this classic lounge in the Chateau Victoria Hotel make their own syrups and bitters and use fresh juices in their traditional and contemporary drinks. ⊠ *Chateau Victoria Hotel, 740 Burdett Ave., Downtown* ☎ *250/361–5684* ⊕ *www.clivesclassiclounge.com.*

The Guild. Pacific Northwest craft beers and microbrews—with a dozen on tap and 40 more available in bottles—feature at this atmospheric Downtown pub, which opened in 2014 in a historic waterfront chandlery. Local farms supply the fixings for such pub classics as fish pie and Welsh rarebit. ⊠ *1250 Wharf St., Downtown* ☎ *250/385–3474* ⊕ *theguildfreehouse.com* ⊗ *Closed Mon. and Tues. in winter.*

Little Jumbo. Well-executed farm-to-fork small plates and possibly the city's longest list of spirits are draws at this welcoming little spot, tucked away off Fort Street. Authenticity is serious business here: even the water served with the single malts is imported from Highlands. ⊠ *506 Fort St., Downtown* ⊹ *at the end of the corridor* ☎ *778/433–5535* ⊕ *www.littlejumbo.ca.*

Veneto Tapa Lounge. Signature cocktails (the bartenders get bylines on the menu), tapas, and charcuterie plates draw a chic after-work crowd to the Hotel Rialto's hip cocktail lounge. ⊠ *Hotel Rialto, 1450 Douglas St., Downtown* ☎ *250/383–7310* ⊕ *www.venetodining.com.*

Vista 18. You can take in lofty views of the city at this lounge on the 18th floor of the Chateau Victoria Hotel. There's live music Thursday, Friday, and Saturday night. ⊠ *Chateau Victoria Hotel, 740 Burdett Ave., Downtown* ☎ *250/382–9258* ⊕ *www.vista18.com.*

DANCE CLUBS

Club 9ONE9. This nightclub often hosts live bands, guest DJs, and other special events. Also in the building are a restaurant, a pub, and several bars, including a sports bar and a hillbilly-theme bar—not to mention beach volleyball played on the roof in summer. ✉ *Strathcona Hotel, 919 Douglas St., Downtown* ☎ *250/383-7137* ⊕ *www.strathconahotel.com.*

Paparazzi. Victoria's longest-running gay club draws a mixed crowd with fun drag, karaoke, and club nights. ✉ *642 Johnson St., Downtown* ☎ *250/388-0505* ⊕ *www.paparazzinightclub.com.*

MUSIC CLUBS

Hermann's Jazz Club. Dinner, dancing, and live jazz are on the menu at this venerable Downtown restaurant and jazz club. ✉ *753 View St., Downtown* ☎ *250/388-9166* ⊕ *www.hermannsjazz.com.*

Lucky Bar. DJs, live bands, and a friendly crowd of locals make the most of Lucky's great sound system and dance floor. ✉ *517 Yates St., Downtown* ☎ *250/382-5825* ⊕ *www.luckybar.ca.*

PUBS

The Bard and Banker Pub. This sumptuously decorated Scottish pub, which occupies a historic bank building on Victoria's main shopping street, has bangers-and-mash and shepherd's pie on the menu, plus a great selection of ales and live music every night. ✉ *1022 Government St., Downtown* ☎ *250/953-9993* ⊕ *www.bardandbanker.com.*

Canoe Brewpub. One of Victoria's biggest and best pub patios overlooks the Gorge, the waterway just north of the Inner Harbour. The interior of the former power station has been stylishly redone with high ceilings, exposed bricks, and wood beams. There's a wide range of in-house brews, top-notch bar snacks, and an all-ages restaurant. ✉ *450 Swift St., Downtown* ☎ *250/361-1940* ⊕ *www.canoebrewpub.com.*

Irish Times Pub. Stout on tap, live music nightly, a lively summertime patio, and a menu of traditional and modern pub fare draw tourists and locals to this former bank building on Victoria's main shopping strip. ✉ *1200 Government St., Downtown* ☎ *250/383-7775* ⊕ *www.irishtimespub.ca.*

Swans Brewpub. A stunning array of First Nations masks and other artworks hangs from the open rafters in this popular Downtown brewpub, where jazz, blues, and swing bands play nightly. ✉ *506 Pandora Ave., Downtown* ☎ *250/361-3310* ⊕ *www.swanshotel.com.*

VIC WEST

PUBS

Spinnakers Gastro Brewpub. You can hop on an Inner Harbour Ferry to this local favorite on the Inner Harbour's north shore. Canada's first modern-day brewpub, it also has the city's longest menu of traditionally made in-house brews. A covered waterfront deck, a double-sided fireplace, excellent pub grub, and an all-ages in-house restaurant make this a popular hangout. ✉ *308 Catherine St., Vic West* ☎ *250/386-2739* ⊕ *www.spinnakers.com.*

PERFORMING ARTS

MUSIC

Summer in the Square. Free jazz, classical, and folk concerts; cultural events; and more run all summer at Centennial Square, which is next to City Hall. Free lunchtime concerts are offered Tuesday to Thursday from noon to 1, from July through September. ⊠ *Centennial Square, Pandora Ave. and Douglas St., Downtown* ☎ *250/361–0388* ⊕ *www. victoria.ca/cityvibe.*

Victoria Jazz Society. Watch for music events hosted by this group, which also organizes the annual TD Victoria International JazzFest in late June and the Vancouver Island Blues Bash in early September. ☎ *250/388–4423* ⊕ *www.jazzvictoria.ca.*

Victoria Symphony. With everything from solo performances to chamber music concerts to full-scale orchestral works, the Victoria Symphony has something for everyone. Watch for Symphony Splash on the first Sunday in August, when the orchestra plays a free concert, accompanied by fireworks, from a barge in the Inner Harbour. ☎ *250/385–6515* ⊕ *www.victoriasymphony.ca.*

THEATER

Belfry Theatre. Housed in a former church, the Belfry Theatre has a resident company that specializes in contemporary Canadian dramas. ⊠ *1291 Gladstone Ave., Fernwood* ☎ *250/385–6815* ⊕ *www.belfry.bc.ca.*

The David Foster Foundation Theatre. Dinner theater performances and film screenings are presented at this lavish venue in the Oak Bay Beach Hotel. ⊠ *The Oak Bay Beach Hotel, 1175 Beach Drive, Oak Bay* ☎ *250/668–7758.*

Langham Court Theatre. The Victoria Theatre Guild, one of Canada's oldest community theater groups, stages works by internationally known playwrights at this 177-seat venue near the Victoria Art Gallery. ⊠ *Langham Court Theatre, 805 Langham Ct., Rockland* ☎ *250/384–2142* ⊕ *www.langhamtheatre.ca.*

Phoenix Theatre. University of Victoria theater students stage productions at this on-campus venue. ⊠ *University of Victoria, 3800 Finnerty Rd., University of Victoria Campus* ☎ *250/721–8000* ⊕ *www. phoenixtheatres.ca.*

Theatre Inconnu. Victoria's oldest alternative theater company, housed in a venue across the street from the Belfry Theatre, offers a range of performances at affordable ticket prices. ⊠ *1923 Fernwood Rd., Fernwood* ☎ *250/360–0234* ⊕ *www.theatreinconnu.com.*

Theatre SKAM. This alternative troupe stages summer shows at such offbeat venues as the Galloping Goose Bike Path (the audience pedals from one performance to the next) and the back of a pickup truck in city parks. ☎ *250/386–7526* ⊕ *www.skam.ca.*

Victoria Fringe Festival. Each August and September, a vast menu of original and intriguing performances takes place at several venues around town. It's part of a circuit of fringe-theater events attracting performers—and fans—from around the world. ☎ *250/383–2663* ⊕ *www.victoriafringe.com.*

SPORTS AND THE OUTDOORS

BEACHES

FAMILY **Cadboro-Gyro Park.** A long sandy, driftwood-strewn beach backed by a grassy park with plenty of picnic tables and shade trees draws families to this sheltered bay, accessible via the Scenic Marine Drive. Kids enjoy the sea creature structures in the play area (including a replica of the legendary "Cadborosaurus" sea serpent said to live in these waters). Hiking trails, a boat launch, and tennis courts keep adults busy; swimming is safe here, if you don't mind the cold (or the sea creature). Snacks can be had at nearby Cadboro Village. **Amenities:** parking (free); toilets. **Best for:** walking; sunrise. ⊠ *Sinclair Rd., Saanich* ✦ *Off Cadboro Bay Rd.* ☎ *250/475–5522* ⊕ *www.saanich.ca.*

FAMILY **Cordova Bay.** Walkers, swimmers, and sunbathers flock to this long stretch of forest-backed sand, pebble, and driftwood beach, which is just north of Mount Douglas Park. There are several access points along Cordova Bay Road. The Beachhouse Restaurant, perched on the sand about midway along the beach (at 5109 Cordova Bay Road), serves take-out snacks plus casual lunches and dinners. **Amenities:** food and drink; toilets (May 1–October 30). **Best for:** swimming; walking. ⊠ *Cordova Bay Rd., Saanich* ⊕ *www.saanich.ca.*

FAMILY **Willows Beach.** This sandy beach with its calm waters, playground, and shady picnic spots, is a summertime favorite among Victorian families. It's just a few miles from Downtown in the very British Oak Bay neighborhood—there's even a teahouse on the beach. **Amenities:** food and drink; parking; toilets. **Best for:** swimming. ⊠ *Dalhousie St., at Beach Dr., Oak Bay* ⊕ *www.oakbay.ca.*

FAMILY **Witty's Lagoon Regional Park.** About 30 minutes west of downtown Victoria, this park has a sandy beach, forest trails, marshlands, and a large lagoon—and it's home to 160 species of birds. There's also a nature house that presents interpretive programs. **Amenities:** parking; toilets. **Best for:** solitude; walking. ⊠ *Metchosin Rd., West Shore* ✦ *Between Duke Rd. and Witty Beach Rd.* ☎ *250/478–3344* ⊕ *www.wittyslagoon.com.*

BIKING

Victoria is a bike-friendly town with more bicycle commuters than any other city in Canada. Bike racks on city buses, bike lanes on Downtown streets, and tolerant drivers all help, as do the city's three long-distance cycling routes, which mix car-free paths and low-traffic scenic routes.

BC Ferries will transport bikes for a nominal fee (just C$2 from Vancouver). You can also rent bikes, bike trailers, and tandem bikes at several Victoria outlets for a few hours, a day, or a week. Helmets are required by law and are supplied with bike rentals.

The Gulf Islands are also popular with cyclists. The scenery is wonderful, but the steep narrow roads and lack of dedicated bike paths can be frustrating.

8

BIKE ROUTES

Galloping Goose Regional Trail. Following an old rail bed, this 55-km (35-mile) route officially starts at the Vic West end of Johnson Street Bridge, which connects Downtown Victoria to Vic West. The multi-use trail runs across old rail trestles and through forests west to the town of Sooke, finishing just past Sooke Potholes Provincial Park. Just north of Downtown it links with the Lochside Regional Trail to the BC Ferries terminal at Swartz Bay, creating a nearly continuous 55-mile car-free route. ⊠ *Johnson St. Bridge, Vic West* ☎ *250/478–3344* ⊕ *www.crd.bc.ca/parks.*

Lochside Regional Trail. This fairly level, mostly car-free route follows an old rail bed for 29 km (18 miles) past farmland, wineries, and beaches from the ferry terminals at Swartz Bay and Sidney to downtown Victoria. It joins the Seaside Touring Route at Cordova Bay and meets the Galloping Goose Trail just north of downtown Victoria. ⊠ *Sidney* ☎ *250/478–3344* ⊕ *www.crd.bc.ca/parks.*

Victoria Seaside Touring Route. Starting at the corner of Government and Belleville streets on the Inner Harbour, this 29-km (18-mile) route along city streets and coastal roads, marked with bright yellow signs, leads past Fisherman's Wharf and along the Dallas Road waterfront to Beacon Hill Park. It then follows the seashore to Cordova Bay, where it connects with Victoria's other two long-distance routes: the Lochside and Galloping Goose regional trails. ⊠ *Government and Belleville Sts., Inner Harbour, Downtown* ⊕ *www.trailsbc.ca/loops-journeys/vancouver-island/loop-victoria-seaside-touring-39-km.*

BIKE RENTALS AND TOURS

Cycle BC Rentals. This centrally located shop rents bikes for adults and children, as well as bike trailers, motorcycles, and scooters. ⊠ *685 Humboldt St., Downtown* ☎ *250/380–2453, 866/380–2453* ⊕ *www.cyclebc.ca.*

Cycletreks. Besides renting bikes, this company runs bike tours of Victoria, multiday trips to the Gulf Islands, and vineyard tours of the Saanich Peninsula and the Cowichan Valley. Their self-guided trips include bikes, maps, and a ride to Butchart Gardens or the end of the Galloping Goose or Lochside trail so that you can pedal back. ⊠ *1000 Wharf St., Downtown* ☎ *250/386–3147* ⊕ *www.cycletreks.com* ☉ *May–Sept. only.*

The Pedaler Bicycle Tours and Rentals. Pedal and sample your way around Victoria's craft breweries, wineries, culinary sites, and bike-friendly neighborhoods on these behind-the-scenes bike tours; the company rents bikes, too. ⊠ *719 Douglas St., Downtown* ☎ *778/265–7433* ⊕ *www.thepedaler.ca.*

GOLF

You can golf year-round in Victoria and southern Vancouver Island. Victoria alone has several public golf courses, ranging from rolling seaview fairways to challenging mountaintop sites.

Golf Vancouver Island. This organization has details about the island's courses. ⊠ ☎ *888/465–3239* ⊕ *www.golfvancouverisland.ca.*

Bear Mountain Golf & Country Club. Built near the top of a 1,100-foot mountain about 30 minutes north of Victoria, this purpose-built resort is home to Canada's only Nicklaus-designed 36-hole duo. Created by Jack Nicklaus and his son Steve, the rugged Mountain Course is known for its elevation changes and views—especially from the 14th hole, which is built on a cliff ledge with striking views across the city. The more user-friendly Valley Course offers plenty of challenge at a slightly lower elevation. The two courses are the centerpiece of a resort that includes a hotel, a spa, and several restaurants. ⊠ *1999 Country Club Way, off Millstream Rd. and Bear Mountain Pkwy., West Shore* ☎ *250/744-2327, 888/533-2327* ⊕ *www.bearmountain.ca* ⊠ *C$149* ⅉ *Mountain Course: 18 holes. 6,891 yards. Par 70. Valley Course: 18 holes. 6,807 yards. Par 71.*

Olympic View Golf Club. The distant peaks of the Olympic Mountains are the backdrop to this bucolic par-72 course, home to two waterfalls and 12 lakes. The first BC course played by Tiger Woods, it's about 30 minutes' drive west of downtown Victoria. ⊠ *643 Latoria Rd., off Veterans' Memorial Parkway, West Shore* ☎ *250/474-3673, 800/446-5322* ⊕ *www.olympicviewgolf.com* ⊠ *C$60* ⅉ *18 holes. 6,534 yards. Par 72.*

HIKING AND WALKING

Victoria is one of the most pedestrian-friendly cities in North America. Waterfront pathways make it possible to stroll virtually all around Victoria's waterfront. For some interesting self-guided walks around the city's historic areas, check out ⊕ *www.victoria.ca/tours* or pick up a free walking-tour map at the city's visitor information center. Though popular with cyclists, the area's long-distance paths are also great for long walks. For views and elevation, check out the trail networks in the area's many provincial and regional parks.

Goldstream Provincial Park. This wilderness park, just 16 km (10 miles) north of town, has a vast network of trails, from wheelchair-accessible paths through ancient Douglas fir and cedar forests to challenging hikes to the view-blessed peak of Mt. Finlayson. Trails also lead to the 47-meter-tall (154-foot) Niagara Falls. ⊠ *Hwy. 1, at Finlayson Arm Rd., West Shore* ☎ *250/478-9414* ⊕ *www.env.gov.bc.ca/bcparks.*

Mount Douglas Park. Trails through the forest to the 260-meter (853-foot) summit of Mt. Douglas reward hikers with a 360-degree view of Victoria, the Saanich Peninsula, and the mountains of Washington State. ⊠ *Off Cedar Hill Rd., Saanich* ☎ *250/475-5522* ⊕ *www.saanich.ca.*

FAMILY **Swan Lake Christmas Hill Nature Sanctuary.** This sanctuary, with its 23-acre lake set in 150 acres of fields and wetlands, is just a few minutes from downtown Victoria. From the 2.4-km (1½-mile) Lake Loop Trail and floating boardwalk, birders can spot a variety of waterfowl and nesting birds year-round. For great views of Victoria, take the 2.4-km (1½-mile) round-trip hike to the top of Christmas Hill. The sanctuary's Nature House is open weekdays 8:30–4 and weekends noon–4. ⊠ *3873 Swan Lake Rd., Saanich* ☎ *250/479-0211* ⊕ *www.swanlake.bc.ca* ⊠ *Free* ⊙ *Daily dawn–dusk.*

8

Victoria: Whale-Watching

The thrill of seeing whales in the wild is, for many, one of the most enduring memories of a trip to Victoria. In summer (roughly April to October), about 85 orca, or "killer whales," reside in the Strait of Georgia between Vancouver and Victoria. They live in pods, and because their movements are fairly predictable, chances are high that you will see a pod on any given trip. Some operators claim sighting rates of 90%; others offer guaranteed sightings, meaning that you can repeat the tour free of charge until you spot a whale.

It's not unheard of to see whales from a BC Ferry en route to Victoria—but the ferries don't alter their routes to take advantage of whale-watching, so your best bet is to take a dedicated tour. A number of companies leave from Victoria's Inner Harbour, a few are based in Richmond (near Vancouver), and others leave from Sidney and Sooke, outside of Victoria.

Not all tours are alike, and the kind of boat you choose determines the kind of experience you're likely to have—though most companies have naturalists on board as guides, as well as hydrophones that, if you get close enough, allow you to listen to the whales singing and vocalizing.

Motor launches, which carry from 30 to 80 passengers, are comfortable, with restrooms, protection from the elements, and even concessions. Seasickness isn't usually a problem in the sheltered waters near Victoria, but if you're not a good sailor, it's wise to wear a seasickness band or take antinausea medication. Ginger candy often works, too.

Zodiacs are open inflatable boats that carry about 12 passengers. They are smaller and more agile than cruisers and offer both an exciting ride bouncing over the waves and an eye-level view of the whales. Passengers are supplied with warm, waterproof survival suits. Zodiac tours are not recommended for people with back or neck problems, pregnant women, or small children.

Note that the kind of boat you choose does not affect how close you can get to the whales. For the safety of whales and humans, government and industry regulations require boats to stay at least 100 meters (328 feet) from the pods, though closer encounters are possible if whales approach a boat when its engine is off.

And, although the focus is on whales, you also have a good chance of spotting marine birds, Dall's porpoises, dolphins, seals, sea lions, and minke, gray, and humpback whales as well as other marine life. And, naturally, there's the scenery of forested islands and distant mountains.

Johnstone Strait, off Telegraph Cove on Vancouver Island's northeast coast, has one of the world's largest populations of orca in summer and is an important center for whale research. Tofino and Ucluelet, on the island's west coast, draw whale-watchers every March and April when an estimated 20,000 Pacific gray whales cruise by on their annual migration.

There are dozens of whale-watching operators in the area. The following recommendations are among the more established: Great Pacific Adventures, Prince of Whales, and Springtide Whale Tours & Charters. ⇨ *For more information on these companies, see Whale Watching.*

KAYAKING

The Upper Harbour and the Gorge, the waterways just north of the Inner Harbour, are popular boating spots.

Island Boat Rentals. You can rent a kayak, canoe, motorboat, or rowboat at this outlet at the Canoe Marina on the Upper Harbour. ⊠ *Canoe Marina, 450 Swift St., Downtown* ☎ *250/995–1661* ⊕ *www. greatpacificadventures.com/rentals.*

Victoria Kayak. Setting out from the Inner Harbour, this company runs 2½-hour tours to see seals and other marine life around Seal Island. It's a good tour for beginners. The company runs evening sunset tours and rents kayaks, too. ⊠ *950 Wharf St., Downtown* ☎ *250/216-5646* ⊕ *www.victoriakayak.com.*

SCUBA DIVING

The waters off Vancouver Island have some of the best cold-water scuba diving in the world, with clear waters and rich marine life; visibility is best in winter. The Ogden Point Breakwater and Race Rocks Underwater Marine Park are popular spots close to town. In Brentwood Bay on the Saanich Peninsula are the Glass Sponge Gardens, a sea mountain covered with sponges that were thought to be extinct at one point. Off Thetis Island, near Chemainus, divers can explore a sunken 737 jetliner. Dive BC (⊕ *www.dive.bc.ca*) has details.

Ogden Point Dive Centre. Guided dives, weekend charters, PADI courses, and equipment sales and service are all available at this PADI-certified dive center at the Ogden Point Breakwater near downtown Victoria. Great shore dives start along the breakwater right outside the shop. ⊠ *199 Dallas Rd., Downtown* ☎ *250/380–9119, 888/701–1177* ⊕ *www.divevictoria.com.*

Rockfish Divers. Based at the Brentwood Bay Resort on the Saanich Peninsula, this internationally accredited PADI dive outfitter offers charters, courses, and equipment rentals. ⊠ *Brentwood Bay Resort & Spa, 849 Verdier Ave., Brentwood Bay* ☎ *250/516–3483,* ⊕ *www.rockfishdivers.com.*

WHALE WATCHING

The following companies provide whale-watching excursions from Victoria. ⇨ *For more information, see the feature "Victoria: Whale Watching."*

FAMILY **Great Pacific Adventures.** This company offers year-round tours with both Zodiacs and covered vessels. Boats are equipped with hydrophones and all guides are marine biologists. In summer a three-hour tour starts at C$105. ⊠ *950 Wharf St.* ☎ *250/386–2277, 877/733–6722* ⊕ *www. greatpacificadventures.com.*

FAMILY **Prince of Whales.** Victoria's biggest whale-watching company offers a whole range of marine excursions, from three-hour boat or Zodiac tours from Victoria, to five-hour trips that include a stop at Butchart Gardens, to one-way or round-trip crossings between Vancouver and Victoria; all sailings have naturalists on board. Zodiac trips cost

8

C$115 and leave year-round; covered boat sailings on the *Ocean Magic II* are C$110 and run from April to October; and Victoria to Butchart Garden trips run from late May to late September (the C$145 fare includes admission to the gardens). The company's Vancouver to Victoria crossings, running from late May to late September on the 74-passenger *Ocean Magic*, are a great time-saver, combining a sailing to or from Victoria with a whale-watching trip. A stop at the Butchart Gardens or return flights by floatplane or helicopter are options, too. The most popular trip, billed as The Ultimate Day Trip, includes a whale-watching trip from Vancouver to Victoria, a stop in Downtown Victoria, a bus transfer to Butchart Gardens, and a sunset sailing back to Vancouver. This C$300 trip runs daily from late May to late September. The company's Victoria office is on the Inner Harbour Causeway, below the Visitor Info Centre. ✉ *812 Wharf St., Lower Causeway Level, Downtown* ☎ *250/383–4884, 888/383–4884* ⊕ *www.princeofwhales.com.*

FAMILY **SpringTide Whale Watching & Eco Tours.** Using marine biologists as guides, this company runs tours on Zodiacs and on 61-foot motor yachts. Summer tours are three hours long, and the boats are equipped with hydrophones. Rates are C$105. ✉ *1119 Wharf St., Downtown* ☎ *250/384–4444, 800/470–3474* ⊕ *www.victoriawhalewatching.com.*

SHOPPING AND SPAS

VICTORIA SHOPPING

In Victoria, as in the rest of BC, the most popular souvenirs are First Nations arts and crafts, which you can pick up at shops, galleries, street markets, and—in some cases—directly from artists' studios. Look for silver jewelry and cedar boxes carved with traditional images and, especially around Duncan (in the Cowichan Valley), the thick handknit sweaters made by the Cowichan people. BC wines, from shops in Victoria or directly from the wineries, make good souvenirs, as most are unavailable outside the province. Shopping in Victoria is easy: virtually everything is in the Downtown area on or near Government Street stretching north from the Fairmont Empress hotel.

Shopping in Victoria is easy: virtually everything is in the Downtown area on or near Government Street stretching north from the Fairmont Empress hotel.

DOWNTOWN

AREAS AND MALLS

Antique Row. Fort Street between Blanshard and Cook streets is home to antiques, curio, and collectibles shops along with a growing number of shops selling artisanal food and eco-friendly fashions. ✉ *Downtown.*

Bay Centre. Downtown Victoria's main shopping mall has about 100 boutiques and restaurants. ✉ *1150 Douglas St., Downtown* ☎ *250/952–5680* ⊕ *www.thebaycentre.ca.*

Fan Tan Alley, in Victoria's Chinatown, is said to be the narrowest street in Canada.

Chinatown. Exotic fruits and vegetables, children's toys, wicker fans, fabric slippers, and other Chinese imports fill the shops along Fisgard Street. Fan Tan Alley, a narrow lane off Fisgard Street, has more nouveau-hippie goods, with a record store and yoga studio tucked in among its tiny storefronts. ⊠ *Downtown.*

Design District. The area where Wharf Street runs into Store Street contains a cluster of Victoria's home decor shops. ⊠ *Downtown* ⊕ *www. victoriadesigndistrict.com.*

Fodor'sChoice ★ **Lower Johnson Street.** This row of candy-color Victorian-era shopfronts in LoJo (Lower Johnson) is Victoria's hub for independent fashion boutiques. Storefronts—some closet size—are filled with local designers' wares, funky boutiques, and shops selling ecologically friendly clothes of hemp and organic cotton. ⊠ *Johnson St., between Government and Store Sts., Downtown.*

Trounce Alley. Art Galleries and high-end fashion outlets line this pedestrian-only lane north of View Street between Broad and Government streets. ⊠ *Downtown.*

MARKETS

Victorians seem to relish any excuse to head outdoors, which may explain the boom in outdoor crafts, farmers', and other open-air markets around town.

Bastion Square Public Market. Crafts vendors and entertainers congregate in this historic square Thursdays, Fridays, and Saturdays from May through September. On Sunday, area farmers join the mix, selling local produce, homemade baked goods, cheeses, jams, and other goodies.

⊠ *Bastion Square, off Government St., Downtown* ☎ *250/885–1387* ⊕ *www.bastionsquare.ca.*

James Bay Community Market. Organic food, local produce, creative crafts, and live music draw shoppers to this summer Saturday market south of the Inner Harbour. Look for it behind the Parliament Buildings. ⊠ *Superior and Menzies Sts., James Bay, Downtown* ☎ *250/381–5323* ⊕ *www.jamesbaymarket.com.*

Moss Street Market. "Make it, bake it, or grow it" is the rule for vendors at this street market, held 10 to 2 on Saturdays from May through October. ⊠ *Fairfield Rd. at Moss St., Fairfield* ☎ *250/361–1747* ⊕ *www. mossstreetmarket.com.*

Ship Point Night Market. Music and local crafts are spotlighted at this night market, held Friday and Saturday evenings in summer on the Inner Harbour. ⊠ *Ship Point Pier, Downtown* ⊹ *Just below the Visitor Info Centre on the Inner Harbour* ☎ *250/413–6828* ⊕ *www.gvha.ca.*

Sidney Thursday Night Market. More than 150 vendors of food, arts, crafts, and more take over the main street of this town, a 30-minute drive north of Victoria, each Thursday evening from mid-May through August. ⊠ *Beacon Ave., Sidney* ⊕ *www.sidneystreetmarket.com.*

RECOMMENDED STORES

Artina's. Canadian-made jewelry—all handmade, one-of-a-kind pieces—fills the display cases at this unique jewelry shop. ⊠ *1002 Government St., Downtown* ☎ *250/386–7000* ⊕ *www.artinas.com.*

Cook Culture. A hive of foodie activity, this upscale kitchenware store in the Atrium Building is also a cooking school, offering workshops on topics like knife skills and how to make sushi or Indian street food. ⊠ *1317 Blanshard St., Downtown* ☎ *250/590–8161* ⊕ *www. cookculture.com.*

Cowichan Trading. First Nations jewelry, art, moccasins, and Cowichan sweaters are the focus at this long-established outlet. ⊠ *1328 Government St., Downtown* ☎ *250/383–0321* ⊕ *www.cowichantrading.com.*

Hill's Native Art. Of the many First Nations stores you'll come across, Hill's is one of the best, offering everything from affordable souvenirs to original First Nations totems, masks, and jewelry as well as Inuit sculptures. ⊠ *1008 Government St., Downtown* ☎ *250/385–3911* ⊕ *www.hills.ca.*

idar. This tiny Tudor-framed shop on Fort Street (look for the three brass honeybees in the sidewalk) houses the workshop of one of the few goldsmiths in North America still forging gold by hand. All the pieces here, in gold, silver, and platinum, are made entirely by hand in original designs reflecting Northwest, Celtic, Nordic, and other traditions. ⊠ *946 Fort St., Downtown* ☎ *250/383–3414* ⊕ *www.idar.com.*

Irish Linen Stores. In business since 1917, this tiny shop has kept Victorians in fine linen, lace, and hand-embroidered items for generations. ⊠ *1019 Government St., Downtown* ☎ *250/383–6812* ⊕ *www. irishlinenvictoria.com.*

Munro's Books. Move over, Chapters: this beautifully restored 1909 former bank now houses one of Canada's best-stocked independent bookstores. Deals abound in the remainders' bin. ⊠ *1108 Government St., Downtown* ☎ *250/382-2464* ⊕ *www.munrobooks.com.*

Murchie's. You can choose from more than 90 varieties of tea to sip here or take home, plus coffees, tarts, and cakes at Victoria's oldest tea purveyor (the company's been around since 1894). ⊠ *1110 Government St., Downtown* ☎ *250/383-3112.*

Rogers' Chocolates. The staff at Rogers' has been making chocolates since 1885, and they're getting pretty good at it. Victoria creams are a local favorite. The current shop dates to 1903. ⊠ *913 Government St., Downtown* ☎ *250/881-8771* ⊕ *www.rogerschocolates.com.*

Fodor's Choice ★ **Silk Road.** Tea aspires to new heights in this chic emporium. Shelves are stacked with more than 300 intriguing varieties; some you can enjoy in flights at an impressive tasting bar, and others have been restyled into aromatherapy remedies and spa treatments, including a green tea facial, which you can try out in the tiny spa downstairs. ⊠ *1624 Government St., Downtown* ☎ *250/704-2688* ⊕ *www.silkroadtea.com.*

SPAS

Since health, nature, and relaxing seem to be the major preoccupations in Victoria, it's not surprising that the city has enjoyed a boom in spas. Aesthetics are important, but natural healing, ancient practices, and the use of such local products as wine and seaweed are more the focus here. Local specialties include vinotherapy (applying the antioxidant properties of wine grapes externally, rather than internally).

Haven Spa. Aesthetics, massages, and facials are the focus at this full-service spa on the Saanich Peninsula. A pre-treatment steam room and post-treatment lounge add to the pampering. ⊠ *Sidney Pier Hotel & Spa, 9805 Seaport Pl., Sidney* ☎ *250/655-9797* ⊕ *www.havenspasalon.ca.*

Le Spa Sereine. A custom-built pedicure room with fully reclining chairs and sunken basins is a draw at this independent Downtown spa. Set in an atmospheric old building, it's also known for salt glows, hydrotherapy, reflexology, and Indian head massages. ⊠ *1411 Government St., Downtown* ☎ *250/388-4419* ⊕ *www.lespasereine.ca.*

Silk Road Spa. Essential oils and organic skin and body products are the draw at this serene Chinatown spa, located inside the Silk Road tea shop. The green-tea facial is especially popular. ⊠ *1624 Government St., Downtown* ☎ *250/704-2688* ⊕ *www.silkroadtea.com.*

SORA Spa. Traditional Thai, Swedish, and hot stone massage, as well as facials and beauty treatments, are among the offerings at this intimate Asian-inspired spa at the Hotel Grand Pacific. ⊠ *Hotel Grand Pacific, 463 Belleville St., Downtown* ☎ *250/380-7862* ⊕ *www.hotelgrandpacific.com.*

Spa at Delta Victoria Ocean Pointe Resort. Organic skin-care products and harbor-view treatment rooms are among the draws at this popular hotel spa. Patrons have access to the hotel's gym and pool. ⊠ *Delta Victoria Ocean Pointe Resort, 45 Songhees Rd., Downtown* ☎ *250/360-5938, 800/575-8882* ⊕ *www.thespadeltavictoria.com.*

8

Spa Magnolia. Organic products, couples treatments, and a hydrotherapy tub are the hallmark of this spa at the Hotel Magnolia. ⊠ *Magnolia Hotel & Spa, 625 Courtney St., Downtown* ☎ *250/920–7721* ⊕ *www. spamagnolia.com.*

Willow Stream Spa at the Fairmont Empress Hotel. Victoria's most luxurious spa is actually a pretty good value, especially if you arrive, as suggested, an hour before your appointment to soak in the Hungarian mineral bath, sauna, and steam room. ⊠ *Fairmont Empress Hotel, 633 Humboldt St., Downtown* ☎ *250/995–4650, 866/854–7444* ⊕ *www. willowstream.com.*

VANCOUVER ISLAND

WELCOME TO VANCOUVER ISLAND

TOP REASONS TO GO

★ **Storm Watching in Tofino:** Its beaches and rain forests make Tofino one of BC's most sublime warm-weather environments; come November, the rampant fury of its coastal storms is an even more extraordinary experience.

★ **Enjoying the rustic charms of the Gulf Islands:** Whether you choose well-developed Salt Spring Island, pretty Galiano Island, historic Mayne Island, beachy Pender Island, or remote Saturna Island, you'll find a wealth of experiences.

★ **Exploring the Cowichan Valley:** With excellent food, wine, and First Nations culture, the valley makes a great excursion from Victoria for foodies or families.

★ **Traveling to Sooke and Beyond:** Bike or hike along the Galloping Goose Trail to Sooke, or drive scenic Highway 14 to the wilderness beaches and trails of the island's southwest coast.

Campbell River

Alaska Inside Passage 101

Powell River

28

Strathcona Provincial Park

Courtenay

Strait of Georgia

19

Sproat Lake

Parksville

VANCOUVER ISLAND RANGES

Port Alberni

4

Tofino

VANCOUVER ISLAND

Long Beach

Wild Pacific Trail

Ucluelet

COAST

Pacific Rim National Park Reserve

Broken Group Islands

Lake Cowich

Barkley Sound

Bamfield

RANGE

PACIFIC

Carmanah Walbran Provincial Park

1 Sooke and the Southwest Coast. Just 45 minutes west of Victoria (and continuing another 48 miles along the coast toward Port Renfrew), the southwest coast of Vancouver Island is heavily forested and beautiful.

Juan de Fuca Provincial Park

Port Renfrew

Juan de Fuca

OCEAN

0   30 mi

0   30 km

112

2 The Cowichan Valley. This fertile region less than an hour north of Victoria is filled with great restaurants, wineries, and farm stands, and its towns offer a wealth of First Nations culture, making it an excursion suitable for either adults or families.

3 The Gulf Islands. There are hundreds of islands in Georgia Strait between Vancouver Island and mainland BC, but five of the biggest are easily reached by ferry from Sidney, just north of Victoria, and have

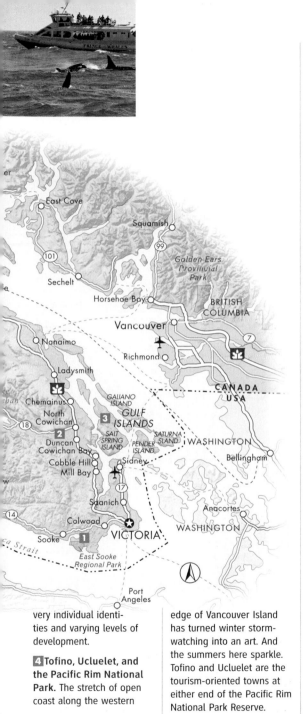

GETTING ORIENTED

The two most popular and accessible regions of southern Vancouver Island are the forested southwest coast between Sooke and Port Renfrew and the Cowichan Valley, with its comfortable B&Bs, wineries, great food, and myriad activities. For a great road trip, take the long, winding Pacific Marine Circle Route around the two regions. It's also an easy escape to the Gulf Islands, reachable by ferry from Sidney; Victoria residents take full advantage of the islands on weekends, so you should too. If you have the time, Vancouver Island's wild west coast, home to crashing surf, deserted beaches, old growth forests, and Tofino, the cutest surf town north of California, makes an unforgettable trip. It's a four-hour drive through the island's mountainous heart or a quick flight—and you'll need at least three days to explore the area.

9

very individual identities and varying levels of development.

4 **Tofino, Ucluelet, and the Pacific Rim National Park.** The stretch of open coast along the western edge of Vancouver Island has turned winter storm-watching into an art. And the summers here sparkle. Tofino and Ucluelet are the tourism-oriented towns at either end of the Pacific Rim National Park Reserve.

With a few days in the area, you have time to explore farther on Vancouver Island than just Victoria. Sooke and the Southwest Coast, the Cowichan Valley, or one of the Gulf Islands can make an easy day-trip from Victoria, though any of them can warrant a weekend or longer for more serious exploration. These three regions around Victoria can be connected, so you don't have to retrace your steps. More time? Head northwest for the stunning coastal wilderness of Tofino, Ucluelet, and the Pacific Rim National Park Reserve.

How to choose? For wilderness beaches and forested hiking trails, take Highway 14 or cycle the Galloping Goose Trail to Sooke and the southwest coast. For food, wine, and First Nations culture, head north over the stunning Malahat drive to the Cowichan Valley. Arts, crafts, kayaking, white-shell beaches, and a touch of neo-hippie island culture await those who visit Salt Spring Island, especially on market Saturdays (Salt Spring is also the only side trip easily manageable by public transport). You can truly get away from it all on the islands of Galiano, Mayne, or Pender. For families, the Cowichan Valley, with its interesting nature centers, has the most obvious kid appeal, though all three destinations have beaches, forests, and cute farm animals.

Wherever you go, food will play a big part in your experience. Vancouver Islanders are often credited with starting the "locavore" movement. Wild salmon, Pacific oysters, locally made artisanal cheeses, forest-foraged mushrooms, organic vegetables, local microbrews, and even wines from the island's family-run wineries can all be sampled here.

PLANNING

WHEN TO GO

July and August are, not surprisingly, peak season on Vancouver Island. That's when the weather is fine, and all that hiking, camping, boating, and outdoor fun is at its best. September, with its quieter pace, harvest festivals, and lingering sunshine, may be the perfect time to visit. Increasingly, storm-watchers are flocking to Tofino and Ucluelet in winter to watch dramatic tempests pound the coast. April is also a prime month for the west coast: that's when 20,000 gray whales swim by on their way to Alaska and when the Pacific Rim Whale Festival welcomes visitors.

MAKING THE MOST OF YOUR TIME

If you're driving (and a car really is essential for exploring the island), pick a circular route to avoid retracing your steps: drive the Pacific Marine Circle Route through Sooke and the Cowichan Valley, link the Saanich Peninsula and Cowichan Valley with a ride on BC Ferries' Mill Bay Ferry, or combine a trip to the Saanich Peninsula or Cowichan Valley with a visit to Salt Spring Island. For the Gulf Islands, it's best to pick one or two islands to explore; the ferry schedules are not conducive to island-hopping. In a hurry? Floatplanes serve the Gulf Islands and the Cowichan Valley from Vancouver, and the experience is unforgettable. Another option? Pick a resort or seaside inn, fly in, stay there, and relax.

Tofino, a five-hour drive across the island from Victoria, is a separate trip altogether; but flying in and renting a car in Tofino is always an option. Three full days are about the minimum: once you've made the trek from Vancouver, it takes a day to unwind and allow the place get into your consciousness. A quick conversation with your host will help you hit the highlights—the best spots to view wildlife, the top trails (some get washed out in stormy weather), when to browse the galleries (some close Monday), and what musicians are playing (if nightlife is on your list).

9

FESTIVALS

Festivals are a great way to explore the region's food and wine scene in the Cowichan Valley. The Pacific Rim has various festivals throughout the year.

MAR.: The **Pacific Rim Whale Festival** (⊕ *www.pacificrimwhalefestival. com*) marks the spring migration of as many as 22,000 Pacific gray whales between Mexico and the Arctic with crafts, food, and cultural events for the whole family. You can try everything from building sand-sculptures to decorating sea creature–cookies.

APR.–MAY: Fishers, diners, and chefs gather to celebrate local fisheries and boat-to-table cuisine at **Feast Tofino** (⊕ *www.feastbc.com*), a monthlong culinary event in May. The **Tofino Shorebird Festival** (⊕ *www. tourismtofino.com*) celebrates the thousands of shorebirds that migrate north from Central and South America to tundra breeding grounds in Alaska. The date changes annually, so check with Tourism Tofino.

JUNE: Area lodges and food and wine producers sponsor the three-day **Tofino Food and Wine Festival** (⊕ *www.tofinofoodandwinefestival.com*) at venues around town.

JULY: The **Pacific Rim Summer Festival** (⊕ *www.pacificrimarts.ca*) is a celebration of music, dance, and the arts during the first two weeks of July.

AUG.: Hundreds of imaginatively crafted lanterns make the **Tofino Lantern Festival** (⊕ *www.tourismtofino.com*) a sight to behold. It's usually held in August.

SEPT.: September is the time for food festivals that celebrate the bounty of the Cowichan Valley. The **Cowichan Wine and Culinary Festival** offers a week of wine and food events. The same month, the **Vancouver Island Feast of Fields** is a lavish celebration of local food on an area farm.

Cowichan Wine and Culinary Festival. Cowichan Valley wineries and restaurants celebrate the region's bounty with a week of wine and culinary events every September. ⊕ *wines.cowichan.net*.

Vancouver Island Feast of Fields. This lavish celebration of local food is held on an area farm, generally in September. ⊕ *www.farmfolkcityfolk.ca*.

NOV.: The humble bivalve is celebrated during the **Clayoquot Oyster Festival** (⊕ *www.oystergala.com*), a five-day gastronomic adventure.

GETTING HERE AND AROUND

AIR TRAVEL

The major airports on Vancouver Island are Victoria International Airport (YYJ), Nanaimo Airport (YCD), and Comox Valley Airport (YQQ). You can also fly into the tiny Tofino-Ucluelet Airport (YAZ) from Vancouver year-round and from Victoria from May through October.

Float planes serve many of the region's islands and coastal areas. For the Gulf Islands, Harbour Air Seaplanes has regular service from downtown Vancouver to Salt Spring and Pender islands. Seair Seaplanes fly from Vancouver Airport to the Southern Gulf Islands. Saltspring Air flies from downtown Vancouver and Vancouver International Airport to the Southern Gulf Islands and to Maple Bay, near Duncan, in the Cowichan Valley. Kenmore Air has summer floatplane service from Seattle to the Gulf Islands. There is no scheduled floatplane service between Victoria and the Gulf Islands.

Orca Air and KD Air fly regularly scheduled flights (on small eight-passenger planes) into Tofino from Vancouver year-round. Orca Air also serves Tofino from Victoria between May and October. Northwest Seaplanes runs charter flights from its terminal at Renton, near Seattle, to Tofino and Ucluelet. Harbour Air Seaplanes runs seaplane charters from Vancouver, Victoria, Nanaimo, and other BC destinations. ⇨ *For information on these airlines, see Air Travel in Travel Smart.*

BOAT AND FERRY TRAVEL

BC Ferries has frequent, year-round passenger and vehicle service to Vancouver Island: it's a 1½-hour crossing from Tsawwassen, about an hour south of Vancouver, to Swartz Bay, about 30 minutes north of Victoria on the Saanich Peninsula. There are also regular sailings from Horseshoe Bay (a 45-minute drive north of Vancouver) to Departure

Bay, 3 km (2 miles) north of Nanaimo, and from Tsawwassen to Duke Point, 15 km (9 miles) south of Nanaimo; these are a good choice if you're en route to Tofino; from Depature Bay it's another two- to three-hour drive, via Port Alberni, to Ucluelet and Tofino. Vehicle reservations can be made for any of these ferry routes. BC Ferries also sail to the Southern Gulf Islands from Vancouver and Vancouver Island (⇨ *see the Gulf Islands section for details*); ferries cross several times a day between Brentwood Bay on the Saanich Peninsula and Mill Bay in the Cowichan Valley. ⇨ *For information on ferry companies, see Boat and Ferry Travel in Travel Smart.*

Lady Rose Marine Services takes passengers on a packet freighter from Port Alberni to various points on Vancouver Island's west coast. The MV *Francis Barkley* sails from Port Alberni to the Broken Group Islands and Ucluelet on Monday, Wednesday, and Friday between early June and late September, and to Bamfield and waypoints on Tuesday, Thursday, and Saturday year-round. Sunday stops (in summer) are Bamfield and the Broken Group Islands, where the company operates Sechart Lodge, a floating base for kayakers. Round-trip fares are C$78 to Ucluelet, and C$74 to Bamfield or the Broken Group Islands.

Contacts Lady Rose Marine Services. ☎ *250/723–8313, 800/663–7192* ⊕ *www.ladyrosemarine.com.*

BUS TRAVEL

Pacific Coach lines runs several times a day between downtown Vancouver and downtown Victoria. Tofino Bus Island Express connects Victoria and Nanaimo to Ucluelet and Tofino. Tofino Bus Island Express also runs Tofino Transit, which offers a summer-only shuttle service in the Tofino area. Greyhound also serves Tofino and most other towns on Vancouver Island. BC Transit provides city bus service in several Vancouver Island communities. BC Transit's Victoria network extends as far as Sooke, Sidney, and Swartz Bay. Cowichan Valley Regional Transit, a separate BC Transit network, offers a limited service in Duncan and the Cowichan Valley. Salt Spring Island has a small BC transit system serving the ferry terminals and the village of Ganges, but it doesn't meet every ferry. The other Gulf Islands don't have transit services. ⇨ *For information on bus companies, see Bus Travel in Travel Smart.*

HOTELS

Accommodations on Vancouver Island range from cozy farmstays to lavish seaside resorts, from homey country inns to funky beach houses. Typically one-of-a-kind and independently run, hotels here make the most of their stunning forest and seaside settings.

In Tofino and Ucluelet, prices for lodging and dining are relatively high since this is such a remote destination. Rates vary widely through the seasons, winter being the lowest: luxury lodge stays during the winter storm-watching season can cost as little as a third of summer rates.

RESTAURANTS

Rich farmland, plentiful seafood, and even a nascent wine industry make locavore dining a no-brainer on Vancouver Island, where even take-out places offer wild salmon and organic greens. Global influences, from fish tacos to sushi, have made their mark on the menus, but the ingredients are resolutely local. Must tries? Cowichan Valley wines, cedar plank salmon, and Nanaimo bars—the ubiquitous sweet treats named for the Vancouver Island city. As you move further from Victoria, prices keep going up, and though food is pricey in this remote area, it's consistently good—even in the humblest spots. Tofino and, to a lesser extent, Ucluelet, offer a range of eateries, from view-blessed resort dining to funky local hangouts; one thing you won't find is a chain restaurant or fast food outlet. Everything is owner-operated and one-of-a-kind here. Enjoy.

WHAT IT COSTS IN CANADIAN DOLLARS				
	$	$$	$$$	$$$$
Restaurants	under C$12	C$13–C$20	C$21–C$30	over C$30
Hotels	under C$125	C$126–C$195	C$196–C$300	over C$300

Prices in the restaurants reviews are the average cost of a main course or equivalent combination of small dishes at dinner or, if dinner is not served, at lunch. Prices in the hotel reviews are the lowest cost of a standard double room in high season, including taxes. For expanded reviews, please visit ⊕ www.fodors.com.

VISITOR INFORMATION

For visitor information for individual destinations on Vancouver Island, see the destinations. Destination BC also offers a good amount of information on Vancouver Island.

Contacts Tourism Vancouver Island. ☎ 250/754–3500, 888/655–3483 ⊕ www.vancouverisland.travel.

SOOKE AND THE SOUTHWEST COAST

Sooke is 28 km (17 miles) west of Victoria on Hwy. 14.

The village of Sooke, on the shore of Juan de Fuca Strait about a 45-minute drive west of Victoria, has two claims to fame: it's home to Sooke Harbour House, one of Canada's best-known country inns, and it's the last stop for gas and supplies before heading out to the beaches and hiking trails of the island's wild and scenic southwest coast.

From Sooke, the narrow and winding Highway 14 runs 77 km (48 miles) through birch and fir woods, with occasional sea views, to the fishing village of Port Renfrew. The area around Sooke is home to some excellent restaurants and high-end B&Bs, but as you head west, other services are few.

The tiny fishing village of Port Renfrew has national and regional parks in all directions. At the end of Highway 14 you'll find the grueling West Coast Trail and the more accessible but still daunting Juan de Fuca Marine Trail. Salmon fishing is also a big reason for visiting the area. The town has a general store, a pub, restaurants, fishing lodges, B&Bs, a campsite, and a range of rustic cabins. There's no garage in town, but gas is usually available at the marina (it's best to play it safe and fill up your tank before leaving Sooke). From Port Renfrew, a 48-km (30-mile) paved back road leads inland to Lake Cowichan in the Cowichan Valley.

To avoid retracing your steps to Victoria, you can follow the signs for the Pacific Marine Circle Route. This self-guided road trip follows Highway 14 from Victoria to Port Renfrew, where it takes a well-maintained back road through the forest to the village of Lake Cowichan. From here, Highway 18 leads to Highway 1 and back through the Cowichan Valley to Victoria. Driving time is about three hours, but watch your fuel gauge, as there are no gas stations between Sooke and Lake Cowichan and no services at all on the 48 km (30 miles) between Port Renfrew and Lake Cowichan.

Watch for the red-and-white lighthouse lamp at the first traffic light as you enter Sooke on Highway 14. It sits in front of the Sooke Visitor Information Centre, which also houses a small museum displaying local First Nations artifacts.

GETTING HERE AND AROUND

Sooke is a 45-minute drive, mostly via Highway 14, west from Victoria, or a pleasant three- to four-hour cycle along the car-free Galloping Goose Trail. BC Transit also runs buses from downtown Victoria as far as the town of Sooke.

VISITOR INFORMATION

Contacts **Sooke Region Museum and Visitor Centre.** ☎ *250/642–6351, 866/888–4748* ⊕ *www.sooke-portrenfrew.com.*

TOP ATTRACTIONS

Juan de Fuca Provincial Park. Extending from Jordan River to near Port Renfrew, Juan de Fuca Provincial Park takes in several beaches, including China Beach, with soft, sandy beaches dotted with driftwood; Sombrio Beach, a popular surfing spot; and Botanical Beach, with its amazing tidal pools. The **Juan de Fuca Marine Trail** is a tough 48-km (30-mile) hike running along the shore from China Beach, west of Jordan River, to Botanical Beach, near Port Renfrew. Several trailheads along the way—at China Beach, Sombrio Beach, Parkinson Creek, and Botanical Beach—allow day hikers to walk small stretches of it. ⊠ *Hwy. 14, between Jordan River and Port Renfrew, Sooke* ☎ *250/474–1336* ⊕ *www.env.gov.bc.ca/bcparks.*

WORTH NOTING

Carmanah Walbran Provincial Park. Logging roads west of Port Renfrew lead to this vast wilderness park, home to some of the world's largest spruce trees, some more than 800 years old, and ancient cedars over 1,000 years old. Be prepared with supplies, because this is an extremely remote region with no services. Watch for logging trucks en route and bears once you're inside the park. ⊠ *Off Highway 14, Port Renfrew* ⊕ *www.env.gov.bc.ca/bcparks.*

East Sooke Regional Park. Hiking trails, tide pools, beaches, and views of the Olympic Mountains draw visitors to this more than 3,500-acre park 2½ km (4 miles) east of Sooke on the south side of Sooke Harbour. ⊠ *East Sooke Rd., Sooke* ⊕ *www.crd.bc.ca.*

9

Vancouver Island's Grape Escape

Thanks to a Mediterranean climate, rich soil, and loads of sunshine—not to mention dedicated winemakers and appreciative consumers—southern Vancouver Island is blossoming into one of North America's fastest-growing, if least known, wine regions. Cool-climate varietals—such as Pinot Noir, Ortega, and Pinot Gris—do well here, at a latitude equivalent to northern France, but it's not all about grapes: English-style craft cider, berry wines, mead, and traditionally made balsamic vinegar are also among the local specialties.

The region centers around the Cowichan Valley, a bucolic area about a 45-minute drive north of Victoria. Dubbed "The New Provence" for its proliferation of organic farms, wineries, restaurants, and specialist food producers, the valley is home to more than a dozen wineries. More are on the Saanich Peninsula, about 20 minutes north of Victoria and, increasingly, dotted across the offshore Gulf Islands.

Touring is easy and wonderfully low-key: burgundy-and-white Wine Route signs, as well as maps available in local tourist offices, show the way. BC Ferries' Mill Bay Ferry links the Cowichan Valley to the Saanich Peninsula.

Most of Vancouver Island's wineries are small, family-run, labor-of-love operations. Finding the wineries, hidden down winding country lanes, tucked between farm stands and artist studios, is part of the fun. Not all the wineries have enough staff to offer tours, but most offer tastings—it's always a good idea to call ahead. Some of the area's best lunches are served on winery patios.

COWICHAN VALLEY WINERIES
There are four notable wineries in the Cowichan Valley.

■ Cherry Point Estate Wines in Cobble Hill

■ Merridale Ciderworks in Cobble Hill

■ Unsworth Vineyards in Mill Bay

■ Zanatta Winery in Duncan

SAANICH PENINSULA WINERIES
Several wineries and other drink artisans can be found in greater Victoria itself. ⇨ *See Chapter 8, Victoria for information on the following wineries.*

■ Church & State Wines in Brentwood Bay, Central Saanich

■ Muse Winery in North Saanich

■ Sea Cider Farm & Ciderhouse in Saanichton

FAMILY **French Beach Provincial Park.** This provincial park, 21 km (13 miles) west of Sooke, comprises a sand-and-pebble beach, a campground, and seaside trails. Whales like to feed in the area, and sometimes can be seen from shore. ⊠ *Hwy. 14, Shirley* 🕾 *250/474–1336* ⊕ *www.env.gov.bc.ca/bcparks*.

Sooke Potholes Provincial Park. Locals and visitors come to cool off at Sooke Potholes Provincial Park, home to a series of natural swimming holes carved out of sandstone by the Sooke River. ⊠ *Sooke River Rd., off Hwy. 14, Sooke* ⊕ *www.crd.bc.ca*.

Tugwell Creek Honey Farm and Meadery. Ever tried mead? Here's your chance. At this little farm about 10 minutes west of Sooke, beekeeper

Bob Liptrot produces traditional honey wine, also known as mead, from his own hives. ✉ *8750 West Coast Rd., Sooke* ☎ *250/642–1956* 🌐 *www.tugwellcreekfarm.com* 🕒 *May–Sept., Wed.–Sun. noon–5; Oct.–Dec. and Feb.–Apr., weekends 12–5.*

Whiffen Spit. West of the village of Sooke, you'll reach this mile-long natural breakwater that makes a scenic walk with great bird-watching. ✉ *Whiffen Spit Rd., off Highway 14, Sooke.*

WHERE TO EAT

$ PACIFIC NORTHWEST 🍴 **Markus' Bistro and Dinner Club.** Two cozy rooms, one with a fireplace, and a small patio overlook Sooke Harbour from this former fisherman's cottage. The European-trained chef-owner makes the most of the local wild seafood and organic produce, much of it from the restaurant's own garden, for his daily-changing lunch menus. Shrimp cakes, grilled prawns, a rich seafood soup, or a tender pulled-pork ciabatta may appear. Set dinners are offered for groups by reservation. [$] *Average main: C$11* ✉ *1831 Maple Ave. S, Sooke* ☎ *250/642–3596* 🌐 *www.markuswharfsiderestaurant.com* 🕒 *No dinner. No lunch Mon.*

$ CAFÉ FAMILY 🍴 **Shirley Delicious.** Heading to the beach? Fuel up with a breakfast burrito, a chai latte, or an organic chocolate brownie at this welcoming café 18 km (11 miles) west of Sooke. Virtually everything, from the quiche and corn fritters to the organic bread and wholesome treats (many gluten-free and vegan) are made from scratch at this cute little A-frame in the woods. The great food and effusively friendly owners make this a favorite stop for locals, surfers, and road-trippers alike. [$] *Average main:* ✉ *2794 Sheringham Point Rd., Shirley* ☎ *778/528–2888* 🕒 *No dinner.*

$$$$ PACIFIC NORTHWEST Fodor's Choice ★ 🍴 **Sooke Harbour House.** The relaxed, ocean-view dining room at this art-filled lodge is the stage for some of the country's most innovative meals. The nightly three- or four-course menus rely almost entirely on local provisions, including seafood from nearby waters, traditional First Nations foods, and about 100 varieties of herbs, vegetables, and edible flowers from the inn's own certified organic garden. You can also book a Gastronomic Adventure—a multicourse tasting menu with optional wine pairings. The wine cellar is exceptional—cellar tours run on request. Don't want a big meal? On Sunday afternoons a less formal à la carte lunch is served. [$] *Average main: C$70* ✉ *1528 Whiffen Spit Rd., Sooke* ☎ *250/642–3421, 800/889–9688* ✉ *info@sookeharbourhouse.com* 🌐 *www.sookeharbourhouse.com* 🕒 *No lunch Mon.–Sat. Check for off-season closures.*

WHERE TO STAY

$$ HOTEL 🏨 **Best Western Premier Prestige Oceanfront Resort.** This four-story colonial-style hotel opened in 2011 on Sooke's waterfront as the area's first full-service complex, complete with a spa, indoor pool, fitness center, restaurant, and convention center. **Pros:** full-service, including valet parking and 24-hour room service; free Wi-Fi throughout; nice recreational activities like a large pool and spa. **Cons:** can get busy with conventions, weddings, and reunions; hotel doesn't really evoke BC. [$] *Rooms from: C$179* ✉ *6929 West Coast Rd., Sooke* ☎ *250/642–0805* 🌐 *www.prestigehotelsandresorts.com* 🛏 *111 rooms, 11 suites* 🍽 *No meals.*

9

$$ HOTEL FAMILY 🏨 **Point No Point Resort.** About 24 km (15 miles) west of Sooke, this cabin compound sits on a bluff next to a long stretch of private beach, with views of Juan de Fuca Strait and the Olympic Mountains; no wonder the 24 rooms are often booked well ahead by repeat visitors. **Pros:** remote and scenic; self-contained cottages assure privacy; good restaurant. **Cons:** remote; no phones or TVs; Wi-Fi in lobby only. [$] *Rooms from: C$190* ✉ *10829 West Coast Rd., Shirley* ☎ *250/646–2020* 🌐 *www.pointnopointresort.com* 🕒 *Restaurant closed Jan. No dinner Mon. and Tues.* 🛏 *24 cabins, 1 4-bedroom house* 🍴 *No meals.*

$$$ B&B/INN Fodor's Choice ★ 🏨 **Sooke Harbour House.** Art, food, and gardens work together seamlessly at one of Canada's best-loved country inns. **Pros:** beautiful decor; water views; great food. **Cons:** no pool; pricey. [$] *Rooms from: C$250* ✉ *1528 Whiffen Spit Rd., Sooke* ☎ *250/642–3421, 800/889–9688* 🌐 *www.sookeharbourhouse.com* 🕒 *Call for seasonal closures* 🛏 *28 rooms* 🍴 *Breakfast.*

SPORTS AND THE OUTDOORS

ZIP LINES

A fast-growing sport, zip-trekking involves whizzing through the forest while attached to a cable or zip line.

FAMILY **Adrena Line Zipline Adventure Tours.** About 40 minutes west of Victoria (behind the 17 Mile Pub on the road to Sooke), this adventure center has two suspension bridges and eight zip line routes ranging in length from 150 feet to 1,000 feet. Open daily March to October, it also offers night zipping on full moon nights. Between May and September, a shuttle bus runs twice daily from the Inner Harbour. ✉ *5128C Sooke Rd., Sooke* ☎ *250/642–1933, 866/947–9145* 🌐 *www.adrenalinezip.com.*

THE COWICHAN VALLEY

The Cowichan people were onto something when they called this fertile valley north of Victoria "the Warm Land." The region, roughly from Mill Bay to Ladysmith, is said to be blessed with the warmest year-round temperatures and more hours of sunshine each year than anywhere else in Canada. Home to a quarter of Vancouver Island's productive farmland, and among the most artists per capita anywhere in the country, the Cowichan Valley has earned another moniker, "The New Provence," thanks to its wealth of wineries, small organic farms, and burgeoning local-food culture.

Highway 1 from Victoria cuts north–south through the valley, while winding side roads lead to studios, wineries, and roadside farm stands. Duncan, the valley's main town, is home to the Quw'utsun' Cultural and Conference Centre, one of BC's leading First Nations cultural centers. A 30-minute drive north is Chemainus, a cute if touristy little town decorated with outdoor murals. Ladysmith, at the valley's north end, has a historic town center and a sandy ocean beach. About 10 minutes south of Duncan are Cowichan Bay, a tiny fishing village with houses built on stilts over the water, Cobble Hill, home to a cluster of wineries, and Mill Bay, where you can catch a ferry to the Saanich Peninsula. Lake

Cowichan and Shawnigan Lake draw campers, boaters, and summer cottagers. The Cowichan Valley Rail Trail, a long-distance foot-and-bike path, connects the two lakes.

GETTING HERE AND AROUND

There are three ways to get here from Victoria: make the hour's drive north on Highway 1 over the scenic Malahat Summit; take the Mill Bay Ferry from Brentwood Bay on the Saanich Peninsula; or travel via a back road from Port Renfrew, west of Sooke, following the Pacific Marine Circle Route. You can also get here from Salt Spring Island, on a ferry to Crofton, 20 minutes north of Duncan.

VISITOR INFORMATION

Contacts **Tourism Cowichan.** ☏ *800/665–3955* ⊕ *www.cvrd.bc.ca.*

MILL BAY

42 km (26 miles) north of Victoria on Trans-Canada Hwy., or Hwy. 1.

From Mill Bay, home to a cluster of shops and cafés at the southern end of the Cowichan Valley, ferries sail across the Saanich Inlet to Brentwood Bay on the Saanich Peninsula. South of Mill Bay, Highway 1 crosses the Malahat, a stunning ocean view route to Victoria.

EXPLORING

Unsworth Vineyards. A relative newcomer among Cowichan Valley wineries, this small producer offers tastings of its Pinot Gris, Pinot Noir, and port-style dessert wine. Any tasting fees are refunded upon a wine purchase. The property is also home to Unsworth Restaurant, a contemporary bistro in a restored 1895 farmhouse that serves lunch and dinner Wednesday through Sunday from May to October. ⊠ *2915 Cameron Taggart Rd., Mill Bay* ☏ *250/929–2292* ⊕ *www.unsworthvineyards. com* ⊠ *C$5 for tastings* ⊗ *Mid-May–mid-Oct., Wed.–Sun. 11–6 (call for off-season closures).*

COBBLE HILL

7½ km (4¾ miles) north of Mill Bay.

Cobble Hill, at the heart of the Cowichan Valley wine district, is centered on a cluster of shops at the junction of Cobble Hill and Hutchinson roads. Wine is the big draw here, but consider stopping for a latte at Old School Coffee, complete with a drive-through window, in a historic schoolhouse.

EXPLORING

Cherry Point Estate Wines. The highly-rated Amusé Bistro is a draw at this family-owned and -operated Cowichan Valley winery. Tastings of Pinot Noir, Pinot Blanc, Pinot Gris, Ortega, and a popular blackberry dessert wine are offered daily in summer; winery tours can be pre-booked (call for hours in winter). The winery's bistro serves lunch Wednesday to Sunday and dinner on Friday and Saturday evenings. ⊠ *840 Cherry Point Rd., Cobble Hill* ☏ *250/743–1272* ⊕ *www.cherrypointvineyards. com* ⊠ *Free* ⊗ *Daily 10–5.*

NEED A BREAK?

Old School Coffee. Stop by this local spot for a good cup of coffee or a snack. ✉ *3515 Cobble Hill Rd., Cobble Hill* ☎ *250/743-6908.*

Merridale Ciderworks. Cider is made in the traditional English way at this cidery and distillery; in addition to several varieties of cider and fortified wines, they also make spirits, like brandy, vodka, and an apple *eau de vie*. Visitors can tour the cidery, taste the wares, and linger over lunches of local fare served on the orchard-view patio. There's also a shop selling ciders, juices, baked goods, and jams, and you can even spend the night in a glamorous yurt on the property. ✉ *1230 Merridale Rd., Cobble Hill* ☎ *250/743–4293, 800/998–9908* 🌐 *www.merridalecider.com* 🎟 *C$5 for tastings* 🕒 *May–Oct., Mon.–Thurs. 11–6, Fri.–Sat. 11–5, Sun. 11–9; Nov.–Apr., call for hours.*

WHERE TO EAT

$ CONTEMPORARY

🍴 **Bistro at Merridale.** Neighboring farms supply much of the fare at this bistro, tucked down a country lane at Merridale Ciderworks. The bistro, part of the gambrel-roofed cider house, showcases local art on whitewashed walls within, and orchard and forest views from the wide, covered veranda. You can match house-made ciders to your meal of, say, a porchetta sandwich, cider-braised pork ribs, or a simple salad of organic greens, goat cheese, and spiced nuts tossed in an apple cider vinaigrette. On Summer Sundays, locals flock here for brick-oven pizza and live music. [$] *Average main: C$12* ✉ *1230 Merridale Rd., Cobble Hill* ☎ *250/743–4293, 800/998–9908* 🌐 *www.merridalecider.com* 🕒 *Closed Jan. No dinner.*

WHERE TO STAY

$$ B&B/INN

🏨 **Damali B&B.** A convenient base for touring the Cowichan Valley wineries, this casual and friendly B&B has two rooms in a contemporary farmhouse set amid lavender fields. **Pros:** pastoral setting; genial owners share tips about the region. **Cons:** no phones. [$] *Rooms from: C$169* ✉ *3500 Telegraph Rd., Cobble Hill* ☎ *250/743–4100, 877/743–5170* 🌐 *www.damali.ca* 🛏 *2 rooms* 🍽 *Breakfast.*

SPORTS AND THE OUTDOORS

Arbutus Ridge Golf Club. Mountain and ocean views from the course and the clubhouse are the draws at this challenging par-71 course, 40 minutes north of Victoria in the Cowichan Valley. ✉ *3515 Telegraph Rd., Cobble Hill* ☎ *250/743–5000* 🌐 *www.arbutusridgegolf.com* ⛳ *18 holes. 6,193 yds. Par 71. Greens Fee: C$54/C$59.*

COWICHAN BAY

8 km (5 miles) north of Cobble Hill.

Often called Cow Bay, this funky little town about 10 minutes south of Duncan (take Cowichan Bay Road off Highway 1) is made up largely of houseboats and houses built on pilings over the water. Seafood restaurants, nautical shops, boat builders, kayaking outfitters, and B&Bs line the waterfront.

EXPLORING

FAMILY **Cowichan Bay Maritime Centre.** The interesting Cowichan Bay Maritime Centre has maritime paraphernalia, including historic vessels and model boats, displayed along a pier, which is also a great place to take in views of the village and boats at harbor. You may also be able to watch boat builders at work in the attached studio. ✉ *1761 Cowichan Bay Rd., Cowichan Bay* ☎ *250/746–4955* 🌐 *www.classicboats.org* 🎟 *Free* 🕒 *Daily 9 am–dusk.*

WHERE TO EAT

$$$ CONTEMPORARY 🍴 **The Masthead.** You know a chef cares about local food when his menu lists how far each ingredient has traveled to reach your plate. At this historic seaside roadhouse in Cowichan Bay, the mussels and clams come from within 5 miles of the restaurant, and the poached Dungeness crab is from the bay outside the door. Many other ingredients—bison, wild salmon, duck breast—are sourced from within 200 miles. The 1863 wood-paneled room offers sea views throughout, but waterside deck tables are favored by the loyal clientele. The long wine list has a good selection of Cowichan Valley labels. [$] *Average main: C$28* ✉ *1705 Cowichan Bay Rd., Cowichan Bay* ☎ *250/748–3714* 🌐 *www.themastheadrestaurant.com* 🕒 *No lunch.*

SHOPPING

Arthur Vickers Gallery. This well-regarded gallery displays the well-known artist's work, with West Coast and First Nations themes, in a historic shipyard space. The gallery has irregular hours in winter. ✉ *1719 Cowichan Bay Rd., Cowichan Bay* ☎ *250/748–7650* 🌐 *www.arthurvickers.com.*

Hilary's Cheese. This shop draws foodies with its artisanal cheeses. A café on-site serves soup and sandwich lunches, and next door, True Grain Bread offers organic baked goods. ✉ *1737 Cowichan Bay Rd., Cowichan Bay* ☎ *250/748–5992.*

9

DUNCAN

9.7 km (6 miles) north of Cowichan Bay.

Duncan, the largest town in the valley, is nicknamed the City of Totems for the more than 40 totem poles that dot the small community. Between May and September, free walking tours of the totems leave hourly from the south end of the train station building on Canada Avenue (contact the Duncan Business Improvement Area Society, at *250/715–1700*, for more information). On Saturdays year-round, the City Square at the end of Craig Street hosts an outdoor market, where you can browse for local produce, crafts, and specialty foods. Duncan is also home to the world's largest hockey stick—look for it on the outside wall of the Duncan arena on the west side of Highway 1 as you drive through town.

EXPLORING

FAMILY **British Columbia Forest Discovery Centre.** Kids adore riding the rails at the British Columbia Forest Discovery Centre, a 100-acre outdoor museum just north of Duncan. Pulled by a 1910 steam locomotive, a

The town of Duncan, in the Cowichan Valley, is nicknamed the City of Totems because there are more than 40 totem poles dotting the community.

three-carriage train toots through the woods and over a trestle bridge across a lake, stopping at a picnic site and playground on the way. Forestry-related exhibits around the site include a 1930s-era logging camp, historic logging equipment, and indoor exhibits about the modern science of forestry. Interpretive trails through the forest lead to ancient trees, one dating back more than 500 years. During July and August, the steam train runs daily every half hour. In May, June, and September, the train may be replaced with a gas locomotive. ✉ *2892 Drinkwater Rd., Duncan* ☎ *250/715–1113, 866/715–1113* ⊕ *www.bcforestdiscoverycentre.com* ✉ *C$15* ⊙ *June–early Sept., daily 10–4:30; early Sept.–mid-Oct. and mid-Apr.–May, Thurs.–Mon. 10–4.*

Cowichan Valley Museum & Archives. This small museum, in a 1912 train station, has exhibits and artifacts about the region's First Nations culture and pioneer history. ✉ *130 Canada Ave., Duncan* ☎ *250/746–6612* ⊕ *www.cowichanvalleymuseum.bc.ca* ✉ *Donations accepted* ⊙ *June–Sept., Mon.–Sat. 10–4; Oct.–May, Wed.–Fri. 11–4, Sat. 1–4.*

FAMILY **Quw'utsun' Cultural and Conference Centre.** This village of cedar long-houses, occupying six acres of shady riverbank, is one of Canada's leading First Nations cultural and educational facilities. A 20-minute video in a longhouse-style theater introduces the history of the Cowichan people, BC's largest aboriginal group, and a 30-minute walking tour reveals the legends behind the site's dozen totem poles. Crafts demonstrations and dance performances are occasionally offered during summer, and the many indigenous plants on-site are labeled with information about their traditional uses. The gift shop stocks, among other things, the hand-knit Cowichan sweaters that the area is known for, and the Riverwalk Café offers a rare opportunity to sample First Nations fare. ✉ *200 Cowichan Way, Duncan* ☎ *250/746–8119, 877/746–8119* 🎟 *C$15* 🕒 *June–Sept., Tues.–Sat. 10–4.*

FAMILY **The Raptors Centre.** At this conservation center about 10 minutes northeast of Duncan, you can see owls, hawks, falcons, and eagles in natural settings. Free-flying bird demonstrations are held daily; you can also join a trainer on a brief falconry or ecology course. ✉ *1877 Herd Rd., Duncan* ☎ *250/746–0372* 🌐 *www.pnwraptors.com* 🎟 *C$14* 🕒 *Mar. and Oct., daily 12–3; Apr.–Sept., daily 11–4:30; Nov. and Dec. Thurs.–Sun. 12–3.*

Teafarm. Can tea grow in Canada? The proprietors of this small organic farm just north of Duncan hope so. While their crop is still maturing, they've opened a tea shop and gallery (in the former milking room of a barn), blending and selling teas, offering tastings, and showcasing the ceramics work of co-owner Margit Nellemann and other area artists. ✉ *8350 Richards Trail, North Cowichan* ☎ *250/748–3811, 855/748–3811* 🌐 *www.teafarm.ca* 🕒 *Wed.–Sun. 10–5.*

Vigneti Zanatta Winery. A local favorite is Vigneti Zanatta Winery, which produces lovely Ortega, Pinot Grigio, and Damasco entirely from grapes grown on its own 25 acres. If you can, time your visit for an Italian-style lunch on the veranda at Vinoteca, a restaurant and wine bar in the winery's 1903 farmhouse. ✉ *5039 Marshall Rd., Duncan* ☎ *250/748–2338 winery, 250/709–2279 Vinoteca Restaurant* 🌐 *www.zanatta.ca* 🕒 *Apr.–Sept., Wed.–Sun. noon–4:30.*

WHERE TO EAT

$$ CANADIAN 🍴 **Riverwalk Café.** This little riverside café, part of Duncan's Quw'utsun' Cultural and Conference Centre, offers a rare opportunity to try traditional BC First Nations fare. All meals start with warm fried bread with blackberry jam and salmon spread. From there, the menu offers both the familiar (salads, burgers, seafood pasta, and fish-and-chips made with salmon) and the more unusual (clam fritters, venison chili, or a seafood stew with salmon, cod, prawns, and sea aparagus). For a treat try the Salish Afternoon Tea for two, which includes candied and smoked salmon, crab cakes, blackberry bread, and more—all served on a cedar platter. A kids' menu and river-view patio in a parklike environment make this a pleasant family spot. [$] *Average main: C$14* ✉ *Quw'utsun' Cultural and Conference Centre, 200 Cowichan Way, Duncan* ☎ *250/746–4370* 🕒 *Closed Sun. and Mon. and mid-Sept.–May. No dinner.*

$$$$ CONTEMPORARY 🍴 **Stone Soup Inn.** Chef-owner Brock Windsor grows his own vegetables, forages for mushrooms and herbs, raises pigs to cure his own bacon, and sources most other provisions from farmers, fishers, and growers in the nearby Cowichan Valley. Thursday to Saturday nights he prepares a five-course "chef's choice" dinner in his homey, candlelit farmhouse dining room. His years of experience are revealed in dishes like miso-marinated black cod served with a gingery squash puree, or braised rabbit paired with wild mushrooms, purple carrots, and polenta. Dishes are matched with Vancouver Island wines. Reservations are recommended; vegetarians and those with food allergies can be accommodated with

9

advance arrangements. The inn is in the forest about 20 minutes west of Duncan. If you don't want to drive back to civilization after your meal, you can spend the night in one of the two simple B&B rooms upstairs. [$] *Average main: C$65* ✉ *6755 Cowichan Lake Rd., Lake Cowichan* ☎ *250/749–3848* 🌐 *www.stonesoupinn.ca* 🕓 *Closed Sun.–Wed. (call for off-season closures). No lunch.*

WHERE TO STAY

$$ B&B/INN FAMILY 🏨 **Fairburn Farmstay and Guesthouse.** This 1896 homestead on 130 pastoral acres is the centerpiece of a historic farm, Canada's first water-buffalo dairy; kids, in particular, enjoy watching the milking. **Pros:** peaceful rural surroundings; family-friendly atmosphere. **Cons:** old-fashioned rooms; at the end of a country road some distance from town. [$] *Rooms from: C$129* ✉ *3310 Jackson Rd., Duncan* ☎ *250/746–4637* 🌐 *www.fairburnfarm.bc.ca* 🕓 *Closed Nov.–Mar.* 🛏 *5 rooms, 1 cottage* 🍴 *Breakfast.*

CHEMAINUS

20 km (12 miles) north of Duncan.

Chemainus is known for the bold epic murals that decorate its townscape, as well as for its beautifully restored Victorian homes. Once dependent on the lumber industry, the small community began to revitalize itself in the early 1980s when its mill closed down. Since then the town has brought in international artists to paint more than 40 murals depicting local historical events around town. Footprints on the sidewalk lead you on a self-guided tour of the murals. Tours by horse and carriage, replica-train rides, free outdoor concerts, a weekly night market, and plenty of B&Bs, cafés, and crafts shops all help pass the time here. Catch, if you can, a show at the Chemainus Theatre Festival, which offers several professional musical and dramatic productions between March and December. The Chemainus Visitor Information Centre (🌐 *www.chemainus.bc.ca*) has details.

PERFORMING ARTS

Chemainus Theatre. The Chemainus Theatre presents popular live musicals and dramas from March to December. ✉ *9737 Chemainus Rd., Chemainus* ☎ *250/246–9820* 🌐 *www.chemainustheatrefestival.ca.*

SPORTS AND THE OUTDOORS

BIKING

For those who want to get outdoors, biking is great around the Lake Cowichan area.

Cowichan Valley Trail. This 76-mile path, part of the Trans-Canada trail, runs from Shawnigan Lake to Lake Cowichan in the Cowichan Valley. A rails-to-trails conversion, the route crosses eight historic bridges, including the 614-foot-long Kinsol Trestle, one of the tallest timber rail trestles in the world. 🌐 *www.cvrd.bc.ca* 🎟 *Free.*

THE GULF ISLANDS

Of the hundreds of islands sprinkled across Georgia Strait between Vancouver Island and the mainland, the most popular and accessible are Galiano, Mayne, Pender, Saturna, and Salt Spring. A temperate climate, white-shell beaches, rolling pastures, and forests are common to all, but each island has a unique flavor. Though rustic, they're not undiscovered. Writers, artists, and craftspeople as well as weekend cottagers and retirees from Vancouver and Victoria take full advantage of them. Hotel reservations are a good idea in summer. Only Salt Spring has a town, but food and accommodation are available on all of the islands.

GETTING HERE AND AROUND

BC Ferries sail from Swartz Bay, on the Saanich Peninsula, just north of Victoria, to all five of the islands, several times a day; these routes don't take reservations, so arrive early if you're taking a car—a good rule of thumb is 45 minutes to an hour early in summer and half an hour in winter. Sailings range from half an hour to more than an hour, depending on stops. Bikes, pets, and foot passengers are welcome. Ferries from the BC mainland leave from Tsawwassen, just south of Vancouver. On these routes to and from the mainland, car reservations are highly recommended; for busier sailings, they're required. The ferry journey from Tsawwassen to Salt Spring takes 90 minutes to three hours (depending on the number of intermediate stops) and less for the other islands.

Travel between the islands on BC Ferries is possible but generally requires an overnight stay at one of the islands. A fun, low-cost way to cruise the islands is to take one of BC Ferries' Gulf Islands Day Trips—traveling as foot passenger from Swartz Bay, around the islands and back, without disembarking. It's also possible to visit Mayne and Galiano from Salt Spring via water taxi, which doubles as the island school boat.

Salt Spring Island has the most frequent ferry service, as well as service from three terminals. Ferries from Swartz Bay, near Victoria, arrive at Fulford Harbour, on the southern tip of the island, 15 km (9 miles) from Ganges, the main town. Ferries from the BC mainland arrive at Long Harbour, on the island's east coast, closer to Ganges. Salt Spring also has BC Ferry service from the Cowichan Valley, with sailings every hour or so from Crofton, 20 minutes north of Duncan, to Vesuvius Bay on Salt Spring.

A BC Transit minibus runs from all three ferry terminals to the town of Ganges, but it doesn't meet every ferry; check online schedules first. For a taxi on Salt Spring, call Silver Shadow Taxi.

Transport on the other islands is limited: Pender has the Pender Island Cab Company. Most island accommodations collect guests from the ferry terminal if asked. Cycling is popular on the islands, despite the hilly terrain.

Contacts Gulf Islands Water Taxi. ☎ *250/537–2510* ⊕ *www.saltspring.com/watertaxi.* **Pender Island Cab Company.** ☎ *250/629–2222* ⊕ *www.penderislandcab.com.* **Silver Shadow Taxi.** ☎ *250/537–3030* ⊕ *www.saltspringtaxi.com.*

VISITOR INFORMATION

Contacts Galiano Island Travel InfoCentre. ☎ *250/539–2233* ⊕ *www.galianoisland.com.* **Mayne Island Community Chamber of Commerce.** ☎ *250/539–3571* ⊕ *www.mayneislandchamber.ca.* **Pender Island Chamber of Commerce.** ⊕ *www.penderislandchamber.com.* **Salt Spring Island Visitor Information Centre.** ☎ *250/537–5252, 866/216–2936* ⊕ *www.saltspringtourism.com.*

SALT SPRING ISLAND

28 nautical miles from Swartz Bay, 22 nautical miles from Tsawwassen.

With its wealth of studios, galleries, restaurants, and B&Bs, Salt Spring is the most developed, and most visited, of the Southern Gulf Islands. It's home to the only town in the archipelago (Ganges) and, although it can get busy on summer weekends, has not yet lost its relaxed rural feel. Outside of Ganges, the rolling landscape is home to small organic farms, wineries, forested hills, quiet white-shell beaches, and several swimming lakes.

What really sets Salt Spring apart is its status as a "little arts town." Island residents include hundreds of artists, writers, craftspeople, and musicians, many of whom open their studios to visitors. To visit more than 35 local artists in their studios, pick up a free Studio Tour map from the tourist information center in Ganges.

The ferries to Salt Spring arrive at three different docks, in or near the island's three villages. Boats from the mainland and from the other southern Gulf Islands dock at Long Harbour, just east of Ganges. Salt Spring's main commercial center is the seaside village of Ganges, about 15 km (9 miles) north of the Fulford Ferry Terminal. It has about a dozen art galleries, as well as the essentials: restaurants, banks, gas stations, grocery stores, and a liquor store. At the south end of Salt Spring Island, the ferries from Victoria dock at the tiny village of Fulford, which has a restaurant, a café, and several offbeat boutiques. Ferries from Crofton, on Vancouver Island, arrive on the west side of Salt Spring Island at the small coastal community of Vesuvius, with a restaurant, a tiny grocery store–cum-café, and crafts studios.

EXPLORING

Every weekend, the Salt Spring Island Saturday Market is one of the island's biggest draws. Everyone will be there. And watching the cheesemakers at Salt Spring Island Cheese is another popular activity for many visitors. ⇨ *See Shopping.*

FAMILY **Burgoyne Bay Provincial Park.** Easy hikes and a pretty pebble beach are the draws at this provincial park, at the end of a dirt road toward the southern end of the island. ⊠ *Burgoyne Bay Rd., at Fulford-Ganges Rd., Salt Spring Island* ⊕ *www.env.gov.bc.ca/bcparks.*

Garry Oaks Winery. This small winery, home to valley-view vineyards and a meditative labyrinth, produces estate-grown Pinot Gris, Pinot Noir, a Chardonnay-Gewürztraminer blend, and an intriguing red made from Zweigelt grapes. It's open for tastings daily in July through early September and on weekends in spring and fall (call ahead). Tours are offered by appointment. ✉ *1880 Fulford-Ganges Rd., Salt Spring Island* ☎ *250/653–4687* ⊕ *www.garryoakswine.com* 🖃 *C$2 for tasting (fee deducted from wine purchases)* ⊙ *July–early Sept., daily noon–5; call for off-season hrs.*

Mistaken Identity Vineyards. This organic vineyard and winery, just north of Ganges, produces Pinot Noir, Merlot, and a variety of signature blends. The offbeat name was inspired by tasters who guessed the wine was from Europe, Australia, or anywhere but western Canada. ✉ *164 Norton Rd., Salt Spring Island* ☎ *250/538–9463, 8//918–2783* ⊕ *www.mistakenidentityvineyards.com* 🖃 *C$4 for tasting (deducted from wine purchases)* ⊙ *June–Sept., daily 12–6; call for off-season hrs.*

FAMILY **Mount Maxwell Provincial Park.** Near the center of Salt Spring Island, Baynes Peak in Mount Maxwell Provincial Park has spectacular views of south Salt Spring, Vancouver Island, and other Gulf Islands. The last portion of the drive is steep, winding, and unpaved. ✉ *Mt. Maxwell Rd., off Fulford–Ganges Rd., Salt Spring Island* ⊕ *www.env.gov.bc.ca/bcparks.*

FAMILY **Ruckle Provincial Park.** This provincial park is the site of an 1872 homestead and extensive fields that are still being farmed. Several small sandy beaches and 8 km (5 miles) of trails winding through forests and along the coast make this one of the islands' most appealing parks. A lovely and very popular campground has walk-in tent sites on a grassy slope overlooking the sea as well as a few drive-in sites in the woods. ✉ *Beaver Point Rd., Salt Spring Island* ☎ *250/539-2115, 877/559–2115* ⊕ *www.env.gov.bc.ca/bcparks.*

Salt Spring Vineyards. Salt Spring Vineyards produces a dozen wines, including Pinot Gris, Pinot Noir, and blackberry port, almost entirely from island-grown fruit. Be sure to try one of the Evolution series, made with a grape variety developed right on Salt Spring Island. Tastings are free and, in summer, paired with local, seasonal food. Wine by the glass, as well as bread, cheese, smoked fish, and other fixings are available for summer picnics on the vineyard-view patio. Live bands entertain on Friday and Sunday afternoons in summer; events, from food tests to outdoor theater, happen regularly too. If you don't want to leave, there's a two-room B&B. ✉ *151 Lee Rd., off Fulford-Ganges Rd., Salt Spring Island* ☎ *250/653–9463* ⊕ *www.saltspringvineyards. com* 🖃 *Free* ⊙ *Mar.–Apr., weekends noon–4; May–mid-June, Fri.–Sun. noon–5; mid-June–Aug., daily 11–5; Sept., daily noon–5; Oct., Fri.–Sun. noon–5; rest of year by appointment.*

Sculpture Trail. At Hastings House Country House Hotel near Ganges, a Sculpture Trail—with intriguing art installations in the woods—is open to the public. The trail access is on Churchill Road. ✉ *Hastings House Country House Hotel, 160 Upper Ganges Rd., Ganges, Salt Spring Island.*

WHERE TO EAT

$$$ ✕**Auntie Pesto's.** Fresh local ingredients and made-from-scratch fare
MODERN keep regulars and visitors well fed at this family-run spot on Gan-
CANADIAN ges' waterfront boardwalk. Settle in at lunchtime for a hearty sand-
wich (try the Grace Point Grill with local chèvre, pesto, and roasted vegetables), homemade soup, or any of almost a dozen pastas. Come

9

evening, chef Shawn Walton takes it up a notch with, for example, duck confit with pear-and-gorgonzola ravioli, or beef tenderloin with port demi-glace. The art-filled interior is welcoming, and on warm evenings the marina-view patio is positively romantic. $ *Average main: C$21 ⊠ Grace Point Sq., 2104–115 Fulford Ganges Rd., Ganges, Salt Spring Island* ☎ *250/537–4181* ⊕ *www.auntiepestos.com* ☉ *Closed Sun. Closed Sept.–mid-May.*

$$$
SEAFOOD

✕ **Calvin's Bistro.** Seafood—whether in the form of a wild salmon fillet, baby-shrimp linguine, or good old halibut-and-chips—tops the menu at this comfortable marina-view bistro in Ganges. A long list of burgers, offered at lunch and dinner, includes local lamb, wild salmon, and even schnitzel. Inside booths are cozy, while the big patio has great harbor views. Friendly Swiss owners account for the house-made European desserts and welcoming service. $ *Average main: C$21 ⊠ 133 Lower Ganges Rd., Ganges, Salt Spring Island* ☎ *250/538–5551* ⊕ *www. calvinsbistro.ca* ☉ *Closed Sun. and Mon.*

$$
CANADIAN
FAMILY

✕ **Harbour House Restaurant.** An organic farm on-site provides everything from herbs and vegetables to honey and big-leaf maple syrup at this farm-to-fork dining room overlooking Ganges Harbour. Hearty breakfasts, healthy lunches, and casual dinners (try the seafood chowder, Salt Spring Island mussels, or the local lamb burger) are made from scratch with sustainable, local ingredients. There's been an inn here since 1916; the current modern hotel has comfortable seaview rooms and even a yoga studio. Farm tours, foodie events, and live music on weekend evenings add to the fun. $ *Average main: ⊠ Harbour View Hotel, 121 Upper Ganges Rd., Ganges, Salt Spring Island* ☎ *250/537–4700* ⊕ *www.saltspringharbourhouse.com.*

$$$
SCANDINAVIAN

✕ **House Piccolo.** Piccolo Lyytikainen, the Finnish-born chef-owner of this tiny restaurant in a quaint village house, serves beautifully prepared and presented European cuisine. Creations include Scandinavian-influenced dishes such as BC venison with a juniper-and-lingonberry demi-glace and charbroiled fillet of beef with Gorgonzola sauce. For dessert, the chocolate terrine Finlandia and vodka-moistened lingonberry crepes are hard to resist. The 250-item wine list includes many hard-to-find vintages. The indoor tables are cozy and candlelit; the outdoor patio is a pleasant summer dining spot. $ *Average main: C$27 ⊠ 108 Hereford Ave., Ganges, Salt Spring Island* ☎ *250/537–1844* ⊕ *www.housepiccolo.com* ☉ *Closed Sun.–Tues. Call ahead for winter hrs. No lunch.*

$$
ECLECTIC

✕ **Rock Salt Restaurant & Cafe.** You can watch the ferry coming across the harbor from the sea-view windows of this Fulford Harbour eatery. Wholesome goodies run the gamut from slow-baked ribs to seafood curries to much-loved yam quesadillas. The made-from-scratch breakfasts are worth getting up early for, and the take-out counter offers provisions for your onward journey. $ *Average main: C$18 ⊠ 2921 Fulford Ganges Rd., Fulford, Salt Spring Island* ☎ *250/653–4833* ⊕ *www. rocksaltrestaurant.com.*

$$
ECLECTIC
FAMILY

✕ **The Tree House Café.** Gulf Island charm flourishes at this Ganges outdoor café, where handmade wooden booths are gathered under a spreading plum tree so folks can sit and hear live music playing every summer night. Visitors and locals flock here for big wholesome breakfasts (think

French toast with real maple syrup) and made-from-scratch burgers, wraps, and quesadillas. It's all yummy, but favorites include the lamb burger, the Thai green curry, and the butternut squash stew. On summer evenings, grab a table early as this is *the* place to be. [$] *Average main:* ✉ *106 Purvis Lane, Ganges, Salt Spring Island* ☎ *250/537–5379* 🌐 *www.treehousecafe.ca* ✍ *Reservations not accepted.*

WHERE TO STAY

$$ RENTAL FAMILY 🏨 **Foxglove Farm.** This 120-acre organic farm and education center on the road to Mount Maxwell has been developed on one of the island's oldest homesteads. **Pros:** beautiful, secluded rural setting; good for kids. **Cons:** far from town; two- or three-night minimum. [$] *Rooms from: C$150* ✉ *1200 Mount Maxwell Rd., Salt Spring Island* ☎ *250/537–1989* 🌐 *www.foxglovefarmbc.ca* 🛏 *3 cabins* 🍴 *No meals.*

$$$$ HOTEL Fodor's Choice ★ 🏨 **Hastings House Country House Hotel.** The centerpiece of this 22-acre seaside estate—with its gardens, meadows, and harbor views—is a 1939 country house, built in the style of an 11th-century Sussex manor. **Pros:** wonderful food; top-notch service; historic character. **Cons:** no pool; some rooms overlook a nearby pub; rates are high. [$] *Rooms from: C$395* ✉ *160 Upper Ganges Rd., Ganges, Salt Spring Island* ☎ *250/537–2362, 800/661–9255* 🌐 *www.hastingshouse.com* ⏲ *Restaurant closed Nov.–Feb.* 🛏 *3 rooms, 14 suites* 🍴 *Breakfast.*

$$ B&B/INN 🏨 **Hedgerow House.** A great choice for a car-free vacation, this three-room inn on a quiet Ganges village street is just a five-minute walk to restaurants, cafés, shops, and the popular Saturday Market. **Pros:** close to town; hosts are tourism industry pros; free Wi-Fi. **Cons:** no kids under 12; showers only (no tubs); no ocean views. [$] *Rooms from: C$170* ✉ *238 Park Dr., Ganges, Salt Spring Island* ☎ *250/538–1716* 🌐 *hedgerowhouse.ca* 🛏 *3 rooms* 🍴 *Breakfast.*

SHOPPING

To visit local artists in their studios, follow the Salt Spring Studio Tour map, listing more than 30 locations. You can either download the map from 🌐 *www.saltspringstudiotour.com* or pick it up at any of the local artist studios, Salt Spring Island Cheese, or at any of the island's hotels.

FAMILY **Salt Spring Island Cheese.** You can watch the cheesemakers at work at this farm and cheese shop north of Fulford Harbour, where tasting is encouraged. Kids can walk through the farmyard to see the animals that provide the milk for the goat's and sheep's milk cheeses. ✉ *285 Reynolds Rd., off Beaver Point Rd., Salt Spring Island* ☎ *250/653–2300* 🌐 *www.saltspringcheese.com* ⏲ *May–Sept., daily 11–5; Oct.–Apr., daily 11–4.*

Fodor's Choice ★ **Salt Spring Island Saturday Market.** Locals and visitors alike flock to Ganges on summer Saturdays for this weekly market, held in Centennial Park from April through October. It's one of the island's most popular attractions. Everything sold at this colorful outdoor bazaar is made or grown on the island; the array and quality of crafts, food, and produce is dazzling. Centennial Park also hosts a farmers' market on summer Tuesdays. ✉ *Centennial Park, Fulford-Ganges Rd., Ganges, Salt Spring Island* ☎ *250/537–4448* 🌐 *www.saltspringmarket.com.*

GALIANO ISLAND

With its 26-km-long (16-mile-long) eastern shore and cove-dotted western coast, Galiano is arguably the prettiest of these islands. It's certainly the best for hiking and mountain biking, with miles of trails through the Douglas fir and Garry Oak forest. Mt. Galiano and Bodega Ridge are classic walks, with far-reaching views to the mainland. Most shops and services—including cash machines, gas pumps, galleries, and a bookstore—are clustered near the Sturdies Bay ferry terminal. A visitor information booth is to your right as you leave the ferry.

EXPLORING

Montague Harbour Marina. You can rent a kayak, boat, or moped at Montague Harbour Marina, or grab a snack at the café on-site. ✉ *Montague Rd., Galiano Island* ☎ *250/539–5733, 250/539–2226 Restaurant* 🌐 *www.montagueharbour.com.*

QUICK BITES

Max & Moritz Spicy Island Food House. This catering van at the Sturdies Bay Ferry Terminal offers German and Indonesian takeout. ✉ ***Sturdies Bay Ferry Terminal, Sturdies Bay Rd., Galiano Island*** ☎ ***520/539–5888*** 🕓 ***Closed Nov.–Mar.***

FAMILY **Montague Harbour Provincial Marine Park.** This provincial park on the island's southwest shore has a long shell beach famed for its sunset views. ✉ *Montague Park Rd., off Montague Rd., Galiano Island* ☎ *250/539–2115* 🌐 *www.env.gov.bc.ca/bcparks.*

WHERE TO EAT

$ CANADIAN 🍴 **Sea Blush Cafe.** At the Montague Harbour Marina, stay for a home-cooked meal on the seaview deck at the popular Sea Blush Café (try the wild salmon sandwich or the fish tacos). It's open for breakfast and lunch every day and serves dinner on summer weekends. Keep an eye out for the local wildlife, including herons, eagles, and even river otters. Reservations are recommended for dinner. [$] *Average main: C$10* ✉ *Montague Harbour Marina, off Montague Park Rd., Galiano Island* ☎ *250/539–5733* 🌐 *www.montagueharbour.com/restaurant.php* 🕓 *Closed Oct.–Apr. No dinner Mon.–Thurs.*

$ CAFÉ 🍴 **Sturdies Bay Bakery & Cafe.** Stop into this cheerful local favorite near the ferry terminal for freshly made pastries and sandwiches. The bread is highly praised, and you can often find roasted organic chicken or other cooked food for taking lunch to the beach. [$] *Average main:* ✉ *2540 Sturdies Bay Rd., Galiano Island* ☎ *250/539–2004* 🕓 *No dinner.*

WHERE TO STAY

$$$ RESORT Fodor's Choice ★ 🏨 **Galiano Oceanfront Inn & Spa.** Just a block from the ferry and local shops, this inviting waterfront retreat on Sturdies Bay, which has both a nice restaurant and great spa, is an ideal spot for a car-free vacation. **Pros:** the staff picks you up at the ferry; well-equipped suites encourage long stays; quiet and lovely environment. **Cons:** no pool. [$] *Rooms from: C$299* ✉ *134 Madrona Dr., Galiano Island* ☎ *250/539–3388, 877/530–3939* 🌐 *www.galianoinn.com* 🛏 *10 rooms, 10 suites* 🍽 *No meals.*

Fresh crab is a delicacy around the Gulf Islands, especially in Ganges Harbour, on Salt Spring Island.

NIGHTLIFE

Hummingbird Pub. The Hummingbird Pub is a friendly local hangout, with live music on summer weekends, plus a family-friendly restaurant and a lawn with a play area for kids. Also in summer, the pub runs a free shuttle bus to the Montague Harbour, stopping at both the marina and the campsite. ⊠ *47 Sturdies Bay Rd., Galiano Island* ☎ *250/539–5472* ⊕ *www.hummingbirdpub.com.*

MAYNE ISLAND

The smallest of the Southern Gulf Islands, Mayne also has the most visible history. The buildings of Miners Bay, the island's tiny commercial center, date to the 1850s, when Mayne was a stopover for prospectors en route to the gold fields.

As the quietest and least hilly of the islands, Mayne is a good choice for cycle touring. It's also a popular spot for kayaking.

EXPLORING

FAMILY **Campbell Point.** Part of the Gulf Islands National Park Reserve, this waterfront area has walking trails and, at Bennett Bay, one of the island's most scenic beaches. ⊕ *www.pc.gc.ca.*

Georgina Point Heritage Park and Lighthouse. This waterfront park overlooking Active Pass is part of the Gulf Islands National Park Reserve. It's also home to the Georgina Point Lighthouse; built in 1885, it still signals ships into the busy waterway. The grassy grounds are great for picnicking. ⊠ *Georgina Point Rd., Mayne Island.*

Japanese Garden. Built entirely by volunteers, this 1-acre garden at Dinner Bay Park honors the island's early Japanese settlers. It's about ½ mile south of the Village Bay ferry terminal. ✉ *Dinner Bay Rd., Mayne Island* 🎟 *Free.*

Mt. Parke. A 45-minute hike up this 263-meter (863-foot) peak leads to the island's highest point and a stunning view of the mainland and other Gulf Islands. ✉ *Montrose Rd., off Fernhill Rd., Mayne Island* 🌐 *www.crd.bc.ca/parks.*

Plumper Pass Lockup. Built in 1896, this former jail is now a minuscule museum chronicling Mayne Island's history. ✉ *433 Fernhill Rd., Miners Bay, Mayne Island* ☎ *250/539–5286* 🎟 *Free* 🕒 *July–Labor Day, Fri.–Mon. 10–2.*

Springwater Lodge. You can stop for a meal or a drink on the deck at this lodge, one of the province's oldest hotels. It's been operating since 1892. ✉ *400 Fernhill Rd., Miners Bay, Mayne Island* ☎ *250/539–5521* 🌐 *www.springwaterlodge.com.*

NEED A BREAK?

Sunny Mayne Bakery Café. Join the locals for homemade soups, sandwiches, and baked treats at this tiny Miner's Bay spot; it's open for breakfast and lunch daily. ✉ ***472 Village Bay Rd., Mayne Island*** ☎ ***250/539–2323*** 🌐 ***www.sunnymaynebakery.com*** 🕒 ***No dinner.***

WHERE TO STAY

$$$ RESORT

🏨 **Mayne Island Resort.** Overlooking Bennett Bay and just steps from Mayne Island's best-loved beach, this chic modern resort enjoys a prime waterfront location and a wealth of amenities, including an indoor pool, a waterfront restaurant, and a spa. **Pros:** waterfront location; hot tub, steam room, and excercise room; private cottages. **Cons:** drop to the water makes it unsuitable for small children; breakfast not included with the cottages, only lodge rooms. [$] *Rooms from: C$299* ✉ *494 Arbutus Dr., Mayne Island* ☎ *250/539–3122, 866/539–5399* 🌐 *www.mayneislandresort.com* 🛏 *14 cottages, 8 rooms* 🍴 *No meals.*

SHOPPING

Farmers' Market. On Saturdays between mid-May and mid-October, check out the Farmers' Market outside the Miners Bay Agricultural Hall. Open from 10 to 1, it sells produce and crafts while local musicians entertain shoppers. ✉ *430 Fernhill Rd., Miners Bay, Mayne Island.*

SPORTS AND THE OUTDOORS

KAYAKING

Bennett Bay Kayaking. This outfitter rents kayaks and standup paddle boards, and leads kayak day tours from mid-April through mid-October. ☎ *250/539–0864* 🌐 *www.bennettbaykayaking.com.*

PENDER ISLAND

Just a few miles north of the U.S. border, Pender is actually two islands: North Pender and South Pender, divided by a canal and linked by a one-lane bridge. Most of the population of about 2,000 cluster on North Pender, whereas South Pender is largely forested and undeveloped. The Penders are blessed with beaches, boasting more than 30 public beach-access points.

There's no town on either island, but you can find groceries, a bakery, gas, a bank, a pharmacy, a liquor store, and a Visitor Information Centre at North Pender's Driftwood Centre. A farmers' market runs on summer Saturdays at Pender Island Community Hall, and crafts shops, studios, and galleries are open throughout the islands.

EXPLORING

Gowlland Point Park. The small pebble beach at Gowlland Point Park, at the end of Gowlland Point Road on South Pender, is one of the prettiest on the islands, with views across to Washington State. ✉ *Gowlland Point Rd., Pender Island.*

Gulf Islands National Park Reserve. Both North Pender and South Pender host sections of the Gulf Islands National Park Reserve. On South Pender a steep trail leads to the 800-foot summit of **Mt. Norman,** with its expansive ocean and island views; in the newer Greenburn Lake section of the park, forest trails circle a pretty freshwater lake. On North Pender, a historic cottage resort called Roesland is now part of the park. One of the circa-1908 cottage on-site houses the Pender Island Museum, hiking trails lead to a small lake, and an easy 15-minute walk leads to a tiny islet. ☎ *250/654–4000* 🌐 *www.pc.gc.ca/pn-np/bc/gulf/index.aspx.*

NEED A BREAK?

The Stand. You can refuel before catching the ferry at the Stand, a rustic take-out shack at the Otter Bay ferry terminal. The burgers—whether beef,salmon, halibut or veggie—are enormous, messy, and delicious. It's strictly cash only. ✉ ***Otter Bay Ferry Terminal, Otter Bay Rd., North Pender Island, Pender Island*** ☎ ***250/629–3292*** 💳 ***No credit cards.***

Hope Bay. A waterview café, an artisans' co-op, and views to Saturna and Mayne islands are the draws at Hope Bay, a lovely cove on North Pender's eastern shore. ✉ *4301 Bedwell Harbour Rd., North Pender Island, Pender Island* ☎ *250/629–3166* 🌐 *www.hopebayrising.com.*

Mortimer Spit. The sandy beach at Mortimer Spit is a sheltered spot for swimming and kayaking; it's near the bridge linking the two islands. ✉ *Mortimer Spit Rd., off Canal Rd., South Pender Island, Pender Island.*

Pender Islands Museum. In a 1908 farmhouse at Roesland on North Pender, part of the Gulf Islands National Park Reserve, this tiny museum houses local historic artifacts. ✉ *2408 South Otter Bay Rd., North Pender Island, Pender Island* ☎ *250/629–6935* 🌐 *www.penderislandmuseum.org* 🎟 *Donations accepted* 🕓 *July–Aug., weekends 10–4; Easter–June and Sept.–mid-Oct., weekends 1–4.*

Sea Star Estate Farm and Vineyards. ✉ *6621 Harbour Hill Dr., North Pender Island, Pender Island* ☎ *250/629–6960* 🌐 *www.seastarvineyards.ca* 🎟 *C$4 for tasting (deducted from wine purchases)* 🕓 *Thurs.–Mon. 12–6.*

WHERE TO STAY

$$$$ RESORT Fodor's Choice ★

🏨 **Poets Cove Resort & Spa.** One of the Gulf Islands' most well-appointed developments fills a secluded cove on South Pender. **Pros:** great views; family-friendly vibe. **Cons:** 20-minute drive from the ferry. [$] *Rooms from: C$309* ✉ *9801 Spalding Rd., South Pender Island, Pender Island* ☎ *250/629–2100, 888/512–7638* 🌐 *www.poetscove.com* 🛏 *22 rooms, 15 cottages, 9 villas* 🍴 *No meals.*

SATURNA ISLAND

With just 300 residents, remote Saturna Island is taken up largely by a section of the Gulf Islands National Park Reserve and is a prime spot for hiking, kayaking, and beachcombing. The most remote of the Southern Gulf Islands, Saturna usually takes two ferries to reach. It has no bank or pharmacy but it does have an ATM, pub, general store, café, and winery. There's also a full-service restaurant at Saturna Lodge.

NEED A BREAK?

Wild Thyme Coffee House. Running for the ferry? Grab a chai or a sandwich at this funky café, housed in a 1963 British double-decker bus. ✉ *109 East Point Rd., Saturna Island* ☎ *250/539–5589* 🌐 *wildthymecoffeehouse.com* 🕑 *No dinner.*

WHERE TO STAY

If you are looking for a place to eat out on the island, the bistro at Saturna Island Family Winery (*8 Quarry Trail, 250/539–3521*) is open from June to September for lunch.

$$ B&B/INN FAMILY

🏨 **Saturna Lodge.** This cozy six-room inn, surrounded by gardens and overlooking pretty, forested Boot Cove, makes a great base for exploring the island. **Pros:** family- and pet-friendly; free ferry and float plane shuttle; free Wi-Fi. **Cons:** restaurant closed some evenings. [$] *Rooms from:* ✉ *130 Payne Rd., Saturna Island* ☎ *250/539–2254, 866/539–2254* ✉ *innkeeper@saturna.ca* 🌐 *saturna.ca* 🕑 *Closed in winter (call for dates)* 🛏 *6 rooms* 🍴 *Breakfast.*

TOFINO, UCLUELET, AND THE PACIFIC RIM NATIONAL PARK RESERVE

Tofino may be the birthplace of North American storm-watching, but the area's tempestuous winter weather and roiling waves are only two of the many stellar attractions you'll find along British Columbia's wildest coastline. Exquisite tide pooling, expansive wilderness beaches, excellent surfing, and the potential to see some of the continent's largest sea mammals lure thousands of visitors to Pacific Rim National Park Reserve, sleepy Ucluelet, and quirkily charming Tofino.

No one "happens" upon Tofino; it's literally at the end of the road, where Highway 4 meets the mouth of Clayoquot Sound. As Canada's premier surfer village, Tofino has shed much of its 1960s-style counter-culture vibe and transformed itself into a happening tourist destination where fine dining, spa treatments, and eco adventures are par for the course. You can enjoy meandering through old-growth forests, exploring pristine beaches and rocky tidal pools, bathing in natural hot springs, and spotting whales, bears, eagles, and river otters in a natural setting.

The harbor towns of Ucluelet and Tofino are chock-a-block with funky shops, services, and eateries. Between them lies the Long Beach section of the Pacific Rim National Park Reserve. Centered on a 16-km (10-mile) stretch of surf-pounded beach backed by old growth forest, this very accessible park is one of Canada's leading natural sights.

Tofino, Ucluelet, and the Pacific Rim National Park

PLANNING

GETTING HERE AND AROUND

Tofino is 314 km (195 miles) from Victoria, about a four- or five-hour drive. If you're coming from Vancouver by ferry (to Victoria or Nanaimo), head north to Parksville via the Trans-Canada Highway (Highway 1) and the Island Highway (Highway 19). From there pick up Highway 4, which crosses the island from Parksville to Port Alberni, Ucluelet, and Tofino. Break up the trip with a lunch or ice-cream break at the Coombs Old Country Market, about 15 km (9 miles) west of Parksville; a good stop for picnic supplies, the store is known for the goats grazing on its sod roof. If you don't want to drive yourself, there's regular bus service from Victoria, but you really need a car to explore the area, so you might have to rent one after arrival.

You can also fly from Victoria or Vancouver, a more expensive but much faster option.

One international car-rental agency (Budget) and one local agency (Tofino Airport Car Rental) rent vehicles at Tofino–Long Beach Airport. Reservations are highly recommended.

Tofino Taxi provides service in Tofino, including airport pick-ups. Book in advance for night or off-hours service. The Tofino Water Taxi is a boat shuttle to Meares Island, Hot Springs Cove in Maquinna Marine Provincial Park, and other remote offshore sites.

Contacts Tofino Airport Car Rental. ⊕ *www.tofinoairportcarrental.com.* **Tofino Taxi.** ☎ *250/725–3333.* **Tofino Water Taxi.** ☎ *250/725–8844, 866/794–2537* ⊕ *www.tofinowatertaxi.com.*

VISITOR INFORMATION

The Pacific Rim Visitors Centre, at the Tofino–Ucluelet junction on Hwy 4, sells park permits and provides free information and maps on the Pacific Rim National Park Reserve and the Tofino-Ucluelet area. The Tofino Vistor Centre, also known as the Cox Bay Visitor Info Centre, is about 10 minutes south of Tofino on Hwy 4. Park passes and information are also available at the Kwisitis Visitor Centre, in the Pacific Rim National Park Reserve.

Contacts Kwisitis Visitor Centre. ⊕ *www.pc.gc.ca/eng/pn-np/bc/pacificrim/ activ/activkwisitis.aspx.* **Pacific Rim Visitors Centre.** ☎ *250/726–4600* ⊕ *www. pacificrimvisitor.ca.* **Tofino Visitor Info Centre.** ☎ *250/725–3414, 888/720–3414* ⊕ *www.tourismtofino.com.*

TOFINO

42 km (26 miles) northwest of Ucluelet, 337 km (209 miles) northwest of Victoria.

Tofino combines the historical roots of the rugged Canadian frontier with the mellow rhythm of a California surf town—think Mendocino in a toque. Old-growth forest meets the relentless surf of the Pacific and explorers from age two to 102 dig into sand, tide pools, and surf. Talk to the locals and you're bound to hear some interesting "How I came to live in Tofino" anecdotes.

The district's 1,800 or so permanent residents host about a million visitors every year, but they've made what could have been a tourist trap into an unconventional little town with several art galleries, good restaurants, and plenty of opportunity to get out to the surrounding wilds. Reservations are recommended any time of year. While many outdoor activities are confined to spring through fall, surfing continues year-round, regardless of the temperature. November through February is devoted to storm-watching (best enjoyed from a cozy waterfront lodge).

EXPLORING

Maquinna Marine Provincial Park. Geothermal springs tumble down a waterfall and into a series of oceanside rock pools at idyllic Hot Springs Cove, accessible only by boat or air from Tofino. Day-trips here, which are offered by several Tofino outfitters, usually include a bit of whale-watching en route. Once you arrive at the park, there's a half-hour boardwalk trail through old-growth forest to the site. If you can't bear to leave, or just like the idea of having the springs to yourself in the evening, book a cabin on the *InnChanter (www.innchanter.com 250/670–1149)*, a historic boat moored near the park. Another popular day-trip is to Meares Island, where an easy 20-minute boardwalk trail leads to trees up to 1,600 years old. ⊕ *www.env.gov.bc.ca/bcparks/ explore/parkpgs/maquinna.*

Tofino Botanical Gardens. Trails wind through displays of indigenous plant life, and the occasional whimsical garden sculpture may catch your eye at Tofino Botanical Gardens. The 12-acre waterfront site, about 2 km (1 mile) south of Tofino on the Pacific Rim Highway, is also home to a café and an affordable ecolodge. The admission fee is good for three days. ✉ *1084 Pacific Rim Hwy., Tofino* ☎ *250/725–1220* 🌐 *www.tbgf.org* 🎟 *C$10* 🕒 *Daily 9–dusk.*

WHERE TO EAT

$ BAKERY 🍴 **The Common Loaf Bake Shop.** This red-turreted village center building has been a bakery and local hangout since the late 1970s. Everything from the panini and muffins to the breakfast pizza is made fresh inhouse. Grab a latte and a Tofino Bar—a popular chocolate treat with a West Coast spin—and climb the winding stairs to the turret room for distant harbor views. Payment is strictly cash only. [$] *Average main:* ✉ *180 First St., Tofino* ☎ *250/725–3915* 💳 *No credit cards.*

$$$$ CANADIAN Fodor's Choice ★ 🍴 **The Pointe.** With 180-degree views of the crashing surf, the Pointe is *the* top-notch Tofino dining experience. It's renowned for its refined West Coast cuisine, which is superbly presented and excellently paired with options from the award-winning wine list. Ingredients from the water—including oysters, shrimp, salmon, and a variety of other seafood—and the land (whatever's in season, such as wild mushrooms and fresh herbs) are used in innovative but not too outlandish dishes. The service is meticulous. For something more casual, stop at the inn's Driftwood Café for high-end snacks and small-plate dinners right on the beach. [$] *Average main: C$35* ✉ *The Wickaninnish Inn, 500 Osprey La., Tofino* ☎ *250/725–3100* 🌐 *www.wickinn.com/restaurant.html.*

$$$ SEAFOOD Fodor's Choice ★ 🍴 **Schooner Restaurant.** An institution in downtown Tofino (it's been run by the same family since 1954), the Schooner's main-floor dining room is comfortable and casually upscale. The seafood dishes change frequently, but ask for the signature halibut filet stuffed with Brie, crab, and shrimp in an apple-peppercorn brandy sauce. The steaming bowl of island clams, mussels, salmon, halibut, and red snapper is another winner. The Schooner also dishes up weekend brunch and hearty lunchtime sandwiches, burgers, and pastas. An oyster bar and summer patio are pluses. From October to May, the whole operation moves upstairs to a more intimate room with exceptional views of Meares Island. [$] *Average main: C$27* ✉ *331 Campbell St., Tofino* ☎ *250/725–3444* 🌐 *www.schoonerrestaurant.ca.*

$$$ CANADIAN 🍴 **Shelter.** This big, bustling spot on the edge of town draws both locals and visitors for burgers, chowder, and fish-and-chips for lunch, and dinners of shucked oysters, pan-seared salmon, and grilled rib-eyes. Choose from the upbeat pub vibe in the lofty wood-beamed first-floor lounge, or opt for a more serene dining experience, with sea views, in the upper-floor restaurant. [$] *Average main: C$29* ✉ *601 Campbell St., Tofino* ☎ *250/725–3353* 🌐 *www.shelterrestaurant.com.*

$$$ ECLECTIC Fodor's Choice ★ FAMILY 🍴 **Sobo.** The name, short for "sophisticated bohemian," sums up the style here: a classically trained chef serving casual fare influenced by international street food. The off-beat concept started in a purple truck before finding a permanent home in this light-filled café and bistro. The truck's long gone, but the food is still eclectic. Starters, like chickpea panelle and bison short rib, and mains, like cedar-plank salmon, wood-oven pizza,

Pacific Rim Storm-Watching

No one's really sure when the concept of "bad weather" morphed into "good weather," but on the tourism-friendly Pacific Rim, nasty storms are usually considered quite fine indeed.

November through March is formally storm-watching season, and thousands of people travel from around the world to witness the spectacularly violent weather. Veteran storm-watchers are known to keep an eye on the weather channels and pack their bags quickly for Tofino or Ucluelet when storm predictions are particularly, well, grim.

Throughout the winter, but particularly during the "peak season" of December through February, as many as 15 "good storms" arrive per month. Winds from the ocean exceed 50 kph (30 mph) and teeming rain—even hail, sleet, or snow—arrives horizontally. Massive waves thunder onto the beaches and crash over the rocky headlands and islets, sending spray soaring. Towering evergreen trees crackle and lean; logs are tossed helter-skelter, high onto kelp-strewn beaches. Unusual storm clouds, mists, and rainbows add to the beauty. And as if the sights weren't enough, expect to hear the eerie sounds of a screaming wind, pounding surf—even the rattling of double-paned windows—unless you happen to be behind reinforced triple-glazed windows, in which case the whole show unfolds in near silence. And that's even more surreal.

The hotels and B&Bs love the storm season because it fills rooms in what could otherwise be a bleak time of year. And it must be admitted that most storm-watching takes place in considerable comfort—particularly at the luxury hotels along Cox Bay, Chesterman Beach, and MacKenzie Beach. These and other waterfront properties in the Tofino-Ucluelet region have shrewdly developed "storm-watching packages," in which treats abound (and rates tumble). Champagne on arrival, fashionable wet-weather gear, complimentary nature walks, and gourmet dinners are among the offerings. Perhaps most important, expect a cozy room, often with a fireplace and a soaker tub with an ocean outlook, in which you can relax in security, while the outer world rages on.

Serious thrill seekers take to the beaches and lookouts to experience storms firsthand. That said, conditions can be decidedly unfriendly, and visitors should remember that people are injured here every year by rogue waves and rolling logs. Storm-watchers planning on walking the Wild Pacific Trail, for example, should go with a companion, and preferably with an experienced naturalist or guide. Long Beach Nature Tours (⊕ www.longbeachnaturetours.com) is a good choice. Other notable storm-watching venues include Wickaninnish Beach, with the largest swells and greatest concentration of logs and driftwood; Long Beach, famed for its rolling swells, wave-washed islands, and panoramic views; Cox Bay, said to receive the largest and most powerful waves; and Chesterman Beach, beloved for its varied conditions and outlooks.

and braised duck ramen with handmade noodles, never fail to impress. The killer fish tacos are legendary. There's a great kids' menu and a bakery counter for take-out treats. [$] *Average main: C$28* ✉ *311 Neill St., Tofino* ☎ *250/725–2341* 🌐 *www.sobo.ca* ⌚ *Closed Dec. and Jan.*

$$$ CONTEMPORARY 🍴 **The Spotted Bear.** Enjoy boat-to-table seafood and other beautifully executed local fare at this popular village-center bistro. An open kitchen, upbeat tunes, and a loyal cadre of local and visiting foodies keeps this tiny place hopping year-round. Grab a seat at the distressed wood bar to watch the chef at work, or settle into one of just seven unadorned tables and see what's on the blackboard specials menu that day. Start with albacore tuna tartare or braised octopus, then try the pork belly and scallops, or the duck breast with parsnip, sweet potato, and pear puree. Alternatively, opt for the daily fish or tagliatelle dish. Finish with a house-made dessert, such as the lavender crème brûlée. The Spotted Bear's Sunday-only brunch is a popular weekend event. [$] *Average main:* ✉ *101 4th Ave., Tofino* ☎ *250/725–2215* 🌐 *www.spottedbearbistro.com* ⌚ *No lunch Mon.–Sat.*

$ MEXICAN 🍴 **Tacofino.** Heading to the beach? Follow the surfers to this orange catering truck at Outside Break, a cluster of driftwood- and cedar-sided shops just south of town. Dubbed "slow food fast," the quick, cheap, and wholesome eats here include burritos, *gringas* (flour tortillas stuffed with meat or beans), and Baja-style fish tacos. Everything, including the salsa, is made from scratch. It's a branch of the original in Vancouver. [$] *Average main:* ✉ *1180 Pacific Rim Hwy., Tofino* ✣ *5 minutes south of Tofino* ☎ *250/726–8288* 🌐 *tacofino.com* ⌚ *Call for seasonal closures.*

$ SEAFOOD 🍴 **Wildside Grill.** Just steps away from the popular Tacofino truck is another take-out, Wildside Grill, where a commercial fisherman and a chef have joined forces to keep Tofitians and visitors supplied with straight-from-the-dock panko-crusted fish-and-chips and juicy fish and beef burgers. Gather a beach picnic, or enjoy a meal under the shade of Wildside's driftwood gazebo. Advance orders are taken by phone. [$] *Average main:* ✉ *1180 Pacific Rim Hwy., Tofino* ✣ *5 minutes south of Tofino* ☎ *250/725–9453* 🌐 *www.wildsidegrill.com* 💳 *No credit cards* ⌚ *Call for seasonal closures.*

9

WHERE TO STAY

$$$ B&B/INN Fodor's Choice ★ 🏨 **Chesterman Beach Bed & Breakfast.** This charming beachside inn, opened as Tofino's first B&B in 1984, is the kind of intimate seaside getaway that brought people to Vancouver Island's West Coast in the first place. **Pros:** gracious owner knowledgeable about area; private and scenic. **Cons:** 10-minute drive to restaurants; breakfast not actually included in rates (and not available at all for the cottage). [$] *Rooms from:* ✉ *1345 Chesterman Beach Rd., Tofino* ☎ *250/725–3726* 🌐 *www.tofinoaccommodation.com* 🍽 *No meals.*

$$$$ RESORT Fodor's Choice ★ FAMILY 🏨 **Clayoquot Wilderness Resort.** People from around the globe arrive via floatplane or a 30-minute boat ride from Tofino to experience one of the region's top wilderness resorts. **Pros:** escapism at its best, with no phone or other distractions; excellent food; a ton of outdoorsy activities. **Cons:** it's extremely pricey; fairly isolated, requiring a long trip. [$] *Rooms from: C$2700* ✉ *Bedwell River, Tofino* ☎ *250/726-8235, 888/333–5405* 🌐 *www.wildretreat.com* ⌚ *Closed Oct.–mid-May* 🛏 *20 tents, 12 with private bath* 🍽 *All meals* ☞ *3-night min.*

$$$ HOTEL **Inn at Tough City.** Vintage furnishings and First Nations art make this harborside inn funky, if a bit cluttered. **Pros:** prime Tofino location; loads of character; restaurant has best sushi in town. **Cons:** the lobby is small and noisy; front-desk staffing friendly but inconsistent. [$] *Rooms from: C$199 ✉ 350 Main St., Tofino ☎ 250/725–2021 🌐 www.toughcity.com ⏲ Closed Dec.–Feb. 🛏 8 rooms 🍴 No meals.*

$$$ HOTEL **Long Beach Lodge Resort.** With handcrafted furnishings, dramatic pieces of First Nations art, and a tall granite fireplace, the great room at this luxury lodge offers front row seats to the surf (and surfers) rolling into miles of sandy beach. **Pros:** exceptional beachfront location; terrific restaurant; cozy areas within the great room. **Cons:** a hot tub, sauna, fitness room, and in-room spa services; beach gets busy with guests from neighboring resorts. [$] *Rooms from: C$299 ✉ 1441 Pacific Rim Hwy., Tofino ☎ 250/725–2442, 877/844–7873 🌐 www.longbeachlodgeresort.com 🛏 41 rooms, 20 cottages 🍴 No meals.*

$$ RESORT **Middle Beach Lodge.** On a bluff overlooking a mile of private beach, this rustically elegant lodge is a great choice for a grown-ups getaway. **Pros:** truly secluded, with an almost exclusive beach; Lodge at the Beach has great rates for the location. **Cons:** limited restaurant hours; kids allowed only in some accommodations. [$] *Rooms from: C$180 ✉ 400 MacKenzie Beach Rd., Tofino ☎ 250/725–2901 🌐 www.middlebeach.com ⏲ Restaurant closed Sun.–Thurs. No lunch 🛏 35 rooms, 10 suites, 19 cabins 🍴 Breakfast.*

$$$ RESORT FAMILY **Pacific Sands Beach Resort.** On 45 acres of lawn and forest along Cox Bay, this resort offers a range of lodge rooms, waterfront suites, and beach villas, all with full kitchens, fireplaces, and private ocean-view decks or patios just steps from the beach.The freshly renovated multilevel beach houses are the nicest, with granite countertops, high ceilings, and soaker tubs; some of the beachfront suites are a bit small and dated. **Pros:** on prime beachfront; good family destination. **Cons:** no restaurant; some suites are on the small side. [$] *Rooms from: C$300 ✉ 1421 Pacific Rim Hwy., Tofino ☎ 250/725–3322, 800/565–2322 🌐 www.pacificsands.com 🛏 22 villas, 57 suites 🍴 No meals.*

$$$$ RESORT Fodor's Choice ★ **The Wickaninnish Inn.** On a rocky promontory with open ocean on three sides and old-growth forest as a backdrop, this cedar-sided inn is exceptional in every sense. **Pros:** at the end of a superb crescent beach; the silence of storms through triple-glazed windows is surreal; excellent staff. **Cons:** pricey and posh; no swimming pool. [$] *Rooms from: C$500 ✉ 500 Osprey La., at Chesterman Beach, Tofino ☎ 250/725–3100, 800/333–4604 🌐 www.wickinn.com 🛏 63 rooms, 12 suites 🍴 No meals.*

SPORTS AND THE OUTDOORS

Thinking about some side trips? Then why not hop onto a boat or floatplane and explore the surrounding roadless wilderness? The most popular day-trip is to Hot Springs Cove in Maquinna Marine Provincial Park, where you can soak in natural rock pools by the sea. Other trips head to Meares Island, where an easy 20-minute boardwalk trail leads to trees up to 1,600 years old. Whale- and bear-watching tours are great options, too; a popular trip combines whale-watching with a visit to Hot Springs Cove, with wildlife-spotting opportunities en route to the thermal springs.

FISHING

Chinook Charters. At Chinook Charters, Captain Mike Hansen is an independent guide born and raised in the area. His custom-designed 30-foot vessel is well-equipped to land a prized coho. Prices are in line with other Tofino operators at around C$600 per day for up to two people. ✉ *331 Main St., Tofino* ☎ *250/726–5221* ⊕ *www.chinookcharters.com.*

Cleanline Sportfishing. Experienced anglers appreciate the expertise of this company, a multiboat operator offering both saltwater and freshwater fishing. Prices are competitive at C$125 per hour in the ocean and about C$800 per day on the rivers. For a spectacular day out, you can be flown into a remote mountain lake where you launch a raft and spend the day fishing for trout as you drift along a river back to the coast; the price for this experience, including the flight, is C$1,500 for two people. ✉ *630a Campbell St., Tofino* ☎ *250/726–3828, 855/726–3828* ⊕ *www.cleanlinesportfishing.com.*

FLIGHTSEEING

In addition to Atleo River Air Service, Tofino Air, which provides small-plane transportation throughout the region, also operates flightseeing tours over outlying forests and beaches to Hot Springs Cove in Maquinna Marine Provincial Park. Other trips take you to the lakes and glaciers of Strathcona Provincial Park. If you can, soar over Cougar Annie's Garden, a century-old wilderness homestead that was once the home of a legendary local character. ⇨ *See Air Travel in Travel Smart.*

Atleo River Air Service. This locally owned company offers breathtaking flightseeing tours around Clayoquot and Barkley sounds, plus fly-in fishing, hot springs tours, and more by both floatplane and helicopter. ☎ *250/725–2205, 866/662–8536* ⊕ *www.atleoair.com.*

HIKING

FAMILY **Long Beach Nature Tours.** Learn about local ecosystems on a beach or forest walk with experienced naturalists. Half- and full-day trips include intertidal and rainforest exploration, treks to remote beaches and, in winter, a chance to watch storms in action. ☎ *250/725–8305* ⊕ *www. longbeachnaturetours.com.*

KAYAKING

Remote Passages. No experience is necessary for these relaxed guided paddles in sheltered waters. Also on offer are whale-watching and bear-watching trips and excursions to Meares Island and Hot Springs Cove in Maquinna Marine Provincial Park. ✉ *71 Wharf St., Tofino* ☎ *250/725–3330, 800/666–9833* ⊕ *www.remotepassages.com.*

Tofino Sea-Kayaking Company. Tofino Sea-Kayaking Company rents kayaks, runs a kayaking school, and provides day and multiday wilderness kayaking trips. No experience is necessary for the day-trips. ✉ *320 Main St., Tofino* ☎ *250/725–4222, 800/863–4664* ⊕ *www. tofinoseakayaking.com.*

SURFING

The coast from Tofino south to Ucluelet is, despite perpetually chilly waters, an increasingly popular surf destination—year-round.

Live to Surf. You can rent boards and other gear at Live to Surf. Jean-Paul Froment runs the business (founded by his parents in 1984) with his sister Pascale from the funky Outside Break commercial hub south of Tofino, which is conveniently close to the major surfing spots of Long Beach, Cox Bay, Chesterman Beach, and MacKenzie Beach. The shop also sells boards, wet suits, and accessories, and provides rentals and lessons. ⊠ *1180 Pacific Rim Hwy.*, *Tofino* ☎ *250/725–4464* ⊕ *www. livetosurf.com.*

Pacific Surf School. This company offers everything from three-hour introductory sessions to multiday camps. ⊠ *430 Campbell St.*, *Tofino* ☎ *250/725–2155*, *888/777–9961* ⊕ *www.pacificsurfschool.com.*

Storm. This hip surf shop in downtown Tofino carries all the latest gear, including boards, clothing, and wet suits. ⊠ *444 Campbell St.*, *Tofino* ☎ *250/725–3344* ⊕ *www.stormcanada.ca.*

Surf Sister. This well-respected school has women-only lessons as well as those for everyone. Check out mother-daughter surf packages, teenager surf camps, and progressive sessions. ⊠ *625 Campbell St.*, *Tofino* ☎ *250/725–4456*, *877/724–7873* ⊕ *www.surfsister.com.*

WHALE-WATCHING AND MARINE EXCURSIONS

In March and April, up to 22,000 Pacific gray whales migrate along the coast here; resident grays can be seen anytime between March and October. In addition, there are humpback whales, sea otters, sea lions, orcas, black bears, and other wildlife. Most whale-watching operators also lead bear-watching trips by sea and excursions along the coast and to the region's outlying islands, including Meares Island and Hot Springs Cove in Maquinna Marine Provincial Park, where you can soak in natural seaside hot springs. Services range from no-frills water-taxi drop-off to tours with experienced guides; prices vary accordingly. Want to stay longer at Hot Springs Cove? Book a cabin on the InnChanter (⊕ *www.innchanter.com*). This historic boat is moored at the cove, and overnights include lavish meals and a chance to have the hot springs to yourself.

Jamie's Whaling Station & Adventure Centre. One of the most established whale-watching operators on the coast, Jamie's has motorized inflatable boats as well as more comfortable 65-foot tour boats. You can book a whole range of adventures, including kayaking, bear-watching, and sightseeing trips to Meares Island or Hot Springs Cove. Jamie's operates from March through October. Jamie's also has a location in Ucluelet and operates Jamie's Rainforest Inn, a 38-room lodge just south of Tofino. ⊠ *606 Campbell St.*, *Tofino* ☎ *250/725–3919*, *800/667–9913* ⊕ *www.jamies.com.*

FAMILY **Ocean Outfitters.** Whale- and bear-watching trips, Meares Island trips, and Hot Springs Cove tours are all on the menu at this popular outfitter. ⊠ *368 Main St.*, *Tofino* ☎ *250/725–2866*, *877/906–2326* ⊕ *www. oceanoutfitters.bc.ca.*

Remote Passages Marine Excursions. A well-established operator, Remote Passages offers whale-watching and bear-watching excursions as well as trips to Hot Springs Cove and Meares Island. Tours have an ecological and educational focus. ⊠ *71 Wharf St.*, *Tofino* ☎ *250/725–3330*, *800/666–9833* ⊕ *www.remotepassages.com.*

DID YOU KNOW?

Surfing in Tofino is not for the faint of heart.

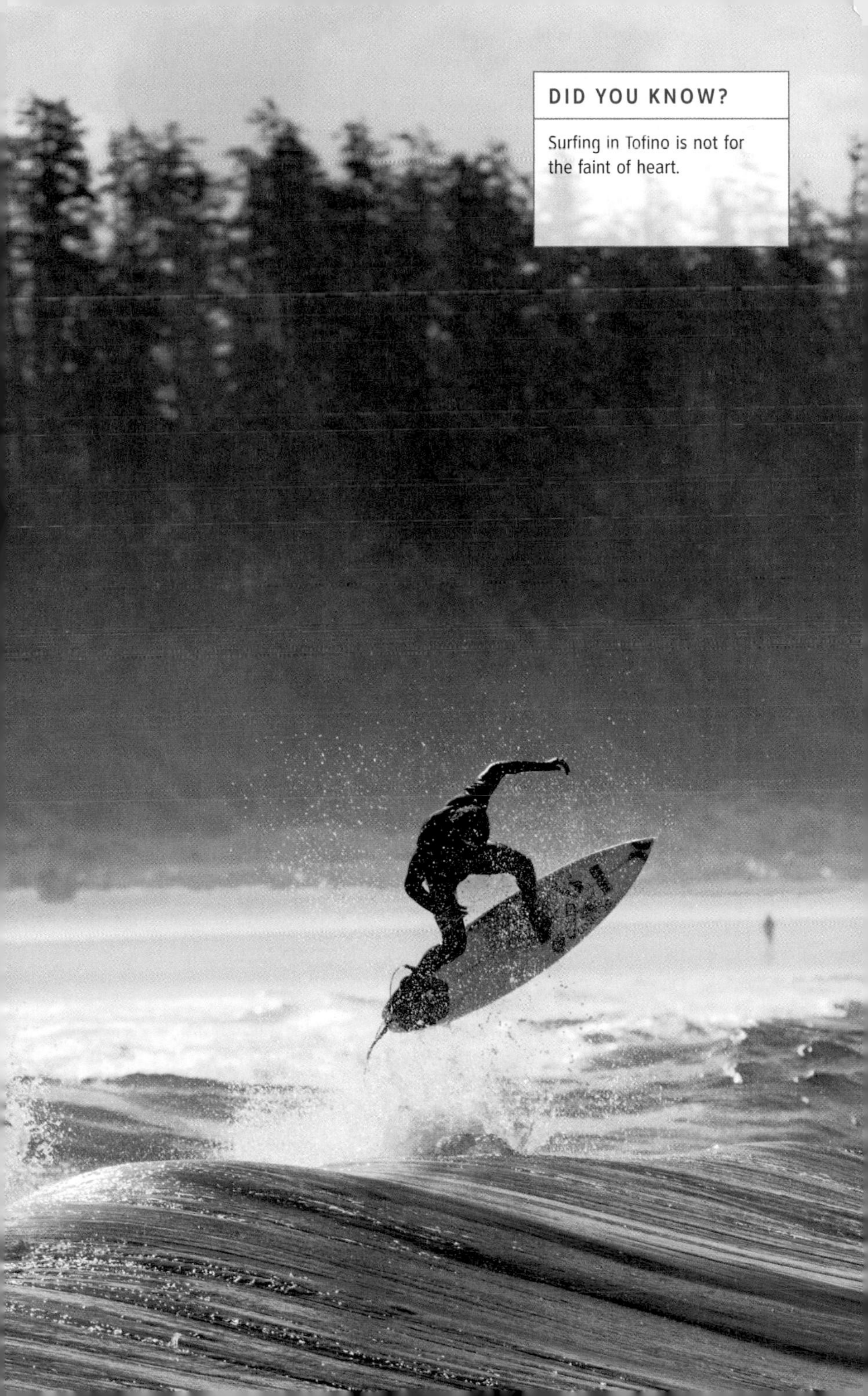

FAMILY **West Coast Aquatic Safaris.** If comfort is a priority, check out this company's covered, wheelchair-accessible all-weather tour boats, with heated cabins and inside seating as well as viewing decks. The company offers whale- and bear-watching trips, Hot Spring Cove trips, and fishing charters. ⊠ *101 Fourth St., Tofino* ☎ *250 /725–9227, 877/594–2537.*

The Whale Centre. This long-established company has a 40-foot-long gray whale skeleton that you can study while waiting for your boat. It runs whale-watching and bird-watching trips from March to mid-October, and bear-spotting tours between April and October as well as daily, year-round trips to Hot Springs Cove in a 30-foot covered boat. ⊠ *411 Campbell St., Tofino* ☎ *250/725–2132, 888/474–2288* ⊕ *www.tofinowhalecentre.com.*

SHOPPING

ART GALLERIES

Eagle Aerie Gallery. In a traditional longhouse, the magnificent Eagle Aerie Gallery houses a collection of prints, paintings, and carvings by renowned BC artist Roy Henry Vickers. ⊠ *350 Campbell St., Tofino* ☎ *250/725–3235* ⊕ *www.royhenryvickers.com.*

Himwitsa Native Art Gallery. Here's where to find a good selection of First Nations crafts, jewelry, and clothing. The complex also has a seafood restaurant. ⊠ *300 Main St., Tofino* ☎ *250/725–2017* ⊕ *www.himwitsa.com.*

Reflecting Spirit Gallery. More than 200 local artists are showcased here with a wide range of photographs, paintings, carvings, pottery, and jewelry. There's a second location in Ucluelet. ⊠ *411 Campbell St., Tofino* ☎ *250/725–2472* ⊕ *www.reflectingspirit.com.*

BOOK STORES

Mermaid Tales Books. This locally run shop has a carefully curated selection of novels, non-fiction selections, and local-interest books as well as kites and toys. ⊠ *455 Campbell St., Tofino* ☎ *250/725–2125* ⊕ *mermaidbooks.ca.*

FLEA MARKETS

FAMILY **Tofino Public Market.** Head to the Village Green on Campbell Street for food, crafts, and entertainment every Saturday from May to September. ⊠ *Campbell St., Tofino* ⊕ *www.tofinomarket.com* ☉ *May–Sept., Sat. 10–2.*

FOOD

Chocolate Tofino. Everything from the wild blackberry butter creams and lavender truffles to the sorbets and gelatos are handmade in-house at this tiny chocolate and gelato shop just south of Tofino. You can even watch chocolatiers at work in the open kitchen. ⊠ *Outside Break, 1180A Pacific Rim Hwy., Tofino* ✛ *2 miles south of Tofino* ☎ *250/725–2526* ⊕ *www.chocolatetofino.com.*

SPAS

Ancient Cedars Spa. A couple's massage in a private cedar hut on the seashore is just one highlight at this much-loved spa at the Wickaninnish Inn. On the edge of the open Pacific and framed by forest, Ancient Cedars induces serenity with hot stone massages, lomilomi treatments, hatha yoga classes, and more. ✉ *Wickaninnish Inn, Osprey Lane at Chesterman Beach, Tofino* ☎ *250/725–3113, 800/333–4604* 🌐 *www.wickinn.com/ancient-cedars-spa.*

Sacred Stone Spa. A small spa above the harbor in downtown Tofino, Sacred Stone specializes in different styles of massages, including hot stone, Ayurvedic, and Thai foot massage. ✉ *421 Main St., Tofino* ☎ *250/725–3341* 🌐 *www.sacredstone.ca.*

UCLUELET

295 km (183 miles) northwest of Victoria.

Ucluelet, which in the Nuu-chah-nulth First Nations language means "people with a safe landing place," along with the towns of Bamfield and Tofino, serves the Pacific Rim National Park Reserve. Ucluelet is quieter than Tofino and has a less sophisticated ambience. Despite a growing number of crafts shops, restaurants, and B&Bs, it's still more of a fishing village than an ecotourism retreat, although Black Rock Resort competes with Tofino's upscale dining-and-lodging market.

Like in Tofino, whale-watching is an important draw as are the winter storms. Ucluelet is the regional base for fishing and for kayaking in the Broken Group Islands, part of the Pacific Rim National Park Reserve. Various charter companies take boats to greet the 20,000 gray whales that pass close to Ucluelet on their migration to the Bering Sea every March and April.

EXPLORING

FAMILY **Ucluelet Aquarium.** Possibly the world's first catch-and-release aquarium, this intriguing attraction on Ucluelet's waterfront displays local sea life and returns it all to the sea at the end of each season. Touch pools, tanks, and displays reveal the secrets of life right outside the aquarium's doorstep. ✉ *180 Main St., Ucluelet* ☎ *250/726–2782* 🌐 *www.uclueletaquarium.org* 🕒 *Mid-Mar.–Nov. daily 10–5.*

Wild Pacific Trail. Ucluelet is the starting point for the Wild Pacific Trail, a hiking path that winds along the coast and through the rain forest; it's a work in progress that will eventually link Ucluelet to Pacific Rim National Park Reserve. A 2.7-km (1.7-mile) loop starts at He-Tin-Kis Park off Peninsula Road and can also be reached from the Amphitrite Point Lighthouse at the end of Coast Guard Road. Take note of the sea-facing trees, bent at right angles in a face-off against the wild and stormy winds. Another 4-km (2½-mile) stretch starts at Big Beach at the end of Matterson Road and continues to the bike path just outside Ucluelet. 🌐 *www.wildpacifictrail.com.*

WHERE TO EAT

$$$ CONTEMPORARY 🍴 **Matterson House.** In a tiny 1931 cottage with seven tables and an outdoor deck, husband-and-wife team Sandy and Jennifer Clark serve generous portions of seafood, prime rib, and veal cutlets. It's simple food, prepared well with fresh local ingredients; everything, including soups, desserts, and the wonderful bread, is made on the premises and can be accompanied by various local wines. [$] *Average main: C$22* ✉ *1682 Peninsula Rd., Ucluelet* ☎ *250/726–2200* 🕒 *Closed Mon. and Tues.*

9

$$$ ECLECTIC 🍴 **Norwoods.** There's a happening vibe at this cozy little wine bar and bistro on Ucluelet's main street. The food, from the busy open kitchen, is pretty darn good, with lots of regional fare, including freshly caught seafood and picked-today produce. The menu changes frequently, but you can count on innovative fare and a choice of small plates or mains. Starters include albacore tuna sashimi in ponzu and sweet pulled pork with house-made kimchi. Mains like miso-glazed salmon hint at the chef's travels around Asia, while duck breast with caramelized fennel puree and grilled beef tenderloin give a nod to European cuisine. Everything is paired with predominantly BC wines. [$] *Average main: C$30* ✉ *1714 Peninsula Rd., Ucluelet* ☎ *250/726–7001* 🌐 *www.norwoods.ca* 💳 *No credit cards* 🕘 *No lunch.*

WHERE TO STAY

$$$ HOTEL 🏨 **Black Rock Oceanfront Resort.** On a rocky ledge at the edge of a shallow inlet, Black Rock Resort is Ucluelet's first upscale, full-service resort. **Pros:** gorgeous views at every turn; chic aesthetic; lovely spa. **Cons:** limited beach access. [$] *Rooms from: C$270* ✉ *596 Marine Dr., Ucluelet* ☎ *250/726–4800, 877/762–5011* 🌐 *www.blackrockresort.com* 🛏 *133 suites* 🍽 *No meals.*

$$ B&B/INN 🏨 **Majestic Ocean Bed and Breakfast.** Longtime kayaking-business operator Tracy Eeftink and her husband Ted have three fetching ground-level rooms opening onto Ucluelet Harbour. **Pros:** on Ucluelet Harbour; hearty breakfasts; picnic lunch on request. **Cons:** a long walk into town; no nearby restaurant. [$] *Rooms from: C$170* ✉ *1183 Helen Rd., Ucluelet* ☎ *250/726–2868, 800/889–7644* 🌐 *www.majesticoceanbb.ca* 🛏 *3 rooms* 🍽 *Breakfast.*

$$$ B&B/INN 🏨 **A Snug Harbour Inn.** On a cliff above the ocean, this couples-oriented B&B has some of the most dramatic views anywhere. **Pros:** friendly vibe; unique location; hot tub. **Cons:** a bit off the beaten track; no on-site dining; no children allowed. [$] *Rooms from: C$270* ✉ *460 Marine Dr., Ucluelet* ☎ *250/726–2686, 888/936–5222* 🌐 *www.awesomeview.com* 🛏 *6 rooms* 🍽 *Breakfast.*

$$$$ RENTAL FAMILY 🏨 **Wya Point Resort.** Choose from ocean-view cedar cottages, rustic yurts, or a family-friendly campground at this new resort-style development tucked into 600 acres of coastal rainforest between Ucluelet and the Pacific Rim National Park Reserve. **Pros:** stunning views; free Wi-Fi; swimmable beach. **Cons:** no restaurant or spa (though both are planned for 2015). [$] *Rooms from:* ✉ *2695 Tofino-Ucluelet Hwy., Ucluelet* ☎ *250/726–2625* 🌐 *www.wyapoint.com* 🛏 *9 cottages, 15 yurts* 🍽 *No meals.*

SPORTS AND THE OUTDOORS

FISHING

Island West Fishing Resort. A fleet of 24- to 26-foot boats, knowledgeable guides, and all the gear you need are draws at this full-service fishing resort in Ucluelet. The staff will clean and ice-pack the fish you caught for your departure home. ✉ *1990 Bay St., Ucluelet* ☎ *250/726–7515* 🌐 *www.islandwestresort.com.*

KAYAKING

Majestic Ocean Kayaking. Excursions range from three-hour paddles around the harbor to trips to the Broken Group Islands and Barkley Sound, as well as multiday adventures to Clayoquot Sound and the Deer Group Islands. ⌧ *1167 Helen Rd., Ucluelet* ☎ *250/726–2868, 800/889–7644* ⊕ *www.oceankayaking.com.*

SURFING

Ucluelet, like Tofino, is a popular year-round surf destination with waters that are equally as cold, so bring your full dry suit summer and winter.

Relic Surf Shop and Surf School. These guys are cool dudes, with a shop packed with surf boards and gear. Private and group lessons are offered year-round; they also offer rentals and lessons for stand-up paddleboards. ⌧ *1998 Peninsula Rd., Ucluelet* ☎ *250/726–4421* ⊕ *www.relicsurfshop.com.*

Wya Point Surf Shop & Cafe. Just north of the Tofino-Ucluelet Junction, this friendly little surf shop, run by the local Ucluelet First Nation, rents boards and wet suits, sells gear, and offers lessons at all levels. Most of the instructors grew up surfing here and know the local breaks intimately. A food truck parked on-site fuels surfers with homemade breakfasts, elk burgers, and salmon wraps. Heading home? Savvy road-trippers grab a meal here before the long drive to Port Alberni. ⌧ *2201 Pacific Rim Hwy., Ucluelet* ✚ *just north of the Junction between Tofino and Ucluelet* ☎ *250/726–2992* ⊕ *www.wyapointsurfshop.com.*

WHALE-WATCHING

Jamie's Whaling Station. If you don't see a whale on your first trip with this well-regarded company, you can take another at no charge. You can book a range of adventures, including kayaking trips and hot-springs tours. The season runs mid-March through October. ⌧ *168 Fraser La., Ucluelet* ☎ *250/726–7444, 877/726–7444* ⊕ *www.jamies.com.*

Subtidal Adventures. This company specializes in whale-watching and nature tours to the Broken Group Islands. Choose between trips on an inflatable Zodiac or a 36-foot former coast-guard rescue boat. ⌧ *1950 Peninsula Rd., Ucluelet* ☎ *250/726–7336, 877/444–1134* ⊕ *www.subtidaladventures.com.*

9

PACIFIC RIM NATIONAL PARK RESERVE

105 km (63 miles) west of Port Alberni, 9 km (5 miles) south of Tofino.

This national park has some of Canada's most stunning coastal and rain-forest scenery, abundant wildlife, and a unique marine environment. It comprises three separate units—Long Beach, the Broken Group Islands, and the West Coast Trail—for a combined area of 123,431 acres, and stretches 130 km (81 miles) along Vancouver Island's West Coast.

More than 100 islands of the Broken Group Islands archipelago in Barkley Sound can be reached only by boat. The islands and their clear waters are alive with sea lions, seals, and whales, and because the inner waters are much calmer than the surrounding ocean, they provide an excellent environment for kayaking. Guided kayak and charter-boat tours are available from outfitters in Ucluelet, Bamfield, and Port Alberni. ⇨ *See Kayaking in Ucluelet for more information.* The most popular part of the park, and the only section that can be reached by car, is the Long Beach section. Besides the beach, the Long Beach section of the park is home to rich stands of old growth forest, a wealth of marine and terrestrial wildlife (including black bears, cougars, and sea lions), and a network of coastal and rain forest hiking paths.

EXPLORING

FAMILY **Kwisitis Visitor Centre & Feast House.** A good first stop in the park is this interpretive center and restaurant, perched on a point about a mile off the highway on Wickaninnish Beach. The park-run center offers insights into local flora and fauna, First Nations traditions, local history, and conservation efforts; don't miss the stunning life-size carving of a whaling canoe. Park rangers here can answer questions about further park exploration. A stroll on the long, sandy windswept beach just outside should work up an appetite for a seafood meal at the the Kwisitis Feast House on-site, where First Nations-inspired lunches and dinners (think Dungeness crab, oysters, mussels, and halibut) are served against a backdrop of crashing surf. The Feast House is open for extended hours in the summer, after the visitor center closes. ⊠ *485 Wick Rd., Ucluelet* ✚ *Off the Pacific Rim Highway, in the Pacific Rim National Park Reserve* ☎ *250/726–3524 Visitor Centre, 250/726–2628 Feast House* ⊕ *www.pc.gc.ca* ✉ *Visitor Centre admission included with park pass* ⊙ *May–mid-Oct., daily 10–4:30; call for winter hours.*

Long Beach. The most accessible—and visited—section of the park is the Long Beach Unit, the highlight of which is a 15-km (9-mile) stretch of pristine forest-backed sand just off Highway 4 between Ucluelet and Tofino. Four-hour 'beach walk' passes are available at Long Beach Parking Lot only. **Amenities:** parking (fee); toilets. **Best for:** surfing; walking. ⊠ *Hwy. 4* ✚ *18 km (11 miles) south of Tofino* ⊕ *www.pc.gc.ca/eng/ pn-np/bc/pacificrim/index.aspx* ✉ *C$4.90 per adult, or C$12.25 per group (four-hour beach pass only).*

Pacific Rim National Park Visitor Centre. A first stop for anyone visiting the Pacific Rim, this visitor center, which doubles as the Ucluelet Visitor Information Office, sits at the point where Highway 4 arrives at the coast. You can pick up maps and information, and pay park entrance fees here. ⊠ *2791 Pacific Rim Hwy., Ucluelet* ☎ *250/726–4600* ⊕ *www. pacificrimvisitor.ca* ✉ *Park admission C$7.80 per person per day or C$19.60 per vehicle* ⊙ *Daily 10–4:30.*

West Coast Trail. Running along the coast from Bamfield to Port Renfrew, this is an extremely rugged 75-km (47-mile) trail for experienced hikers only. It takes an average of six days to complete and is open from May 1 to September 30. A quota system helps the park manage the number of hikers, and reservations, through Parks Canada, are highly recommended between mid-June and mid-September. Hiking requires payment of a reservation fee, ferry fares, and an overnight use fee. ☎ *877/737–3783 trail reservations* ⊕ *parkscanada.gc.ca* ✉ *C$127.50 overnight use fee; C$32 ferry fees; C$24.50 reservation fee.*

WHISTLER

WELCOME TO WHISTLER

TOP REASONS TO GO

★ **Skiing Whistler and Blackcomb:** With more than 8,000 acres of skiing terrain, this is one of North America's premier mountain resorts.

★ **Getting to Whistler:** The incredibly scenic Sea-to-Sky Highway gets you from Vancouver to Whistler in about two hours (longer if you stop off in Squamish to try the awe-inspiring Sea-to-Sky Gondola that opened in 2014).

★ **The Peak2Peak Condola:** One of Whistler-Blackcomb's signature activities, the 11-minute trip that is the longest, highest, and most spectacular ride of its kind in the world.

★ **Zipping through Whistler's Wilds:** The adrenaline-infused zipline through stands of hemlock, across canyons, and over raging rivers lets you feel Whistler up-close-and-personal.

★ **Catching the Olympic spirit:** Surge down the bobsled course, ski with an Olympian, or climb into one of the rings for a digital moment.

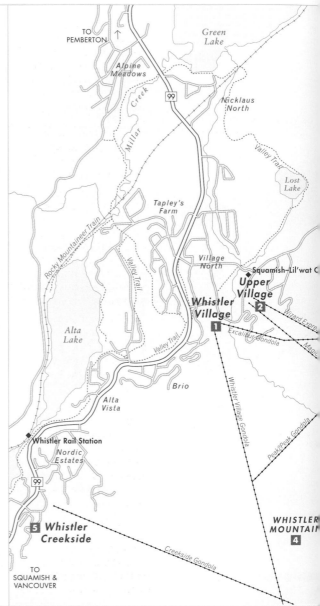

British Columbia

1 Whistler Village. The pedestrian-only, compact core of the resort offers a network of paths, trails, and covered walkways lined with shops, eateries, and people-watching opportunities. The bases of Whistler and Blackcomb mountains are at the Village edge, so you can even ski to the door of many hotels and condos.

2 Upper Village. The petit Upper Village—Blackcomb Mountain's base and home to the luxurious Four Seasons Resort—remains somewhat isolated from Whistler Village, but a wonderful footpath connects the two areas.

3 Blackcomb Mountain. At 5,280 feet in elevation, Blackcomb is the resort's snowboarding center, with its main base in the Upper Village.

4 Whistler Mountain. At 5,020 feet, the shorter of the resort's two mountains, Whistler has more skiable terrain and can accommodate 35,500 skiers per hour, with its main base in Whistler Village.

5 Whistler Creekside. Located 10 minutes south of Whistler Village on Highway 99, Creekside is the newest shopping and dining development at the resort.

GETTING ORIENTED

Whistler is a sophisticated alpine community lying within an easy—and stunningly beautiful—two-hour drive of Vancouver. It is the gateway to year-round, outdoor adventures for every age, ability, and pocketbook. In winter, there are snow activities galore alongside mountain-top fondues. In summer, it's all about mountain biking, picnics on a glacier, fishing, hiking, and rafting. Neighboring Squamish and Pemberton offer pastoral valleys, organic farms, and a gentler pace of life.

10

Lost Lake

0 |—————| 1/2 mi

0 |—————| 1/2 km

sh–Lil'wat Centre

Wizard Express Lift

Magic Lift

BLACKCOMB MOUNTAIN
3

Peak Gondola

WHISTLER MOUNTAIN
4

Updated By
Chris McBeath

With two breathtaking mountains—Whistler and Blackcomb—enviable skiing conditions, championship golf courses, more than 200 shops, 90 restaurants and bars, an array of accommodations, spas, hiking trails, and what experts consider the best mountain-bike park in the world, it's no surprise that Whistler consistently ranks as the top ski resort in North America.

Back in the early 1960s, when Whistler's early visionaries designed the ski resort as a car-free village, they had the 1968 Winter Olympics in mind. That dream was finally realized four decades later when the resort hosted the 2010 Winter Olympic Games. With that came the widening of Highway 99 and other Olympic-size benefits, such as the Squamish-Lil'Wat Centre, a cultural focal point for these proud First Nations who have occupied and explored this wilderness region for millennia.

Whistler Resort, which includes Whistler and Blackcomb mountains, has the largest ski area and two of the longest vertical drops on the continent, as well as one of the world's most advanced lift systems. But there's more to Whistler than skiing and snowboarding; each winter people flow into the resort with no intention of riding a chairlift, preferring to explore the many spas, shops, and restaurants, as well as the varied nightlife. During the rest of the year, they come to play four championship golf courses, race down the world's largest downhill bike park, and hike the hundreds of miles of trails. Then there's horseback riding along mountain ridges, zip-lining across Fitzsimmons Valley, or hopping aboard a helicopter ride to have lunch on one of dozens of nearby glaciers. Whistler is also now a member of The Mountain Collective, a ski- and perk-pass program that's good for half a dozen other top-notch resorts including Aspen and Jackson Hole.

The drive into the Coast Mountains from Vancouver is a stunning sampler of mainland British Columbia. You'll follow the Sea-to-Sky Highway (Highway 99) past fjordlike Howe Sound, through the historic mining community of Britannia Beach, past the logging town of

Squamish, and into Whistler Resort. Once you're in Whistler, you don't really need a car; anywhere you want to go within the resort is reachable by foot or a free shuttle bus. Parking lots ring the village, although as a hotel guest, you may have access to coveted (and often pricey) underground parking. Unless you're planning to tour the region, cars can be an expensive hindrance.

The bases of Whistler and Blackcomb mountains are just at the village edge, and many slope-side accommodations boast ski-to-the-door locations. If you can ski directly to your room, though, be sure not to miss the fun of the après-ski parade through the pedestrian-only village, a bold urban-design decision that has resulted in an incredibly accessible resort. Families take to the Village Stroll in search of Cows Ice Cream and its racks of novelty, bovine-themed T-shirts. Couples shop for engagement rings or the latest Roots sportswear styles. Skiers and snowboarders shuffle through the crowd, leaning their skis and boards against the buildings to dip into the vibrant après-ski scene on a dozen outdoor heated patios. The Village warren continues to expand, and Village North (or Marketplace) has all but been absorbed.

Against this backdrop, Whistler has also been building its identity as a progressive, livable, and sustainably green city, with programs for accessible housing and strong schools. Though only 8% of the 161 square km (100 square miles) that comprise Whistler is designated for development, North America's premier four-season resort continues to grow, especially now that the world has visited during the 2010 Winter Games.

PLANNING

WHEN TO GO

Whistler teems with partying Vancouverites, especially during the off-season. Three days provide plenty of time for zipping, skiing, biking, or whatever your alpine adventure may be, but you'll quickly discover that it's a very happening place almost every day, with open-air concerts throughout the summer and weekly shows in winter with the area's best skiers and riders jumping through blazing rings of fire.

10

FESTIVALS

JAN./FEB.: During **Winterpride Whistler** (⊕ *gaywhistler.com*), held every January or February, the resort heats up for a week with naughty nightlife, fine dining, fabulous après-ski, and slope-side fun.

APR.: The raucous **Telus World Ski & Snowboard Festival** (⊕ *www.whistler.com*) end-of-the-season bash fills 10 days with music, arts, fashion shows, and extreme sports.

JUNE: When the going gets tough, hundreds of die-hard warriors head for the two-day **Tough Mudder** (⊕ *www.whistler.com*), a gruelling military-style obstacle course that tests more than physical stamina.

JULY: More than 100 daredevil racers from all over the world hurtle down S-bends at breakneck speeds during **Whistler Longboard Festival** (⊕ *www.whistlerlongboard.com*).

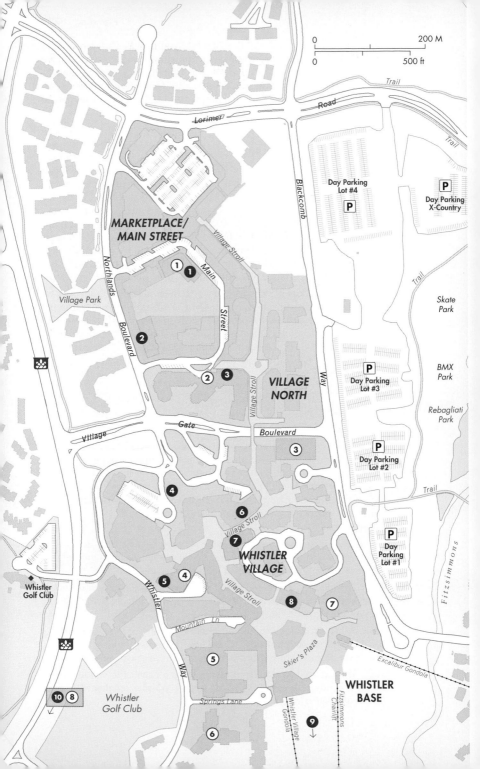

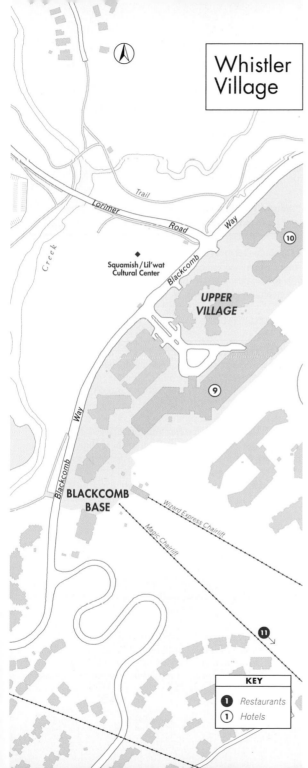

Whistler Village

AUG.: The annual **Kokanee Crankworx** (⊕ *www.crankworx.com*) mountain-bike festival showcases the sport's boldest and most talented athletes as they whip down double black-diamond runs; there are also daily concerts and a huge downhill biking scene.

SEPT.: The four-day, suds-filled **Whistler Village Beer Festival** (⊕ *wvbf.ca*) celebrates everything that makes the craft beer movement one of the world's fastest growing drinking phenomenons.

NOV.: There's a little bit of everything at **Cornucopia** (⊕ *www. whistlercornucopia.com*), an annual festival for foodies and oenophiles. The grand gala do is a veritable who's who in the Pacific Northwest wine industry.

DEC.: The annual **Whistler Film Festival** (⊕ *www.whistlerfilmfestival.com*) features world premieres from top directors, industry events, and parties, all with a Canadian focus.

GETTING HERE AND AROUND

Just 120 km (75 miles) north of Vancouver on Highway 99 (Sea-to-Sky Highway), Whistler is easy to get to from Vancouver, depending on your budget. You won't need a car once you're here; even if you choose to stay outside the village, you can get around easily with public shuttle buses or taxis. The closest airport is Vancouver International Airport, about 135 km (84 miles) away.

AIR TRAVEL

If you've got the money, you can travel in style from the airport to the slopes: Glacier Air has charter helicopter and airplane service between Whistler and Vancouver International Airport or Vancouver Harbour for anywhere from C$330 to C$3,000. Harbour Air connects Victoria and Whistler, from June through September, for C$295. Its affiliate, Whistler Air, runs two daily flights between Vancouver's Coal Harbour and the Whistler area from mid-May to early October; the company also partners with Rocky Mountaineer's Whistler Mountaineer service to offer fly-rail packages for around C$345. In the winter, Harbour Air manages many of the online bookings for Westcoast Air and Whistler Air. ⇨ *For more information on these companies, see Air Travel in Travel Smart.*

BUS TRAVEL TO WHISTLER

Perimeter Whistler Express has daily bus service to Whistler from Vancouver International Airport and from many Vancouver hotels (eight times a day in ski season, five times a day in summer). One-way fares from the airport start at C$85, and from downtown Vancouver fares start at C$40; reservations are recommended. Departing from various stops in Vancouver (check the website during the season for stop details), the Snow Bus is a winter-only luxury coach with snacks and movies. Whistler Direct Shuttle provides year-round service from the airport only. Finally, both Greyhound Canada and Pacific Coach lines offer service to Whistler from downtown Vancouver and from Vancouver Airport. (⇨ *For more information on these bus companies, see Bus Travel in Travel Smart.*)

Contacts Perimeter Whistler Express. ☎ *604/266–5386, 877/317–7788* ⊕ *www.perimeterbus.com.* **Snow Bus.** ☎ *877/451–1777* ⊕ *www.snowbus.com.* **Whistler Direct Shuttle.** ☎ *888/405–2410* ⊕ *www.whistlerdirectshuttle.com.*

BUS TRAVEL AROUND WHISTLER

The Whistler and Valley Express (WAVE) bus system operates a free, year-round public-transit system within Whistler village, as well as paid public transit throughout the Valley and north to Pemberton. It's operated by BC Transit. ⇨ *See Bus Travel in Travel Smart for more information.*

CAR TRAVEL

Driving from Vancouver to Whistler takes approximately two hours along the scenic Sea-to-Sky Highway (aka Highway 99). It's recommended to check weather conditions during the winter season; in spite of considerable improvements for the Olympics, rockslides still occur and can cause delays. ⇨ *For information on car rentals at the Vancouver airport or in Vancouver itself, see Car Travel in Travel Smart.*

LIMO TRAVEL

LimoJet Gold runs a stretch limo service from Vancouver International Airport to Whistler for C$320 per trip. Pearl International Limousine Service has limos, sedans, and 10-passenger vans—all equipped with blankets, pillows, bottled water, and videos so you can enjoy the ride. Rates start at about C$300. Vancouver All-Terrain Adventures charters four-wheel drives from Vancouver International or downtown Vancouver to Whistler. Vehicles travel in all weather and will stop for sightseeing. The cost starts at C$350 one way. ⇨ *For more information see Ground Transportation in Travel Smart.*

TAXI TRAVEL

For a cab in the Whistler area call Whistler Taxi. Service is available around the clock.

Contacts Whistler Taxi. ☎ *604/938–3333* ⊕ *www.whistlertaxi.com.*

TRAIN TRAVEL

The Whistler Mountaineer is a three-hour, premier train journey from North Vancouver to Whistler. It's an "experience" train trip, providing passengers with commentary and refreshments while taking in the Sea-to-Sky's jaw-dropping scenery. The service runs May to September; fares start at C$270 round-trip, including bus transfers from downtown to North Vancouver.

Contacts Whistler Mountaineer. ☎ *888/687–7245* ⊕ *www.rockymountaineer.com.*

HOTELS

Affordable Whistler is not an oxymoron. Prices may have soared here before the 2010 Vancouver Olympics, but every effort has been made to keep the mountains accessible to as many kinds of pocketbooks as possible. Sure, there are some up-in-the-stratosphere prices to be found, but the range of options among the condos, B&Bs, self-service suites, and hotel rooms means that Whistler is as accessible to families and active boomers as it is with the youthful crowd who take advantage of sharing suites with sofa beds, bunk beds, and dorm-style accommodations. The farther away from the Village, the cheaper the price. Nevertheless, ski-in

10

ski-out hotels and lodges command premium rates. Unless otherwise noted, hotels offer free Wi-Fi. If yours does not, Wi-Fi HotSpot passes are available at C$8 per day. Contacting Central Reservations is the most efficient way of securing the best accommodations to fit your budget.

Price categories are based on January–April ski-season rates; prices will be higher during Christmas and school breaks, but lower in summer and considerably lower in the shoulder seasons. Minimum stays during all holidays are pretty much the rule. Also, Whistler Village has some serious nightlife: if peace and quiet are important to you, ask for a room away from the main pedestrian thoroughfares, book in the Upper Village, or stay in one of the residential neighborhoods outside the village.

Hotel reviews have been shortened. For full information, visit Fodors.com.

RESTAURANTS

Whistler's restaurant scene is varied enough to please the palates of its nearly 10,000 residents and sophisticated enough to cater to the tastes of its thousands of international visitors. You can relax with a cappuccino in an unpretentious back-alley coffee shop; chill out (and people watch) on a patio with a dish of homemade fusilli, or splurge on award-winning cuisine with magnificent wine pairings. Although some restaurants do close during the shoulder seasons for a brief respite, no one goes hungry here, especially when you realize that many of Vancouver's celebrity chefs now call Whistler home. Today, some of the top ski-resort restaurants in the world take advantage of the growing locavore or "slow food" movement—as evidenced during four months of Sunday farmers' markets and organic bounty—to provide diners with a surprising array of Northwest cuisine. Foodies will especially enjoy Whistler's Cornucopia Festival, which showcases culinary talents and BC wineries every November. Then there's the relatively new Beer Festival, a sudsy celebration of craft brews from the Pacific Northwest (widely considered the birthplace of North America's craft beer movement) and beyond. And for grazers? Tasting tours will while away an afternoon or evening.

For those on lower dining budgets, there are plenty of sandwich and coffee shops scattered around the village. There is also a full-scale grocery store should you land a room with a kitchen.

WHAT IT COSTS IN CANADIAN DOLLARS			
$	$$	$$$	$$$$
Restaurants	under C$13	C$13–C$20	C$21–C$30	over C$30
Hotels	under C$126	C$126–C$195	C$196–C$300	over C$300

Prices in the restaurants reviews are the average cost of a main course or equivalent combination of small dishes at dinner or, if dinner is not served, at lunch. Prices in the hotel reviews are the lowest cost of a standard double room in high season, including taxes.

VISITOR INFORMATION

Contacts Tourism Whistler. ☎ *800/944-7853* ⊕ *www.whistler.com.*
Whistler Visitor Information and Activity Center. ☎ *604/932-0606* ⊕ *www.whistler.com.*

EXPLORING

Fodor's Choice ★ FAMILY

Peak 2 Peak Gondola. The longest and tallest gondola in the world delivers jaw-dropping views as it travels 2.7 miles from Whistler's Roundhouse to Blackcomb's Rendezvous Lodge, which sits at an elevation of 7,000 feet. Two gondolas have a glass-floor viewing area that are worth the extra few minutes wait; there's a separate line-up for these. A day-pass may seem costly until you realize that you can ride Peak-2Peak as many times as you wish. In summer, the ski runs and the rest of the mountain sides open up to incredible hiking. Discounts are offered for multiple days. ✉ *Roundhouse Lodge, Whistler Mountain* ☎ *800/766–0449* 🌐 *www.whistlerblackcomb.com* 🎟 *C$50* 🕒 *Daily 10–5 (but varies by season).*

Fodor's Choice ★ FAMILY

Squamish-Lil'wat Centre. A collaborative project of the neighboring Squamish Nation and Lil'wat Nation, this cultural center is designed to share and preserve the heritage and traditions of these two peoples. The concrete, cedar, and fir structure melds the longhouse concept of the coastal Squamish people with the traditional Lil'wat pit house. Inside, carvings adorn the walls and displays of art, artifacts, and tools reveal the similarities and differences of the cultures. Try to catch one of the regularly scheduled storytelling sessions. The on-site café, which serves contemporary food with a First Nations twist—think Lil'wat venison chili, a "mountain hoagie" with bison salami and wild-boar prosciutto, or a "Caesar" salad of romaine and Parmesan with bannock croutons—is worth a visit itself. ✉ *4584 Blackcomb Way* ☎ *866/441–7522* 🌐 *www.slcc.ca* 🎟 *C$18 (Mon. by donation)* 🕒 *Daily 9:30–5.*

WHERE TO EAT

WHISTLER VILLAGE

$$$$ CONTEMPORARY

🍴 **Araxi.** Terra-cotta tiles, well-chosen antiques, and original artwork create a vibrantly chic atmosphere for what has always been one of Whistler's top fine-dining restaurants. Local farmers grow produce exclusively for Araxi's chef, who also makes good use of regional cheeses, game, and fish. The food is fresh and innovative, best described as Pacific Northwest cuisine with a nod to Italy. Seafood is a specialty, so while you can certainly order a superbly prepared beef tenderloin, it's dishes like alder-smoked Arctic char or handmade pasta with wild prawns, scallops, and mussels that steal the show. The two-tier seafood tower is a must-try for seafoodies who love to graze and share. Wine aficionados take note: the wine list is 27 pages long. A heated patio is open in summer, and the lounge is a popular afternoon and après-ski spot, especially for its oyster bar. [$] *Average main: C$35* ✉ *4222 Village Sq.* ☎ *604/932–4540* 🌐 *www.araxi.com* 🕒 *No lunch Oct.–May* 👔 *Reservations essential.*

$$$$ FRENCH FUSION Fodor's Choice ★

🍴 **Bearfoot Bistro.** As one of Whistler's top destination restaurants, this elegant bistro never fails to impress. The French-inspired cuisine means that the menu choices, which change daily depending on the availabilty of local products, may include anything from a rack of wild caribou with sweet corn to pepper-crusted elk carpaccio to steamed

10

ON-MOUNTAIN EATING OPTIONS

Like the world's best ski resorts, Whistler has a great variety of on-mountain eating options. You'll find them all listed on the trail/resort map, but these are the key ones to know about.

Both Whistler and Blackcomb have a day lodge, accessible from the gondola, with a cafeteria that serves an array of soup, sandwiches, and hot food options. At the other end of the spectrum, there is fine dining at Christine's in Blackcomb's Rendezvous day lodge and at Steep's in Whistler's Roundhouse. Should you be moving about on one plank or two, don't miss Whistler's Harmony Hut and Blackcomb's Horstman Hut for chili and other comfort foods to go with spectacular views. Crystal Hut is where to find terrific Belgian waffles and fondues. In-the-know skiers head to the Glacier Creek Lodge for a shorter lunch line.

Dungeness crab with garlic herbed butter. If everything looks too delicious to decide, the chef will customize a tasting menu according to your preferences, or you can simply go for the all-inclusive, three-course table d'hôte menu. Allow the sommelier to do the wine pairings for a really masterful meal. [$] *Average main: C$33* ✉ *4121 Village Green* ☎ *604/932–3433* 🌐 *www.bearfootbistro.com* 🕒 *No lunch.*

$$ CANADIAN 🍴 **Elements.** Locals consistently rank Elements, which is found in Summit Lodge, as having the best tapas in the area. It's a hip eatery where everyone from animated thirtysomethings to jet-setting families with young children occupy the comfy suede banquettes and booths. The draw here is the open-concept kitchen that produces locally inspired small plates that are perfect for sharing. Steamed Salt Spring Island mussels with lemongrass, kaffir lime, and coconut green curry are yummy, as are the spicy chicken drumsticks, venison mini-burgers with Gruyère, and the signature bruschetta. Pair your small plates with fine Canadian wines. The restaurant is open for breakfast, too, when several variations of eggs Benedict are the stars. [$] *Average main: C$15* ✉ *Summit Lodge, 4359 Main St.* ☎ *604/932–5569* 🌐 *www.elementswhistler.com.*

$ BAKERY 🍴 **Hot Buns Bakery.** You may think this sweet spot has been transported from a rural French town, with its stone floors, vintage skis hanging from the ceiling, and simple wooden tables and chairs. But the reason to come here is not the look of the place: It serves the best *pain au chocolat,* lattes, and crepes in town. And the cinnamon buns? Delicious. Choose a savory Tex-Mex crepe for a quick lunch or a decadent pear-and-chocolate crepe to satisfy your après-ski sweet tooth. It's not a bad way to start—or end—the day. The address is a bit misleading, because the main entrance is actually on Sunrise Alley, behind La Brasserie des Artistes. [$] *Average main: C$8* ✉ *4232 Village Stroll* ☎ *604/932–6883* 🌐 *www.hotbuns.moonfruit.com* 🕒 *No dinner.*

$$$$ STEAKHOUSE 🍴 **Hy's Steakhouse.** If beef's your passion, then you don't get much better than Hy's, a hardcore steakhouse that's famous for the quality of its sirloins, filet mignons, porterhouses, and T-bones. Roasted prime rib comes with Yorkshire pudding, and the combos are accompanied by king crab or lobster. This is he-man food, although the menu will appeal

to everyone, even vegetarians. The place is dark, moody, and just right for a candlelit dinner, a secret rendezvous, or a more formal affair. Service is impeccable and discreet. [$] *Average main: C$50* ✉ *Delta Whistler Village Suites, 4308 Main St.* ☎ *604/905–5555* 🌐 *www.hyssteakhouse.com* 🕓 *No lunch.*

$$ EUROPEAN 🍴 **La Brasserie des Artistes.** "The Brass," as it's known, has one of the area's best patios, situated in the square where people-watching is as entertaining as the street performers and free concerts. With this kind of location the food doesn't have to be outstanding, but you can nevertheless get reasonably priced bistro fare, from burgers to steaks. It opens for breakfast with an assortment of egg dishes and keeps going until the après-ski crowd finally departs around midnight. As popular as this place is, tables turn over quickly so getting a seat doesn't take long. [$] *Average main: C$20* ✉ *4232 Village Stroll* ☎ *604/932–3569* 🌐 *www.labrass.moonfruit.com.*

$$$$ ITALIAN 🍴 **Quattro at Whistler.** Vancouverites in search of fine Italian fare flock to the Pinnacle Hotel for warming après-ski meals. The dining room exudes a whimsical Venetian style with ornamental ironwork, picturesque tiles, and hand-painted chandeliers. For a splurge try *L'Abbuffata,* a five-course Roman feast that comes on family-size platters meant for sharing. Other popular dishes include spaghetti *pescatore* (with prawns, scallops, and clams), pistachio-crusted sea bass, pressed Cornish game hen, and a plate of five pastas for two to share for a reasonable fixed price. The cellar is filled with 900 wine varieties and an impressive grappa selection. [$] *Average main: C$33* ✉ *Pinnacle Hotel, 4319 Main St.* ☎ *604/905–4844* 🌐 *www.quattrorestaurants.com* 🕓 *No lunch.*

$$ JAPANESE 🍴 **Sushi Village.** If you don't equate sushi with social buzz, then you haven't been to this perennial Whistler hot spot, which offers everything from après-ski to late-night dining. The chef's choice sashimi is a favorite, as are the dozen different house special rolls, including one tasty combination of shrimp tempura, avocado, scallops, and salmon. There are also teriyaki dinners and hot pots served family-style as well as a gluten-free menu. A score of sakes (and sake margaritas) accentuate the festive environment. Phoning ahead for take-out orders lets you jump the line. [$] *Average main: C$20* ✉ *4272 Mountain Sq.* ☎ *604/932–3330* 🌐 *www.sushivillage.com* 🕓 *No lunch Mon.–Thurs.*

WHISTLER MOUNTAIN

$$$ PACIFIC NORTHWEST 🍴 **Steeps Grill & Wine Bar.** Although it's atop Whistler Mountain, you're likely to see as many non-skiers as skiers in the crowd dining here. That's because Steeps Grill & Wine Bar is located inside the enormous Roundhouse Lodge at the top of Whistler Village Gondola, and lots of the visitors are simply sightseers. While other mountain dining outlets tend to cater to the grab-and-go crowd, this venue is a stay-a-while, full-service dining affair offering lots of West Coast favorites like smoked salmon chowder and Dungeness crabcakes. [$] *Average main: C$22* ✉ *Roundhouse Lodge, Whistler Mountain* ☎ *604/905–2379* 🌐 *www.whistlerblackcomb.com* 💳 *No credit cards* 🕓 *No dinner spring and fall (actual dates vary).*

BLACKCOMB MOUNTAIN

$$ ✕ **Christine's on Blackcomb Mountain.** On-mountain dining is surprisingly
CANADIAN accessible to those without skis. On Blackcomb Mountain, there's
Christine's, offering classic dishes such as roasted red pepper bisque, a
Mediterranean tagine, or a showy salad with roasted asparagus with
savory almonds. The place is also a hot spot for weekend brunch.
Once only accessible to skiers, now you can get here via the gondola
from Whistler. Because of this, most patrons tend to be decked out in
full snow gear. Christine's is open in summer. $ *Average main: C$20*
✉ *Rendezvous Lodge, Blackcomb Mountain* ☎ *604/938-7437* ⊕ *www.
whistlerblackcomb.com* ⊗ *Winter ski season and summer adventure
season* ⊗ *No dinner spring and fall (actual dates vary).*

WHISTLER CREEKSIDE

$$$$ ✕ **Rim Rock Café.** About 3 km (2 miles) south of the village, this restau-
SEAFOOD rant is a perennial favorite as much for its cozy, unpretentious dining
room as for its great seafood. If deciding on only one item is hard, why
not go for one of the samplers: the Rim Rock Trio combines sea bass
in an almond-ginger crust, grilled prawns, and rare ahi tuna marinated
in soy sauce, sake, and mirin. Although seafood takes precedence on
the menu—try the raw oysters with champagne—Alberta beef and local
game will satisfy carnivores. If you want a booth or a coveted table near
the fireplace, dine on the early side or make a reservation. Otherwise, be
prepared to wait. $ *Average main: C$42* ✉ *2117 Whistler Rd., Whistler
Creekside* ☎ *604/932-5565, 877/932-5589* ⊕ *www.rimrockwhistler.
com* ⊗ *No lunch.*

WHERE TO STAY

Whistler Central Reservations. Tourism Whistler is a good source for infor-
mation on lodging and often features online discounts at selected hotels.
☎ *800/944-7853* ⊕ *www.whistler.com.*

WHISTLER VILLAGE

$$$ ⌂ **Adara Hotel.** Whistler's only true boutique hotel is the Adara, sister to
HOTEL Vancouver's Opus Hotel and equally as hip. **Pros:** free boxed breakfast
in winter; hip environment; pet friendly. **Cons:** no on-site restaurant; no
bathtubs, just showers. $ *Rooms from: C$260* ✉ *4122 Village Green*
☎ *866/502-3272, 604/905-4009* ⊕ *www.adarahotel.com* ⇗ *20 rooms,
21 suites* ⊗ *No meals.*

$$$ ⌂ **Delta Whistler Village Suites.** Not only is the Southwestern-style decor
HOTEL warm and inviting, the apartment-size studio and one- and two-bed-
FAMILY room suites are great choices for families and were renovated in 2014.
Pros: central location; nice mountain views; free ski and bike storage.
Cons: rooms are small; some street noise; high parking fee. $ *Rooms
from: C$295* ✉ *4308 Main St.* ☎ *604/905-3987, 888/299-3987*
⊕ *www.deltahotels.com* ⇗ *225 suites* ⊗ *No meals.*

$$$$
HOTEL
Fodor's Choice
★
FAMILY

🛏 **Fairmont Château Whistler Resort.** Just steps from the Blackcomb ski lifts, this imposing-looking fortress is a self-contained, ski-in, ski-out resort-within-a-resort with its own shopping arcade, golf course, and impressive spa. **Pros:** ski-in and ski-out option; a terrific spa; shopping and golf on-site. **Cons:** bustling with guests and kids; not particularly intimate; regular guests must pay for Wi-Fi. $ *Rooms from: C$475* ✉ *4599 Château Blvd.* ☎ *604/938–8000, 800/257–7544* ⊕ *www.fairmont.com* ↘ *550 rooms, 56 suites* ⭐ *No meals.*

$$$
RESORT
FAMILY

🛏 **Hilton Whistler Resort.** With a wealth of family-friendly facilities, this resort hotel sits at the base of the Whistler and Blackcomb gondolas. **Pros:** steps from the chairlift; huge rooms; pet friendly. **Cons:** small spa; some unremarkable street views. $ *Rooms from: C$300* ✉ *4050 Whistler Way* ☎ *604/932–1982, 800/515-4050* ⊕ *www.hiltonwhistler.com* ↘ *287 rooms, 24 suites* ⭐ *No meals.*

$$$$
HOTEL

🛏 **Nita Lake Lodge.** Within easy reach of the lifts and amenities of Whistler Creekside, this lovely lodge is Whistler's only lakefront hotel, so it feels a world away from the madding crowd. **Pros:** unique lake location; laid-back lounge; next door to the train station. **Cons:** shuttle required to access slopes; away from the Village action. $ *Rooms from: C$375* ✉ *2131 Lake Placid Rd.* ☎ *604/966–5700, 888/755–6482* ⊕ *www.nitalakelodge.com* ↘ *37 studios, 38 suites, 2 villas* ⭐ *Breakfast.*

$$$$
HOTEL

🛏 **Pan Pacific Whistler Mountainside.** With the very lively Dubh Linn Gate Old Irish Pub on the premises, this hotel tends to attract the younger set, most of whom seem to spend their time on the large deck cheering on skiers as they reach the bottom of the slope. **Pros:** about as close to the ski lift as you can get; on-site pub at your door. **Cons:** gets booked up quickly; common areas can get noisy. $ *Rooms from: C$350* ✉ *4320 Sundial Crescent* ☎ *604/905–2999, 888/905–9995* ⊕ *www.panpacific.com* ▭ *No credit cards* ↘ *120 suites* ⭐ *No meals.*

$$$$
HOTEL

🛏 **Pan Pacific Whistler Village Centre.** Although it bills itself as an all-suites boutique hotel, the Pan Pacific feels more like a beautiful apartment building with a fabulous concierge service. **Pros:** extraordinarily friendly staff; free breakfast buffet; central location. **Cons:** loud ground-floor rooms; limited services. $ *Rooms from: C$350* ✉ *4299 Blackcomb Way* ☎ *604/966–5500, 888/966–5575* ⊕ *www.panpacific.com* ↘ *82 rooms* ⭐ *Breakfast.*

$$$
HOTEL

🛏 **Summit Lodge & Spa.** Tucked away in a quiet part of the village, this friendly boutique hotel offers gracious service and one of the area's best values in luxury accommodations. **Pros:** quiet rooms; quality spa; free shuttle to the Village Gondola. **Cons:** small parking spots; lots of pets (and their dander), so it's not recommended for those with allergies. $ *Rooms from: C$285* ✉ *4359 Main St.* ☎ *604/932–2778, 888/913–8811* ⊕ *www.summitlodge.com* ↘ *75 rooms, 6 suites* ⭐ *Breakfast.*

$$$$
HOTEL

🛏 **The Westin Resort & Spa.** This luxury hotel has not only a prime location on the edge of the village but also a long list of upscale amenities that will make you want to stay here. **Pros:** boot-warming services; quiet yet central location; excellent spa. **Cons:** expensive extras, especially the parking; you must pay for Wi-Fi. $ *Rooms from: C$450* ✉ *4090 Whistler Way* ☎ *604/905–5000, 888/634–5577* ⊕ *www.westinwhistler.com* ↘ *419 suites* ⭐ *No meals.*

10

UPPER VILLAGE

$$$$ HOTEL Fodor's Choice ★ FAMILY

Four Seasons Resort Whistler. This plush nine-story hotel gives alpine chic a new twist with warm earth tones and wood interiors, big leather chairs beside the fireplace in the lobby, and amazingly spacious rooms. **Pros:** top-notch spa; great fitness classes; free village shuttles. **Cons:** a long walk to restaurants and nightlife; expensive parking; free Wi-Fi is frustratingly slow (a paid upgrade is available). [$] *Rooms from: C$450* ✉ *4591 Blackcomb Way, Upper Village* ☎ *604/935–3455, 888/935–2460* 🌐 *www.fourseasons.com/whistler* 🛏 *273 studios and suites, 3 town homes* 🍴 *No meals.*

SPORTS AND THE OUTDOORS

Adventurers pour into Whistler during every season and from every corner of the world. In winter, you'll meet Australian and New Zealander skiers and guides who follow the snows around the globe; in summer there are sun-baked guides who chase the warm months to lead white-water rafting or mountain-biking excursions. These globe-trotters demonstrate how Whistler's outdoor sports culture now operates on a global, all-season scale.

The staging of sliding (bobsled, luge, skeleton) and alpine and cross-country skiing events in Whistler during the Olympic Games has yielded a host of opportunities for the adventurous, including a world-class cross-country center (and lodge) operated by the Whistler Legacies Society. The sliding center remains a professional training facility (the ice is rumored to be the fastest on the planet), as well as a public venue for those who've always wanted to experience the 100-km-per-hour (62-mile) thrill of a sliding sport. The mountains changed little after the games, other than having some commemorative signage to indicate what happened where.

Hikers and anglers, downhill and touring cyclists, free skiers and ice climbers, kayakers and golfers—there really is something for everyone here. Whistler and Blackcomb mountains are the reasons why most people are here, but the immediate environs are equally compelling. Garibaldi Provincial Park, adjacent to the Whistler area, is a 78,000-acre park with dense mountainous forests splashed with hospitable lakes and streams for fishing and kayaking. At Alta Lake, you'll see clusters of windsurfers weaving across the surface, dodging canoeists. At nearby Squamish, the Stawamus Chief, the second largest granite monolith in the world behind Gibraltar, attracts serious rock climbers, although there are milder climbs for novices.

Whether online or in person, **Tourism Whistler** has information on all aspects of the resort. It also runs an online reservation center for accommodations, guides, and virtually anything else you might need.

Whistler Visitor Information and Activity Center. A good first stop for most Whistler outdoor activities, here's where to pick up hiking, biking, and cross-country maps or find out about equipment rentals. They'll help organize your stay and even book activities. ✉ *4010 Whistler Way* ☎ *800/944–7853* 🌐 *www.whistler.com.*

CLOSE UP

Mountain Biking

Ski resorts everywhere have latched onto the popularity of downhill biking. Whistler and Blackcomb were not only among the first to realize the potential of converting ski runs to fat-tire trails, they also established the best downhill-biking center in the world. Located on lower Whistler Mountain, the trails—more than 200 km (124 miles) of them—are marked green through double diamond and groomed with as much care as their winter counterparts.

Riding custom bikes designed specifically for the Whistler terrain, cyclists bomb down the single-track trails, staying high on the steeply banked turns and taking air on the many tables and jumps. Expert riders might add 30-foot rock drops, leaps over streambeds, and 100-foot platform bridges to their brake-free sprints through the forest. Beginners can find plenty of comfortable dirt lanes to follow, though, and you can keep your fingers ready at the hydraulic brake should the speed become uncomfortable. After their first taste of the sport, most novice riders can't wait to sit back on the specially designed chairlift, transition onto the blue terrain, invite a few bumps, and maybe grab some air before the day is through. Downhill biking provides pure, if muddy, adrenaline-fueled bliss.

Whistler Mountain Bike Park, with experienced instructors, is a great place to learn how to downhill bike.

BIKING AND HIKING

The 28-km (45-mile) paved, car-free Valley Trail links the village to lakeside beaches and scenic picnic areas. For more challenging routes, ski lifts whisk hikers and bikers up to the alpine, where marked trails are graded by difficulty. The Peak Chair operates in summer to take hikers to the top of 7,160-foot-high Whistler. Among the most popular routes in the high alpine-trail network is the High Note Trail, an intermediate, 8-km (5-mile) route with an elevation change of 1,132 feet and fabulous coastal mountain views. Trails are clearly marked—you take the lift up and choose whichever way you want to come down, just as if you were skiing. The casual stroller can also experience the top of the mountain on the Peak2Peak Gondola, the largest free-span gondola expanse in the world: it crosses Fitzsimmons Valley, connecting Whistler and Blackcomb mountains in just 11 minutes. Free trail maps are available from Tourism Whistler and the Whistler Activity Center.

Fanatyk Co. Ski and Cycle. This outfit rents bikes, arranges for repairs, and books bike tours. The staff is passionate and knowledgeable about pedals and wheels. ⊠ *6–4433 Sundial Pl.* ☎ *604/938–9455* ⊕ *www. fanatykco.com.*

G1 Rentals. G1, the nickname for Garbanzo Bike & Bean, is where biking enthusiasts, novice or expert, can get geared up rentals. Inside the gondola building and next to the access point for Whistler Mountain Bike Park, here's where to find out about lessons, equipment, safety gear, and park passes. ⊠ *Whistler Gondola Base* ☎ *604/905–2252* ⊕ *bike.whistlerblackcomb.com.*

10

Whistler is well known as a ski destination, but many of the trails are also accessible in summer for mountain biking.

Whistler Alpine Guides. This year-round outfitter offers everything from avalanche safety courses in winter to mountaineering in summer. Among its signature activities is a hike named Via Ferrata, Italian for "Iron Way," so named because it's straight up a vertical pathway using fixed cables and metal-rung ladders. Surprisingly, no experience is necessary. Even older children can tackle it. Besides, it's great for bragging rights. Ice climbing, glacier walks, and backcountry overnights add to the roster of activities. ✉ *4314 Main St.* ☎ *604/938–9242* ⊕ *www. whistlerguides.com.*

Fodor's Choice ★ **Whistler Mountain Bike Park.** There's something for riders of every skill level at the Whistler Mountain Bike Park, from gentle rides that satisfy novices to steep rock faces that will challenge the experts. High-season rates range from C$55 for a day to C$159 for a three-day pass. The park is open from mid-May to early October, and rentals are available. The park is accessed from the Whistler Village Gondola or Fitzsimmons Express. ✉ *Whistler Mountain* ☎ *604/967–8950* ⊕ *www.bike. whistlerblackcomb.com.*

BOATING

Canoe and kayak rentals are available at Alta Lake at both Lakeside Park and Wayside Park. A perfect place for canoeing is the River of Golden Dreams, which connects Alta Lake with Green Lake, both within a couple of miles of the village.

Canadian Outback Adventure Company. Contact this adventure specialist for guided river-rafting trips in the Whistler area. It has easygoing trips for families and those not wanting to tackle rollicking rapids. The company offers free pickups at all Whistler area resorts. ☎ *604/921–7250, 800/565–8735* ⊕ *www.canadianoutback.com.*

Wedge Rafting. Specializing in whitewater rafting adventures, this company offers two-hour to full-day tours on the Green, Birkenhead, or Elaho-Squamish river. Tours depart from the village and include all equipment and experienced guides. Adventures are suitable for all levels. ⊠ *218-4293 Mountain Sq.* ☎ *604/932 7171, 888/932–5899* ⊕ *www.wedgerafting.com.*

> ## SUMMER SKIING
>
> Whistler is a summer hiking and outdoors destination, but dedicated skiers can still get their fix up on Horstman Glacier. Glacier skiing is recommended only for intermediate to advanced skiers. One of the fun perks is the stares you'll get in the village as you walk around in your downhill gear in the summer temps.

Whistler Jet Boating. Owner-operator Eric Pehota runs three daily excursions from May to September, cutting his jet boat through swirling channels and rushing rapids right up to the base of Nairn Falls. Like many Whistler guides, he operates via cell phone and through the activity center. Meeting points vary depending on water levels and weather. Trips are C$109. ⊠ *Whistler Activity Center, 4010 Whistler Way* ☎ *604/905–9455, 604/894–5845* ⊕ *www.whistlerjetboating.com.*

CROSS-COUNTRY SKIING

The meandering trail around the Whistler Golf Course from the village is an ideal beginners' route. The 28 km (17 miles) of track-set trails that wind around scenic Lost Lake, Chateau Whistler Golf Course, the Nicklaus North Golf Course, and Green Lake include routes suitable for all levels; 4 km (2½ miles) of trails around Lost Lake are lighted for night skiing from 4 to 10 each evening. Trail maps and rental equipment are available in sports shops throughout the village.

Whistler X-Country Ski & Hike. Operating out of the Whistler Nordic Center at Whistler Olympic Park—the same place you can hitch a ride on a bobsleigh—Whistler Cross Country Ski & Hike and Coast Mountain Guides team up to give lessons or guided cross-country ski tours that are ideal for beginners and advanced skiers. The countryside is considered one of the largest Nordic recreational areas in North America. They have two Nordic-gear retail outlets: here and in Squamish. You can also connect with these folks via the Whistler Activity Centre. ⊠ *Whistler Nordic Center at Olympic Park, 5 Callaghan Valley Rd.* ☎ *604/964–2454, 604/567–2232.*

10

One of the reasons Whistler is so popular is because it's great for avid skiiers, and beginners, too!

DOWNHILL SKIING AND SNOWBOARDING

When Whistler and Blackcomb Ski Resorts merged in 1997, they created a snow behemoth not seen in these parts since the last sighting of a Sasquatch. Whistler had already garnered top-notch status, but the addition of Blackcomb left the competition buried in the powder. The numbers are staggering: 410 inches of annual snowfall, over 8,000 skiable acres, 200 named runs, 12 alpine bowls, three glaciers, and the world's most advanced lift system. Point yourself downward on Blackcomb, and you can ski or snowboard for a mile from top to bottom. And there are lots of ways to get to the top, either via the Whistler Village, Creekside, or Blackcomb Excalibur gondola or by taking one of several chairs from the base up the mountain. According to the locals, many of whom are world-class competitors, picking the day's mountain depends on conditions, time of day, and time of year. While most residents swear by Whistler's bowls and steeps, some prefer the long glade runs and top terrain park of Blackcomb. You can do both in the same day, thanks to the Peak2Peak Gondola, which whisks riders along the 2.7-mile journey in just 11 minutes.

Ultimate Ski Adventures. Whether your goal is to gain confidence and control on the runs or to tackle the best terrain the mountain has to offer, these folks will show you how with one-on-one instruction or in small groups. ✉ *7273 Fitzsimmons Rd. S* ☏ *604/263–2390* ⊕ *www.ultimateski.com.*

Whistler Alpine Guides Bureau. These expert mountain guides offer group tours, instructional clinics, and customized one-on-one trips to get you shredding untouched backcountry powder. ✉ *4314 Main St.* ☏ *604/938–9242* ⊕ *www.whistlerguides.com.*

Whistler/Blackcomb Hi Performance Rentals. Equipment rentals, including some of the best brands on the market, are geared toward intermediate and advanced skiers. The company (G1 Rentals) has several outlets in the village, but the main office is at the Whistler gondola base. ⊠ *Whistler Gonodola Base, 3434 Blackcomb Way* ☎ *604/905–2252* ⊕ *www.whistlerblackcomb.com.*

Fodor's Choice ★ **Whistler/Blackcomb Ski and Snowboard School.** The school offers lessons for skiers and snowboarders of all levels. You can even choose to ski with an Olympian. Whistler Kids remains one of the best children's ski schools anywhere. ⊠ *4545 Blackcomb Way* ☎ *604/967–8950, 800/766–0449* ⊕ *www.whistlerblackcomb.com.*

FISHING

Tourists first developed this region for the fishing. All five area lakes—Alta, Alpha, Lost, Green, Nita—are stocked with trout.

Whistler Fishing Guides. Local guides offer fishing excursions throughout the region, including heli-fishing for the more adventurous angler. They look after all transportation, gear, and even lunch on full-day trips. ☎ *604/932–4267* ⊕ *www.whistlerfishingguides.ca.*

Whistler Fly Fishing. These fly-fishing specialists target five species of Pacific salmon, steelhead, trout, and char on dozens of rivers lakes in the area. They take care of all the details including equipment, licenses, and transportation to and from your Whistler accommodation. ☎ *888/822–3474* ⊕ *www.whistlerflyfishing.com.*

10

GOLF

Few visitors associate Whistler with golf, but the four championship courses vie with some of the best in the Pacific Northwest. Golf season in Whistler runs from May through October; greens fees range from C$99 for twilight specials to C$235 for prime-time slots.

Golf Whistler. You can arrange advance tee-time bookings through Golf Whistler, an online service that also features last-minute specials and accommodation packages. ☎ *866/723–2747* ⊕ *www.golfwhistler.com.*

GOLF CLUBS AND COURSES

Fodor's Choice ★ **Big Sky Golf and Country Club.** Facing some impressive glaciers, this links-style course follows the Green River. Located 30 minutes north of Whistler, Big Sky sits at the base of 8,000-foot Mt. Curie. It's a favorite with locals, and for good reason. Check out the imaginative metal sculptures along the way. ⊠ *1690 Airport Rd.* ☏ *604/894–6106, 800/668–7900* ⊕ *www.bigskygolf.com* ✉ *C$155* ⚑ *18 holes. 7,001 yds. Par 72.*

Chateau Whistler Golf Club. Carved from the side of Blackcomb Mountain, this challenging and breathtaking course was designed by prominent golf-course architect Robert Trent Jones Jr. Make sure to carry plenty of balls, though you can reload at the turn. ⊠ *4612 Blackcomb Way* ☏ *604/938–2092, 877/938–2092* ⊕ *www.fairmontgolf.com* ✉ *C$155* ⚑ *18 holes. 6,635 yds. Par 72.*

Nicklaus North Golf Course. Jack Nicklaus designed this challenging 18-hole track, which finishes beside lovely Green Lake. It's one of the few courses in the world that bears the famous golfer's name. ⊠ *8080 Nicklaus North Blvd.* ☏ *604/938–9898, 800/386–9898* ⊕ *www. nicklausnorth.com* ✉ *C$155* ⚑ *18 holes. 6,961 yds. Par 71.*

Whistler Golf Club. Often overlooked, this Arnold Palmer–designed course is frequently ranked among the best in the country. It's surprisingly challenging, especially around Bear Island, and it has some spectacular practice facilities. Five after 5 specials run as little as C$19. ⊠ *4001 Whistler Way* ☏ *604/932–3280, 800/376–1777* ⊕ *www.whistlergolf. com* ✉ *C$139* ⚑ *18 holes. 6,722 yds. Par 72.*

HELI-SKIING AND HELI-HIKING

The Coast Mountains of western Canada have more glaciers than almost anywhere else on the planet. The range is bordered by the Fraser River in the south and the Kelsall River in the north. Helicopter adventures consist of skiing, glacier hikes, and picnics.

Blackcomb Aviation. Sightseeing tours over Whistler's stunning mountains and glaciers are offered year-round: there are heli-hiking, -biking, -fishing, -picnics, -golfing, and even heli-weddings in summer. The company also operates tours out of Vancouver. ⊠ *9960 Heliport Rd.* ☏ *604/938–1700, 800/330–4354* ⊕ *www.blackcombaviation.com.*

Coast Range Heli-Skiing. This heli-skiing operator offers a shuttle service from Whistler to their base in Pemberton for unique backcountry powder experiences. A seasonal desk operates out of Whistler Village. ⊠ *Mountain Sq.* ☏ *604/218–4293 Whistler seasonal service desk, 800/701–8744* ⊕ *www.coastrangeheliskiing.com.*

Fodor'sChoice
★
Whistler Heli-Skiing. Intended for intermediate to expert skiers and snowboarders, Whistler Heli-Skiing offers guided day trips with three or more glacier runs. Prices start at C$899 per person. Heli-hiking is available all year long, and guided tours can be tailored to your group's abilities. You can also enjoy a specially prepared picnic lunch in an old-growth forest, pastoral meadow, or on a 12,000-year-old glacier. ⊠ *4545 Blackcomb Way* ☏ *604/932–4105, 888/435–4754* ⊕ *www. whistlerheliskiing.com.*

HORSEBACK RIDING

The ultimate gentle summer activity, horseback riding in Whistler can take you through alpine meadows, old-growth forests, and along riverside beaches.

Adventure Ranch. Perched alongside the Lillooet River, this 10-acre ranch north of Whistler has vast tracts of wilderness in every direction. It offers two-hour rides (C$79), as well as longer excursions. The facilities include a swimming pool, volleyball court, and snack bar with a pleasant patio. The ranch is open from mid-May to mid-September. ⊠ *1641 Airport Rd.* 🕾 *604/894–5200* ⊕ *www.adventureranch.net.*

SNOWMOBILING, SNOWSHOEING, AND SLEIGH RIDES

Blackcomb Snowmobile. You can book guided snowmobile trips through the backcountry, learn to mush a dog sled, or follow a First Nations trapper's trail on snowshoes. Trips start at C$189 for two hours; snowshoeing comes in at C$89 for two hours. ⊠ *Hilton Whistler Resort, 4050 Whistler Way* 🕾 *604/932–8484* ⊕ *www.blackcombsnowmobile.com.*

Fodor's Choice
★
Canadian Wilderness Adventures. Snowmobiles, dog sleds, and snowshoes are just some of the transportation choices here. After a day in the snow you can reward yourself with a candlelit fondue dinner in a beautiful log cabin. Seasoned outdoorspeople can take an avalanche skills training course. In summer, transport changes to ATVs and canoes. ⊠ *Carleton Lodge, 4290 Mountain Sq.* 🕾 *604/938–1616* ⊕ *www.canadianwilderness.com.*

TUBING

FAMILY **Coca-Cola Tube Park.** Located on Blackcomb Mountain, this fabulous tube park is all about family fun. The park has 1,000 feet of lanes rated green, blue, and black diamond, a magic carpet to get to the top, a fire pit, a play area, and a snack station. There are even minitubes for the little ones. Catch the Fire & Ice Show on Sundays from mid-December through March. ⊠ *Blackcomb Excalibur Gondola, 4010 Whistler Way, Blackcomb Mountain* 🕾 *604/935–3357* ⊕ *www.whistlerblackcomb.com.*

10

ZIP-LINING AND CANOPY TOURS

Fodor's Choice
★
Ziptrek Ecotours. In a rain forest between Whistler and Blackcomb mountains, Ziptrek offers tours ranging from Tree Trek walks along suspension bridges through the forest to 10-line, five-hour adrenaline-filled zipline extravaganzas, including a combo package with the Peak 2 Peak Gondola. None of them requires any experience, although if you're afraid of heights you should know that the full course includes a heady zip over a canyon far, far below you. (The company claims to have the "longest, highest, and fastest zip lines in North America.") With runs ranging from 200 to 2,400 feet in length, this is a heart-thumping experience worth splurging on for the whole family. ⊠ *4282 Mountain Sq.* 🕾 *604/935–0001, 866/935–0001* ⊕ *www.ziptrek.com.*

NIGHTLIFE

Whistler has a legendary après-ski scene, and on any given weekend, there may be more nonskiers than skiers filling the local patios, clubs, and saloons. Stag and stagette parties wander the pedestrian-only village stroll, and people line up early to get inside Buffalo Bills or the Garibaldi Lift Company, where DJs and bands from Vancouver and beyond come to spin.

The night begins with après, when skiers, bikers, and hikers alike unwind on patios such as the one at the Longhorn Saloon & Grill— think happy hour for the hyped up—and the clubs usually stay open until 2 am except for Sundays and holidays. The minimum age is 19 and smoking is only allowed outside, although even some patios are smoke-free zones. When the bars close, the local constables lead a (usually) well-behaved cattle drive through the village and back to the hotels.

For entertainment listings, pick up Whistler's weekly newsmagazine, the *Pique,* available at cafés and food stores.

WHISTLER VILLAGE

BARS AND PUBS

Fodor'sChoice ★ **Belvedere Ice Room at Bearfoot.** The Bearfoot claims that its ice room is the only sub-zero vodka tasting room in Canada. Coming it at a chilly -32°C (-26°F), the experience (C$48) includes the use of cozy, Canada Goose parkas, four boot-shaped shot-glass tasters from a selection of 50 vodka varieties, and one definite "wow" moment to remember. ⊠ *4121 Village Green* ☎ 604/932–3433 ⊕ *www.bearfootbistro.com/the-experience.*

Black's Pub. You'll find Whistler's largest selection of whiskeys (more than 40 varieties) and 99 beers from around the world at this pleasant pub. The adjoining restaurant is reasonably priced, offering mainly pizzas and pastas. ⊠ *4270 Mountain Sq.* ☎ *604/932–6945* ⊕ *www. blackspub.com.*

BrewHouse. You'll come for the house-brewed ales and lagers and you'll stay to relax in the woodsy atmosphere, complete with fireplaces, pool tables, and a slew of TVs turned to sports channels. Brewery tours are offered Thursday and Saturday afternoon. The adjacent restaurant and patio are good places for casual meals. ⊠ *4355 Blackcomb Way* ☎ *604/905–2739* ⊕ *www.mjg.ca.*

Dubh Linn Gate Irish Pub. As its name implies, this place is full of the Irish blarney, with an interior that was actually transported all the way from the Emerald Isle. The staff pours a decent pint of Guinness, and the menu includes solid Irish fare like steak and Guinness pie. Celtic music is a highlight most nights. ⊠ *Pan Pacific Hotel, 4320 Sundial Crescent* ☎ *604/905–4047* ⊕ *www.dubhlinngate.com.*

Fodor'sChoice ★ **Garibaldi Lift Company.** At the base of the Whistler Gondola, this popular joint attracts a lively crowd to its restaurant, lounge, and club, in large part because it's a great venue for live bands. It's a cozy place to chill out and watch the latest ski and snowboard videos during the day; in the evening, though, things get hopping. Friday night house parties are

An inuksuk—a stone landmark—stands sentry over Whistler and Blackcomb mountains.

legendary—the music isn't run-of-the-mill Top 40—and in addition to live bands, it's a venue for top DJ talent from Canada and the U.S. ⊠ *4165 Springs La.* ☎ *604/905–2220.*

Longhorn Saloon & Grill. A veritable institution among Whistler's drinking establishments, the Longhorn has been around since the mid-1980s. It still packs them in until the wee hours, with the crowds moving from the saloon to the patio overlooking the base of Blackcomb. The interior calls to mind Steamboat Springs or Crested Butte, but the variety of local brews makes it clear that you're in BC. The menu is strictly pub food. ⊠ *Carleton Lodge, 4284 Mountain Sq.* ☎ *604/932–5999* ⊕ *www. gibbonshospitality.com/longhorn.*

DANCE CLUBS

Buffalo Bill's Bar & Grill. Across from the Whistler Gondola, this club features 1980s music for the younger crowd; well-known regional bands jam here once or twice a month. If you can't get onto the small dance floor, there's a pool table. ⊠ *4122 Village Green* ☎ *604/932–6613* ⊕ *www.gibbonshospitality.com/buffalobills.*

Garfinkle's. One of Whistler's most cavernous clubs, Garfinkle's hosts live rock, hip-hop, funk, and jazz performances. It's a hangout for a young crowd, many of whom are weekend partiers from Vancouver. It's a high point (literally) on any Whistler trip. ⊠ *1–4308 Main St.* ☎ *604/932–2323* ⊕ *www.gibbonshospitality.com/garfinkles.*

Maxx Fish. Located below Amsterdam Cafe, this dance club attracts a who's who of DJs from around the world. The crowd is hip and young, the music is eclectic, and the vibe is cool. ⊠ *4232 Village Stroll* ☎ *604/932–1904* ⊕ *www.maxxfish.com.*

Moe Joe's. Its hot central location makes Moe Joe's a perennial favorite. Theme nights from Ladies Night Saturday to Check-in Fridays (via Facebook for free cover) to Glow-in-the-Dark giveaways on Sundays appeal to a diverse crowd. If you're traveling in a group, reserve a party booth or snag a VIP pass to skip the lines. ⊠ *4115 Golfers Approach* ☎ *604/935–1152* ⊕ *www.moejoes.com.*

Tommy Africa's. The club's been around forever, and depending on what's happening on any given night it's definitely worth a look. Guest DJs play alternative and progressive dance music, and with so many youthful patrons drinking the club's trademark shooters (shot glasses of undiluted alcoholic concoctions), it's not long before someone is dancing on the stage. ⊠ *4216 Gateway Dr.* ☎ *604/932–6090* ⊕ *www.tommyafricas.com.*

SHOPPING AND SPAS

Whistler has almost 200 stores, including chain and designer outlets, gift shops, and outdoor-clothing and ski shops. Most are clustered in the pedestrian-only Whistler Village Centre; more can be found a short stroll away in Village North, Upper Village, and in the shopping concourses of the major hotels.

Where there's skiing, there are spas. Whistler has several outstanding hotel spas—including those at the Four Seasons Resort Whistler and the Westin Resort & Spa—which offer mostly mainstream and European treatments; the Fairmont Château Whistler Resort also has a menu of Ayurvedic therapies, while you can get traditional Javanese treatments in the spa at the Summit Lodge & Spa.

WHISTLER VILLAGE

CLOTHING

Amos and Andes. Amid the endless sweater shops, this one stands out. The handmade sweaters and dresses have offbeat designs and fabulous colors. They're really comfortable, especially those made with silky-soft merino wool. ⊠ *2–4321 Village Gate Blvd.* ☎ *604/932–7202* ⊕ *www.whistlersweatershop.com.*

Helly Hansen. Here's where to find high-quality Norwegian-made skiing, boarding, and other outdoor wear and equipment. There's a second location at the Westin Resort. ⊠ *4295 Blackcomb Way* ☎ *604/932–0143* ⊕ *www.hellyhansen.com.*

Lululemon Athletica. Best known for its yoga gear, this iconic Canadian retailer carries a wide range of ultra-comfortable and flattering athletic wear. ⊠ *Unit 118-4154 Village Green* ☎ *604/938–9642* ⊕ *www.lululemon.com.*

Open Country. There are several upscale clothing shops in Whistler, but here you'll find many designer labels all under one roof: leisure wear classics for men and women by Tommy Hilfiger, Jack Lipson, Kenneth Cole, Michael Kors, and Ralph Lauren. ⊠ *Fairmont Chateau Whistler Resort, 4599 Chateau Blvd.* ☎ *604/938–9268.*

Roots. This Canadian-owned enterprise is known for its sweatshirts and cozy casuals, and it's something of a fixture in Whistler. It outfits the Canadian Olympic team, and has clothed many American and U.K. Olympians in the past. ⊠ *4154 Village Green, Unit 100* ☎ *604/938–0058* ⊕ *www.canada.roots.com.*

JEWELRY

Rocks & Gems. This interesting shop has an amazing selection of trilobites featuring specimens from around the globe, including rare finds from BC. This is the shop to go to whether you're searching for a one-of-a-kind collector fossil, an exotic stone like ammolite, or a handcrafted necklace or ring. ⊠ *4154 Village Green* ☎ *604/938–3307.*

GALLERIES

Adele Campbell Fine Art Gallery. This gallery has a broad range of paintings and sculptures, many with wildlife and wilderness themes, by both established and up-and-coming BC artists. You'll usually be able to find some affordable pieces. ⊠ *Westin Resort, 4090 Whistler Way* ☎ *888/938–0887* ⊕ *www.adelecampbell.com.*

ArtWalk. Organized by the Whistler Arts Council, ArtWalk is a self-guided tour throughout July and August where you can check out the work of the many talented artists who live in the Sea-to-Sky Corridor. Venues include galleries, hotel lobbies, shops, and art studios which display their ceramics, photography, jewelry, and mixed media art. Guests can meet the artists while enjoying appetizers and live music. ⊠ *Maurice Young Millennium Place, 4335 Blackcomb Way* ☎ *604/935–8410* ⊕ *www.artswhistler.com.*

Black Tusk Gallery. Specializing in quality regional art, Black Tusk is a showcase for Pacific Northwest Coast Native artists, both from Canada and the U.S. Works include limited-edition silk-screen prints and traditional crafts such as masks, paddles, bowls, jewelry, and totem poles. ⊠ *Hilton Whistler Resort, 4293 Mountain Sq.* ☎ *604/905–5540* ⊕ *www.blacktusk.ca.*

Plaza Galleries. The range of artists represented at the Plaza Galleries is inspired. Many, such as acclaimed wildlife artist Robert Bateman, hail from British Columbia, though you're just as likely to see the efforts of international names who are just starting to make their mark in North America. You can also buy art by old-time Hollywood stars that include Anthony Quinn and Red Skelton. ⊠ *Whistler Town Plaza, 22–4314 Main St.* ☎ *604/938–6233* ⊕ *www.plazagalleries.com.*

10

Whistler Village Art Gallery. With a focus on contemporary painting, sculpture, and glass, this well-established gallery has earned a loyal following from those looking for innovative work by Canadian artists. There's a second location at the Four Seasons Resort Whistler. The hotel has a different entrance, at 4050 Whistler Way. ⊠ *Hilton Whistler Resort, 4293 Mountain Sq.* ☎ *604/938–3001* ⊕ *www.whistlerart.com.*

SPORTING GOODS

Can-Ski. With more than 40 years in the business, Can-Ski is synonymous with everything having to do with snow. It has a good selection of brand-name ski gear, clothing, and accessories, and does custom boot fitting and repairs. Can-Ski has other locations at Glacier Lodge, Deer Lodge, and Whistler Creekside (winters only). ⊠ *Crystal Lodge, 4154 Village Green* ☎ *604/938–7755* ⊕ *www.whistlerblackcomb.com/stores.*

Fanatyk Co. In winter you can buy off-the-rack skis and boots, as well as order custom-made boots. In summer the shop specializes in top-of-the-line mountain bikes as well as bike rentals, repairs, and tours. ⊠ *6–4433 Sundial Pl.* ☎ *604/938–9455* ⊕ *www.fanatykco.com.*

Showcase Snowboards. Considered by locals to be the town's best snowboard shop, this place is staffed by guys who live for the board: snow, skate, and surf. The 3,500-square-foot shop showcases of all the best gear. ⊠ *Sundial Hotel, 4340 Sundial Crescent* ☎ *604/905–2022* ⊕ *www.showcasesnowboards.com.*

SPAS

Fodor's Choice
★
Scandinave Spa. Nudging up to the edge of Lost Lake, a 10-minute drive north of Whistler Village, this place is a find. Following the traditions of Scandinavia, these pools and hydrotherapy baths are intended to soothe sore muscles, relax the body, and improve blood circulation. The circuit involves a eucalyptus steam bath, a Finnish sauna, a soak in the heated outdoor pools—especially wonderful when it's snowing—and then relaxation in a number of lounge areas and solariums. The Bearfoot Bistro is in charge of the café, so you know the food is spa superlative. Day passes are C$58. ⊠ *8010 Mons Rd.* ☎ *604/935–2424* ⊕ *www.scandinave.com/en/whistler.*

Taman Sari Royal Heritage Spa. True to its name, this spa celebrates the royal wellness traditions and rich stylings of Java and Bali. Exotic-sounding treatments and products include Javanese deep-tissue massage, a sun flower facial, body scrubs, and holistic therapies such as reflexology. It has two locations, at the Summit Lodge and also at the Hilton. ⊠ *Summit Lodge & Spa, 4359 Main St.* ☎ *604/938–5982* ⊕ *www.tamansarispa.com.*

UPPER VILLAGE

Although there is little to no shopping in the Upper Village, the posh Four Seasons resort there does have one of the most luxurious spas in Whistler.

SPAS

The Spa at Four Seasons Resort Whistler. Without a doubt, this is the most luxurious and decadent spa in town, featuring 14 treatment rooms, a relaxation lounge, a full-service health club, outdoor pools, whirlpools, steam rooms, and a fitness studio. ⊠ *Four Seasons, 4591 Blackcomb Way, Upper Village* ☎ *604/935–3400* ⊕ *www.fourseasons.com/whistler.*

THE OKANAGAN VALLEY

WELCOME TO THE OKANAGAN VALLEY

TOP REASONS TO GO

★ **Okanagan Wines:** The little-known wineries of the Okanagan Valley are producing some highly acclaimed wines and earning top honors in international circles, though they don't often make their way to U.S. stores.

★ **Explore diverse landscapes:** The region's diverse geography creates an Eden for outdoor activities and agriculture: cattle ranches, golf courses, orchards, lakeside vineyards, marble canyons, trestle train tracks, and Canada's only desert.

★ **Skiing:** The Okanagan's arid microclimate translates into bountiful powder snows. Ski resorts may not have the same caché as Whistler, but for value, quality snow, and family appeal, these mountains are hidden treasures.

★ **The Kettle Valley Railway:** While a steam locomotive still travels along a preserved section of this historic railway, most of the railbed caters to cyclists and hikers. The scenery, views, waterfalls, and trestle bridges are stunningly beautiful. ↙

1 Kelowna and Vernon. As the regional hub of the Okanagan, Kelowna is a vibrant, busy commercial town that manages to juxtapose designer dining with an anything-goes casualness. It's a great base for any style of getaway. Nearby Vernon is far smaller and surrounded by picturesque communities and rural landscapes that offer some of the region's finest golf, horseback riding trails, and vacation retreats.

2 Summerland and Peachland. On Okanagan Lake, in the heart of the Okanagan Valley, these small, historic communities are within 22 km (13.5 miles) of each other and about a 40-minute drive south of Kelowna. As their names suggest, orchards, beaches, and sunshine offerings abound.

3 Penticton and Naramata. Located 68 km (42 miles) south of Kelowna on the Okanagan Lake stretch of Highway 97, Penticton is the junction point for the Naramata Benchlands running up the east side of the lake; Highway 3A, which winds west toward the coast; and the continuation of Highway 97 south toward Osoyoos. Serious grape lovers often head to this region first.

4 Oliver and Osoyoos. Surrounded by the arid landscapes of Canada's only desert, it seems anomalous that vineyards should thrive here. But they do. In summer, Osoyoos Lake transforms the community into vacationville central. Oliver is 42 km (26 miles) south of Penticton and Osoyoos is 21 km (13 miles) further south, only 2 km from the U.S. border.

British
Columbia

GETTING
ORIENTED

Long known as the fruit-growing capital of Canada, the Okanagan has also become a significant wine-producing area that is about a five-hour drive from Vancouver. Within the Okanagan region, the valley stretches about 174 km (108 miles) from the gateway town of Vernon, just north of Kelowna, to Osoyoos, near the U.S. border.

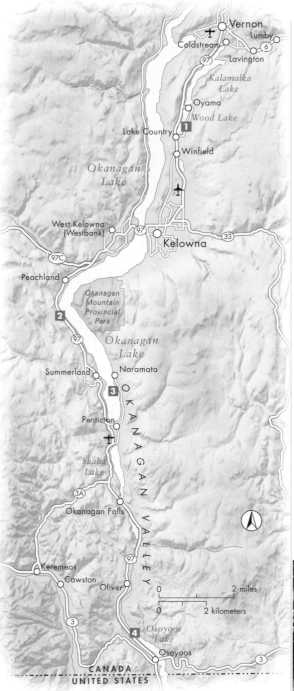

If you think that "wine country" and "British Columbia" have as much in common as "beaches" and "the Arctic," think again. The Okanagan region, roughly five hours east of Vancouver by car or one hour by air, has earned another moniker: "Napa of the North," for its award-winning blends. Admittedly, wine production is a literal drop in the bucket compared to that of the Napa Valley; but still, the Okanagan is a magnet for wine enthusiasts—novice and expert alike.

Its lakeside and scenic vineyards aren't the Okanagan's only draw. Add to that the region's arid summer climate, water activities, numerous golf courses, mountain trails, and abundant snow in winter, and you have a perfect short getaway from Vancouver and the British Columbia coast as well as a perfect setting for a longer stay.

The Okanagan's wineries are concentrated in three general areas: around the city of Kelowna and north toward Vernon, along the Naramata Bench outside the town of Penticton, and in the area between Oliver and Osoyoos, just north of the U.S. border. If you're planning a short trip, you might want to stick to just one of these areas, especially since each one has developed its own wine trail to accommodate visitors with time constraints. That said, with approximately 200 wineries throughout the Okanagan, each area also offers enough to occupy several days of tasting.

As more urbanites, celebrity chefs, and city escapees discover the Okanagan's year-round appeal, the region's restaurants, amenities, and services are growing in sophistication, with wineries taking the lead. Many of them have created unique places to stay as well as spectacular destination dining on patios, in-house, and even safari-style, in the middle of the vineyards themselves.

It may only be about 125 km (75 miles) between Kelowna and Osoyoos, but wine touring, when coupled with unexpected digressions such as visiting a garden in spectacular bloom, an art studio, or a historic site along the way, can turn a two-hour sojourn into a full day of meandering adventure. Just be sure to stop by one of the roadside stalls to pick up a pint of cherries, a box of apricots, apple chutney, peach jam, and honey.

The Okanagan's sandy lake beaches and hot dry climate have long made it a family-holiday destination for Vancouverites and Albertans, and the region is still the fruit-growing capital of Canada.

PLANNING

WHEN TO GO

The Okanagan hosts a wine festival in May, to open the season, and in early October, to close the season; both weekends are fun and busy times to visit. High season is defined as the time between the festivals.

The hot dry summer, especially July and August, is peak season here, and weekends get crowded. May and June are quieter, and most wineries are open, so either month can be a good alternative to the mid-summer peak.

However, September just might be the best time for an Okanagan wine-tasting trip. Everything is still open, the weather is generally fine, and the vineyards are full of grapes ready to pick. Many wineries release new wines in the fall, so there are more tasting options.

In winter, the Okanagan becomes a popular ski destination, with several low-key but first-rate resorts. If your main objective is wine touring, though, many wineries close or reduce their hours from November through April.

MAKING THE MOST OF YOUR TIME

Three days from Vancouver is barely enough time to enjoy the Okanagan; five days to a week would be optimal.

The best place to start a wine-tasting tour is at one of the two area wine info centers (Kelowna or Penticton). You can get an overview of the area's wines, get help in organizing your time, and usually taste a wine or two.

We've included a selection of the best wineries, but our list is only a fraction of the Okanagan's more than 200 producers. Because new wineries open every year, ask for recommendations at your hotel, or simply stop in when you see an appealing sign.

FOOD AND WINE FESTIVALS

Festivals are a great way to explore the region's food and wine scene. In addition to Winefests every Spring and Fall throughout the region, many of the smaller communities put on harvest fairs. Penticton's PeachFest (⊕ *www.peachfest.com*) has run for over 60 years, celebrating peaches every August with beach fun, square dancing, sand sculpting competitions, and concerts. In September, Kelowna hosts the HopScotch Festival (⊕ *www.hopscotchfestival.com/kelowna*), where Scotch whiskies from around the world vie for tasting attention alongside other spirits and craft beers. Even Osoyoos gets into the foodie-act with its Oyster Festival (⊕ *www.oooysterfestival.com*) in April.

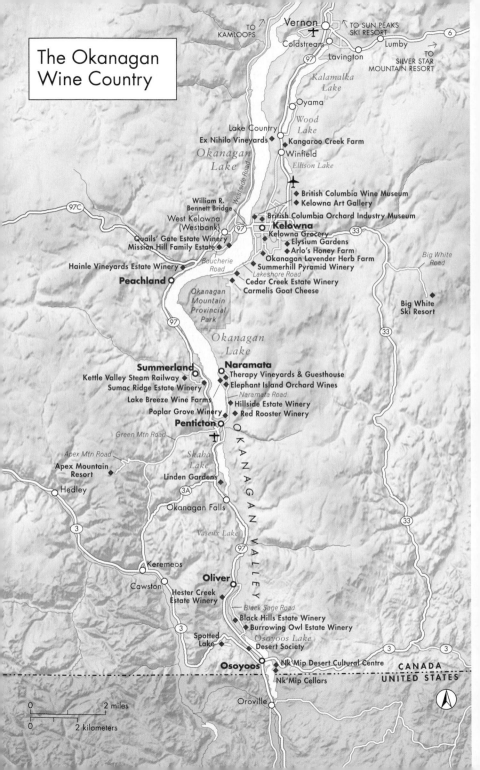

The Okanagan Wine Country

TO KAMLOOPS

Vernon

TO SUN PEAKS SKI RESORT

Coldstream

Lumby

6

TO SILVER STAR MOUNTAIN RESORT

Lavington

97

Kalamalka Lake

Oyama

Wood Lake

Lake Country

Ex Nihilo Vineyards

◆ Kangaroo Creek Farm

Okanagan Lake

Winfield

Ellison Lake

Westside Road

◆ British Columbia Wine Museum
◆ Kelowna Art Gallery

William R. Bennett Bridge

◆ British Columbia Orchard Industry Museum

West Kelowna (Westbank)

97

Kelowna

33

Kelowna Grocery

Quails' Gate Estate Winery
Mission Hill Family Estate

◆ Elysium Gardens
◆ Arlo's Honey Farm

Hainle Vineyards Estate Winery

◆ Okanagan Lavender Herb Farm
◆ Summerhill Pyramid Winery

Boucherie Road

Lakeshore Road

Big White Road

Peachland

◆ Cedar Creek Estate Winery
◆ Carmelis Goat Cheese

Okanagan Mountain Provincial Park

Big White Ski Resort

97

33

Okanagan Lake

Summerland

Naramata

◆ Therapy Vineyards & Guesthouse

Kettle Valley Steam Railway ◆
Sumac Ridge Estate Winery

◆ Elephant Island Orchard Wines

Naramata Road

Lake Breeze Wine Farms

◆ Hillside Estate Winery

Poplar Grove Winery

◆ Red Rooster Winery

Penticton

Green Mtn Road

Apex Mtn Road

Skaha Lake

Apex Mountain Resort

◆ Linden Gardens

Hedley

3A

Okanagan Falls

3

Vaseux Lake

Keremeos

97

Cawston

Oliver

Hester Creek Estate Winery ◆

Black Sage Road

3

◆ Black Hills Estate Winery
◆ Burrowing Owl Estate Winery

Spotted Lake

◆ Desert Society

Osoyoos Lake

Osoyoos

◆ Nk'Mip Desert Cultural Centre

3

3

CANADA

UNITED STATES

Nk'Mip Cellars

Oroville

0   2 miles

0   2 kilometers

GETTING HERE AND AROUND
AIR TRAVEL

The main airport for the Okanagan wine country is in Kelowna. There's also a small airport in Penticton.

Air Canada and WestJet both fly into Kelowna from Vancouver. From Vancouver, Air Canada also serves Penticton; flights take about one hour. Taxis generally meet arriving flights at the Kelowna Airport.

Let's Go! provides shuttle transportation several times daily from the Kelowna Airport to local hotels for C$21 per person, as well as to Big White, Silver Star, Apex, and Crystal ski mountains. Okanagan Airport Shuttle offers transit service to Vernon for C$37 and to Silver Star for C$85, with slight discounts on the return trip. Big White Shuttle runs scheduled service between various downtown locations and the resort for C$25 round-trip.

Airport Transfer Contacts Big White Shuttle. ☎ *800/663–2772* ⊕ *www.bigwhite.com.* **Let's Go Transportation.** ☎ *778/821–0101* ⊕ *www.letsgotransportation.ca.* **Okanagan Airport Shuttle.** ☎ *250/542–7574,* ⊕ *premierpacific.com/bus/main.php?cat_id=6.*

BUS TRAVEL

Greyhound Canada runs buses from Vancouver to Vernon, Kelowna, and Penticton, with connections to smaller Okanagan towns. The Kelowna Regional Transit System operates buses in the greater Kelowna area.

Contacts Kelowna Regional Transit System. ☎ *250/860–8121* ⊕ *www.bctransit.com/regions/kel.*

CAR TRAVEL

To get to the Okanagan by car from Vancouver, head east on Highway 1 (Trans-Canada Highway). Just east of Hope, several routes diverge. For Oliver or Osoyoos in the South Okanagan, take Highway 3 east through the winding roads of Manning Park. For the Kelowna area, the fastest route is Highway 5 (the magnificent Coquihalla Highway) north to Merritt, then follow Highway 97C (the Okanagan Connector) toward Kelowna. To reach Penticton and Naramata, you can either take the Coquihalla to 97C, then turn *south* on Highway 97, or take Highway 3 to Keremeos, where you pick up Highway 3A north, which merges into 97 *north*. Allow about five hours of driving time from Vancouver to the Okanagan region.

If you're traveling from Whistler, consider the back route. Highway 99 travels through Pemberton to Lillooet. From here, take Highway 12 to Cache Creek, where you'll join Highway 1 traveling east to Kamloops. Take the Highway 97 exit to Vernon, the northernmost town of the Okanagan Valley. This is not a road to drive in winter, and whenever you go remember that gas stations are few and far between. In summer, the 561-km (350-mile) drive can take about seven to eight hours.

Several major agencies, including Avis, Budget, Enterprise, Hertz, and National, have offices in Kelowna.

HOTELS

The wine industry has added a quiet sophistication with the development of higher-end lodgings and boutique inns geared to wine-and-food lovers. This means that from July to September you need to reserve early, especially if you're planning on visiting on a weekend. The Kelowna region is more urban (and less picturesque), but it has a greater range of accommodations and other services. The Naramata and Oliver/Osoyoos areas are both prettier and more rural.

Hotel reviews have been shortened. For full information, visit Fodors.com.

RESTAURANTS

Like the California wine regions, Okanagan has attracted gourmands and the restaurants reflect that. They also benefit from the amazing fruit harvest here. From summer to fall, every month reaps a harvest of different fruits, from cherries and plums to nectarines, peaches, and several varieties of apples.

WHAT IT COSTS IN CANADIAN DOLLARS			
$	$$	$$$	$$$$
Restaurants	under C$13	C$13–C$20	C$21–C$30	over C$30
Hotels	under C$125	C$125–C$195	C$196–C$300	over C$300

Prices in the restaurants reviews are the average cost of a main course or equivalent combination of small dishes at dinner or, if dinner is not served, at lunch. Prices in the hotel reviews are the lowest cost of a standard double room in high season, including taxes. For expanded reviews, please visit ⊕ www.fodors.com

TOUR OPTIONS

Arbutus Routes. Arbutus Routes rents bikes and offers biking tours of the Okanagan wine country, including some multiday itineraries. ☎ 604/935–7566 ⊕ www.arbutusroutes.com.

Monashee Adventure Tours. Monashee Adventure Tours has full- or half-day bike- and wine-tour combinations, and other tours around the Okanagan. ☎ 250/762–9253, 888/762–9253 ⊕ www.monasheeadventuretours.com.

Distinctly Kelowna Tours. Distinctly Kelowna Tours pairs winery visits with walking excursions, zip-lining, and other adventures. ☎ 250/979–1211, 866/979–1211 ⊕ www.distinctlykelownatours.ca.

Okanagan Wine Country Tours. Okanagan Wine Country Tours offers narrated three-hour, four-hour, and full-day wine-country tours. There's even a floatplane tour over the lush valleys to the Okanagan's Golden Mile near Oliver. ☎ 250/868–9463, 866/689–9463 ⊕ www.okwinetours.com.

Okanagan Limousine. With Okanagan Limousine you can tour the wine area in chauffeur-driven style. It offers half-day and full-day tours to wineries in Kelowna, Summerland/Peachland, Naramata, Oliver/Osoyoos, and Okanagan Falls. ☎ 250/717–5466, 866/336–3133 ⊕ www.ok-limo.com.

VISITOR INFORMATION

The knowledgeable staff at the British Columbia VQA Wine Information Centre will tell you what's new at area wineries and help you plan a self-drive winery tour. The center also stocks more than 500 local wines and offers complimentary tastings daily. It's a good place to stop and find out about places to stay and eat.

Hello BC has information about the province, including the Okanagan. The Thompson Okanagan Tourism Association is the main tourism contact for the Okanagan. Towns like Osoyoos, Kelowna, and Penticton have visitor information centers, though not all are open year-round. Some, like Discover Naramata, are virtual only.

Contacts British Columbia VQA Wine Information Centre. ☎ *250/490–2006* ⊕ *www.pentictonwineinfo.com.* **Destination Osoyoos.** ☎ *250/495–5070, 888/676–9667* ⊕ *www.destinationosoyoos.com.* **Discover Naramata.** ⊕ *www. discovernaramata.com.* **Hello BC.** ☎ *800/435–5622* ⊕ *www.hellobc.com.* **Penticton & Wine Country Visitor Information Centre.** ☎ *250/493–4055, 800/663–5052* ⊕ *www.tourismpenticton.com.* **Thompson Okanagan Tourism Association.** ☎ *250/860–5999* ⊕ *www.totabc.org.* **Tourism Kelowna.** ☎ *250/861–1515, 800/663–4345* ⊕ *www.tourismkelowna.com.*

KELOWNA AND VERNON

Kelowna is 390 km (242 miles) northeast of Vancouver, 68 km (42 miles) north of Penticton; Vernon is 55 km (34 miles) north of Kelowna

The largest community in the Okanagan Valley, with a regional population of more than 180,000, Kelowna makes a good base for exploring the region's beaches, ski hills, wineries, and numerous golf courses. Although its edges are untidily urban, with strip malls and office parks sprawling everywhere, the town's walkable downtown runs along and up from Okanagan Lake. So even though the city continues to expand, you can still enjoy a stroll in the restful lakeside park.

Okanagan Lake splits Kelowna in two. On the east side of the lake is Kelowna proper, which includes the city's downtown and the winery district south of the city center that the locals call the Mission. On the west side of the lake is the community of West Kelowna, which is frequently still known by its former name, Westbank. Several wineries are on the west side, on and off Boucherie Road. The William R. Bennett Bridge connects the two sides of the lake.

Vernon is at the northernmost point of the Okanagan Valley. Lying in the heart of Lake Country and snuggled against the Monashee Mountains, Vernon is growing in popularity as a year-round vacation destination, most notably because the city's proximity to Kalamalka Lake makes it an ideal summer getaway with sandy beaches and miles of fresh, emerald green water for every kind of water sport. Predator Ridge Golf Resort and Sparkling Hill Resort have put Vernon on the map for international visitors and small, rural communities nearby such as Armstrong (famous for its cheese) and Enderby, on the banks of the Shuswap River, make for exploring a very lush, and quaint part of the Okanagan. And for winter visitors, it's near Silver Star Mountain Resort.

GETTING HERE AND AROUND

As the regional hub of the Okanagan Valley, options for getting to Kelowna include air, bus, and car. If traveling from Whistler, a car is your best option to maneuver the back roads and stop along the way to take in the scenery, and such stops are likely to be frequent. Kelowna's transit system runs buses throughout the city and to outlying areas, as well as to Vernon, and shuttle services provide transportation to specific resorts and ski mountains. If you're intent on touring at all, go by car or take a tour.

EXPLORING

British Columbia Orchard Industry Museum. Housed in the same building as the Wine Museum, this museum might be modest, but it's extremely well done. Displays describe the history of the area's fruit industry and put the entire region into a larger context. ⊠ *1304 Ellis St.* ☎ *778/478–0347* ⊕ *www.kelownamuseums.ca* ⊠ *By donation* ☉ *Weekdays 10–5, Sat. 10–4.*

British Columbia Wine Museum. A good place to start your wine country exploration is this museum in a history-filled packing house in the museum district. The staff is knowledgeable and can provide information about local wineries and wine tours. It hosts daily wine tastings and occasional wine-related exhibits. ⊠ *1304 Ellis St.* ☎ *250/868–0441* ⊕ *www.kelownamuseums.ca* ⊠ *By donation* ☉ *Weekdays 10–6, Sat. 10–5, Sun. 11–5.*

Elysium Gardens. Carved out of an apple orchard, these gorgeous gardens have lovely views of the lake. The four-acre oasis includes manicured lawns, ornamental grasses, and masses of peonies. Don't miss the simplicity of the Japanese Garden. If you see something you like, there's also a nursery on the premises. ⊠ *2834 Belgo Rd.* ☎ *250/491–1368* ⊕ *www.elysiumgardennursery.com* ⊠ *C$10; C$12 for guided tour* ☉ *May–late Sept., Tues.–Sun. 10–5.*

Kangaroo Creek Farm. You don't have to go Down Under to catch up with a kangaroo or a wallaby. At this farm you can get up close and personal with these creatures, and even hold a joey. The 'roo wrangler determines hours monthly according to weather and the mob (that's what a group of kangaroos is called), so call ahead because the hours can vary. ⊠ *3193 Hill Rd.* ☎ *250/766–4823* ⊕ *www.kangaroocreekfarm. com* ⊠ *C$5 (suggested donation)* ☉ *May–Sept., daily 10–2 (hrs vary, so call ahead).*

Kelowna Art Gallery. Works by contemporary Canadian artists make up the majority of the gallery's permanent collection. It's also an elegant venue for temporary local and international exhibits, including many for children (worth noting for rainy days). ⊠ *1315 Water St.* ☎ *250/762–2226* ⊕ *www.kelownaartgallery.com* ⊠ *C$5; free Thurs.* ☉ *Tues.–Sat. 10–5 (Thurs. until 9), Sun. 1–4.*

OKANAGAN TOURING TIPS

OKANAGAN WINERIES: LARGE OR SMALL?

Starting your trip at a larger winery can be a useful orientation. The big ones generally have organized tours, where you can learn about the types of wine they make and the winemaking process, and you can pick up general information about the region as well. They usually have restaurants, too, where you can refuel.

On the other hand, at the smaller producers you may get to talk with the owners or winemakers themselves and get a more personal feel for their wines and the winemaking business. Our recommendation is to include a mix of larger and smaller wineries in your itinerary.

OKANAGAN: NORTH OR SOUTH?

The Okanagan is a large region. Just remember that the number of wineries dwindles the farther north you travel; however, those en route to Vernon (within an easy drive of Kelowna) are worth visiting. If your time is limited, consider concentrating on one area:

■ **Go to Osoyoos/Oliver:** if you prefer smaller wineries, a more rural setting, and a dry, desertlike climate.

■ **Visit Penticton/Naramata:** for smaller wineries and if you prefer cycling or other outdoor adventures; there are several biking and hiking options nearby.

■ **Head for Kelowna:** if you're arriving by plane (it has the region's only significant airport), if you prefer a more urban setting, or if you want to check out the largest wineries. Kelowna isn't appealing, though,

so if you're envisioning idyllic wine country, go farther south.

WHAT TO DO BESIDES WINERIES?

Before becoming such a hip wine-and-food destination, the Okanagan was a family holiday spot, best known for its "beaches and peaches"—the lakes with their sandy shores, boating and waterskiing opportunities, and waterfront lodges and campgrounds, as well as the countless farm stands offering fresh produce. The beaches and peaches are still there, and the Okanagan still welcomes families. With its mild, dry climate, the region is also popular with golfers, and there are gardens to visit as well as trails for hiking and biking.

The restaurant scene in the Okanagan is evolving, too, and a growing number of high-end eateries emphasize food-and-wine pairings. Some of the best are at the wineries, especially the Sonora Room at Burrowing Owl in Oliver and the Terrace at Mission Hill in the Kelowna area. Surprisingly, outside of Kelowna, it can be hard to find good-quality, cheap eats: your best bet, particularly in the summer and fall, is to stop at one of the many roadside farm stands to pick up fruits, veggies, and picnic fare. Some wineries have "picnic licenses," which means that they're allowed to sell you a glass (or a bottle) of wine that you can enjoy on the grounds, paired with your own picnic supplies or with picnic fare that the winery sells. Check out ⊕ *www. KelownaFarmtoTable.com* for food-oriented touring ideas that include markets, honey farms, lavender fields, and herbal gardens.

WINERIES

Almost all of the wineries in and around Kelowna offer tastings and tours throughout the summer and during the Okanagan Wine Festivals held in May and October; several have restaurants, and most also have shops open year-round. Many wineries charge a nominal fee (C$3–C$8) for tastings, more if a tour is involved.

■TIP➔ As you plan your tour route, note that Cedar Creek and Summerhill are on the east side of the lake, while Mission Hill and Quails' Gate are on the west.

Cedar Creek Estate Winery. South of Kelowna, the award-winning Cedar Creek—now a part of the Mission Hill family—is in a lovely spot overlooking the lake. Tours of the winery run daily from May through October, and the shop is open for tastings year-round. With salads, sandwiches, and other light contemporary fare, the outdoor Vineyard Terrace Restaurant serves lunch from mid-June through mid-September, weather permitting. If you like these wines, visit Cedar Creek's sister winery, Greatna Ranch Estates, 9 km (5½ miles) south of Peachland. ⊠ *5445 Lakeshore Rd.* ☏ *250/764–8866, 800/730–9463* ⊕ *www. cedarcreek.bc.ca* ▨ *Tours C$8, tastings C$3; private tours C$13* ☽ *Tours May–Oct., daily 11, 1, and 3. Wineshop May–Oct., daily 10–6; Nov.–Apr., daily 11–5.*

Ex Nihilo Vineyards. Canada is the world's largest producer of ice wine, a specialty of Ex Nihilo Vineyards, a 10-minute drive north of Kelowna. This small but enterprising winery was among the first in the area to court celebrity endorsements, and struck a deal with the Rolling Stones to label its Riesling ice wine "Sympathy for the Devil." The tasting room is open May to October; the tasting fee is waived if you make a purchase, as is the case at most wineries. ⊠ *1525 Camp Rd.* ☏ *250/766–5522* ⊕ *www. exnihilovineyards.com* ▨ *Tasting C$5* ☽ *May–Oct., daily 10–6.*

Mission Hill Family Estate. Sitting atop a hill overlooking Okanagan Lake, Mission Hill Family Estate is recognizable for its 12-story bell tower. It was built, as the owner describes it, to resemble "a combination monastery, Tuscan hill village, and French winery." With a vaulted cellar blasted from volcanic rock, the well-established vineyard produces a wide variety of award-winning wines and offers several different winery tours, from a basic 60-minute tour with a tasting of three wines, to a more in-depth visit that includes wine-and-food pairings. An outdoor amphitheater hosts art events, music, and theater. The Terrace Restaurant is one of the Kelowna area's best dining options. Mission Hill took over Cedar Creek Winery in 2013. ⊠ *1730 Mission Hill Rd.* ☏ *250/768–6448, 800/957–9911* ⊕ *www.missionhillwinery. com* ▨ *Tastings and tours C$8–C$95* ☽ *July–early Sept., daily 9:30–7; Apr.–June and early Sept.–early Oct., daily 10–6; early Oct.–Nov., daily 10–5; Dec.–Mar., daily 10–4.*

Quails' Gate Estate Winery. Set on 125 acres above the western edge of Okanagan Lake, Quails' Gate Estate Winery runs tours several times daily from May to mid-October (though the exact times vary) and by appointment for the rest of the year. The family-owned winery produces more than a dozen different varieties, although it's best known

CLOSE UP

A Crash Course in Okanagan Wines

11

GETTING ORIENTED

A great source of information about Okanagan wines is the British Columbia Wine Institute (⊕ *www.winebc. com*). The website includes a helpful guide to BC wines, as well as detailed itinerary suggestions for Okanagan wine touring. It also includes a calendar of wine-related dinners, tastings, and other events around the province.

A DROP OF HISTORY

Most wine experts agree that back in the dark ages (aka the 1970s), the wine produced in British Columbia was, to put it charitably, plonk. Okanagan Riesling and sparkling Lambrusco were the best sellers. Beginning in the late 1970s, however, growers began replacing their vines with high-quality Vinifera varieties to start producing more sophisticated wines. In 1984, BC had 13 wineries; today there are more than 200.

WHAT TO DRINK

In British Columbia overall, the top white varietals are Chardonnay, Pinot Gris, Gewürztraminer, Pinot Blanc, and Sauvignon Blanc. The top reds are Merlot, Pinot Noir, Cabernet Sauvignon, Syrah, and Cabernet Franc. Many Okanagan wineries also produce ice wine, a late-harvest dessert wine made from grapes that have frozen on the vine.

WHAT IS VQA?

British Columbia wines that carry a "VQA" (Vintners Quality Alliance) label must meet certain production and quality standards. A professional tasting panel approves each VQA wine. Participation in the VQA program is voluntary, and there are plenty of fine BC wines that have opted not to take part.

TO SPIT OR NOT TO SPIT?

On a day-long wine-tasting excursion, you can taste a good deal of wine. To avoid getting fatigued, or overly inebriated, do as the pros do: sip, swirl, and spit. Most wineries have a bucket on the tasting bar for that purpose, so don't be shy. You'll enjoy your tour more in the long run. And if the sample in your glass is more than you can drink, simply pour it into the bucket.

TRANSPORTING WINE

If you're buying bottles at the wineries, be sure you have some way to keep them cool, particularly in summer when soaring temperatures can spoil them quickly. If you must transport wine in your car, put it in a cooler or keep it on ice.

Most wineries will ship wines for you, but *only within Canada;* they cannot send wine over the border. If you're traveling back to the United States, have your wine packed for travel and transport it yourself.

UH-OH: SOLD OUT?

It's not uncommon for smaller Okanagan wineries to sell out of their wine in a given year. And when there's limited wine left, they generally close or reduce the hours in their tasting rooms. If you have your heart set on visiting a particular winery, check its website or phone in advance to be sure it has wine available.

for its award-winning Chardonnay and Pinot Gris, which were served to the Duke and Duchess of Cambridge during their Canadian visit. Complimentary tastings are offered in the spacious wineshop, and the Old Vines Restaurant is open year-round. The garden patio, open only in summer, is a lovely spot for Sunday brunch. ✉ *3303 Boucherie Rd.* ☎ *250/769–4451, 800/420–9463* 🌐 *www.quailsgate.com* 🎫 *Tastings C$5; Tours C$10* 🕒 *Tours May–mid-Oct.; times vary, call for schedule. Wineshop May and June, daily 10–7; July–early Sept., daily 9:30–7; early Sept.–Apr., daily 10–6.*

Summerhill Pyramid Winery. On the east side of the lake is Summerhill Pyramid Winery, an organic producer best known for its sparkling and ice wines. What startles visitors, though, is the four-story-high replica of the Great Pyramid of Cheops, used to age and store the wine. As a venue for summer concerts, the pyramid's fabulous acoustics are unparalleled. You can tour the pyramid and winery and visit the shop year-round. The Summerhill Sunset Bistro, with a veranda overlooking Okanagan Lake, serves lunch and dinner daily (except from January to early February). If the evening is cool, there's plenty of room inside. ✉ *4870 Chute Lake Rd.* ☎ *250/764–8000, 800/667–3538* 🌐 *www.summerhill.bc.ca* 🎫 *Tours C$10, tastings C$5* 🕒 *Tours May–mid-Oct., daily noon, 2, and 4; mid-Oct.–Apr., daily noon and 2. Wineshop May–mid-Oct., daily 10–7; mid-Oct.–Apr., daily 10–5.*

WHERE TO EAT

$$$ FRENCH 🍴 **Bouchons Bistro.** Lots of windows and crisp white-linen tablecloths make this restaurant as bright as a French café, and the menu offers an array of classics. Signature dishes include a mouthwatering bouillabaisse containing everything from fresh salmon and halibut to scallops, shrimp, and mussels; and a hearty cassoulet that includes duck confit, smoked pork belly, and Toulouse sausage over white beans. For dessert, you might opt for a cheese plate or go sweet with classic crème caramel or lavender soufflé served on passionfruit nectar. Can't make up your mind? Go for the Chef's Table d'Hôte menu of the week, a veritable showcase of whatever is in season at the time. The bistro is justifiably proud of its sommeliers and its wine list of roughly 170 bottles, primarily Okanagan and French labels. [$] *Average main: C$29* ✉ *105–1180 Sunset Dr.* ☎ *250/763–6595* 🌐 *www.bouchonsbistro.com* 🕒 *No lunch.*

$$ AMERICAN 🍴 **Minstrel Cafe & Bar.** Although it looks unpretentious, the Minstrel is one of the few places that offers a taste of nightlife in Kelowna. The café-style menu includes sharing plates of tapas, gourmet burgers, pasta, sirloins, and curries—and all are very tasty—while the bar flaunts its style with provocative martinis and a thirst-quenching sangria. The real story is the live entertainment that usually includes an eclectic mix of blues, jazz, and folk music from a surprisingly impressive bank of talent. For that reason alone, reservations are a good idea as the place can be busy. [$] *Average main:* ✉ *4638 Lakeshore Rd.* ☎ *250/764–2301* 🌐 *www.minstrelcafe.com* 🕒 *Closed Mon.–Tues. Nov.–Apr.*

$$$ CONTEMPORARY 🍴 **Old Vines Restaurant.** This contemporary eatery at Quails' Gate Winery is open throughout the year, making it a good choice for off-season visits. When the weather is fine, you can dine on the patio overlooking the lake. Menu choices are a balance of seafood (such as steamed West Coast mussels or soy-marinated sablefish) and meat (braised wild boar or duck breast with fennel and hazelnut pearl barley). There's plenty here for vegetarians (double-baked goat cheese and rosemary soufflé is delish), alongside salads like the quinoa and vegetable mix that are as colorful as they are tasty. The staff is attentive and knowledgeable about wine pairings. [$] *Average main: C$30* ✉ *3303 Boucherie Rd.* ☎ *250/769–2500* 🌐 *www.quailsgate.com* 🕒 *Mon.–Sat. 11:30–9, Sun. 10:30–9.*

$$$ CANADIAN 🍴 **RauDZ.** Rod Butters, one of BC's best-known chefs, created this contemporary eatery to deliver a culinarily interesting yet casual dining experience. The restaurant's interior is simple, with an open kitchen, a 21-foot communal table, and exposed brick and beams revealing the historic building's architectural roots. The kitchen emphasizes seasonal, locally sourced fare and is not afraid to offer chili dogs (made with merguez sausage) or cheeseburgers (topped with artisanal cheddar or blue) alongside more innovative dishes. Look for wild boar scallopini, bison meatballs, and jumbo scallops paired with a root vegetable torte and celeriac fondue. If you're into desserts, the "liquid" variety are worth your consideration; a favorite is Ripple-icious: buttermilk rippled with espresso, and punched with vodka and Baileys. P.S.: The name is pronounced "Rod's." [$] *Average main: C$30* ✉ *1560 Water St.* ☎ *250/868–8805* 🌐 *www.raudz.com* 🕒 *No lunch* ✍ *Reservations not accepted.*

$$$ PACIFIC NORTHWEST 🍴 **Summerhill Sunset Organic Bistro.** When the sun cooperates, the skies here become a dazzling array of salmon, orange, pink, and turquoise as dusk approaches. The food is impressive enough, though, that you'll be lingering over every mouthful long after the sun goes down. In addition to salads and soups—the prawn bisque over dried tomato foam is melt-in-your-mouth smooth—there are expertly prepared dishes like beef Bourguignon, chicken breast with yam-thyme gnocchi, and a coffee-and-pepper-crusted venison strip loin. There are also options for those who have vegan and gluten-free diets. Make sure to share a plate of artisan cheeses and breads. House-made desserts include a decadent chocolate trio, and a quince mousse served with poached pear, Agassiz hazelnut wafers, and Syrah syrup. Be sure to try the wines named for Robert Bateman, Canada's foremost wildlife artist. Before dinner, try to schedule a tour of the winery's pyramid, fashioned after the one in Egypt. [$] *Average main: C$30* ✉ *4870 Chute Lake Rd.* ☎ *250/764–8000* 🌐 *www.summerhill.bc.ca* 🕒 *Closed Jan.–mid-Feb.*

$$$ MODERN CANADIAN 🍴 **The Terrace at Mission Hill.** With its panoramic views across the vineyards and the lake, this outdoor eatery at the Mission Hill Family Estate is a winner for alfresco dining for lunch and early dinners to catch ths sunset. It's tough to compete with such a classic wine-country locale, but the innovative kitchen here is up to the task. You might start with a simple salad of perfectly ripe tomatoes and locally made feta cheese, or a tart of duck prosciutto, leeks, and potatoes before moving on to

pan-seared sablefish paired with a pea puree, or braised venison with figs. Every item is matched with an appropriate wine. Stay a while to enjoy a tasting plate of cheeses or a decadent assortment of chocolate creations. If the weather's cool, there are heaters and blankets. If the weather's inclement, service stops. [$] *Average main: C$30* ✉ *1730 Mission Hill Rd.* ☎ *250/768–6467* 🌐 *www.missionhillwinery.com* 🕘 *Closed early Oct.–Apr.*

WHERE TO STAY

$$ B&B/INN 🏨 **Apple Blossom Bed & Breakfast.** On the western slopes above Okanagan Lake, this cheery B&B offers terrific views and genuine hospitality. **Pros:** warm welcome from owners Jeanette and John Martens; moderate prices. **Cons:** a bit twee—if you need high style, look elsewhere. [$] *Rooms from: C$135* ✉ *3582 Apple Way Blvd.* ☎ *250/768–1163, 888/718–5064* 🌐 *www.applebnb.com* 🕘 *Closed mid-Oct.–mid-Apr.* 🛏 *4 rooms* 🍴 *Breakfast.*

$$$$ RESORT FAMILY 🏨 **The Cove Lakeside Resort.** The guest suites at this resort on the western shore of Okanagan Lake have all the comforts of home and then some: fully equipped kitchens complete with special fridges to chill your wine, 42-inch plasma TVs, washer-dryers, and fireplaces. **Pros:** lakeside location; marina and moorage available for guests. **Cons:** high season gets busy (and noisy) with young families. [$] *Rooms from: C$325* ✉ *4205 Gellatly Rd.* ☎ *250/707–1800, 877/762–2683* 🌐 *www.covelakeside.com* 🛏 *150 suites* 🍴 *No meals.*

$$$ RESORT 🏨 **Delta Grand Okanagan Resort.** On the shore of Okanagan Lake, this resort is a five-minute stroll from downtown Kelowna, though you may never want to leave the grounds because of all the amenities—there's even a casino and show lounge. **Pros:** a full menu of resort activities for kids and adults; within minutes of Kelowna's entertainment and shopping district. **Cons:** feels like a big convention hotel; pricey parking; not the hippest choice in town. [$] *Rooms from: C$299* ✉ *1310 Water St.* ☎ *250/763–4500, 800/465–4651* 🌐 *www.deltahotels.com* 🛏 *260 rooms, 60 condominiums, 70 villas* 🍴 *No meals.*

$$$ HOTEL 🏨 **Four Points Kelowna Airport.** For jet-lagged travelers on their way to winecountry and wishing to bypass Kelowna, a 25-minute drive away, this new hotel, which opened in mid-2013, fits the bill as a resting stop. **Pros:** close proximity to Kelowna International Airport; breakfast included in rates; new hotel. **Cons:** away from city "action"; typical chain hotel. [$] *Rooms from:* ✉ *5505 Airport Way* ☎ *855/900–5505* 🌐 *www.fourpointskelownaairport.com* 🛏 *120 rooms* 🍴 *Breakfast.*

$$$ HOTEL 🏨 **Hotel El Dorado.** Combining a 1926 building with a modern addition, this boutiquey lakeside lodging is one of Kelowna's more stylish options. **Pros:** eclectic style; lake views; on-site boat rentals. **Cons:** a short drive from downtown; busy on-site liquor store—a benefit to some, a nuisance for others. [$] *Rooms from: C$275* ✉ *500 Cook Rd.* ☎ *250/763–7500, 866/608–7500* 🌐 *www.hoteleldoradokelowna.com* 🛏 *49 rooms, 6 suites* 🍴 *No meals.*

$$$ RESORT FAMILY 🏨 **Manteo Resort Waterfront Hotel & Villas.** This striking Tuscan-style resort, painted in vivid reds and ochres, sits on a sandy swimming beach directly on Okanagan Lake. **Pros:** lots of activities for kids; guest

barbecue facilities. **Cons:** rooms are rather generic; a short drive from downtown. *Rooms from: C$275 ✉ 3762 Lakeshore Rd. ☎ 250/860–1031, 800/445–5255 🌐 www.manteo.com ⇨ 48 rooms, 30 suites, 24 villas 🍴 No meals.*

$$$$ RESORT **Predator Ridge Golf Resort.** Set on two stunning 18-hole golf courses that are part of a vacation-home community, this full-service resort offers a wide range of accommodations, from studio, one-, and two-bedroom units in the modern Craftsman-style lodge to two- and three-bedroom cottages. **Pros:** you can stumble out of bed onto the links; wilderness landscape; proximity to Sparkling Hill Resort. **Cons:** feels understaffed at times; location is rather remote, especially for wine touring. *Rooms from: C$350 ✉ 301 Village Centre Pl. ☎ 250/542–3436, 888/578–6688 🌐 www.predatorridge.com ⇨ 75 suites, 51 cottages 🍴 No meals.*

$$$$ RESORT Fodor's Choice ★ **Sparkling Hill Resort.** Carved into a granite hillside, this stunning resort has walls made of glass, so views of the Monashee Mountains and the northern shores of Lake Okanagan are always striking, whether from your beautifully furnished room, the excellent restaurant, the state-of-the-art gym, or the heated infinity pool. **Pros:** a mind-boggling spa; unforgettable views; pet-friendly vibe. **Cons:** no in-room coffee; not a central location, especially for wine-touring. *Rooms from: C$405 ✉ 888 Sparkling Place ☎ 250/275–1556, 877/275–1556 🌐 www.sparklinghill.com ⇨ 146 rooms, 3 penthouses 🍴 Breakfast.*

$$ B&B/INN **A View of the Lake B&B.** Owner Steve Marston and his wife Chrissy run this bed-and-breakfast in their contemporary home—he's a former restaurant chef who whips up elaborate breakfasts and offers periodic dinners and cooking demonstrations in his lavish kitchen. **Pros:** lake views; to-die-for kitchen (take a class if you can). **Cons:** guest room furnishings are a bit minimalist for some. *Rooms from: C$185 ✉ 1877 Horizon Dr. ☎ 250/769–7854 🌐 www.aviewofthelake.com ⇨ 4 rooms 🍴 Breakfast.*

SPORTS AND THE OUTDOORS

BIKING AND HIKING

Kettle Valley Rail Trail. This former railroad route runs through some of the Okanagan's prettiest and most dramatic countryside. Bikers and hikers can follow the trail in sections, the most popular being from Brodie (along Highway 5) to just east of Midway (on Highway 3). Other sections run between Penticton and Naramata and through the Kelowna area. Pick up trail maps from the visitor center in Kelowna. 🌐 *www.kettlevalleyrailtrail.com.*

GOLF

With more than 35 courses in the Okanagan Valley—19 in the Kelowna region alone—golf is a big draw. Several courses have joined forces to create Golf Kelowna (🌐 *www.golfkelowna.com*), a one-stop shop for tee times, accommodation, and visitor information.

Gallagher's Canyon Golf and Country Club. Located about 15 km (9 miles) southeast of downtown Kelowna, Gallagher's Canyon is part of a golf community development and has an 18-hole championship course that meanders among ponderosa pines, as well as a shorter nine-hole course. Greens fees include use of a cart. It's a challenging course, and the vistas of the mountains, orchards, and vineyards are a nice bonus. ✉ *4320 Gallagher's Dr.* W ☎ *250/861–4240, 800/446–5322* ⊕ *www. golfbc.com/courses/gallaghers_canyon* ✉ *C\$159 for 18 holes; C\$27 for 9 holes* ⸙ *18 holes. 6,802 yds. Par 72.*

Harvest Golf Club. Surrounded by lush vineyards and orchards (you can pick peaches, apricots, pears, and five kinds of apples while you play), the 18-hole Harvest Golf Club is aptly named. The championship course has bent-grass fairways and multiple tees so you're always challenged. Greens fees include a cart. Open from mid-March to mid-November, the Harvest Grille serves breakfast and lunch consisting of sandwiches, salads, and other casual fare; more substantial dishes are added to the menu in the evening. ✉ *2725 KLO Rd.* ☎ *250/862–3103, 800/257–8577* ⊕ *www.harvestgolf.com* ✉ *C\$125* ⸙ *18 holes. 7,109 yds. Par 72.*

Okanagan Golf Club. With their Okanagan Valley views, the two courses at the Okanagan Golf Course are a feast for the eyes. The Quail Course is a challenging hillside course with dramatic changes in elevation and tight, tree-lined fairways. The Jack Nicklaus–designed Bear Course is more forgiving. High-season greens fees include a cart. ✉ *3200 Via Centrale* ☎ *250/765–5955, 800/446–5322* ⊕ *www.golfbc.com/courses/ bear* ✉ *C\$159 for either course* ⸙ *Quail Course: 18 holes. 6,794 yds. Par 72. Bear Course: 18 holes. 6,885 yds. Par 72.*

SKIING

Ski the Okanagan? Outside of British Columbia, the Okanagan's ski resorts may not be that well known, but they're quite popular with Vancouverites and other Canadians. Unlike coastal ski resorts, such as Whistler-Blackcomb, which tend to have damp weather, the Okanagan resorts are blessed with dry powdery snow and bright sunny days. Okanagan mountains may not have the glam factor of more celebrated ski destinations, or as many high-brow dining options, but they are easy to navigate and really know how to cater to families.

Ski season generally begins in late November or early December and continues through mid-April. The busiest times are the Christmas/New Year holidays and in mid-March when many schools in the western U.S. and Canada have their spring break. In summer, the resorts turn to mountain biking and championship golf. For more information about skiing and other winter activities in the Okanagan, contact the Thompson Okanagan Tourism Association. (⇨ *See Visitor Information in Planning.*)

Big White Ski Resort. With an average annual snowfall of more than 750 cm (24 feet), this family-oriented resort is a hot favorite. The mountain has a vertical drop of 777 m (2,550 feet) and a good mix of more than 118 runs, served by 16 up-to-date lifts. You can ski or walk anywhere in the compact village, which has more ski-in/ski-out accommodations than any other Canadian resort. There are excellent day-care and children's programs, a ski school, and night skiing five times a week. Three snowboard parks, 25 km (15 miles) of cross-country trails, snowmobiling, ice-skating, horse-drawn sleigh rides, dog sledding, a 60-foot ice climbing wall, and Canada's largest snow-tubing park, round out the resort's myriad options. Shuttles run regularly from the Kelowna Airport to the mountain; on weekends and holidays, there's also shuttle service from several Kelowna-area hotels. ⊠ *Big White Rd., off Hwy. 33 about 1 hr southeast of Kelowna* ☎ *250/765–8888, 800/663-2772, 250/765-7669 snow reports* ⊕ *www.bigwhite.com* ▧ *One-day lift ticket C$84.*

Silver Star Mountain Resort. The friendly Silver Star Mountain Resort, 22 km (14 miles) northeast of Vernon, has six chairlifts, a vertical drop of 2,500 feet, 115 runs on 3,065 skiable acres, and night skiing. The resort also has 60 km (37 miles) of groomed, track-set cross-country trails; two half pipes for boarders; snow tubing, snowmobile, or snowshoe tours; sleigh rides, and skating. The Victorian-style village has several ski-in, ski-out hotels and lodges, restaurants, and a day spa. Although only 65 km (40 miles) from Kelowna International Airport, this smaller mountain is usually quieter than its "big sisters" so line-ups are less time-consuming. That holds true in the summer, too, when ski runs convert to mountain bike trails. ⊠ *Silver Star Rd.* ☎ *250/542–0224, 800/663–4431 reservations* ⊕ *www.skisilverstar.com* ▧ *One-day lift ticket C$81.*

Sun Peaks Resort. With a 2,891-foot vertical drop, 3,678 skiable acres on three mountains, lots of sunshine, powder snow, and a 2,500-foot-long snowboard park, Sun Peaks Resort can keep most powderhounds happy. Twelve lifts serve the 122 downhill runs. This family-friendly resort also offers a ski school, day care, 30 km (18 miles) of groomed and tracked cross-country trails, snowshoeing, dog-sledding, snowmobiling, and sleigh rides. The compact Tyrolean-themed village has a number of ski-in, ski-out hotels and places to eat. The mountain is 53 km (33 miles) north of Kamloops, and shuttle services will transport skiers from Kamloops Airport. There's also a twice-a-week shuttle from the Vancouver Airport. Note: In summer, Sun Peaks becomes one of British Columbia's top mountain-bike destinations, and also opens up its 18-hole championship golf course. ⊠ *1280 Alpine Rd.* ☎ *250/578– 5484, 800/807–3257* ⊕ *www.sunpeaksresort.com* ▧ *One-day lift ticket C$84; Nordic skiing C$18.*

SHOPPING

Arlo's Honey Farm. This is a mom-and-pop operation where the bees receive a lot of TLC. A small demonstration area puts glass between you and the bees while honey is harvested. Of course there's a shop filled with honey-related items. ⊠ *4329 Bedford La.* ☎ *250/764-2883* ⊕ *www.arloshoneyfarm.com.*

Carmelis Goat Cheese. The drive to Carmelis is up the side of the mountain, so bring your camera to take photos of the stupendous views. Save some shots for the goats—they're responsible for the array of cheeses you can sample (and buy, of course). Call a week ahead to arrange a tour of the cheese-production facilities and the goat barns. ⊠ *170 Timberline Rd.* ☎ *250/764–9033* ⊕ *www.carmelisgoatcheese. com* ▧ *Tours C$5.*

Okanagan Grocery. A good place to start if you're assembling a picnic, this first-rate bakery sells a variety of hearty loaves. It also offers a selection of local cheeses and other gourmet items. ⊠ *Guisachan Village, 2355 Gordon Dr.* ☎ *250/862–2811* ⊕ *www.okanagangrocery.com.*

Okanagan Lavender Herb Farm. You can wander through more than 60 varieties at this pick-your-own farm, which has taken a cue from the surrounding wineries and opened to the public. There's a gift shop, small café, and deck where you can enjoy a cool lavender lemonade or lavender ice cream. Arlo's Honey Farm is just around the corner. ⊠ *4380 Takla Rd.* ☎ *250/764–7795* ⊕ *www.okanaganlavender.com* ⊙ *May–Oct., daily 10–5:30.*

SUMMERLAND AND PEACHLAND

Summerland is 52 km (31 miles) south of Kelowna; Peachland is 25 km (15 miles) southwest of Kelowna.

Between Kelowna and Penticton, Highway 97 winds along the west side of Okanagan Lake, past vineyards, orchards, fruit stands, beaches, picnic sites, and some of the region's prettiest lake and hill scenery.

GETTING HERE AND AROUND

BC Transit runs bus services between Kelowna to Osoyoos with stops at Summerland and Peachland. Both are small, walkable communities. Touring is best done with a tour company or independently by car or bicycle.

EXPLORING

Kettle Valley Steam Railway. One way to tour the area is aboard the historic Kettle Valley Steam Railway, pulled by a restored 1912 steam locomotive. The 90-minute trips take you along 16 km (10 miles) of a century-old rail line. Several times a year there's a "Great Train Robbery" reenactment with a barbecue dinner and musical entertainment. ⊠ *18404 Bathville Rd.* ☎ *877/494–8424* ⊕ *www.kettlevalleyrail.org* ⊠ *C$22* ⊙ *Mid-May–mid-June and early Sept.–early Oct., Sat.–Mon. 10:30 and 1:30; mid-June–early Sept., Thurs.–Mon. 10:30 and 1:30.*

WINERIES

Hainle Vineyards Estate Winery. Hainle Vineyards Estate Winery is a hidden gem: British Columbia's first organic winery and the first to make ice wines. It is a small producer open for tastings (though not tours), and its award-winning wines are likely to become more coveted since the vines are still recovering from the 2012 Peachland fires. ⊠ *5355 Trepanier Bench Rd.* ☎ *250/212-5944* ⊕ *www.hainle.com* ⊠ *Tasting C$5* ⊙ *May.–Oct., daily 11–5; Nov.–Apr., by appointment only.*

Sumac Ridge Estate Winery. One of the area's first vineyards, Sumac Ridge has earned a fine reputation for its Merlot, Meritage, and sparkling ice wine. There are two tours: a 45-minute "Private Reserve" tour that includes tastings and food pairings, as well as a 90-minute tour (C$35) that combines tastings with a generous platter of hand-crafted cheese and lavender crème brûlée. This a great mid-morning or mid-afternoon stop and the shop is open year-round. ✉ *17403 Hwy. 97 N* ☎ *250/494–0451* ⊕ *www.sumacridge.com* ☛ *Tours C$10 or C$35. Tastings by donation to Food Bank (C$3 suggested)* ⊘ *Tours May–late June, daily at 11 and 2; late June–early Oct., daily at 11, 1, and 3. Wineshop late June–early Sept., daily 9:30–9; early Sept.–late June, daily 10–8.*

WHERE TO EAT AND STAY

$ ✕ **Bliss Bakery and Bistro.** Across the street from Okanagan Lake, this
CAFÉ café on Peachland's tiny commercial strip epitomizes the small-is-good philosophy. It's the best place in the area for muffins, pastries, and coffee. The hearty breads are excellent, too, and there's a small selection of sandwiches and soups for lunch. Popular items often sell out, so come early in the day. $ *Average main: C$9* ✉ *4200 Beach Ave.* ☎ *250/767–2711* ⊕ *www.blissbakery.ca* ⊘ *No dinner* ⚑ *Reservations not accepted.*

$$$$ 🛏 **Summerland Waterfront Resort.** Designed for families who like the feel
RESORT of a summer cottage but want the amenities of a resort, the rooms at
FAMILY this modern lakeside hotel are bright and beachy. **Pros:** prime location on the lake; spa; welcomes pets. **Cons:** not many dining options nearby. $ *Rooms from: C$329* ✉ *13011 Lakeshore Dr. S* ☎ *877/494–8111* ⊕ *www.summerlandresorthotel.com* ⟿ *115 suites* ⦿ *No meals.*

PENTICTON AND NARAMATA

16 km (10 miles) south of Summerland, 395 km (245 miles) east of Vancouver.

With its long, sandy beach backed by motels and cruising pickup trucks, Penticton is all about nostalgia-inducing family vacations. But drive through the city center to the east side of Okanagan Lake and you'll be in the heart of the flourishing Naramata wine country. The route is so peppered with wineries that the seemingly short drive could take all afternoon.

GETTING HERE AND AROUND

BC Transit runs bus services between Kelowna to Osoyoos with stops at Penticton; Penticton Transit provides services only within the city, and Okanaga-Similkameen Transit schedules buses to Naramata. Touring is best done with a tour company, or independently by car or bicycle.

EXPLORING

Linden Gardens. This former family fruit farm has morphed into a breathtaking nine-acre garden of flowers, trees, ponds, and streams. A path winds through a maze of constantly changing colors, passing over footbridges and beside jungles of wildflowers. Benches are strategically placed beneath weeping willows for shade or beside plants that draw butterflies and hummingbirds. The Frog City Café is an excellent stop for a late breakfast or light lunch. ✉ *351 Linden Ave.* ☎ *250/497–6600* ⊕ *www.lindengardens.ca* ☛ *C$5* ⊘ *Mid-Apr.–Oct., call for hrs.*

DID YOU KNOW?

Lake Breeze Vineyards, overlooking Okanagan Lake, is an enticing stop for a wine tasting or for lunch at the Patio restaurant.

WINERIES

May through October is high season for the Naramata wineries. Many of the smaller vineyards close or scale back their hours between November and April.

Elephant Island Orchard Wines. Although many vintners take advantage of the nearby orchards, this funky winery makes a specialty out of fruit wine. Using recipes that are generations old, it creates some delightful table and dessert wines from pears, cherries, and black currants. Best of all, tastings are complimentary. ⊠ *2730 Aikens Loop* ☎ *250/496–5522* ⊕ *www.elephantislandwine.com* ✉ *Free* ☉ *May–mid-Oct., daily 10:30–5:30; mid-Oct.–Apr., by appointment.*

Hillside Estate Winery. As you drive along the road between Penticton and Naramata, it's hard to miss the 72-foot tower at Hillside Estate Winery. Its first commercial release was in 1989, and the Old Vines Gamay Noir, Cabernet Franc, Syrah, and Pinot Gris are all award winners. It also produces an unusual white wine called Muscat Ottonel. The Hillside Bistro is open between April and mid-October. ⊠ *1350 Naramata Rd.* ☎ *250/493–6274* ⊕ *www.hillsideestate.com* ✉ *Tastings C$5* ☉ *Apr.–Oct., daily 10–6; Nov.–Mar., by appointment.*

Lake Breeze Wine Farms. On the Naramata Benchlands above Okanagan Lake, Lake Breeze Wine Farms is one of the region's most attractively located small wineries. Its white wines, particularly their Gewürztraminer, Pinot Gris, and Pinot Blanc, are well regarded. The tasting room and garden patio make for a lovely setting; the outdoor Patio Restaurant is open for lunch (weather permitting) between May and mid-October. ⊠ *930 Sammet Rd.* ☎ *250/496–5659* ⊕ *www.lakebreeze.ca* ✉ *Tastings C$3* ☉ *Apr., Fri.–Sun. 12–4; May–mid-Oct., daily 11–5:30.*

Poplar Grove. Poplar Grove makes respected Merlot, Chardonnay, and Pinot Gris, and the winery's Vanilla Pod restaurant is a seasonal favorite that really struts its foodie stuff—with pairings—serving organic fare in a simple setting overlooking the lake. Further up the road is Poplar Grove Cheeses, which sells first-rate soft and pungent double-cream Camembert and an intense Tiger Blue. It's not affiliated with the winery, but the cheese shop's restaurant takes full advantage of its neighbor's offerings. ⊠ *425 Poplar Grove Rd.* ☎ *250/493–9463 winery* ⊕ *www.poplargrove.ca* ✉ *Tastings C$5* ☉ *Call for winery hrs.*

Red Rooster Winery. Sampling wine at Red Rooster is a cultural experience. In addition to showcasing the recent vintages, the bright, spacious tasting room sells the work of local artists as well as dining-oriented lifestyle paraphernalia, and the Pecking Room Patio & Grill is a great place to try wine pairings. If owning a vineyard is your fantasy, Red Rooster's "Adopt A Row" program could be the next best thing. You "own" a row of 50 vines for the season and are guaranteed a case of wine. ⊠ *891 Naramata Rd.* ☎ *250/492–2424* ⊕ *www.redroosterwinery.com* ✉ *Tastings C$5; private tastings C$10* ☉ *Apr.–Oct., daily 10–6; Nov.–Mar., daily 11–5.*

Therapy Vineyards & Guesthouse. With wines that carry such names as Super Ego, Pink Freud, and Freudian Sip, you may feel like running for the analyst's couch. But never fear, this small vineyard combines its whimsical humor with a number of quality wines, especially its Merlot and Pinot Noir varietals. The winery often hosts special weekends focusing on culinary and yoga programs. But with only a handful of rooms in the guest house, most participants reserve early or stay elsewhere. ✉ *940 Debeck Rd.* ☎ *250/496–5217* 🌐 *www.therapyvineyards.com* 🍷 *Tastings C$3* 🕐 *May–Oct., weekdays 10–5, weekends 10–6.*

WHERE TO EAT

$ CAFÉ 🍴 **Bench Artisan Food Market.** In the morning, the smell of coffee is likely to draw you into this foodie-friendly market and café, where just-from-the-oven pastries or homemade granola will tempt you to stay a while. At midday there are soups, salads, and sandwiches. The staff will make picnic platters to go (you can order these the day before), or you can assemble your own from the locally made cheeses, fresh-baked breads, and signature molten-chocolate brownies. [$] *Average main: C$12* ✉ *368 Vancouver Ave.* ☎ *250/492–2222* 🌐 *www.thebenchmarket.com* 🕐 *No dinner.*

$$$ MODERN CANADIAN 🍴 **Hillside Bistro.** Hillside Estate Winery's straightforward lunch menu—salads, sandwiches, pizzas, and pastas—is presented with style. The two patios and rustic dining room tend to attract tour groups during the day. In the evening the vibe is more intimate, making this a good choice for traditional favorites like grilled sirloin steak with blue cheese, roasted chicken with grilled peaches, or honey-glazed salmon. [$] *Average main: C$25* ✉ *Hillside Estate Winery, 1350 Naramata Rd.* ☎ *250/493–6274, 888/923–9463* 🌐 *www.hillsidewinery.ca* 🕐 *Closed mid-Oct.–early Apr. No dinner Apr. No dinner Mon.–Thurs. May and June.*

$$ MODERN CANADIAN 🍴 **Patio at Lake Breeze.** A seat at this beautifully landscaped patio is one of the hottest tickets in town, so plan on an early lunch if you hope to get a table. Among the wine-friendly dishes, you might find a warm seafood salad with a chipotle-lime cream sauce, pan-roasted halibut with tomato confit and Chardonnay cream, or a sirloin burger topped with locally made cheese. Or simply spend the afternoon sharing a charcuterie plate. The tables are outdoors, meaning the restaurant closes in inclement weather. Reservations are accepted for groups of six or more. [$] *Average main: C$17* ✉ *930 Sammet Rd.* ☎ *250/496–5659* 🌐 *www.lakebreeze.ca* 🕐 *No dinner. Closed mid-Oct.–Apr.*

WHERE TO STAY

$$$$ B&B/INN 🏨 **Apple D'Or.** A palatial log cabin with gardens to match the views of Okanagan Lake, this guesthouse makes for a luxurious home-base for exploring the Naramata Bench. **Pros:** great wine-tasting home base for Naramata; lovely gardens. **Cons:** Naramata location precludes visiting other wineries if time is short; strict cancellation policies. [$] *Rooms from: C$325* ✉ *2587 Naramata Rd.* ☎ *250/496–4045* 🌐 *www.appledor.ca* 🕐 *Closed Nov.–Mar.* 🛏 *3 suites* 🍽 *Breakfast.*

$$$ B&B/INN 🏨 **God's Mountain Estate.** Filled with intriguing nooks and crannies, this quirky Mediterranean-style villa has a gorgeous white-washed exterior and sits on 115 rambling acres overlooking Skaha Lake. **Pros:** romantic atmosphere; dinners are extraordinary. **Cons:** the eccentric style is not for everyone; two-night minimum stay. [$] *Rooms from: C$200* ✉ *4898 Lakeside Rd.* ☎ *250/490–4800* 🌐 *www.godsmountain.com* 🛏 *10 rooms, 4 suites* 🍴 *Breakfast.*

$$$ HOTEL 🏨 **Naramata Heritage Inn & Spa.** At this hotel dating back to 1908, many of the Mission-style furnishings, wood floors, and claw-foot tubs are original, but plenty of the amenities—heated bathroom floors, fluffy duvets, central air-conditioning—are au courant. **Pros:** great choices at the wine bar; soothing spa. **Cons:** guest rooms are small. [$] *Rooms from: C$225* ✉ *3625 1st St.* ☎ *250/496–6808, 866/617–1188* 🌐 *www.naramatainn.com* 🕒 *Closed Nov.–Jan.* 🛏 *11 rooms, 1 suite* 🍴 *Breakfast.*

$$$ B&B/INN 🏨 **Therapy Vineyards And Guesthouse.** Independent travelers who want to get away from it all might consider a room at this cozy winery guesthouse. **Pros:** lake views; private. **Cons:** no common space for guests; few amenities. [$] *Rooms from: C$200* ✉ *940 Debeck Rd.* ☎ *250/496–5217* 🌐 *www.therapyvineyards.com* 🕒 *Closed Nov.–Apr.* 🛏 *6 rooms* 🍴 *Breakfast.*

SPORTS AND THE OUTDOORS

SKIING

Apex Mountain Resort. Known for its intimate ambience and soft powder snow, Apex Mountain Resort is a lesser known ski gem offering snow-bunnies 68 trails, 4 lifts, a vertical drop of 2,000 feet, and a peak elevation of 7,197 feet. Located 33 km (21 miles) west of Penticton, the resort has night skiing, a ski school, a terrain park and half pipe for boarders, a snow-tube park, an outdoor ice rink, a skating trail through the forest, snow-shoeing and snowmobile tours. Accommodation options near the mountain include a couple of inns, plus condos and townhouses. ✉ *Apex Mountain Rd., off Green Mountain Rd.* ☎ *250/292–8222, 877/777–2739* 🌐 *www.apexresort.com* 🎫 *One-day lift ticket C$66; Nordic pass C$18; snow tube park C$15.*

OLIVER AND OSOYOOS

58 km (36 miles) south of Penticton, 400 km (250 miles) east of Vancouver.

South of Penticton, between the southern tip of Lake Okanagan and the U.S. border, Highway 97 passes through the country's only desert and runs along a chain of lakes: Skaha, Vaseaux, and Osoyoos. With a hot, dry climate, the lakeshore beaches can be crowded with families in summer; this is also a popular winter destination for snowbirds from the Canadian prairies. The climate makes this a prime wine-producing area, and the roads on both sides of Osoyoos Lake between the towns of Oliver and Osoyoos are lined with vineyards.

Oliver bills itself as the "Wine Capital of Canada" and this sleepy town of about 4,700 does have an ever-growing number of wineries. The community hopes to construct a "wine village" that will include an upscale inn and spa, although the plan has been on the table for the past several years.

The southernmost town in the Okanagan region, Osoyoos, has a significant First Nations population among its roughly 5,000 residents. The Osoyoos Indian Band operates North America's first aboriginal-owned winery and also runs an informative desert cultural center that's well worth a visit.

GETTING HERE AND AROUND

BC Transit runs bus services between Kelowna to Osoyoos; stops include Penticton. South Okanagan Transit provides bus transportation in and around Osoyoos, including to Oliver 22 km (13 miles) away. Touring is best done with a tour company or independently by car or bicycle.

EN ROUTE

If you're approaching the Oliver/Osoyoos area from the west along Highway 3, keep your eye out for **Spotted Lake.** Containing one of the world's highest concentrations of minerals, this 38-acre lake dries up as the summer progresses, leaving mineral deposits in a distinctive "spotted" pattern. The Osoyoos Indian Band, which lives in the area, considers the lake sacred, believing its minerals have healing properties. The lake is on private property, but it's visible from the highway; it's east of Cawston and about 8 km (5 miles) west of Osoyoos.

EXPLORING

Desert Society. The northern tip of the Great Basin Desert is home to flora and fauna found nowhere else in the country. Located at the entrance of the society's 67-acre park, the interpretive center shares displays and more about the unique local ecology. You can also take a one-hour guided tour along a boardwalk leading through the desert. ⊠ *146th St., off Hwy. 97* ☎ *250/495–2470, 877/899–0897* ⊕ *www.desert.org* ⊠ *C$7* ⊙ *Late Apr.–mid-May and mid-Sept.–mid-Oct., daily 10–2; mid-May–mid-Sept., daily 9:30–4:30; guided tours mid-May–mid-Sept. at 10, noon, and 2.*

FAMILY **Nk'Mip Desert Cultural Centre.** Run by the Osoyoos Indian Band, this well-designed museum—the name is pronounced "in-ka-meep"—has exhibits about the area's aboriginal community, the region's natural setting, and the animals that make their home in this desert environment. Don't miss "Sssnakes Alive!," a daily show featuring live rattlesnakes and other creatures native to the area. You can also walk to a reconstructed village that includes two pit houses, a tepee, and a sweat lodge. (Bring water, since there's little shade along the trails.) The center's exterior is a striking, environmentally friendly earth wall built of a mix of soil, water, a small amount of cement, and pigment. ⊠ *1000 Rancher Creek Rd.* ☎ *250/495–7901* ⊕ *www.nkmipdesert. com* ⊠ *C$12* ⊙ *Early Mar.–early May, Tues.–Sat. 9:30–4:30; early May–June and Sept.–Oct., daily 9:30–4:30; July–Aug., Thurs.–Tues. 9:30–4:30, Wed. 9:30–4:30 and 5–9.*

WINERIES

Wineries line the roads between Osoyoos and Oliver, and continue north toward the town of Okanagan Falls. Most are fairly small operations, with some notable larger producers. Many wineries close or reduce their operations between November and April, so call first if you're traveling off-season.

Black Hills Estate Winery. On the Black Sage Bench between Osoyoos and Oliver, Black Hills Estate Winery has developed a cult following among Okanagan aficionados and frequently sells out of its much-admired wines. When the wine is gone, the tasting room closes for the season. It's worth calling to check on the status of its Nota Bene (a blend of Cabernet Sauvignon, Merlot, and Cabernet Franc), Alibi (Sauvignon Blanc with a bit of Sémillon), Chardonnay, or whatever the winemaker dreams up next. From May through mid-October, tours of the vineyard and winery depart at 11 am and 1:30 pm and include tastings. ⊠ *30880 Black Sage Rd.* ☎ *250/498–0666* ⊕ *www.blackhillswinery.com* ⊠ *Tours C$10* ⊙ *Tours May–mid-Oct. 11 and 1:30.*

Burrowing Owl Estate Winery. With wines consistently taking home medals in international competitions, Burrowing Owl is one of the area's best known boutique vineyards. Recent award-winning vintages include a 2009 Pinot Noir and a 2008 Pinot Gris, Cabernet Franc, and Merlot. Winery tours are offered on weekends from May through October, and tastings are available year-round. At the 25-foot tasting bar, the donations asked for tastings go toward the Burrowing Owl Recovery Society. To savor the sweeping views of the vineyards and Osoyoos Lake, enjoy a meal at the terrific Sonora Room Restaurant. ⊠ *100 Burrowing Owl Pl., off Black Sage Rd.* ☎ *250/498–0620, 877/498–0620* ⊕ *www. bovwine.ca* ⊠ *Tours C$5, tastings C$3* ⊙ *Tours May–Oct., weekends 11 and 2. Wineshop May–mid-Oct., daily 10–5; call for off-season hrs.*

Hester Creek Estate Winery. Set high on a bluff between Osoyoos and Oliver, Hester Creek has an inviting bistro called Terrafina, a multipurpose tasting venue that includes a main room large enough to host parties, a private dining room for intimate groups, a patio with a wood-fired pizza oven, and a gourmet demonstration kitchen. There's a grassy picnic area where you can enjoy a snack and a glass of wine—Pinot Blanc, Pinot Gris, Merlot, and Cabernet Franc are all top choices. The best part? Tastings are free. ⊠ *13163 326th Ave.* ☎ *250/498–4435* ⊕ *www. hestercreek.com* ⊠ *Free* ⊙ *May–mid-Oct., daily 10–6; mid-Oct.–Apr., daily 10–4.*

Nk'Mip Cellars. A few minutes east of Osoyoos, Nk'Mip Cellars is the country's first winery operated by a First Nations people. On a ridge overlooking Osoyoos Lake, it's part of a stunningly designed resort complex that is, as odd as it sounds, surrounded by arid desert, a lush golf course, and abundant vineyards. The winery released its first vintage in 2002 and now produces 18,000 cases annually, including an award-winning Pinot Blanc, Reisling, Chardonnay, and Syrah. For every bottle sold of its premium label, C$1 goes to support the Desert Cultural Centre Legacy Fund. In addition to wine, the tasting room sells aboriginal art. Stay to enjoy dining at the Patio Restaurant. ⊠ *1400 Rancher*

Creek Rd. ☎ 250/495–2985 ⊕ www.nkmipcellars.com ⊠ Tours C$10 ☼ Tours May–Oct., daily 11, 1, 3 (and 5 in July and Aug.). Wineshop Apr.–May and Sept.–Oct. daily 9–5; June–Aug. daily 9–6; Nov.–Mar. by appointment only.

WHERE TO EAT

$$$ ✕ **The Patio.** On a lovely terrace looking out over the vineyards at
CANADIAN Nk'Mip Cellars, this restaurant offers shady respite from the desert
heat. The menu includes salads, cheese plates, and other light meals, and
dishes sometimes feature aboriginal influences, such as wild salmon or
bison steak. Like many winery dining rooms, this one is outdoors and
closes when the weather turns. Although it's primarily a place for lunch,
it serves dinner on Friday and Saturday evenings in July and August.
$ *Average main: C$27* ⊠ *Nk'Mip Cellars, 1400 Rancher Creek Rd.*
☎ *250/495–2985* ⊕ *www.nkmipcellars.com* ☼ *Closed Oct.–Apr. No
dinner May–June or Sept; no dinner Sun.–Thurs. July–Aug.*

$$$ ✕ **Sonora Room Restaurant.** Start with a picture-perfect backdrop over-
MODERN looking the vineyards, add a contemporary market-driven menu, top
CANADIAN it off with expert service, and the result is one of the Okanagan's finest
Fodor's Choice dining experiences. With its high-beamed ceilings and wood floors, the
★ interior is rustic, but the best seats are on the terrace looking out across
the fields. Opt for a West Coast seafood cioppino, duck breast with
cabbage and apple slaw, or a sophisticated vegetarian plate that might
include chickpea-crusted tofu, a salad of quinoa and Brussels sprouts, or
roasted cauliflower puree. The restaurant is open for lunch and dinner
daily from May through mid-October, but keeps more limited hours
off-season. $ *Average main: C$26* ⊠ *Burrowing Owl, 100 Burrowing
Owl Pl.* ☎ *250/498–0620, 877/498–0620* ⊕ *www.bovwine.ca* ☼ *Oct.–
mid-Dec., closed Mon.–Wed. Closed mid-Dec.–late Apr.*

$$ ✕ **Watermark Wine Bar and Patio.** Part of the swanky Watermark Beach
WINE BAR Resort, this wine bar sits on the water and has terrific views. Guests
FAMILY from other resorts head here for a night out, grazing on more than
30 tapas ranging from Thai-style skewered meats to yam fries with
spicy mayonnaise to lamb merguez sausage. More substantial dishes,
such as chicken with wild mushrooms, are offered for dinner. Many
of the featured wines are limited editions from local wineries, so if
you didn't taste them during your afternoon touring, you may find
them here. $ *Average main: C$15* ⊠ *Watermark Beach Resort, 15
Park Pl.* ☎ *250/495–5508* ⊕ *www.watermarkbeachresort.com* ⊟ *No
credit cards.*

WHERE TO STAY

$$$$ ⊞ **The Guesthouse at Burrowing Owl.** You could be forgiven for thinking
B&B/INN you're in Tuscany while sitting on your balcony sipping a glass of Char-
donnay, overlooking the vineyards, at this romantic inn. **Pros:** great
views over the vineyards; excellent service. **Cons:** no resort-style ame-
nities. $ *Rooms from: C$350* ⊠ *100 Burrowing Owl Pl.* ☎ *250/498–
0620, 877/498–0620* ⊕ *www.bovwine.ca* ☼ *Closed mid-Dec.–Feb.*
⇨ *10 rooms, 1 suite* ⊩◎⊨ *Breakfast* ⌣ *2 night min. June–mid Oct.*

$$$ RESORT FAMILY 🏨 **Spirit Ridge Vineyard Resort & Spa.** At this Southwestern-style resort (the only full-service resort in Osoyoos), all the accommodations—from the one-, two-, and three-bedroom suites to the one- and two-bedroom villas—have gourmet kitchens, living rooms with fireplaces, and expansive balconies. **Pros:** there's plenty to do; family-friendly environment. **Cons:** lake access is a little awkward; away from the center of town. [$] *Rooms from: C$290* ✉ *1200 Rancher Creek Rd.* ☎ *250/495–5445, 877/313–9463* 🌐 *www.spiritridge.ca* 🛏 *226 suites* 🍴 *No meals.*

$$$ B&B/INN 🏨 **The Villa at Hester Creek.** All the rooms in this Mediterranean-style B&B overlook rows of vines at the Hester Creek Estate Winery. **Pros:** serene environment; spacious rooms. **Cons:** no common areas. [$] *Rooms from: C$299* ✉ *13163 326th Ave.* ☎ *250/498–4435, 866/498–4435* 🌐 *www.hestercreek.com* ⏲ *Closed Nov.–mid-Feb.* 🛏 *5 rooms, 1 suite* 🍴 *Breakfast* ☞ *2 night min. June–mid-Oct.*

$$$ RESORT 🏨 **Walnut Beach Resort.** With its own sandy beach on the shores of Okanagan Lake, this lovely resort has an away-from-it-all ambience, helped by the fact that it's at the end of a road in a quiet residential neighborhood. **Pros:** relaxed atmosphere; great food; friendly staff. **Cons:** popular wedding venue; a bit difficult to find; limited evening entertainment. [$] *Rooms from: C$285* ✉ *4200 Lakeshore Dr.* ☎ *250/495–5400, 877/936–5400* 🌐 *www.walnutbeachosoyoos.com* 🛏 *112 rooms* 🍴 *No meals.*

SPORTS AND THE OUTDOORS

BIKING AND HIKING

International Bicycling and Hiking Trail. If you want to travel from winery to winery under your own power, follow the International Bicycling and Hiking Trail. This relatively flat trail begins at the north end of Osoyoos Lake and runs north along the Okanagan River for 18 km (11 miles). There are also plenty of shorter trails, around Mt. Kobau as an example. To get to the trail parking lot from Osoyoos, follow Highway 97 north for 8 km (5 miles), then head east on Road 22. 🌐 *www.destinationosoyoos.com.*

TRAVEL SMART
VANCOUVER

GETTING HERE AND AROUND

Most visitors to British Columbia arrive by car via the I–5 interstate highway (called Highway 99 in Canada) or fly into the province's main airport in Vancouver. For visitors who plan to rent a car, well-maintained roads and highways make it easy to drive to destinations such as Victoria, Ucluelet, and Tofino on Vancouver Island, Whistler (two hours outside Vancouver), or the Okanagan. Public transportation in Vancouver is accessible and well run.

▌AIR TRAVEL

Flying time to Vancouver is 5½ hours from New York, 6½ hours from Montréal, 4 hours from Chicago, and 2½ hours from Los Angeles.

Security measures at Canadian airports are similar to those in the United States. Be sure you're not carrying anything that could be construed as a weapon: a letter opener, Swiss Army knife, a pair of scissors, or a toy weapon, for example.

Passengers departing from Vancouver must pay an airport-improvement fee before they can board their plane; however, this fee is now included directly in the cost of tickets, simplifying the process. The fee is C$5 for flights within British Columbia and the Yukon and C$20 for all other flights.

Airline Security Issues Transportation Security Administration. ⊕ *www.tsa.gov.*

AIRPORTS

The major airport is Vancouver International Airport (YVR), in the suburb of Richmond about 16 km (10 miles) south of downtown Vancouver.

Vancouver International Airport is Canada's second-busiest airport, but it's easy to get around this spacious facility. Getting through the immigration process, though, can add 45 minutes to your travel time, so plan on getting there early. Extensive duty-free shopping, dining, spa, children's play areas, and other services are available, plus free Wi-Fi. Regular courtesy shuttles run between the Main and South Terminals.

Vancouver Island is served by Victoria International Airport. Otherwise, there are domestic airports in or near many towns on the island, including Campbell River, Comox, and Nanaimo. The tiny Tofino/Long Beach airport is 6 miles outside Tofino. Smaller communities without airports are served by floatplanes.

Vancouver International Airport is the closest airport to Whistler. The main airport for the Okanagan wine country is in Kelowna.

GROUND TRANSPORTATION

There are many options for getting downtown from Vancouver International Airport, a drive of about 20 to 45 minutes, depending on traffic. If you're driving, go over the Arthur Laing Bridge and north on Granville Street (also signposted as Highway 99). Signs direct you to Vancouver city center.

The fastest and cheapest way to travel downtown or to points en route is via the Canada Line, part of TransLink, Vancouver's rapid-transit system, which delivers you Downtown from the Vancouver International Airport in 25 minutes. The station is inside the airport, on level four, between the domestic and international terminals. The trains, which are fully wheelchair accessible and allow plenty of room for luggage, leave every six minutes from the airport and every three minutes from downtown Vancouver. Fares are C$8.75 each way which represents a regular bus fare and a C$5 "airport travel" add-on for out-of-Richmond destinations. If you're stopped by the transit authorites carrying a ticket that does not have the surcharge, they'll fine you C$75-C$150.

Taxi stands are in front of the terminal building on domestic- and international-arrivals levels. The taxi fare to Downtown is about C$38. Area cab companies include Black Top and Yellow.

LimoJet Gold and Pearl International both have limo service between the airport and downtown Vancouver for about C$75 to C$95 one way; both also offer service from the airport to Whistler for about C$320 each way.

Taxis and Shuttles Black Top and Checker Cabs. ☎ *604/731–1111* ⊕ *www.btccabs. ca.* **Limojet Gold Limousine Services.** ☎ *604/273–1331, 800/278–8742* ⊕ *www. limojetgold.com.* **Pearl International Limousine Service.** ☎ *604/732–7897, 877/977–3275* ⊕ *www.pearllimousine.ca.* **TransLink.** ☎ *604/953–3333* ⊕ *www.translink. ca.* **Yellow Cab.** ☎ *604/681–1111* ⊕ *www. yellowcabonline.com.*

FLIGHTS

Of the large U.S. airlines, American, Delta, Northwest, and United fly to Vancouver. Among smaller carriers, Horizon Air (an affiliate of Alaska Airlines) flies to Vancouver and Victoria from many western U.S. cities. Many international carriers fly to Vancouver, including Air Canada, Lufthansa, Quantas, and British Airways. Canadian charter companies Air Transat and Canadian Affair fly to Vancouver, usually at lower rates than the other airlines offer.

Within Canada, regularly scheduled flights to every major city and to most smaller cities are available on Air Canada. WestJet, a regional carrier, serves most Canadian cities.

Several companies offer floatplane and small-plane service between Vancouver, Victoria, Whistler, and other destinations in British Columbia. Among these are Harbour Air (which also encompasses Whistler Air and West Coast Air), Kenmore Air, KD Air, Northwest Seaplanes, Orca Air, Pacific Coastal Airlines, Saltspring Air, and Seair Seaplanes.

Additionally, the well-heeled may be interested in helicopter transfers. Among the companies operating in the Vancouver and Victoria area are Glacier Air and Helijet.

Floatplane, Helicopter, and Regional Air Contacts Helijet. ☎ *604/273–4688, 800/665–4354* ⊕ *www.helijet.com.* **KD Air.** ☎ *800/665–4244* ⊕ *www.kdair.com.* **Kenmore Air.** ☎ *425/486–1257, 866/435–9524* ⊕ *www. kenmoreair.com.* **Northwest Seaplanes.** ☎ *425/277–1590, 800/690–0086* ⊕ *www. nwseaplanes.com.* **Orca Air.** ☎ *888/359–6722* ⊕ *www.flyorcaair.com.* **Pacific Coastal Airlines.** ☎ *800/663–2872* ⊕ *www.pacific-coastal.com.* **Saltspring Air.** ☎ *250/537–9880, 877/537–9880* ⊕ *www.saltspringair.com.* **Seair Seaplanes.** ☎ *604/273–8900, 800/447–3247* ⊕ *www.seairseaplanes.com.*

▪ BIKE TRAVEL

Despite British Columbia's demanding landscape, bicycle travel is extremely popular. Nicknamed Canada's Cycling Capital, Victoria is especially bike-friendly, and Vancouver is not far behind, with a growing number of bike-only lanes in the heart of Downtown and many designated bike thoroughfares via the most picturesque streets and beachfronts. One of the most spectacular routes follows the abandoned 600-km-long (370-mile-long) Kettle Valley Railway through the mountains of the BC Interior; Tourism Kelowna has details. Gentler options include the 100-km (62-mile) Galloping Goose Regional Trail near Victoria and the rolling hills of the Gulf Islands. Cycle Vancouver Island has information about bike touring on Vancouver Island and the Gulf Islands. Mountain-biking enthusiasts gravitate toward the trails on Vancouver's North Shore Mountains and at Whistler.

Bike Maps Cycle Vancouver Island. ☎ *250/592–4753* ⊕ *www. cyclevancouverisland.ca.* **Galloping Goose Regional Trail.** ☎ *250/478–3344* ⊕ *www. gallopinggoosetrail.com.* **Tourism Kelowna.** ☎ *250/861–1515, 800/663–4345* ⊕ *www. tourismkelowna.com.*

▮ BOAT AND FERRY TRAVEL

Ferries play a central role in British Columbia's transportation network. In some areas, ferries provide the only access (besides floatplanes) to remote communities. For visitors, ferries are one of the best ways to get a sense of the region and its ties to the sea. BC Ferries operates one of the largest ferry fleets in the world, serving about 40 ports of call on BC's west coast. The ferries carry vehicles as well as bicycles and foot passengers.

Reservations are recommended between Vancouver and Vancouver Island and on most sailings between Vancouver and the Southern Gulf Islands, especially on weekends and holidays.

BC Ferries operates two ferry terminals outside Vancouver. From Tsawwassen (an hour south of downtown Vancouver), ferries sail to Swartz Bay near Victoria, to Nanaimo on Vancouver Island, and to the Southern Gulf Islands. From Horseshoe Bay (45 minutes north of Downtown), ferries sail to the Sunshine Coast and to Nanaimo on Vancouver Island. Vehicle reservations on Vancouver to Victoria and Nanaimo and Vancouver to the Sunshine Coast routes are optional (but recommended especially for Vancouver to Victoria) and cost an additional C$15 to C$22. There is no charge for reservations on Gulf Island routes.

There are several options for getting to Vancouver Island from Washington State: Black Ball Transport operates the MV *Coho,* a car ferry, daily year-round between Port Angeles, Washington, and Victoria's Inner Harbour. The car and passenger fare is US$62; bikes are US$6.50. The *Victoria Clipper* runs daily, year-round passenger-only service between downtown Seattle and downtown Victoria. Trips take about three hours, and the one-way fare from mid-May to late September is US$96; bicycles and pets are an extra US$10, and reservations are recommended. Washington State Ferries runs a car ferry daily from April through December from Anacortes, Washington, to Sidney (some runs make stops at different San Juan Islands), about 30 km (18 miles) north of Victoria. Trips take about three hours. One-way high-season fares are US$59.85 for a vehicle and driver, and bikes are US$6.

Boat and Ferry Information BC Ferries. ☎ *888/223-3779, 888/223-3779 in BC, Alberta and Washington State* ⊕ *www. bcferries.com.* **Black Ball Ferry Line.** ☎ *250/386-2202, 360/457-4491* ⊕ *www. cohoferry.com.* **Clipper Navigations.** ☎ *250/382-8100, 800/888-2535* ⊕ *www. clippervacations.com.* **Washington State Ferries.** ☎ *206/464-6400, 888/808-7977* ⊕ *www.wsdot.wa.gov/ferries.*

▮ BUS TRAVEL

IslandLink Bus operates bus service to most towns on Vancouver Island and connects with BC Ferries in Nanaimo. The same company operates AirportLink, ValleyLink, and WhistlerLink buses, which serve Vancouver International Airport, the Fraser Valley, and Whistler. Pacific Coach Lines operates frequent service between Victoria and Vancouver (both Downtown and the airport) on BC Ferries. The Tofino Bus provides daily service from Vancouver, Vancouver Airport, Victoria, Nanaimo, and points en route to Port Alberni, Tofino, and Ucluelet. From May to September, the West Coast Trail Express shuttles hikers from Victoria and Nanaimo to the trailheads of the West Coast and Juan de Fuca trails. All bus companies ban smoking, and most long-distance buses have restrooms on board. Some even play videos.

Greyhound serves most towns in the province and provides frequent service on popular runs, including from Victoria to Tofino.

Contacts Greyhound. ☎ *800/661-8747 in Canada, 800/231-2222 in U.S.* ⊕ *www. greyhound.ca.* **IslandLinkBus.** ⊕ *www. islandlinkbus.com.* **Pacific Coach.** ☎ *604/662-7575, 800/661-1725* ⊕ *www.pacificcoach.com.*

Tofino Bus Island Express. ☎ *250/725–2871, 866/986–3466* ⊕ *www.tofinobus.com.* **West Coast Trail Express.** ☎ *250/477–8700, 888/999–2288* ⊕ *www.trailbus.com.*

▌ CAR TRAVEL

Canada's highway system is excellent. It includes the Trans Canada Highway, or Highway 1, the longest highway in the world—running about 8,000 km (5,000 miles) from Victoria, British Columbia, to St. John's, Newfoundland, using ferries to bridge coastal waters at each end. The second-longest Canadian highway, the Yellowhead Highway (Highway 16), follows a route from the Pacific Coast and over the Rockies to the prairies. North of the population centers, roads become fewer and less developed.

The Sea-to-Sky Highway between Vancouver and Whistler is full of twists and turns, and although it was upgraded and widened prior to the 2010 Winter Olympics, drivers should still exercise caution. Landslides occasionally occur along this highway, also noted for its spectacular scenery along Howe Sound.

Within British Columbia, the Trans-Canada Highway (Highway 1), Highway 3, and the Coquihalla Highway (Highway 5) offer easy access to the Okanagan. Speed limits range from 50 kph (30 mph) in cities to a maximum of 100 kph (60 mph) on highways.

FROM THE UNITED STATES

Drivers must carry owner registration and proof-of-insurance coverage, which is compulsory in Canada. The Canadian Non-Resident Inter-Provincial Motor Vehicle Liability Insurance Card, available from any U.S. insurance company, is accepted as evidence of financial responsibility in Canada. If you're driving a car that is not registered in your name, carry a letter from the owner that authorizes your use of the vehicle.

The main entry point into British Columbia from the United States by car is on Interstate 5 at Blaine, Washington, 48 km (30 miles) south of Vancouver. Three highways enter British Columbia from the east: Highway 1, or the Trans-Canada Highway; Highway 3, or the Crowsnest Highway, which crosses southern British Columbia; and Highway 16, the Yellowhead Highway, which runs through northern British Columbia from the Rocky Mountains to Prince Rupert. From Alaska and the Yukon, take the Alaska Highway (from Fairbanks) or the Klondike Highway (from Skagway or Dawson City).

Border-crossing procedures are usually quick and simple. Most British Columbia land-border crossings are open 24 hours; exceptions are the crossing at Aldergrove and smaller border posts in eastern British Columbia, which are typically open 8 am to midnight. The Interstate 5 border crossing at Blaine, Washington, also known as the Douglas, or Peace Arch, border crossing, is one of the busiest border crossings between the United States and Canada. Weekend and holiday traffic tends to be heaviest; listen to local radio traffic reports for information about wait times, which can sometimes be as much as three hours. The Canada Border Services Agency posts estimated wait times on its website. When Aldergrove's C$17 million expansion is finished in 2016, it will be transformed from a cozy backwater to a major crossing that should relieve congestion at the Blaine crossing.

Insurance Information Canada Border Services Agency. ☎ *204/983–3500* ⊕ *www.cbsa-asfc.gc.ca.* **Insurance Corporation of British Columbia.** ☎ *604/661–2800, 800/663–3015* ⊕ *www.icbc.com.*

CAR RENTAL

When you reserve a car, ask about taxes, cancellation penalties, drop-off charges (if you're planning to pick up the car in one city and leave it in another), and surcharges (for being under or over a certain age, for additional drivers, or for driving across state or country borders). All these things can add substantially to your costs. Request car seats and extras such as GPS when you book.

Rates are sometimes—but not always—better if you book in advance or reserve through a rental agency's website. There are other reasons to book ahead, though: for popular destinations, during busy times of the year, or to ensure that you get certain types of cars (vans, SUVs, exotic sports cars).

■**TIP→** Make sure that a confirmed reservation guarantees you a car. Agencies sometimes overbook, particularly for busy weekends and holiday periods.

Renting a car is a good option if you're getting out of the cities but if you plan to spend most or all your time in downtown Vancouver, you won't need a car: parking can be difficult to secure and most attractions are within walking distance or a short cab or bus ride away. Downtown Victoria is even more compact. Rates in Vancouver begin at about C$40 a day or C$230 a week, usually including unlimited mileage. Car rentals in BC also incur a 12% tax as well as a vehicle-licensing fee of C$1.99 per day. An additional 17% Concession Recovery Fee (also known as a premium location fee), an extra fee charged by the airport authority for retail space in the terminal, is levied at airport locations. Some companies located near Vancouver International Airport offer free customer pick-up and drop-off at the airport, enabling you to avoid the latter fee. Some companies also tack on other fees, such as an Energy Recovery Fee, or a Vehicle Maintenance Fee, of about C$1 per day. If you prefer a manual-transmission car, check whether the rental agency of your choice offers stick shifts; some companies don't in Canada.

Car-rental rates vary by supply and demand, so it pays to shop around and to reserve well in advance. Vancouver's airport and downtown locations usually have the best selection. When comparing

costs, take into account any mileage charges: an arrangement with unlimited mileage is usually the best deal if you plan to tour the province. You'll find the usual car rental agencies, such as Alamo, Avis, Budget, Hertz, and National Car Rental. The local Lo-Coast Rent A Car is also a good option.

Additional drivers are charged about C$10 per day. Child seats and booster seats, which are required for children up to age 9, also cost about C$10 per day, so if you need one for more than a few days, it's worth bringing your own or buying one locally.

CAR RENTAL RESOURCES
Local Agencies Lo-Cost Rent A Car.
☎ 888/556–2678 ⊕ www.locostrentacar.com.

Major Agencies Alamo. ☎ 877/222–9075 ⊕ www.alamo.ca. **Avis.** ☎ 800/230–4898 ⊕ www.avis.ca. **Budget.** ☎ 800/268–8900 ⊕ www.budget.ca. **Hertz.** ☎ 800/654–3131 ⊕ www.hertz.ca. **National Car Rental.** ☎ 800/227–7368 ⊕ www.nationalcar.ca.

GASOLINE
Gasoline prices vary significantly from neighborhood to neighborhood in British Columbia. Expect to pay at least C$1.50 per liter (1 gallon = 3.78 liters), with prices slightly higher in Vancouver. In BC, the price includes federal and provincial taxes, a gradually increasing carbon emissions tax, and in the Greater Vancouver region, 15 cents per liter of local transit tax. The total tax for every liter is more than C$1.

Most gas stations are self-serve and most are automated, so you can pay at the pump using a credit card; major credit cards are widely accepted. A British Columbia law requires customers to pay for the gas before it's dispensed, so if you want to pay cash you'll have to estimate how much you'll need. It's not customary to tip attendants.

PARKING

More than 300 parking lots (above- and belowground) are available in Vancouver. Underground parking prices downtown typically run C$3 to C$5 per hour, depending on location. Parking meters are in effect 9 am to 8 or 10 pm daily and are strictly monitored. On street parking can be hard to find downtown, especially during workdays and on weekends. Read signs carefully to avoid being towed or fined; be aware that some spots must be vacated by the time rush hour begins at 3 pm. Fines run between C$35 and C$75, plus the cost of the tow truck.

ROAD CONDITIONS

Snow tires are recommended when traveling the Sea-to-Sky Highway between Vancouver and Whistler or driving on the Coquihalla or Trans-Canada highways during the winter.

ROADSIDE EMERGENCIES

In case of emergency anywhere in BC, call 911; if you are not connected immediately, dial "0" and ask for the operator. The British Columbia Automobile Association (BCAA) provides 24-hour roadside assistance to AAA and CAA members.

Emergency Services British Columbia Automobile Association. ☎ *800/222–4357 roadside assistance* ⊕ *www.bcaa.com.*

RULES OF THE ROAD

In Canada your own driver's license is acceptable. By law, you're required to wear seat belts and to use infant seats. In BC, babies under the age of one and under 20 pounds must travel in a rear-facing infant seat and not in a front seat with an active air bag; children over one year old and between 20 and 40 pounds need to be secured in child seats, while kids up to age nine or four-foot-nine inches tall (whichever comes first) must use booster seats. Motorcycle and bicycle helmets are mandatory. Unless otherwise specified,

right turns are permitted on red signals. Speed limits, given in kilometers, are usually within the 50–100 kph (30–60 mph) range outside the cities.

WINTER DRIVING

In coastal areas, the mild damp climate means that roadways are frequently wet. Winter snowfalls are not common (generally only once or twice a year), but when snow does fall, traffic grinds to a halt and the roadways become treacherous and stay that way until the snow melts. Beware of icy roads, especially east of Vancouver.

Tire chains, studs, or snow tires are essential equipment for winter travel in the north and in mountain areas such as Whistler. If you're planning to drive into high elevations, be sure to check the weather forecast beforehand. Even the main-highway mountain passes can be forced to close because of snow conditions. The Ministry of Transportation website has up-to-date road reports.

Road Reports BC Ministry of Transportation. ⊕ *www.drivebc.ca.*

▌CRUISE TRAVEL

Vancouver is a major embarkation point for Alaska cruises, and virtually all Alaska-bound cruise ships call here; some also call at Victoria and Prince Rupert, farther north. Most luxury liners, though, make straight for Alaska, leaving the fjords and islands of BC to smaller vessels and expedition ships. Some operators lead sailing trips around BC's islands; independent travelers can explore the coast on BC Ferries or on one of the coastal freighters serving remote outposts.

The small, expedition-style ships operated by American Safari Cruises and Cruise West explore the British Columbia coast on their way to Alaska; some offer cruises exclusively in BC. Bluewater Adventures has eight- to 10-day sailing cruises of the BC coastline, including the Queen Charlotte Islands.

For less traditional experiences, check out the *Aurora Explorer*, a 15-passenger packet freighter operated by Marine Link Tours that weaves in and out of the Broughton Archipelago. Mothership Adventures operates a 10-passenger restored hospital ship dating from 1956 that offers guided kayak paddles to otherwise inaccessible coastal inlets.

Cruise Lines Bluewater Adventures. ☎ *888/877–1770, 604/980–3800* ⊕ *www. bluewateradventures.ca.* **Marine Link Tours.** ☎ *250/286–3347* ⊕ *www.marinelinktours.com.* **Mothership Adventures.** ☎ *888/833–8887* ⊕ *www.mothershipadventures.com.* **Un-Cruise Adventures.** ☎ *888/862–8881* ⊕ *www. un-cruise.com.*

Reservations are essential on the Rocky Mountaineer and highly recommended on Amtrak and VIA routes. All the train services accept major credit cards, traveler's checks, and cash. VIA Rail will accept U.S. and Canadian currency.

Information Amtrak. ☎ *800/872–7245* ⊕ *www.amtrak.com.* **Rocky Mountaineer Vacations.** ☎ *604/606–7245, 877/460–3200* ⊕ *www.rockymountaineer.com.* **VIA Rail Canada.** ☎ *888/842–7245* ⊕ *www.viarail.ca.*

▌ TRAIN TRAVEL

Amtrak has service from Seattle to Vancouver, providing connections between Amtrak's U.S.–wide network and VIA Rail's Canadian routes. VIA Rail Canada provides transcontinental rail service. In BC VIA Rail has two major routes: Vancouver to Jasper, and Jasper to Prince Rupert with an overnight stop in Prince George. A third route, Victoria to Courtenay on Vancouver Island, is not currently in service, although there is talk of bringing it back. Rocky Mountaineer Vacations operates a variety of spectacular all-daylight rail trips between the Canadian Rockies and the West Coast as well as the Whistler Mountaineer between North Vancouver and Whistler. All trains are no-smoking, and they do not run in winter.

ESSENTIALS

■ ACCOMMODATIONS

In Vancouver and Victoria you have a choice of luxury hotels; moderately priced modern properties; bed-and-breakfasts, both simple and luxurious; and smaller older hotels with perhaps fewer conveniences but more charm. Options in smaller towns include large, full-service resorts; remote wilderness lodges; small, privately owned hotels; roadside motels; and B&Bs. it's always a good idea to reserve in advance.

In addition to Canada's national star-rating system, Canada Select, you can look for a blue Approved Accommodation decal on the window or door of a hotel or motel. Both indicate that the property has met industry association standards for courtesy, comfort, and cleanliness.

Expect accommodations to cost more in summer (except for ski resorts, where winter and spring break are high season). If you're planning to visit in high season, book well in advance. As a rule, hotels in downtown Vancouver are substantially pricier than those located 10 or 15 minutes outside the downtown core. Special events or festivals can fill rooms and raise prices, too. Note also that many out-of-the-way lodgings are closed during the winter.

The lodgings we list are the cream of the crop in each price category. When pricing accommodations, always ask what's included and what costs extra. Properties are assigned price categories based on the range between their least and most expensive standard double rooms at high season (excluding holidays). *Prices in the reviews are the lowest cost of a standard double room in high season.*

Most hotels and lodgings require you to give your credit-card details before they will confirm your reservation. If you don't feel comfortable emailing this information, ask whether you can fax it (some places even prefer faxes). However you book, get confirmation in writing and have a copy of it handy when you check in.

Be sure you understand the hotel's cancellation policy. Some places allow you to cancel without any kind of penalty—even if you prepaid to secure a discounted rate—if you cancel at least 24 hours in advance. Others require you to cancel a week in advance or penalize you the cost of one night. Small inns and B&Bs are most likely to require you to cancel far in advance. Most hotels allow children under a certain age to stay in their parents' room at no extra charge, but others charge for them as extra adults; find out the cutoff age for discounts.

APARTMENT AND HOUSE RENTALS

Rental houses, apartments, and cottages are popular in British Columbia, particularly on the coast and the islands, and in Whistler. Whistler condos are usually time-share or consortium arrangements and can be booked directly through Tourism Whistler. Vacation rentals elsewhere are usually privately owned and range from simple summer cottages to luxurious waterfront homes. Rates range from C$800 per week to several thousands; popular places book up as much as a year in advance.

Local Agents Chalet Select. ☎ *800/741–1617* ⊕ *www.chaletselect.com.* **Make Yourself At Home.** ☎ *604/874–7817* ⊕ *www.makeyourselfathome.com.* **Tourism Whistler.** ☎ *604/664–5625, 800/944–7853* ⊕ *www.tourismwhistler.com.*

BED-AND-BREAKFASTS

B&Bs are found in the country and the cities. In Vancouver, many of the top B&Bs are scattered throughout the West End, between Stanley Park and Downtown. In Victoria, try in the historic neighborhoods of Oak Bay and Rockland or in

James Bay near the Inner Harbour. Room quality varies from house to house as well, so you should ask to see a room before making a choice. Note that some B&Bs require you stay at least a certain number of nights in high season.

Reservation Services (U.S.-based) Bed and Breakfast.com. ☎ 800/462-2632 ⊕ www. bedandbreakfast.com. **Bed & Breakfast Inns Online.** ☎ 800/215-7365 ⊕ www.bbonline. com. **BnB Finder.com.** ☎ 888/469-6663 ⊕ www.bnbfinder.com.

Reservation Services (Canada-based) Hello BC. ☎ 800/435-5622 ⊕ www.hellobc. com. **Victoria Bed and Breakfast Guide.** ⊕ www.bestinnsofvictoria.com.

∎ COMMUNICATIONS

INTERNET

As in most North American cities, Internet cafés and Wi-Fi service can be found throughout Vancouver and Victoria. Most hotels and B&Bs also have Internet connections; many of the larger properties have Wi-Fi, which is usually free. It's harder to find Internet cafés in smaller towns in the Okanagan, Tofino, and Ucluelet, but many lodgings have some kind of connection that you can use. Internet and Wi-Fi access are available free at all 22 branches of the Vancouver Public Library. Internet cafés throughout the city charge about C$3 per half hour.

Contacts Cybercafés. ⊕ www.cybercafes. com. **Vancouver Public Library.** ☎ 604/331-3603 ⊕ www.vpl.vancouver.bc.ca.

PHONES

The good news is that you can now make a direct-dial telephone call from virtually any point on earth. The bad news? You can't always do so cheaply. Calling from a hotel is almost always the most expensive option; hotels usually add huge surcharges to all calls, particularly international ones. Calling cards help keep costs to a minimum, but only if you purchase them locally. And as expensive as mobile phone calls can be, they are still

usually a much cheaper option than calling from your hotel.

CALLING WITHIN CANADA

Vancouver uses 10-digit calling for local calls (e.g., 604/555-1212). The city's area codes are 604 and 778. Whistler and the Sunshine Coast also use a 604 area code, and for the rest of British Columbia, including Victoria and Vancouver Island, it's 250. Pay phones are easy to find, and new ones accept credit cards and prepaid calling cards. Dial 411 for directory assistance, 0 to reach an operator, and 911 for emergencies. All long-distance calls, including calls to the United States, must be prefixed with a 1.

CALLING OUTSIDE CANADA

The country code for the United States is 1.

MOBILE PHONES

If you have a multiband phone (some countries use different frequencies from those used in the United States) and your service provider uses the world-standard GSM network (as do T-Mobile, Cingular, and Verizon), you can probably use your phone abroad. Roaming fees can be steep, however: 99¢ a minute is considered reasonable. And overseas you normally pay the toll charges for incoming calls. It's almost always cheaper to send a text message than to make a call, since text messages have a really low set fee (often less than 5¢).

If you just want to make local calls, consider buying a new SIM card (note that your provider may have to unlock your phone for you to use a different SIM card) and a prepaid service plan in the destination. You'll then have a local number and can make local calls at local rates. If your trip is extensive, you could also simply buy a cell phone in your destination, as the initial cost will be offset over time.

■ **TIP➔** If you travel internationally frequently, save one of your old mobile phones or buy a cheap one on the Internet; ask your cell-phone company to unlock it for you, and take it with you as a travel phone, buying a new SIM card with pay-as-you-go service in each destination.

Contacts Cellular Abroad. ☎ 800/287–5072 ⊕ www.cellularabroad.com. **Mobal.** ☎ 888/888–9162 ⊕ www.mobalrental.com. **Planet Fone.** ☎ 888/988–4777 ⊕ www.planetfone.com.

■ CUSTOMS AND DUTIES

You're allowed to bring goods of a certain value back home without having to pay any duty or import tax. But there's a limit on the amount of tobacco and liquor you can bring back duty-free, and some countries have separate limits for perfumes; for exact figures, check with your customs department. The values of duty-free goods are included in these amounts. When you shop abroad, save all your receipts, as customs inspectors may ask to see them as well as the items you purchased. If the total value of your goods is more than the duty-free limit, you'll have to pay a tax (most often a flat percentage) on the value of everything beyond that limit.

Visitors may bring in the following items duty-free: 200 cigarettes, 50 cigars, and 7 ounces of tobacco; 1 bottle (1.14 liters or 40 imperial ounces) of liquor or 1.5 liters of wine; or 24 355-milliliter (12-ounce) bottles or cans of beer for personal consumption. Any alcohol and tobacco products in excess of these amounts are subject to duty, provincial fees, and taxes. You can also bring in gifts up to a total value of C$60 per gift as long as the gifts do not include alcohol or tobacco.

Information in Canada Canada Border Services Agency. ☎ 204/983–3500, 800/461–9999 in Canada ⊕ www.cbsa.gc.ca. **Canadian Firearms Centre.** ⊕ www.cfc-cafc.gc.ca.

U.S. Information U.S. Customs and Border Protection. ⊕ www.cbp.gov.

■ TRAVELING WITH PETS

No longer relegated to boarding kennels during a vacation, pets are now the norm when it comes to travel. You'll find many hotels and inns have set aside dog-designated rooms. If you are bringing a cat or dog into Canada, it must have a certificate issued by a licensed veterinarian that clearly identifies the animal and certifies that it has been vaccinated against rabies during the preceding 36 months. Assistance dogs are allowed into Canada without restriction.

■ EATING OUT

In Vancouver, where several thousand eateries represent almost every cuisine on the planet, deciding what to eat is as important as deciding what to see and do. Vancouverites are a health-conscious lot, so light, organic, and vegetarian meals are easy to find, and every restaurant and even most pubs ban smoking indoors and out. Good coffee is everywhere—downtown you'll never have to walk more than half a block for a cup of high-test cappuccino.

On-the-go dining, served from mobile trucks, is a fun new phenomenon and street eats are so good that many locals choose them over sit-down restaurants, especially when they're short on time. Neighborhood pubs, both in and outside cities, are another good bet for casual meals. Many have a separate restaurant section where you can take kids.

In Victoria and on Vancouver Island, the farm-to-fork ethos is particularly strong, in part because the island's bounty is so accessible. Many chefs work directly with organic farmers when they are creating their distinctive regional dishes. You'll be pleased to find that in addition to top-draw destinations such as Whistler, you'll discover excellent food even in the most out-of-the-way places in the province.

Although the Canadian dollar is no longer the steal it once was, dining in British Columbia is still one of North America's great bargains. To be sure, high-end entrées, especially where seafood is involved, can top C$35, but C$20 to C$25 is more the norm. Bargains abound: the densest cluster of cheap eats in Vancouver is along Denman Street in the West End. Another budget option is to check out the lunch specials at any of the small Asian restaurants lining the streets in both Vancouver and Victoria. They serve healthy hot meals for about the same cost as a take-out burger and fries. But beware: alcohol is pricey in BC. A bottle of wine can easily double your bill.

MEALS AND MEALTIMES

Despite dwindling stocks, wild Pacific salmon—fresh, smoked, dried, candied, barbecued, or grilled on an alder wood plank in the First Nations fashion—remains British Columbia's signature dish. Other local delicacies served at BC's upmarket restaurants include Fanny Bay or Long Beach oysters and Salt Spring Island lamb. Another homegrown treat is the Nanaimo Bar. Once a Christmas bake-sale standard, this chocolate-and-icing concoction has made its way to trendy city cafés.

Most upscale restaurants in Vancouver, Victoria, and Whistler observe standard North American mealtimes: 5:30 to 9 or so for dinner, roughly noon to 2 if open for lunch. Casual places like pubs typically serve food all afternoon and into the evening. Restaurants that stay open late (meaning midnight or 1 am) usually morph into bars after about 9 pm, but the kitchen stays open. In Vancouver, the West End and Kitsilano have the most late-night choices. In Victoria, pubs and a couple of jazz clubs are your best bet.

Unless otherwise noted, the restaurants listed in this guide are open daily for lunch and dinner.

PAYING

Credit cards are widely accepted, but a few smaller restaurants accept only cash. Discover Cards are little known in Canada, and many restaurants outside of Vancouver do not accept American Express.

RESERVATIONS AND DRESS

Regardless of where you are, it's a good idea to make a reservation if you can. In some places, it's expected. In British Columbia, smart casual dress is acceptable everywhere.

At the hottest restaurants in Vancouver, Victoria, and Whistler, you need to make reservations at least two weeks in advance, perhaps more if you want to dine between 7 and 9, or on a Friday or Saturday night. On weeknights or outside of the peak tourist season, you can usually secure a table by calling the same day.

If you want to dine, but not sleep, at one of BC's better-known country inns, such as the Sooke Harbour House or the Wickaninnish Inn, make your reservation as far ahead as possible. Six months ahead is not unreasonable. Guests staying at these inns are given first choice for dining reservations, which means that space for nonguests is limited. Remember to call the restaurant should you need to cancel your reservation—it's only courteous.

WINES, BEER, AND SPIRITS

Though little known outside the province, British Columbia wines have beaten those from many more established regions in international competitions. A tasting tour of BC's Okanagan wine region is a scenic way to experience some of these vintages, many of which are made in smallish batches and rarely find their way into liquor stores.

British Columbians are also choosy about their beer, brewing and drinking (per capita) more microbrewed ales and lagers than anyone else in the country. You'll find a daunting selection of oddly named brews, since many cottage breweries produce only enough for their local pubs. It's always worth asking what's on draft.

Although the Okanagan is *the* hot spot for wines, good wineries are popping up all over Vancouver Island, alongside cottage breweries and distilleries. There is also a growing number of them in and around Vancouver.

▌ ELECTRICITY

Canada uses the same voltage as the United States, so all of your electronics should make the transition without any fuss. There's no need for adapters.

▌ EMERGENCIES

Foreign Embassies Consulate of the United States. ☎ *604/685-4311* ⊕ *vancouver. usconsulate.gov.*

▌ MAIL

In British Columbia you can buy stamps at the post office or from many retail outlets and some newsstands. If you're sending mail to or within Canada, be sure to include the postal code (six digits and letters). Note that the suite number often appears before the street number in an address, followed by a hyphen. The postal abbreviation for British Columbia is BC.

Within Canada, postcards and letters cost C$1 for a single stamp (C$.85 if purchased in a booklet of 10 stamps) for up to 30 grams, C$1.20 for between 31 and 50 grams, and C$1.80 for between 51 and 100 grams. Letters and postcards to the United States cost C$1.20 for up to 30 grams, C$1.89 for between 31 and 50 grams, and C$2.95 for up to 100 grams.

International mail and postcards are C$2.50 for up to 30 grams, C$3.60 for between 31 and 50 grams, and C$5.90 for between 51 and 100 grams.

Post Office Canada Post. ☎ *604/482-4296, 800/267-1177* ⊕ *www.canadapost.ca.*

SHIPPING PACKAGES

Small packages can be sent via the Small Packets service offered by Canada Post. Rates are determined by weight, size, and method of delivery. You can also use DHL, UPS, or FedEx, or the Canadian shipping companies ICS and Purolator.

Express Services DHL. ☎ *800/225-5345* ⊕ *www.dhl.ca.* **FedEx.** ☎ *800/463-3339* ⊕ *www.fedex.ca.* **ICS Courier.** ☎ *888/427-8729* ⊕ *www.icscourier.ca.* **Purolator.** ☎ *888/744-7123* ⊕ *www.purolator.com.* **UPS.** ☎ *800/742-5877* ⊕ *www.ups.ca.*

▌ MONEY

Throughout this book, unless otherwise stated, all prices, including dining and lodging, are given in Canadian dollars.

■ **TIP→** Banks never have every foreign currency on hand, and it may take as long as a week to order. If you're planning to exchange funds before leaving home, don't wait until the last minute.

ATMS AND BANKS

Your own bank will probably charge a fee for using ATMs abroad; the foreign bank you use may also charge a fee. Nevertheless, you'll usually get a better rate of exchange at an ATM than you will at a currency-exchange office or even when changing money in a bank. And extracting funds as you need them is a safer option than carrying around a large amount of cash.

■ **TIP→** PINs with more than four digits are not recognized at ATMs in many countries. If yours has five or more, remember to change it before you leave home. ATMs are available in most bank and credit-union branches across British Columbia, as well as in many convenience stores, malls, and gas stations. Major banks include RBC Royal Bank, BMO Bank of Montreal, TD Bank Financial Group, HSBC, Scotiabank, and the Canadian Imperial Bank of Commerce.

ITEM	AVERAGE COST
Cup of Coffee	C$3
Glass of Wine	C$8
Glass of Beer	C$5
Sandwich	C$5
One-Mile Taxi Ride	C$7
Museum Admission	C$20

Prices here are given for adults. Substantially reduced fees are almost always available for children, students, and senior citizens.

CREDIT CARDS

Visa and MasterCard are universal throughout British Columbia. Diners Club, also known as En Route, is less widely accepted. Discover is little known in Canada outside major hotel chains, and many small retailers are reluctant to accept American Express cards because of the high fees charged.

It's a good idea to inform your credit-card company before you travel, especially if you're going abroad and don't travel internationally very often. Otherwise, the credit-card company might put a hold on your card owing to unusual activity—not a good thing halfway through your trip. Record all your credit-card numbers—as well as the phone numbers to call if your cards are lost or stolen—in a safe place, so you're prepared should something go wrong. Both MasterCard and Visa have general numbers you can call (collect if you're abroad) if your card is lost, but you're better off calling the number of your issuing bank, since MasterCard and Visa usually just transfer you to your bank; your bank's number is usually printed on your card.

If you plan to use your credit card for cash advances, you'll need to apply for a PI⌐ ᴀt least two weeks before your trip. ⌐ h it's usually cheaper (and safer) ⌐lit card abroad for large pur-
can cancel payments or
⌐ere's a problem), note
⌐ompanies *and* the

banks that issue them add substantial percentages to all foreign transactions, whether they're in a foreign currency or not. Check on these fees before leaving home, so there won't be any surprises when you get the bill.

■TIP➔ Before you charge something, ask the merchant whether or not he or she plans to do a dynamic currency conversion (DCC). In such a transaction the credit-card processor (shop, restaurant, or hotel, not Visa or MasterCard) converts the currency and charges you in U.S. dollars. In most cases you'll pay the merchant a 3% fee for this service in addition to any credit-card company and issuing-bank foreign-transaction surcharges.

Dynamic-currency-conversion programs are becoming increasingly widespread. Merchants who participate in them are supposed to ask whether you want to be charged in U.S. dollars or the local currency, but they don't always do so. And even if they do give you a choice, they may well avoid mentioning the additional surcharges. The good news is that you *do* have a choice. And if this practice really gets your goat, you can avoid it entirely thanks to American Express; with its cards, DCC simply isn't an option.

Reporting Lost Cards American Express. ☎ 800/528–4800 in the U.S. and Canada, 336/393–1111 collect from abroad ⊕ www. americanexpress.com. **Diners Club.** ☎ 800/234–6377 in the U.S. and Canada, 303/799–1504 collect from abroad ⊕ www. dinersclub.com. **MasterCard.** ☎ 800/627–8372 in the U.S. and Canada, 636/722–7111 collect from abroad ⊕ www.mastercard.com. **Visa.** ☎ 800/847–2911 in the U.S. and Canada, 410/581–9994 collect from abroad ⊕ www. visa.com.

CURRENCY AND EXCHANGE

The units of currency in Canada are the Canadian dollar (C$) and the cent, in almost the same denominations as U.S. currency ($5, $10, $20, 5¢, 10¢, 25¢, etc.). The C$1 and C$2 bill have been replaced by C$1 and C$2 coins—known as a "loonie," because of the loon that appears on the coin, and a "toonie," respectively. As of February 2013, Canada phased out its one-cent coin.

U.S. dollars are accepted in much of Canada (especially in communities near the border), but you won't get the exchange rate offered at banks. ATMs are ubiquitous in Vancouver and Victoria, and credit cards are accepted virtually everywhere.

▮ PACKING

In Vancouver and the rest of British Columbia, attire tends to be casual but neat. T-shirts, polo shirts, and slacks are fine at tourist attractions and all but the most upscale restaurants. Waterproof, breathable fabrics are recommended for those planning outdoor excursions. Weather in British Columbia is changeable and varied; you can expect cool evenings and some chance of rain even in summer, so don't forget your umbrella. If you plan on camping or hiking in the deep woods in summer, particularly in northern British Columbia, definitely take insect repellent. In wilderness areas it's also a good idea to carry bear spray and/or wear bells to warn bears of your presence. Both are available in camping and hardware stores in BC.

SHIPPING LUGGAGE AHEAD

Shipping your luggage in advance via an air-freight service is a great way to cut down on backaches, hassles, and stress—especially if your packing list includes strollers, car seats, etc. There are some things to be aware of, though.

First, research carry-on restrictions; if you absolutely need something that isn't practical to ship and isn't allowed in carry-ons, this strategy isn't for you. Second, plan to send your bags several days in advance to U.S. destinations and as much as two weeks in advance to some international destinations. Third, plan to spend some money: it will cost at least US$100 to send a small piece of luggage, a golf bag, or a pair of skis to a domestic destination, much more to places overseas.

Some people use FedEx to ship their bags, but this can cost even more than air-freight services. All these services insure your bag (for most, the limit is US$1,000, but you should verify that amount); you can, however, purchase additional insurance for about US$1 per US$100 of value.

Contacts Luggage Concierge. ☎ 800/288–9010 ⊕ www.luggageconcierge.com. **Luggage Forward.** ☎ 866/416–7447 ⊕ www.luggageforward.com. **Luggage Free.** ☎ 800/361–6871 ⊕ www.luggagefree.com. **Sports Express.** ☎ 866/416–7447 ⊕ www.sportsexpress.com.

▮ PASSPORTS AND VISAS

Citizens of the United States now need a passport to re-enter the United States from Canada. Passport requirements apply to minors as well. Anyone under 18 traveling alone should carry a signed and dated letter from both parents or from all legal guardians authorizing the trip. It's also a good idea to include a copy of the child's birth certificate, custody documents if applicable, and death certificates of one or both parents, if applicable. Citizens of the United States, United Kingdom, Australia, and New Zealand do not need visas to enter Canada for a period of six months or less.

▮TIP➜ Before your trip, make two copies of your passport's data page (one for someone at home and another for you to carry separately). Or scan the page and email it to someone at home and/or yourself.

If you're renewing a passport, you can do so by mail. Forms are available at passport-acceptance facilities and online.

▮ TAXES

Most purchases in British Columbia incur a 5% Goods & Services Tax (GST), as well as a 7% Provincial Sales Tax (PST).

Prices in this book do not normally include taxes.

▌ TIME

Vancouver, Victoria, Vancouver Island, and the nearby areas are within the Pacific time zone, on the same time as Los Angeles and Seattle. It's 19 hours behind Sydney, 8 hours behind London, 3 hours behind New York City and Toronto, 2 hours behind Chicago, and 1 hour ahead of Alaska.

Time Zones Timeanddate.com. ⊕ *www.timeanddate.com/worldclock.*

▌ TIPPING

Tips and service charges are not usually added to a bill in Canada. In general, tip 15% of the total bill. This goes for waiters, barbers and hairdressers, and taxi drivers.

TIPPING GUIDELINES	
Bartender	C$1–C$5 per round of drinks, depending on the number of drinks
Bellhop	C$1–C$5 per bag, depending on the level of the hotel
Hotel Concierge	C$5 or more, if he or she performs a service for you
Hotel Doorman	C$1–C$2 if he helps you get a cab
Hotel Maid	C$1–C$3 a day (either daily or at the end of your stay, in cash)
Hotel Room-Service Waiter	C$1 to C$2 per delivery, even if a service charge has been added
Porter at Airport or Train Station	C$1 per bag
Skycap at Airport	C$1 to C$3 per bag checked
Taxi Driver	15%, but round up the fare to the next dollar amount
Tour Guide	10% of the cost of the tour
Valet Parking Attendant	C$2–C$3, but only when you get your car
Waiter	15%–20%, with 20% being the norm at high-end restaurants; nothing additional if a service charge is added to the bill

▌ TOURS

GUIDED TOURS

Guided tours are a good option when you don't want to do it all yourself. You travel along with a group (sometimes large, sometimes small), stay in prebooked hotels, eat with your fellow travelers (the cost of meals is sometimes included, sometimes not), and follow a schedule.

But not all guided tours are an if-it's-Tuesday-this-must-be-Belgium experience. A knowledgeable guide can take you places that you might never discover on your own, and you may be pushed to see more than you would have otherwise. Tours aren't for everyone, but they can be just the thing for places where making travel arrangements is difficult or time-consuming (particularly when you don't speak the language).

Whenever you book a guided tour, find out what's included and what isn't. A "land-only" tour includes all your travel (by bus, in most cases) in the destination, but not necessarily your flights to and from or even within it. Also, in most cases prices in tour brochures don't include fees and taxes. And remember that you'll be expected to tip your guide (in cash) at the end of the tour.

SPECIAL-INTEREST TOURS
BIKING

AOA Adventures, Rocky Mountain Cycle Tours, and Austin-Lehman Adventures run a variety of comfortable multiday bike trips in Whistler, the Gulf Islands, and the Okanagan.

■ **TIP➜** Most airlines accommodate bikes as luggage, provided they're dismantled and boxed.

Contacts AOA Adventures. ☎ *480/945–2881, 866/455–1601* ⊕ *www.aoa-adventures.com.* **Austin-Lehman Adventures.** ☎ *800/575–1540* ⊕ *www.austinlehman.com.* **Rocky Mountain Cycle Tours.** ☎ *800/661–2453* ⊕ *www.rockymountaincycle.com.*

ECO TOURS

British Columbians are known for their green-friendly practices, whether it's protecting endangered species, instituting responsible climate-change initiatives, or running local recycling programs. And it's all fed into tourism as well. Ecosummer Expeditions hosts a number of outdoor adventure trips in BC, including weeklong hiking trips along the West Coast Trail on Vancouver Island, kayaking tours amid orcas in Johnstone Strait, and inn-based kayaking trips in the Gulf Islands.

Contacts Ecosummer Expeditions. ☎ *250/674-0102, 800/465-8884* ⊕ *www.ecosummer.com.*

GOLF

BC Golf Safaris specializes in complete, customized golf vacations based around courses in Vancouver, Victoria, Whistler, the Okanagan, and the Rockies.

Contacts BC Golf Safaris. ☎ *866/723-2747* ⊕ *www.bcgolfsafaris.com.*

SKIING

Contact Whistler Blackcomb, the host mountain resort of the 2010 Winter Games, to book a complete vacation at one of the world's most popular ski resorts.

Contacts Whistler Blackcomb. ☎ *866/218-9690* ⊕ *www.whistlerblackcomb.com.*

■ VISITOR INFORMATION

Regional visitor information services are available in British Columbia. In addition, Downtown Ambassadors, sponsored by the Downtown Vancouver Business Improvement Association, are easily spotted on Vancouver streets in their red uniforms. They can provide information, directions, and emergency assistance to anyone visiting Vancouver's central business district.

Contacts Aboriginal Tourism Association of British Columbia. ☎ *877/266-2822* ⊕ *www.aboriginalbc.com.* **Canadian Tourism Commission.** ☎ *613/946-1000* ⊕ *www. canada.travel.* **Granville Island Information Centre.** ☎ *604/666-6655* ⊕ *www.*

granvilleisland.com. **Tourism British Columbia.** ☎ *800/435-5622* ⊕ *www.hellobc.com.* **Tourism Victoria InfoCentre.** ☎ *250/953- 2033* ⊕ *www.tourismvictoria.com.* **Vancouver Visitor Centre.** ☎ *604/683-2000* ⊕ *www. tourismvancouver.com.*

ONLINE RESOURCES

Information of particular interest to outdoorsy types is on the website for British Columbia Parks (⊕ *www.bcparks.ca*), which outlines recreation, camping, and conservation initiatives at provincially operated reserves throughout British Columbia. At the site for Parks Canada (⊕ *www.pc.gc.ca*), you can learn about the seven national parks that fall within BC's borders. The Great Outdoor Recreation Page (⊕ *www.gorp.com*) is another fount of information for hikers, skiers, and the like.

There are several useful general-interest sites that deal with travel in British Columbia. One good option is the ever-expanding VancouverPlus.ca (⊕ *www. vancouverplus.ca*), which provides tourism tips and travel suggestions for Vancouver. Among alternative newsweeklies, the *Georgia Straight* offers timely features about exploring the province in its "Outside" section (⊕ *www.straight.com*).

For outdoors enthusiasts, in addition to specific sites mentioned in the book, there are several websites that can provide information. These include the Canadian Cycling Association (⊕ *www. canadian-cycling.com*), the Canadian Recreational Canoeing Association (⊕ *www.paddlingcanada.com*) for canoeing and kayaking, the Alpine Club of Canada (⊕ *www.alpineclubofcanada. ca*) for climbing and mountaineering, and the Royal Canadian Golf Association (⊕ *www.golfcanada.ca*).

INDEX

PHOTO CREDITS

Front cover, Vancouver & Victoria (4th)- Michael Wheatley/age fotostock [Description: Passenger ferry, False Creek, Vancouver]. 1, SharpShooter/Shutterstock. 2-3, Jeremy Koreski/Tourism Vancouver Island. Chapter 1: Experience Vancouver and Victoria: 8-9, Barrett & MacKay/age fotostock. 10, JJ Studio/Shutterstock. 11 (left), Xuanlu Wang/Shutterstock. 11 (right), Jennifer Zhou/Shutterstock. 12, ABC.pics/Shutterstock. 13 (left), Studiotouch/Shutterstock. 13 (right), July Flower/Shutterstock. 15, zhu difeng/Shutterstock. 16 (left), Kenji Nagai. 16 (top center), Michel Teiten/wikipedia.org. 16 (bottom center), WordRidden/Flickr. 16 (top right), Natalia Bratslavsky/Shutterstock. 16 (bottom right), Steve Rosset/Shutterstock. 17 (top left), robcocquyt/Shutterstock. 17 (bottom left), Natalia Bratslavsky/Shutterstock. 17 (top center), Xuanlu Wang/Shutterstock. 17 (top right), Hannamariah/Shutterstock. 17 (bottom right), 009fotofriends/Shutterstock. 18, Rainer Plendl/Shutterstock. 19, MAY FOTO/age fotostock. 20, Ian Wilson/Shutterstock. 21, Tim in Sydney/wikipedia.org. Chapter 2: Exploring Vancouver: 23, Alison Wright/age fotostock. 24, Xuanlu Wang/Shutterstock. 25, Natalia Bratslavsky/Shutterstock. 26, ABC.pics/Shutterstock. 31, Lijuan Guo/Shutterstock. 35, Douglas Williams/age fotostock. 38, Lijuan Guo/iStockphoto. 40-41, Steve Rosset/iStockphoto. 45, Hannamariah/Shutterstock. 46, Foxtongue/Flickr. 48, Dorothy Washbern. 50-51, Jennifer Zhou/Shutterstock. 53, David Leadbitter/Alamy. 56, WordRidden/Flickr. 59, Chris Cheadle/age fotostock. 65, SuperStock/age fotostock. 68, Gary Blakeley / Shutterstock. 70, Lijuan Guo/Shutterstock. 73, Douglas Williams/age fotostock. 76, Tourism Richmond. Chapter 3: Outdoors and Sports: 77, Steve Rosset/Shutterstock. 78, Andrew Ferguson/ Shutterstock. 85, Rolf Hicker/age fotostock. 88, Rich Wheater/age fotostock. 94-95, Chris Cheadle/age fotostock. Chapter 4: Shopping: 97, Kenji Nagai. 98, goose3five/Flickr. 101, Barrett & MacKay/age fotostock. 106, Ansgar Walk/wikipedia.org. 114, lululemon athletica/Flickr. Chapter 5: Nightlife and the Performing Arts: 117, Stu Ross Photography/Flickr. 118, Atlantide S.N.C./age fotostock. 126, Opus Hotel Vancouver. Chapter 6: Vancouver Where to Eat: 133, Azia. 134, Foxtongue/Flickr. 136, sashafatcat/Flickr, [CC BY 2.0]. 137 (top), kimberrywood/Shutterstock. 137 (bottom), Geoff604/Flickr. Chapter 7: Vancouver Where to Stay: 161, Relais & Chateaux. 162, Relais & Chateaux. Chapter 8: Victoria: 175, Xuanlu Wang/Shutterstock. 176 and 177, 2009fotofriends/Shutterstock. 178, ciapix/Shutterstock. 185, Barrett & MacKay/age fotostock. 188-89, North Light Images/age fotostock. 191, Tracy O/wiki pedia.org. 203, Lindsay Douglas/Shutterstock. 229, Chuck Pefley/Alamy. Chapter 9: Vancouver Island: 233-236, Landon Sveinson Photography/Tourism Vancouver Island. 248, Chris Cheadle/age fotostock. 257, Boomer Jerritt/age fotostock. 269, Jeremy Koreski/age fotostock. Chapter 10: Whistler: 275, Randy Lincks/age fotostock. 277 (top), Thomas Quine/wikipedia.org. 277 (bottom), David P. Lewis/ Shutterstock. 278, Steve Rosset/Shutterstock. 292, Randy Lincks/age fotostock. 294, Randy Lincks/ age fotostock. 298, robcocquyt/Shutterstock. Chapter 11: The Okanagan Valley: 303, Henry Georgi / age fotostock. 304, Edcorey | Dreamstime.com. 305, Max Lindenthaler / Shutterstock. 306, Richard Cavalleri / Shutterstock. 324-25, Dave Blackey/age fotostock. Back cover: Xuanlu Wang/Shutterstock; Protasov A&N/Shutterstock; Natalia Bratslavsky/Shutterstock. Spine: oksana.perkins/Shutterstock.

About Our Writers: All photos are courtesy of the writers.

NOTES

NOTES

NOTES

NOTES

NOTES

NOTES

NOTES

NOTES

NOTES

NOTES

BOUT OUR WRITERS

A travel writer since 2006, **Chloë Ernst** often explores her British Columbia backyard writing for Fodor's, Zagat, and Travelandleisure.com. While she loves Vancouver's hiking trails and breweries, Chloë has a special affinity for long ferry journeys and out-of-the-way excursions, and her adventures have taken her to abandoned Alaskan gold mines and along jungle roads in Bolivia. More of her writing can be found at ⊕ *www. chloeernst.com.*

Carolyn B. Heller has been enthusiastically exploring—and eating—her way across her adopted city of Vancouver since she relocated here in 2003. She's a regular contributor to the Forbes Travel Guide and Hotel-Scoop.com, and her travel and food articles have appeared in publications ranging from the *Boston Globe* and the *Los Angeles Times,* to *FamilyFun, Real Weddings,* and *Perceptive Travel* magazines. She's the author of two travel books, *Moon Ontario* and *Living Abroad in Canada,* and she's contributed to more than 25 Fodor's guides for destinations from New England to New Zealand.

Freelance writer **Sue Kernaghan** has written about British Columbia for dozens of publications and websites around a world, including several editions of *Fodor's Vancouver and British Columbia.* A fourth-generation British Columbian, she now lives and writes on Salt Spring Island.

Award-winning freelance travel writer **Chris McBeath's** more than 25 years in the tourism industry have given her an insider's eye about what makes a great vacation. British Columbia is her home, so whether routing through backcountry or discovering a hidden-away inn, Chris has combined history, insight, and anecdotes into her contribution to this book. Many of Chris's articles can be found at ⊕ *www.greatestgetaways.com;* her destination videos are available on YouTube.